MW00629546

ADMIRAL NICHOLAS HORTHY:

MEMOIRS

ANNOTATED BY ANDREW L. SIMON

Copyright © 2000 Andrew L. Simon

Original manuscript copyright © 1957, Ilona Bowden

Library of Congress Card Number: 00-101186

Copyright under International Copyright Union

All rights reserved. No part of this book may be reproduced in any form or by any electronic or mechanical means, including information storage and retrieval devices or systems, without prior written permission from the publisher.

ISBN 0-9665734 3-9

Printed by Lightning Print, Inc. La Vergne, TN 37086

Published by Simon Publications, P.O. Box 321, Safety Harbor, FL 34695

Admiral Horthy at age 75.

Publication record of Horthy's memoirs:

- First Hungarian Edition: Buenos Aires, Argentina, 1953.
- German Edition: Munich, Germany, 1953.
- Spanish Edition: AHR - Barcelona, Spain, 1955.
- Finnish Edition: Otava, Helsinki, Finland, 1955.
- Italian Edition, Corso, Rome, Italy, 1956.
- U. S. Edition: Robert Speller & Sons, Publishers, New York, NY, 1957.
- British Edition: Hutchinson, London, 1957.
- Second Hungarian Edition: Toronto, Canada: Vörösváry Publ., 1974.
- Third Hungarian Edition: Budapest, Hungary:Europa Historia, 1993.

Table of Contents

FOREWORD

by Andrew L. Simon, Professor Emeritus, The University of Akron

It is a sure sign of respectability if one is routinely vilified for 80 years by the Communists and for 60 years by the Nazis. Without the opportunity for rebuttal, a fiction repeated often enough, will become 'self evident truth'. Goebbels knew this, so did Beneš, two of the 20th century's master propagandists. When Admiral Nicholas Horthy, Regent of Hungary for a quarter of a century, was re-buried in his family's cript in September of 1993, there was an international uproar in the media. *The Economist* wrote about 'Hungary's shameful past'. The *New York Times* served up a dire warning about the return of Fascism, the *Frankfurter Allgemeine* 'would rather forget it', the Brazilian *Veja* commented that 'Hungary honors a Nazi'. There is no end to the list. One sane opinion appeared in *The Financial Times*: 'western historiography was interested exclusively in his alliance with Hitler, and the Communists characterized the anti-Bolshevik as a monster'.

Admiral Horthy, privy to the domestic policies of the Habsburg empire at the highest level, naval hero, last commandant of the Austro-Hungarian Navy, Regent of a destroyed country that he led into relative prosperity against great odds, an anti-Bolshevik, a prisoner of the Nazis, was indisputably a statesman. Under his rule, to quote Columbia University history professor Istvcn Deck, "Hungary ... was an island in the heart of Europe where a semblance of the rule of law and a pluralistic society had been preserved in a sea of barbarism". Having traveled the world while in the navy, speaking six languages (Hungarian, Croat, Italian, German, French, English), serving as aide-de-camp of Emperor Francis Joseph, he had a solid background for his position. Horthy was not a narrow-minded Nationalist but a patriot who greatly preferred the multi-ethic, multi-religious, multi-lingual diversity of the Monarchy in which he grew up and had an admirable career, even as a Hungarian Protestant in a Austrian Catholic "regime." Above all, he was a gentleman in the old, true sense of the word. His intimate knowledge of the politics of Central Europe during a time that led from the heights of the cultured, law-abiding, modernizing, developing age of the Monarchy to the depths of the Communist reigns of terror throughout the region makes his Memoirs an interesting, informative reading.

•

The death of Communism, (if not the Communists) revived the old ethnic and religious conflicts in Central and Eastern Europe, not only in Bosnia but throughout the Danubian basin. To address these problems western statesmen, and indeed, the general public, must understand them. Alas, this understanding will not come from western history books. As a 1993 survey of standard American college history textbooks indicated, these are saturated with some eighty years worth of propaganda. First, this propaganda was directed toward the dissolution of the Habsburg empire. Then it was a reaction of Hungary's demand of the peaceful return to her historic borders. Hungary lost two thirds of her territory at the end of the first world war; one out of every three Magyars became "ethnic minorities" in their own land of birth. Hungary wanted 'everything back', the Successor States were not prepared to give an inch. The end of the second world war, and the Communist oppression that followed, has placed a lid on the boiling pot. Now the lid is off.

The age-old concept of the Danubian Federation, in the form of the European Union, reemerged from the ashes of nationalistic madness and communist oppression that plagued the region during the 20th century. "The old Austro-Hungarian empire is reemerging in the new political geography" wrote *The Boston Globe* as early as August 20, 1989. Columnist Flora Lewis echoed from Paris that in proposing a Danubian Federation "Kossuth's Idea is Timely" (September 24, 1989). Otto von Habsburg, quoted in *Le Figaro* as saying in 1991: "under Austria one should not consider the present tiny country but a cultural sphere that spread from Czernowitz to Sarajevo. A survey article in *The Economist* (November 18, 1995) David Lawday wrote: "The countries of Central Europe, unavoidably detained for a while, are clamoring to join the European Union. When they do, it will be a homecoming." Hungary's joining NATO in 1999 was the first step toward her reintegration to the European community of nations. Horthy would be pleased.

For this edition, the text was compared to the Hungarian original and its English version was edited accordingly. About 600 footnotes were added to clarify names and some issues the reader may not be familiar with. The sources of these footnotes range from the private letters of Wallenberg to the records of the interrogations of Eichmann by the Israeli police, from long hidden memoirs of Hungarian generals and politicians, and a wide variety of books, articles and private recollections, mainly dealing with Hungary during World

War II, the German occupation of Hungary in the Spring of 1944, Horthy's attempts at saving his country, getting out of the war and his eventual imprisonment by the Nazis. The primary aim of this book is not to present Horthy's memoirs but to describe the history of Hungary during the 'Horthy Era' through a rich mosaic of views and comments of a multitude of participants. The Memoirs, originally published in several languages in the 1950's, serves as the structural support, the skeleton, of the story.

The text was reviewed by Mrs Ilona Bowden, widow of Stephen Horthy, Professor István Deák of Columbia University, Professor Scott F. Korom of the University of North Dakota, and Sandor Balogh, Professor Emeritus, Hudson Valley Community College. Their helpful comments and assistance in minimizing the number of errors in the text is gratefully appreciated. Without the help of Dr. Antal Simon of Budapest, who collected a huge array of reference material, this work could not have been done.

Safety Harbor, Florida, St. Stephen's Day, 1999.

Andrew L. Simon

INTRODUCTION

by Nicholas Roosevelt, former U.S. Minister to Hungary

NICHOLAS HORTHY will figure in European history of the 20th century as the powerful head of a small state who was powerless to prevent the absorption of his country first by the German Nazis and then by the Russian Communists. His failure was due not to incapacity, weakness or blundering on his part, but rather to the simple fact that the Hungarians were outnumbered ten to one by the Germans and twenty to one by the Russians, and that Germany and Russia each regarded occupation of Hungary as a pre-requisite to its own aggrandizement. Hungary had no more chance of effective resistance against either aggressor than a wounded stag attacked by a pack of wolves.

I saw Admiral Horthy from time to time when he was Regent of Hungary and I was United States' Minister to that country. This was in 1930-33. In appearance he was a typical sea-dog, red faced, sturdy, energetic, powerful, though relatively short in stature. Many a retired British admiral could have been mistaken for him. His integrity and courage were outstanding, as was his devotion to duty. Unlike other "strong men" he was singularly lacking in vanity, ambition and selfishness. He did not seek the high offices that were thrust upon him, but rather accepted them in the fervent hope that by so doing he could serve the country that he so dearly loved. Stern when need be, he was fundamentally kind. Proud of his office of regent, and punctilious about official etiquette, he yet was simple in his tastes and courteous and considerate of others. His official life was given over to an unending round of formalities, from which the only relief was escape to the country to hunt wild boars or stags, or shoot game birds. His energy in the field, even when in his sixties, exhausted many a younger man, and his skill with rifle and shotgun placed him among the best shots in a country where shooting as a sport was almost a profession.

Nicholas Horthy had just turned forty-one when, in 1909, the old Austrian Emperor, Franz Josef, appointed him one of his personal aides, thus bringing the future admiral into intimate contact with this survivor of an age that is utterly remote from our own. Franz Josef in his youth had known Prince Metternich, leader of the Congress of Vienna in the winter of 1814-15, and relentless enemy of liberalism in Europe, who had been forced to resign as Chancellor of the Empire just before Franz Joseph was crowned emperor in December of 1848. By the time that Nicholas Horthy came to serve Franz Josef the Emperor had become a legendary figure, *Emperor-King*, for more than sixty years, an autocrat who ruled his court and family with rigid regard for formality, a bureaucrat with a prodigious capacity for work, and, withal, a great gentleman. The admiral several times told me of the admiration, respect and affection which he had for the old man, not the hero-worship of a youth in his twenties, but the considered appraisal of a man in his forties for an employer still vigorous and efficient as he turned eighty. It is a tribute alike to Franz Josef's influence and to Nicholas Horthy's modesty that the Admiral, as Regent of Hungary, when faced with a grave problem of state always asked himself what the old Emperor would have done under the the circumstances.

Admiral Horthy's life, as set forth in this volume, covers the most revolutionary century in the world's history. His early training as a naval cadet was in the age of sails. Electric lighting was almost unknown in Europe when he completed his naval schooling. The Turks were still in control of parts of the Balkan peninsula. Russia's ambition to bring all Slavic-speaking peoples under its sway, while recognized, seemed unlikely ever to be realized. The recently achieved Italian unity was regarded by Austrians and Hungarians as an affront to historic realities. Prussia's domination of the newly created German Empire was resented by Austrians in particular, who looked down on the Prussians as ill-mannered, pushy people who had usurped the position of leadership of German culture which so long had belonged deservedly to the Austrians. As for the United States, it was regarded by European rulers as a small, isolated country inhabited by a bumptious, money-grubbing lot of transplanted Europeans, a nation which deservedly played no role in world affairs.

Yet within thirty years an American President, Woodrow Wilson, with millions of American soldiers backing the Allies against Germany and Austria-Hungary, proclaimed the principle of self-determination which hastened the break-up of the Austro-Hungarian empire and the abdication of Franz Josef's successor, Charles, the last of the Habsburg emperors. Nicholas Horthy, as commander-in-chief of the Austro-Hungarian navy, had the humiliation of carrying out Charles's order to surrender the imperial fleet to the scorned Yugoslavs without any resistance. German Austria proclaimed itself a republic. The Magyar remnant of Hungary, under the leadership of a

Magyar count regarded by his peers as weak, unreliable and unbalanced, declared its independence.

Dominated at first by socialists, it was shortly taken over by communists. In Russia Marxism replaced Czarism. The megalomanic Kaiser William II of Germany fled to Holland and took to sawing wood in his refuge at Doom, soon to see another megalomaniac, this time an Austrian by birth, Adolph Hitler, backed by one of Germany's greatest generals, Ludendorff, make his first (and unsuccessful) attempt to dominate and re-integrate Germany. Ludendorff was soon to be locked up as a lunatic. A decade later Hitler became Fuehrer of the "eternal" German Reich which endured a scant ten years.

Throughout most of the two decades that followed the armistice of 1918 the author of this book was a symbol of sanity, order and stability in an unstable, disordered and sick Europe. As head of the counterrevolutionary movement in Hungary, which, before he was named Regent in 1920, had rescued that country from the Communists, he had incurred the hatred of left wingers inside and out of Hungary[1]. As Regent his policy was to try to restore to Hungary the boundaries it had had before the Habsburg empire broke up, a policy which, however commendable to Magyars, ran counter to the nationalist aspirations and fears of non-Magyars, and was doomed to failure. In the ensuing years most of the supporters of the Habsburgs and many of the landed nobility of Hungary believed this upholder of the *ancien regime* to be "dangerously" liberal and suspected him of wanting to establish a Horthy dynasty to replace the Habsburgs. Royalists never forgave him for having twice thwarted ex-King Charles's attempts to regain the throne of Hungary, attempts which, if successful, would surely have brought about the invasion and occupation of Hungary by the neighbor states. The words put into the mouth of Brutus at Caesar's funeral by Shakespeare could well be paraphrased: "Not that Horthy loved Charles less, but Hungary more." When, twenty years later, Regent Horthy appeared to go along with Hitler, it was because he was faced with force which neither resistance nor appeasement could curb. What the outside world did not realize was that Hitler's hatred of Horthy's independence and fearlessness was one of the reasons why the Fuehrer took over control of Hungary and virtually made the Regent his prisoner.

1   A fact still true in the end of the 1990's. (Ed.)

7

The last time I saw this staunch old admiral was when I paid my farewell visit to him before returning to the United States in 1933. He spoke with passionate earnestness about his conviction that Russia was the greatest threat not only to Hungary but to the western world. For years this subject had been an obsession of his, so much so, in fact, that the members of the diplomatic corps in Budapest in the 1930s discounted it as a phobia. Events have proved that his fears were justified. True, it was the Nazis who started Hungary down the path of destruction. But it was the Russians who crushed the spirit of the Hungarian nation and reduced the economic level of the Magyars to pre-feudal poverty. The Hungarian Regent in this case had foreseen correctly, but he was unable to convince either British or American leaders that Communist Russia was even more rapacious and greedy than Czarist Russia, and that it was folly to believe that if Russia was treated as a friendly ally that country would respond in kind.

If any of Admiral Horthy's critics continue to question his clarity of thinking and his abundant common sense, let them read this book. Written simply and modestly, it is an absorbing record of the life of a gallant man who fought hopelessly but bravely to save as much as he could for his country in the midst of the conflicting jealousies, ambitions and hatreds of Eastern Europe which had been inflamed by World War I. He was a conservator rather than a conservative, a traditionalist rather than a fascist, a practical man rather than an idealist. He would have restored the old order had he been able to do so. Instead, he saw the Iron Curtain close over his beloved Hungary, and retired to Portugal, where, at the age of eighty-eight he is still living with his memories of a world that is gone forever. Fearless, incorruptible, steadfast, his influence, like that of George Washington, stemmed from strength of character rather than brilliance of intellect. Men might disagree with him, but even his enemies respected him. They might question his judgment, but none questioned his integrity and uprightness.

Big Sur, California, April 1956.   Nicholas Roosevelt[2]

---

2   (1893 - 1982) Nicholas Roosevelt served in the U.S. Army during WW1. Ha was American Minister to Hungary between 1930 and 1933.

PREFACE

Twice, and each time without my having striven after it, I have been appointed to a position of leadership. Towards the end of the First World War, His Majesty the Emperor Charles appointed me Commander-in-Chief of the Fleet of the Austro-Hungarian dual monarchy. A few years later the Hungarian people elected me Regent of Hungary, an appointment that made me the virtual head of the Hungarian State. Many honours have come my way unbidden. In this attempt at authorship, I am not seeking fame; circumstances have compelled me to lay down the sword and take up the pen.

When I began jotting down experiences and incidents from my long life during the forced inactivity, first of my imprisonment during the years 1944 and 1945, later of my sojourn in hospitable Portugal, I did so with no other purpose than that of leaving notes as a memento for my family. That these pages are now being offered to the public is the outcome of the insistence of many friends who have overcome my reluctance with the words of Goethe: "The question whether a man should write his own biography is a vexed one. I am of the opinion that to do so is the greatest possible act of courtesy."

This duty of courtesy towards history and my contemporaries is not one I wish to shirk, especially as I am now the only surviving witness of a number of events which have involved other people as well as myself. I am at the same time activated by the wish to speak a word of encouragement to my beloved Hungarian countrymen, who, after the crash of 1919, have now been plunged into the yet deeper abyss of Communist terror and foreign domination. The misfortunes of 1945 cannot and must not be the finale of Hungarian history. I profess my adherence to the words of our great Hungarian poet, Imre Madách, who in his *The Tragedy of Man* sings, "Man, have faith, and in that faith, fight on!"

In this fight, the experience of my life may be of use both to my contemporaries and to posterity. The place destiny has given the Magyars, set between the Slav and German races, is unlikely to suffer change; from it are bound to arise, time and time again, the same problems that presented themselves during my occupation of the office of Regent.

It is the task of the biographer, and this applies even more to the writer of autobiography, to give a picture of events as they appeared at the time,

9

uninfluenced by the impact of subsequent developments. Any fool can be wise after the event. My efforts to perform the task of chronicler have been hampered by two factors: as one's years increase, the capacity of one's memory to hold and retain decreases. Others who have written down their recollections at an advanced age have been able to make good this handicap by referring to diaries and archives. I have never kept a diary, and those official or private documents which were locked away in my safe at the moment of my imprisonment in October, 1944, were either destroyed or left behind in the Royal Palace in Budapest. I was, however, able partly to fill certain gaps with the help of former collaborators on whose assistance I called. To them I owe a debt of gratitude.

Invaluable also was the help given me by my wife and by my daughter-in-law, who have spared no effort in completing and correcting these memoirs. A few documents were to be found in accounts of my life written by the Baroness Lily Doblhoff, Owen Rutter and Edgar von Schmidt-Pauli. I am sure that these writers would not mind the use I have made of such documents, as well as of what they themselves wrote about me, to refresh my memory. The same applies to a number of books written about Hungary since the war.

It has often been painful, yet sometimes cheering, to find how differently the same event has been dealt with by different authors. But that experience is a common one and any public figure soon discovers that it is impossible to please everybody. In such cases, history must be left to pronounce its verdict. And one who, throughout his life, has striven to do his duty to the best of his ability and conscience, need not fear that verdict. That is the spirit in which I place these memoirs before the public and the historians of the future.

Estoril, Portugal, August 20, 1952   Horthy

10

1. Out into the World

I was born on June 18th, 1868, on our family estate of Kenderes in the county of Szolnok in the heart of the Hungarian plains. The tall trees of the extensive park shaded the house in which my ancestors[1] had dwelt since the end of Turkish rule. Before that time, my people had lived for centuries in Transylvania[2].

I was the fifth of nine children[3], seven boys and two girls. Our childhood was one of exuberant happiness, secure in the love of our parents. I adored my mother[4]. Her sunny, warm-hearted and gay temperament set the tone of our family life, and to this day gilds my youthful memories. My father[5] I admired and revered. But Stephen Horthy, devoting himself to the management of his estates, was a man of strong character, a strict disciplinarian, intolerant of disobedience in the home, so that he often engendered in us a certain fear. With my boyish pranks, into which my vivid imagination and love of adventure often led me, he had little sympathy, and even my indulgent mother could not prevent him from sending me at the age of eight away from the home atmosphere to Debrecen, where I joined my two brothers, who were living with a French tutor. From that moment, I found myself in the turmoil of life, and learned early to act for myself and to be responsible for my own actions.

1   His ancestor, István (Stephen in English) Horthy, received his nobility in 1633. Hungarian nobilities were hereditary, and were granted either by the king or by the prince of Transylvania. In addition to an inalienable land grant, nobility meant the right to vote and freedom from taxation. All such privileges were voluntarily rescinded by 1848. After that noble ranks had little more meaning than direct lineage to a Mayflower passenger in the United States.

2   The prefix, "nagybányai", referring to the original land grant, was first used by the son of István Horthy, reformed bishop of Transylvania, also named István, who was secretary to Prince Francis Rákóczi II. Nagybánya is a mining town in northern Transylvania.

3   István (1858-1937), Zoltán (1860-?), Béla (1864-1880), Paula (1863-1906), Erzsébet (1871-?), Szabolcs (1873-1914), Jenô (1874-1876), Jenô (1877-1954).

4   Paula Halassy of Dévaványa (1839-1895).

5   István (1830-1904).

Those who are familiar with Hungarian history will know that, in the year before my birth, 1867, our great and wise statesman, Francis Deák, had concluded the *Ausgleich,* or Compromise, between Austria and Hungary, as the agreement between Vienna and Budapest was called. Since Ferdinand I of Habsburg had been crowned at Székesfehérvár with the Holy Crown of St. Stephen in 1527, two years before the Turks laid siege to Vienna, there had existed between the Magyar nobility and the Habsburgs the same inimical relations as had existed between the princes of the Holy Roman Empire and the Estates. In the revolutionary struggle for freedom in the years 1848-49, the Habsburgs had been declared deposed by the Hungarian insurgents under Kossuth. The young Emperor, Francis Joseph, had been able to re-enter Hungary only with the help of Russian troops, who then set foot: in our land for the first time[6]. In 1867, Hungary had been given an independent constitutional government. Only "Joint Affairs", military matters, foreign policy, and the finances connected with them, were dealt with in Vienna by joint Ministries, which were responsible, however, to delegations appointed on a basis of parity by the Vienna and Budapest Parliaments.

I left the parental home before the Russo-Turkish War, ending in the Congress of Berlin[7], had been fought. That Congress caused considerable changes to be made in the map of Europe. Hitherto the Ottoman Empire had extended as far as Sarajevo and Mostar; now Bosnia-Herzegovina, a dangerous focus of unrest, was occupied by Austria-Hungary and governed from Vienna as a state territory. For the first time, Montenegro was declared an independent state; the small kingdom of Serbia was enlarged by the addition of Nis, Vranje and Pirot, and the independent principality of Bulgaria was created. To the east, the Principalities of Moldavia and Wallachia, which had been united in 1866 under Charles I of Hohenzollern-Sigmaringen[8], to form Rumania, was now our neighbour.

---

6 In the spring of 1849 Austrian armies suffered a series of defeats by the Hungarians. Under the Holy Alliance existing between Austria and Russia, the Austrians asked for Russian help: sixty thousand troops. Russia sent over 200,000. To the anger of the Austrians, Hungary surrendered to Czar's forces, not to Austria. Austrian retributions were harsh. One of these was the execution of twelve leading Hungarian generals at Arad on October 6, 1849.

7 1878.

8 Charles I (1839-1914).

Russia could not reconcile herself to her diplomatic defeats at the Berlin Congress. While the alliance of these three Emperors existed, the statesmanship of Bismarck[9], actively supported as it was by Andrássy[10], the Foreign Minister of the Austro-Hungarian monarchy, succeeded in preventing an outbreak of Austro-Russian antagonism. The 1908 Bosnian crisis, when Austria-Hungary turned occupation into annexation, the Balkan Wars and the murder at Sarajevo were still decades in the future. When I determined to take up the career of naval officer, I thought less of naval battles and victories than of seeing the world and travel.

At Debrecen, I had reached the higher forms of the primary school. I spent my grammar school days at the Lähne Institute in Sopron, where the teaching was in German, for my parents wished me to perfect myself in that language.

It had not been easy to obtain my parents' consent to my entry into the Naval Academy. My brother Béla, older than me by four years, had been seriously wounded in the course of manoeuvres two months before the conclusion of his training as a naval cadet. The surgeon from Budapest who, with my father, had hastened to Fiume[11], had been unable to save his life. Could I ask my parents to let yet another son go into the Navy after so great a sacrifice had been demanded from them already? My mother persuaded my father to agree. Blessing their memory for this decision, I now record my gratitude to them for

9   Otto von Bismarck (1815-1898) German chancellor, on his first official visit to Budapest in 1852 wrote his wife: "If you were here for a moment to see with me the dead silver of the Danube, the dark mountains against the pale-red background and the lights of Pest glittering up to me; Vienna would go down in your appreciation compared with Budapest. You see, I am a worshipper of natural beauty." (Montgomery, J. F.: Hungary, the Unwilling Satellite, New York: Devin-Adair Co., 1947, pp. 15. - Montgomery was the U. S. minister to Hungary between 1933 and 1941.)

10   Gyula Andrássy Sr. (1823-1890) was sentenced to death *in absentia* for his role in the 1848-49 revolution. Pardoned, he became the first constitutional premier of Hungary in 1867, then became Austro-Hungarian foreign minister from 1871 to 1979. He opposed Austrian interference in Hungarian affairs, and supported Magyar supremacy at the expense of other ethnic groups. In the 1878 Berlin Congress he obtained the right to occupy Bosnia-Herzegovina. This was much opposed by the Hungarians who did not want to increase the Slavic element in the empire. As a result, he resigned.

11   Croat: Rijeka.

letting me enter the profession that had been the dream of my boyhood, and for giving me the fulfilment of my most ardent wishes.

I have never ceased to love that profession and my enthusiasm for it has never faded. As Regent of Hungary, I was proud to wear my Admiral's uniform even after the Austro-Hungarian fleet had, to my undying grief, ceased to exist.[12]

Discipline in the Austro-Hungarian Navy was strict. However, the fact that, through rigorous selection, the officers' cadre was particularly homogeneous, though its members came from the most diverse regions of the realm, made the service pleasant. The number of candidates was invariably so large that selection could be meticulous. In my year, 1882, forty-two candidates out of six hundred and twelve, if I remember correctly, were admitted. As all naval officers had to pass through the Naval Academy, their education and training were uniform. The standards were high, which meant that in the course of the four years' training, more than a third of the forty-two originally admitted fell out. Finally only twenty-seven of us emerged as fully fledged naval officers.

I was not one of the more zealous students; I preferred the practical part of the training. As I was among the smaller boys of my year, and good at gymnastics, I became one of the topmen. During an exercise, one of the lifts to the yardarms was let go by mistake, and I was thrown from the height of sixty to seventy feet; as I fell, I tried to catch hold of the ropes, and though I skinned my hands I succeeded in saving my life. The naval hospital had quite a task to put me together again, for I had broken some ribs, an arm and a number of teeth in my lower jaw as I crashed on to the deck. At my urgent request, my parents were not informed, for I had no wish to cause them alarm. The school year ended with the customary two months' cruise in the Mediterranean, after which came four months' leave.

Our education was governed by the maxim which was inscribed in letters of gold on a marble plaque at the college: "Above Life Stands Duty". That maxim has remained my guide throughout life, long after the day, at the end of four years, upon which we achieved the longed-for moment and became midshipmen. After my four months' leave, I was appointed to the frigate *Radetzky*, the flagship of the winter squadron, which consisted of three units. At that time, we were still using sail; the boilers were rarely stoked. Even the armour-clads still carried sail, and one frequently saw captains, trained in the

12 For an unbiased Western view, see the letter in the Appendix.

old school, stopping their engines on entering a narrow harbour and making use of the sails with which they were so much more familiar. Similarly, in harbour, during stormy weather, they would replace the anchor-chains, which they did not trust, with hawsers. Not before the end of the eighties did the construction of modern battleships, cruisers and torpedo-boats start.

The winter squadron sailed from Dalmatia to Spain. The captain of the flagship *Hum* was frigate-captain Archduke Charles Stephen, a brother of the Queen of Spain[13], the mother of the future King Alphonso XIII. This meant that we were exceedingly well received in all the Spanish ports. The Spanish did their utmost to show us the beauty of their country, bullfights, of course, being among the sights. From Malaga, two friends and I went on a marvellous expedition along the coastal plain through forests of orange-trees and across the Sierra Nevada and on to Cordova and Granada, where the Alhambra made a profound impression on me. At Barcelona, many people came to visit us on board. The cadets of the watch had to conduct the principal guests off the ship, and, moreover, see that they had left the ship by five o'clock. I transgressed that order one day, as I could not bring myself to despatch one family which had arrived rather late. For that I lost a fortnight's shore leave, which seemed a very heavy punishment to me, for Barcelona was an attractive and beautiful city where there was much to be seen and done. Was I to be cheated of that? Hardly had my companions left the ship before I was putting on my civilian clothes, creeping over the side into a Spanish boat that I had beckoned over and following them. Near the landing stage, the captain's launch lay waiting. I was hurrying to the café where I knew my friends were going, when I saw my captain in the Calle Larga coming towards me. Whatever happened, he mustn't see me. I covered my face with my handkerchief, dived into an alley and ran back to the harbour as fast as my legs would carry me. I sprang into the captain's launch and hid under the rowing seats. Before long, the captain arrived and was rowed to the ship. Once on the deck of the *Radeczky*, he ordered the officer of the watch to have me called. I heard him giving the order before the sailors had even given me a hand up so that I could climb on board through a porthole. In the cadets' quarters, I rapidly changed into uniform. The cadet who came to look for me thought he was seeing a ghost as his eye fell on me, for he had watched me go ashore. I allowed the time it would have taken for me to be woken from sleep, dress and go on deck to elapse, and then presented myself before the captain, looking as sleepy as I could. He was so dumbfounded that he sent me away without a

13 Arch-Duchess, Marie-Christine (1858-1929).

word. Many years later, when he was an admiral and I an officer, he asked me how I had worked the trick. I had to tell him that it was he who had had the kindness to take me back to the ship in his own launch.

Eighteen months later, I saw Barcelona again. The occasion was a maritime exhibition to which the navies of the world had been invited. The Queen and her eighteen-year-old son were expected to be present. Seventy-six warships had assembled in the roads. We were soon on especially good terms with the Dutch and in their company made a number of cafés sadly unsafe. One day, they held a banquet on their frigate, the *Johan Willem Friso*, one cadet from each nation had been invited. I had the honour of representing our squadron.

On such occasions, the chief aim of the hosts was to put as many of the guests under the table as possible. The dinner began at six o'clock, and at nine o'clock the first 'corpses' were being carried on deck to be lowered into the rowing boats waiting to take them back to their respective ships. I held out for some time, but at last my turn came and the fate of the others overtook me. I woke the next morning to find myself in a delightful but strange cabin. I rang the bell, whereupon a bare-headed sailor entered and addressed me in a language I could not even place. When I went on deck, I discovered that I had been taken to a Russian corvette, where they had looked after me to the best of their ability. All that morning, boats could be seen going the rounds, exchanging strayed cadets.

My second trip to Barcelona was made in the *Prinz Eugen*. After the squadron was laid up, I was transferred to the *Minerva*, a corvette without engine. Under the coast of Sicily, we were once caught in a westerly storm and it was due solely to our captain that we succeeded in battling our way against the furious wind and the towering waves into the well-protected harbour of Malta. He maneeuvred so boldly and so magnificently that we were loudly cheered by the crews of the British Mediterranean squadron that lay anchored there. Before we sailed on to Tunis, where I was to see the ruins of old Carthage, we were given an opportunity of visiting the picturesque island of Malta with its memories of the ancient crusader knights.

Before we set sail again, I bought a parrot, which soon became the pet of all the cadets. He sat on his perch and we all tried in vain to teach him to speak. After the day's work in Tunis we used to play games of tarot in the mess-room. A few weeks after we had sailed, someone, during a game, called "tarot!" and "pagatultimo!" and, to our amazement, the parrot suddenly shrieked, "contra," the one word he must have heard clearly during our games at Tunis.

In November, 1889, I was appointed a sublieutenant and, to my great joy, was transferred to the *Taurus*. That was our Embassy ship, as we used to call the warships which the big powers sent to Constantinople on account of the uncertain conditions prevailing under Sultan Abdul Hamid[14]. In winter we lay moored in front of the Tophane artillery arsenal; in summer we lay anchored opposite the summer residences of the Embassies on the Bosphorus. In summer, also, we would undertake long cruises on the Black Sea, taking us up the Danube as far as Galata or in the Mediterranean along the Turkish coast.

Life in Constantinople was both pleasant and varied. When off duty, we went in for sport. We even had a small pack of hounds, and would go off on a drag-hunt every week with an English attaché as master of the hunt.

After more than a year in Constantinople, the *Taurus* had to have new boilers put in and we went to Pola. On the voyage, we called at Corfu, where I visited the Achilleion, a castle constructed with much taste and loving care on a glorious promontory of the island by our Queen-Empress Elizabeth. The castle owed its name to a statue of Achilles that had been erected in the park. Together with her son, Crown Prince Rudolph, she had planned the building and chosen the site. After the tragic death of the Crown Prince, she never returned to Corfu. The Achilleion passed into the possession of German Emperor Wilhelm II, whose sister Sophie was married to Constantine, the future King of Greece.

The wish of every naval officer, a voyage round the world, was granted to me while serving in the corvette *Saida*, to which I was transferred in the summer of 1892. Her captain was Commander Sachs[15], former aide-de-camp to Emperor Francis Joseph. There were ten officers on board, of whom I was the junior in age and rank. The two years' voyage I made in her still ranks among

14 Turkish Sultan Abd al-Hamid II (1842-1918). After the loss of the Russian-Turkish wars, concluded by the Congress of Berlin in 1878, he pursued an active pro-German policy. For his part of the Armenian massacres between 1892 and 1896 he was called the Great Assassin. Under his reign, in 1908 a coup of reformist army officers, the Young Turks, forced him to adhere to the constitution of 1976. That story is described in the Chapter 2.

15 Moritz Sachs von Hellenau (1844-1933).

the finest memories of my life. Like Ulysses, we saw the cities of many men, and knew their mind. The supremacy of the white race in the whole world was firm and undisputed. Under the rule of Queen Victoria, 'Britannia rules the waves' was true without reservation; we encountered a number of impressive examples of that in the course of our voyage. I could easily fill a volume with the description of that cruise alone, but I shall limit myself to giving a few scenes and comments that may be of interest in showing how times have changed.

We had left Pola under sail, and, the wind being favourable, soon reached Port Said. A short leave made it possible for us to visit the sights of Egypt: the pyramids, the splendid mosques, the rich museums, and also the places of entertainment. I stayed at Shepherd's Hotel, the building which went up in flames in 1952. Opposite the hotel was the shop of the cigarette manufacturer Dimitrino, who was my father's supplier. I paid my father's outstanding account when I bought the cigarettes needed by the officers' mess for the long voyage. Unexpectedly, our leave was prolonged, which presented us with a problem: our purses did not stretch quite as far as that. We put our heads together, and I propounded the happy idea of asking Dimitrino for a loan. I wrote down how much each of us would need, and somewhat diffidently put the matter to Dimitrino. He replied that he was very sorry but he could not give me the sum as his cashier had just left for home. He would, however, send after him and would then despatch a message to our hotel. I took that to be a polite form of refusal. Picture my amazement when, within a quarter of an hour, a messenger called to ask me to go over to Dimitrino's. I found him standing by a large, open safe, filled with gold. With a florid gesture, he asked me to take exactly what I needed. The payment of my father's small account might well have been a trick; but, as a business man, Dimitrino was a good judge of human nature.We were able to reimburse him from Suez. The proverbial heat of the Red Sea caused us considerable trouble, for we were not employing native stokers but using our own men. A steam-pump kept three showers constantly in action on deck and though the temperature of the water was eighty-six degrees, it struck us as cold, and we could not stay under it for long at a time. At Aden, we came across swarms of Persian carpet dealers and Jewish ostrich-feather merchants. Our ship was quickly surrounded by native tree-trunk canoes, from which Somali boys jumped like frogs into the water, diving after coins. The place was alive with sharks. We saw many boys who had lost an arm or a leg while indulging in their dangerous pastime.

18

At Bombay, a British naval officer came on board to welcome us. As we were talking with him on deck, a P.& O. liner happened to pass by, whereupon the Lieutenant-Commander remarked that there was a British major on board her who was being transported to England to a mental asylum. One evening, he told us, while this major was entertaining friends from his cavalry regiment in his bungalow near Poona, he suddenly observed a cobra winding itself round his leg. This snake is not uncommon in those parts and its bite is fatal. The major asked his guests to remain motionless and ordered his servant quickly to warm some milk and put it down with great caution near him. This took some time. Tempted at last by the milk, the venomous snake uncoiled itself and slithered over to the dish, whereupon the servant cut off its head. The guests, released from the almost unbearable tension, began to ease their positions. The major did not move. His reason had fled.

In the neighbourhood of Poona there is a forest high up in the mountains where Europeans go to recuperate. When I heard that panthers abounded there, I asked for a couple of days' leave to go and try my luck with a *sikhari*, a native hunter. He took me to a raised platform after having tethered a lamb in the centre of an empty space within two hundred yards of the last of the bungalows. It was growing dark. I could hardly believe that a panther would venture so near a settlement, for we could still hear the voices of people in one of the bungalows. The *sikhari,* however, told me that only two weeks before a panther had walked into the house of an English lady and, to her horror, had helped himself to her little dog. The bright moonlight would have been excellent for shooting, but no panther appeared. Only after the moon had set were we able, by ear, to follow the tragedy of the lamb below us. We had to remain where we were until day broke. I had unfortunately no time to make a second attempt.

With the aid of a pilot, we steamed up the River Hugly, an arm of the Ganges delta, and dropped anchor opposite Sowgor Island. This island is uninhabited, largely on account of the tigers which come from all directions, especially during the season of rut, swimming across the river. After my disappointment over the panther, I was hoping to bag a tiger. This time, I set out with a calf as bait. The pilot, seeing me set off, informed the captain that I was endangering my life. Before long the signal "No. 1 boat, return" called me back. The next morning we proceeded to Calcutta.

Along the shore, tropical forests alternated with fields tilled by the natives with the help of tame elephants. In the vicinity of the town, along both banks, there were numerous three- and four-masted sailing ships, driven off the seas and condemned to rot by the advance of steam power.

Calcutta at that time had a population of over a million. On the third day of our stay, we were invited by the Viceroy to a dinner and ball, on which occasion we met the cream of Calcutta society. Every day saw some activity: polo, horse-races, parties, theatre shows. It was all so entertaining that I was almost reluctant to go on an excursion to Darjeeling, but, feeling that it was my duty to pay my respects to the memory of the great Hungarian explorer of Tibet, Kőrösi- Csoma[16], by visiting his tomb. I went and have never regretted having seen the Himalayas and the highest mountains on earth with my own eyes.

At polo, I made the acquaintance of the Maharaja of Cooch-Behar in Bengal, who invited me to a tiger hunt on elephant-back, which was to take place two days after we were due to sail. I was in despair, for would I ever have such an opportunity again? I even thought of reporting sick, of having myself taken to hospital and following the *Saida*, after the hunt, to Singapore. But my conscience played me false, though my unconscious did not: in the course of a race, my horse fell and I broke a collarbone. Taking leave of Calcutta was not easy.

What we saw of India testified to the colonizing talents of the British. They had made sure of the Khyber Pass and were holding the unruly tribes along the North-West frontier in check. They had put a stop to the constant conflicts between Hindus and Moslems. In the economic field, they had seen to the regulation of the flow of the big rivers and by irrigation they had brought huge areas in the Punjab under cultivation. They had built roads and railways; in short they had created civilization and wealth, and were maintaining order with relatively small forces. Today India is partitioned, and millions of refugees on either side of the India-Pakistan frontiers have to suffer for the theoretical bliss of liberation.

Singapore, the British Gibraltar of the East, was most impressive. If anyone had told us then that this fortress, so difficult of approach, would one day be

16 Hungarian (Transylvanian) orientalist, Sándor Kőrösi-Csoma (1784-1842).
    He created the first Tibetan-English dictionary.

20

conquered by the Japanese, we should have laughed in derision. The Sultan of Johore received us in audience; the presence, however, of a British aide-de-camp was an indication that his country belonged to the British sphere of influence. Not until later did he acknowledge British sovereignty.

While in Calcutta, I had received a letter from the Siamese royal prince, Mom Rashwongse Krob, who had been a pupil at our Naval Academy and had spent fourteen years in Vienna, where we had met at the home of a mutual friend. In his letter, he promised to meet me at Bangkok. The Menam, on which the capital of Siam[17] is situated, is so shallow that we had to anchor far out, almost out of sight of the coast. A few hours after our arrival, Mom Krob appeared in a small steam yacht and, as I had been given three days' leave, I was able to join him immediately. It took us three hours to reach Bangkok. My host lived within the harem, and, apologizing for his inability to take me to his home, he told me that he had booked a room for me in a hotel which was run in faultless European style. After dinner, we visited the theatre belonging to the Minister of Foreign Affairs, in which all the female parts were played by his wives. The action was made clear by means of pictures at the back of the stage. The dancer, dressed in a golden Buddha costume, moved her fingers and toes to the music of drums, gongs and fifes. It took me a little while before I was able to distinguish a kind of exotic melody. Mom Krob pointed out to me proudly that the orchestra played in unison without using a written score.

Bangkok, with its splendid buildings, its countless pagodas, its museums filled with gold and jewellery, impressed me as a fairytale come true. My three days flew by. I had to forgo being presented at court as I lacked the requisite clothes. I never dreamed that fifty years later I should be entertaining the King's successor, Bama Prajadhipok VII, at Gödöllö as my guest.

In Java, we came into contact with Dutch civilization, which had made the fertile islands of the East Indies into the main producers of rubber, tobacco, coffee, tea and other commodities of world importance. At Batavia, we were the guests of the Governor-General at his summer residence Buitenzorg, which, on account of its altitude, enjoys a delightful climate in spite of its proximity to the Equator. The weather is determined by the monsoons, which for six months of the year blow from the north-east to the south-west between Japan and Cape Town, and the other six months in the opposite direction. Sailing ships have to regulate their voyages accordingly. From Surabaya, we

17 Today's Thailand.

rode to the Bromo, a holy mountain, one of the world's largest volcanoes. It is some eight thousand feet high and the crater measures some two thousand, seven hundred feet across. We rode down a zigzag path, and then ascended another cone. Suddenly, mist came down on us from all sides; the effect was so weird that we thought at first we had run into a volcanic eruption and we quickly mounted our horses and prepared to take a hurried leave of the holy mountain. But the mist turned abruptly into a tropical downpour, similar to one we had experienced the day before.

Our next port of call was Albany in south-west Australia. The distance we had covered was considerable, for we had followed the south-east trade wind nearly to South Africa before we entered the region of prevailing west wind. Since the world first came into existence, a westerly storm has raged incessantly between approximately 35 and 53 degrees south latitude. The cold air of the Antarctic flows towards the tropics and, by the eastern rotation of the earth, is deflected westwards. As the Indian Ocean is some twenty thousand feet deep in those parts, the storms create waves of a magnitude unknown in our latitudes. When these enormous masses of water come rolling along, rapidly overtaking the ship, the spectator has the feeling that, when the wave breaks, ship and all will be swallowed up and vanish into the depths for ever. But such waves only break in shallow water. For weeks on end, it was impossible to eat at a properly laid table; at night one was in constant danger of being hurled out of one's bunk. Nothing was to be seen but masses of foaming water and the gigantic albatrosses which circled round the ship like gliders to snap up any trifle thrown overboard. We were glad to reach smooth water off Albany. Our consul informed us that there was an epidemic raging in town, and our captain decided to confine himself to taking in fresh victuals and to go straight on to Melbourne. We raced along offshore in a fairly smooth sea on a westerly storm, often making fifteen knots.

At that time Melbourne, with its three hundred thousand inhabitants, was the most modern city I had seen. There were still people alive who had been among the first colonists, living in tents, but when I was there the city had been planned with fine broad streets and squares of perfect symmetry.

The Governor of Victoria at that time was the thirty-year-old Earl of Hopetoun[18], whose large fortune enabled him to maintain an almost royal household. He had an excellent stable, for he was an enthusiastic horseman,

18 John Adrian Louis Hope (1860-1908).

taking part in every steeplechase, fox hunt or kangaroo hunt. When I was invited to dinner with him, black coffee was served in the stables. The Earl had a marked predilection for Hungary, which was probably due to our wonderful mare, *Kincsem,* every one of whose fifty-six victories he knew in detail. He invited me to the next steeplechase, and though I had no hunting clothes with me, I accepted his invitation with alacrity.

A special train took us to a certain station where the horses were taken off. We assembled inside a stockade and mounted our horses. A few moments later, the huntsman with the whips and the pack of hounds made his appearance. "Are we ready?" the Governor asked, and, though the gates were open, he rode up to and over the wooden fence. And though I had been riding horses since I was five years old, and have been on many a hunt, never have I seen so high a fence taken, not even in jumping competitions. What was I to do? The mare I had been given was so willing and so surefooted that I could ask even that of her.

I also took part in a kangaroo hunt, for which they beat a wood. The tempo among the trees is very sharp and short, for when the kangaroo tires, it sits down and defends itself against the hounds by kicking. Hounds are flung up into the air, head over tail. The huntsman finally kills the quarry with a pistol-shot. Special saddles are used on these hunts to protect the riders' knees against the trees.

As, on my departure, I was thanking my host for these delights and praising the mare I had ridden, the Governor offered her to me as a gift. Alas, I could not accept her, for there was no place on board of the Saida for a horse, nor could I send her home unaccompanied on some other ship.

In Melbourne, we saw a peculiar mode of public transport: the cable-trams. They were drawn by cable, close to the pavement. The second car of each vehicle was open, and it was easy to jump on or off while it was moving. The passenger had to pay a small coin, which, dropped into a box, gave a discrete tinkle, thus ensuring that each payment was checked by the other passengers. In all things, Melbourne competed with the older Sydney. If the one had a famous large organ, the other had to build not only a larger one but if possible the largest in the world. The concerts given by highly paid Belgian organists were famous far and wide. I never missed one when I had a chance of attending, and counted them among the greatest musical pleasures of my life.

When the *vox humana* stop was pulled, it sounded for all the world like a wonderful tenor, baritone, bass, soprano or contralto.

We did not fail to patronize the Café Vienna, a cafe-restaurant, the proprietor of which was Viennese. Twenty years before, he and a partner had opened a bakery, and their *Kaisersemmel* (fancy bread) and *Kipfel* (horn-shaped roll) had proved so attractive a novelty that their business had grown by leaps and bounds. One of the partners had built the Cafe Vienna, the other had set up racing stables, but success had gone to his head and before long he died insane.

At Sydney, we were naturally asked the stock question: "What do you think of our harbour?" And, truly, Sydney vies with Rio de Janeiro in the fame and beauty of its harbour; it would be difficult to say which of the two is the finest in the world.

We were instructed to be ready to meet the geologist, Baron Foullon-Norbeck[19], who was to sail in the *Saida* to the New Hebrides and the Solomon Islands, where he was going to prospect for nickel, Austria-Hungary having about that time introduced nickel coins. This assignment unfortunately forced us to omit Tahiti, Honolulu and San Francisco from our ports of call. I had been particularly looking forward to visiting Honolulu, which at that time was still the independent kingdom of the Sandwich Islands, ruled over by Queen Lilinokalani, the aunt of my orderly! A sailor had come to the royal residence, the only survivor of a shipwreck, and, quickly learning to speak the language, had made himself useful. A handsome young man, he had fallen in love with the heiress to the throne and had married her. Two years before, this Prince Consort had died, and the Queen had approached our Ministry of Foreign Affairs to enquire after her husband's relatives, he having been a native of Sale on the island of Grossa. Thus I learned that the young sailor had been the uncle of my orderly. I should have been delighted to have been present at the reception of good old Domini (that was his name) at the court of Queen Lilinokalani.

Among the many visitors who came to see our ship at Sydney was a charming old gentleman who, after the War of Independence of 1849[20], had emigrated from Hungary to Australia. He had amassed a tidy fortune and had become a

19 Baron Heinrich Foullon von Norbeck (1850-1896).

20 1848-49.

man of importance, but his prosperity had not compensated for his homesickness. When I asked him, over a meal, why he did not return home, he confessed that he was afraid he might be disappointed. He would be expecting everyone to acclaim his return, but as he no longer knew a soul in Hungary, people were more likely to be indifferent to him. To please him, I gathered together our Hungarian male choir, and we sang one fine Hungarian song after another to him. The old gentleman broke down altogether and, amid his sobs, was hardly able to regain his composure.

After Baron Foullon-Norbeck had come on board, we left Sydney and set sail for New Zealand, where we dropped anchor in Auckland harbour. The northern island is full of volcanoes and bubbling hot springs. At one place somewhere in that region, it is said that trout can be caught in one spring, taken out and lowered into one nearby, where they can be boiled without being removed from the hook! We saw only an occasional Maori; and of the kiwi, the only wingless bird in the world, we saw none. I was surprised at the paucity of wild life in New Zealand. A few years later, when discussing this with Emperor Francis Joseph, I answered a question of his with the remark that I thought it would be an ideal country for chamois. As a result of this comment, a few pair of chamois were sent out there, and, as I heard later, did very well and increased in numbers.

Our next port of call was Noumea, the capital of the French penal colony of New Caledonia. Here the worst types of criminals were sent, and among them was Ravachol, the murderer of the French President. Punishment was very severe and the guillotine was in frequent use. The prisoner on arrival was put in solitary confinement in a dark cell. Only after a long period of good behaviour could he be transferred to a higher grade. The fifth grade was the highest, and, on reaching that, a prisoner could select a wife from among the female prisoners and could till a piece of land. Under these conditions, however, it was no wonder that many of the convicts became insane and had to be sent to the lunatic asylum which it had been found necessary to build next door to the prison. One of the inmates believed himself to be a monkey, and as we crossed the courtyard he was swinging from branch to branch in a large tree with amazing agility. Another believed himself to be the nephew of our Emperor, and on hearing who we were declared himself willing to receive us in audience.

When the captain called on the Governor, he took me with him to act as his interpreter, as our major-domo, a French-speaking Swiss, was supposed to have taught me French in my boyhood. I soon discovered that lack of practice had made my knowledge of the language very rusty.

On New Caledonia there was a kind of deer related to the Sikka deer. I went deer-stalking with a native hunter who hunted by smell like a dog, and very successfully at that.

In our quest for nickel, we sailed from Noumea to the New Hebrides. Owing to the number of treacherous coral reefs and the unreliability of the charts, we used steam while we were among the islands. At that time, the New Hebrides and the Solomon Islands were independent, and I believe that there was a plan to annex some of the islands to Austria-Hungary should Baron Foullon-Norbeck succeed in finding nickel. I have never understood why the Austro-Hungarian monarchy made no attempt to acquire colonies. Admiral Tegetthoff[21] tried to convince those in authority in Vienna of the necessity of colonial possessions, pointing out that they were a means of draining off surplus population without losing it to America. What small countries like Belgium, Holland and Portugal had achieved could surely be achieved by Austria-Hungary? But Admiral Tegetthoff and others who thought as he did received no reply other than that Austria-Hungary did not intend adopting a colonial policy.

The New Hebrides and the Solomon Islands were inhabited solely by head-hunters and cannibals at that time. The Bushmen, an ugly, small, pitch-black, bearded race, were perpetually at war with the salt-watermen, with whom they waged fierce battles to obtain salt. Casualties were eaten. Missionaries often met with the same fate. On first arrival, they were received hospitably and given help in their house-building activities. When they looked fat enough, they were killed and eaten. I was entrusted with the command of the landing party which was to escort Foullon-Norbeck. The captain made me responsible for his safety. After my first experience of progress in the trackless, tangled jungle, I invariably took twenty-five hand-picked men with me, sailors who carried the necessary equipment and who were, moreover, fully armed. On the first island, we climbed the highest

21 Admiral Baron Wilhelm von Tegetthoff (1827-1871). Under his command the Austro-Hungarian navy had a great victory over the Italian navy at Lissa on July 20, 1866.

mountain. The geologist picked up a stone, broke it with a hammer and announced, "coral formation, we can go." On the next island, this was repeated. I would not permit any natives to approach us, as I knew that they carried poisoned javelins and arrows. Whenever they came in sight, I shot down a few coconuts well beyond them to show them how long a range our rifles had. I had a native interpreter with me who spoke fluent English, having been carried off to Australia, where they were in need of labour. Natives used to be enticed on board ship by means of small presents, such as glass beads, matches and hatchets. Once on board, they would be asked to perform some small service below deck, and the moment they had gone below, the anchor was raised. My interpreter had learned to smoke in Australia and was very grateful when I gave him a little of my tobacco, for since his return to his native island he had seen none.

Nickel, and gold also, were finally discovered on Guadalcanal, an island of the Solomon archipelago, which was much in the news during the Second World War. As we were beginning to run short of coal, however, and we would be having to use steam to pass through Torres Strait between Australia and New Guinea, we left Guadalcanal for Thursday Island of Robinson Crusoe fame, where we proposed to bunker. There Baron Foullon-Norbeck, whom I had accompanied on more than thirty landings in perfect concord and amity, left us to travel back to Vienna. The year following, he continued his search for nickel in the Austro-Hungarian warship *Albatross*, an expedition which had a tragic ending.

I assume that Norbeck considered the natives harmless and that he convinced my successor that precautionary measures were unnecessary. At any rate, when he set off to climb yet another mountain he insisted on leaving the major part of his escort at base; the remainder began the ascent accompanied by a large number of natives. The leader of these walked beside the commander of the expedition, Lieutenant Budik[22], and asked him by signs to show him the revolver he was carrying in his belt, and for which he displayed the greatest respect. As Budik was explaining the function of the weapon to him, a number of shots rang out below them, and the natives immediately began to attack the climbing party. The native leader produced his stone axe and began swinging it, but Budik shot him down. Several natives were killed and the rest fled, but our side also had its losses. Poor Foullon-Norbeck had his skull crushed. Midshipman Beaufort was killed and seven of his men with him. The

22 Lt. Ferenc Budik (1870-1918), later became captain.

wounded were carried back to the ship, but when next morning a landing party went to collect the dead, no trace of them could be found.

Though we ourselves had no difficulties, we were nevertheless glad to reach Amboina, a fascinating island in the Moluccas which belonged to the Dutch, and to find ourselves among civilized people again. Our next port of call was Borneo.

When the weather was calm, our ship used to be followed by sharks, which snatched greedily at any food which was thrown overboard. One petty officer on board had been a professional tunnyfisher and would harpoon these monsters from a distance of thirty to fifty feet with amazing sureness of hand. He also caught quite a few sharks for us with a baited hook. To catch one particularly mighty specimen, a large noose was lowered into the water on a strong rope fixed to the main yardarm. The rope ran through a tackle back to the deck, and about a hundred men were holding it. The shark was tempted with pieces of meat and bacon rind to swim into the noose; it did, the sailors hauled on the rope and in a few moments the shark was dangling in the air. It was thrashing so violently that we feared it would damage the deck. In the end, a sailor had himself lowered beside it and threw another noose round its tail. With that aid, we succeeded in getting the monster on board, where it was killed with axe blows. Inside its body we found three large bladders filled with young shark, each the size of an average trout. Thrown into buckets of water, they swam about merrily, and we counted fifty-five of them. *Brehm's Encyclopedia* gave the figure of thirty to fifty eggs hatching inside the female's body.

Between Celebes and Borneo, I took over the midnight watch to the words, "Nothing in sight," one bright and starry night. With all sails set, we were making a regular eight knots, and every half hour the bosun of the watch would sing out, "Lights are burning bright and all's well." For safety's sake, I searched the horizon with my glasses, and suddenly I observed, on the starboard beam, a large four-masted sailing ship, all sails set, but of her navigation lights not a glimmer. She was heading straight for us like the Flying Dutchman. The situation was critical. If I turned to port, and the manoeuvre were to fail, there was a danger of our being rammed. I decided, therefore, to turn to starboard so that, should we fail to pass astern of her, we should ram her and not be rammed. Fortunately the watch was ready and did their work to perfection. The stunsails were taken in at speed, we braced the yards round and passed her, merely brushing a boat that was hoisted over her stern.

On board this other ship there was not a soul to be seen: they were all asleep. To wake them up, I had a signal gun fired on deck. That episode was my most exciting experience of the whole cruise.

We dropped anchor off the village of Kudat in a fine bay in the north-eastern part of Borneo. In this region there were no Europeans. With a view to having some sport, I had bought myself a small single-sculler in Sydney. I had it lowered, and, armed with a rifle, I rowed inshore and up a stream into the jungle, which was the habitat of monkeys and parrots. On returning, I went ashore near the village and, to my astonishment, a freshly shaved Englishman stepped out of one of the huts. He was a well-known big game hunter who was combing the world for rare species and had come to this place in a Chinese junk to hunt bantengo, a kind of wild buffalo. It needed little persuasion on his part to get me to agree to join him on an expedition. Four mornings later, after he had worked out his plans with the Sultan, at that time, north-east Borneo was still an independent sultanate, we set out. He warned me about the alligators, which had been known to attack boats.

Before the day appointed, however, I had decided to try my luck single-handed. I took two midshipmen with me and arranged for the boat to come for us the next morning at six o'clock. We hit nothing. The forest was too dense, but we spent a very romantic New Year's Eve. We had pitched camp in a clearing and ate our supper with a good appetite. On the stroke of midnight, we uncorked the bottle of champagne we had brought with us and drank to our loves, our happy homecoming and to the New Year in general. But we forgot to drink to the weather, which was a mistake. We had hardly turned in before the most fearful downpour woke us up, and, wet and shivering with cold, we realized that the boat would not be calling for us for hours. I have rarely been so cold as on that New Year's morning on the Equator.

The hunting trip with the Englishman was a great success. We stood, concealed by trees, a thousand feet apart on the edge of a clearing where game was wont to appear at dusk. And, indeed, an enormous bull suddenly came out of the forest. Though the distance was great and his position unfavourable, I risked a shot, followed by two more. The Englishman fired

29

also and when at last the bull dropped, he had been hit ten times. We cut off his head and put it on a termite hill. In a singularly short space of time, it had been picked clean by these ants, and as I had fired the first three shots, I was given the skull as a trophy, which I proudly took home with me.

Our voyage, however, should not be regarded as nothing but a succession of hunting expeditions, receptions and sight-seeing. No matter how far from home we were, discipline was rigidly maintained and we had to work at our studies. We were glad to be passing through the Suez Canal again.

We had moored according to canal regulations to make way for a mail steamer, but a trailing rope fouled the propeller and, as it was growing dark, the captain decided to spend the night in the Canal. Our faces fell; we had been away for over two years and were longing to get home as speedily as possible. As I was the diving officer, I asked permission of the captain to inspect the trouble with the aid of a diver. I had the searchlights directed on to the propeller and we succeeded in cutting the rope away. Our labours were considerably complicated by the many fish that were attracted by the bright light.

South of Crete we were beating into a fresh westerly wind. At midnight, I took over the watch and about an hour later we went about just offshore, and began to follow a south-westerly course. Suddenly there was a mighty crash as if the ship had run into shallow ground. Yet the charts showed no shallows there. We were at a loss to explain the incident until we heard later that Crete had been subjected to a violent earthquake, which we had felt as a sea tremor.

Off the Bocche di Cattaro, we picked up a signal ordering us to make for the shore. Field Marshal Archduke Albert and Admiral Baron Sterneck[23], Commander-in-Chief of the Navy, wished to inspect our ship. A great disappointment awaited the midshipmen. Instead of going on leave, they were forthwith distributed among the various warships of the squadron present in the bight. Painful as it was to them, they had to part with their dearly acquired South Sea mementoes.

On voyages across oceans, it was customary for the ship's pendant to be lengthened by a yard for every thousand miles covered. When we entered Pola, our pendant was dragging in the water far astern.

23 Baron Maximilien von Sterneck (1829-1897)

At the end of the voyage, I took the three months' leave to which I was entitled. As I travelled through Hungary and saw our peasants, clad in the picturesque costume they still wore then, harvesting the golden wheat, I could have embraced them. My first evening in Budapest I spent at the National Theatre. My seat was in the front row and there was nothing wrong with my hearing, yet I could scarcely understand a word. For three years, I had heard so little Hungarian that the sound of the language had become almost alien to me. It took me a while to attune my ears to it.

The next day I arrived at Kenderes. After our long separation, my reunion with my parents and brothers and sisters was indeed a profound joy.

2. New Appointments

At the end of my leave, in the autumn of 1894, I was appointed to the staff of Vice-Admiral Baron Spaun[1], the chief of the naval technical committee. In that post, I gained an insight into a number of important and interesting questions, but I also came across far too many shortcomings. As a result either of mistaken opinions or of a shortage of money, the technical committees at Pola and in Vienna often refused to take up important discoveries, thereby doing considerable harm. I remember that, in my time, a draughtsman in the torpedo section handed in an invention which the naval officers recommended without reservation, but it was firmly rejected by the expert engineer for naval artillery matters. Soon afterwards, that engineer retired and went into partnership with Obry[2], a constructional draughtsman. Today every torpedo contains their gyroscope. This invention, which keeps the torpedo on its set course, has vastly increased the torpedo's range.

The first destroyer of the Austro-Hungarian Navy was built at the Schichau yard at Elbing[3]. I belonged to the crew which was to take her over. I made use of the occasion to visit the then expanding capital of the German Empire. If Vienna was the more welcoming and homely city, the ebullient energy of Berlin was more likely to impress a young man. A trade fair that was being held there at the time of my visit held a particular interest for me.

The trial trip of the *Magnet* was most successful. On passing through the newly opened Kaiser Wilhelm Canal, we received a hearty welcome from the people of Schleswig-Holstein. In spite of variable weather, our voyage home was smooth. On the way, we called at Gibraltar and Corfu.

Upon my return, I was fortunate enough to be sent on the torpedo course, which I preferred by far to the three other possibilities: the writing desk, the artillery, or the mine-laying service, since it meant that I would remain at sea all the time, as exercises were frequent. Chances of promotion would also be better. The training, theoretical and practical, covered a year.

1   Adm. Baron Hermann Spaun (1833-1919).

2   Lajos Obry, chief mechanic at the naval shipyard at Pola. He was one of the designer of the Lummis - Whitehead torpedo used by many navies before W.W.I.

3   Today Elblag in Poland.

Following upon that course, I was again chosen as one of the crew that was to take over a ship, and this time we went to England. The Thames Iron Works[4] had built us two extremely fast deep-torpedo-boats. Once again, I seized the opportunity of seeing new countries and admiring new towns. I travelled via Mainz and Cologne to Brussels, and from there, accompanied by a friend, via Ostend, to London. We were very disappointed to hear from our naval attaché that the transfer was to be made the next day; it seemed that sojourn in the metropolis would be limited to a Sunday afternoon. On the first trial trip, however, the condenser casing of the *Cobra* tore, and her sister ship, the *Boa,* had to tow her back to Poplar. Investigation proved that material of inferior quality had been used and the builders had to foot the bill. What was more, we had months in which to enjoy the famous sights and traditions of London.

We were put up at a good hotel, and made the most of our sojourn. The mornings were occupied in Poplar, supervising the work. Names on the Underground like Fenchurch Street Station and Millwall Junction were difficult for us, but vital. If we missed them were liable to get lost in the wilds of London. In the afternoon we were free and that gave us the opportunity to get to know sights of London, and in particular the museums. Their richness left a deep impression on me. We patronized the theatre box-offices in the evenings, and though I cannot, after all these years, remember what else we saw, I recall the brilliance of the famous musical comedy *The Belle of New York.* We naturally went to the races, where we saw for the first time the new 'American seat', introduced by Ted Sloan the jockey, and soon to become universal in England and on the Continent.

I made friends with a very pleasant and intelligent R.N. officer. He gave me a beverage which he called *whisky sour.* I liked it and it seemed harmless enough, with its lemonade taste. Shortly afterwards, when I met several friends at the bar during the interval at a music-hall, I was several times asked to have a drink, and knowing at the time the name of no other, I answered a "*whisky sour*", so that by the time we went to supper the world was turning rapidly round my head! I beat a quick retreat and made for the hotel, and for the next three days had to shun all entertainment. We were not free from money troubles and were more than once obliged to send an SOS to our respective fathers. The fact is that we were often extravagant through ignorance, as, for

4   Horthy is mistaken here. The original documents and publications mention
     Yarrow & Co., not the Thames Iron Works as the manufacturer of these tor-
     pedo boats.

example, when it came to buying seats at the theatre, or hailing a hansom instead of joining the fashionable mob on the horse-bus, a mode of conveyance which the Prime Minister of the day did not despise.

Apart from these diversions, we lieutenants and our superiors, the two Lieutenant- Commanders, made no attempt to take part in London's social life. Even with our own Embassy, we were careful to deal strictly through the naval attaché. The enjoyment of those weeks in England has left in me, despite all the unhappy changes that the years between have wrought, an indelible sense of sympathy as a Magyar with the British nation, and a conviction that our two peoples share their best ideals in common.[5]

After new trials, we began the journey home, first calling at the French port of Brest. When, late that night, I returned from town to the harbour, there was no sign of the *Boa*. After a while, I recognized a crane near which the ship had moored. And then I saw the *Boa*, down in the depths. The rise and fall of the tide at Brest is some forty feet, which I had not reckoned with, being accustomed to measuring the tide at Pola in inches.

On this occasion, we had singularly bad weather on the way home, especially in the Bay of Biscay. The waves washed right over the ship, and for days hot meals were out of the question. It was only just possible to stay on our course. We were extremely relieved to reach Lisbon, where we could recuperate and at the same time learn to know that beautiful city. To visit Cintra, the ancient castle of the Braganzas[6], we had to go on horseback. Along the south bank, there were only a few small clusters of fishermen's cottages. Little did I guess then in what changed circumstances I should be returning to Lisbon.

5   The former editor of *The Economist*, Graham Hutton expressed the same sentiment when he wrote, in 1939, thus: "There is no people in Europe as in-dividualistic as the Hungarian, and the stratification of Hungary's social sys-tem is like that of England as the Hungarian constitution and limited monarchy is like the English equivalents. (Perhaps that is why the English and Hungarian versions of 'democracy' -less essentially democratic than those of other liberal régimes in Europe - have been more successful than those of the German Weimar Republic, France, Czecho-Slovakia, Belgium. For both England and Hungary, with their vestigial aristocracy, their rigidly defined class and caste barriers which every one voluntarily respects, thereby gain in national cohesion.) Hutton, Graham: *Danubian Destiny*, London: Harrap & Co., 1939. pp. 197-198.

6   The Braganza Dynasty reigned in Portugal from 1640 until 1910, also in Brazil from 1822 until 1889.

I remember a visit to the Opera, when the King of Portugal[7] was present. I was surprised at the small amount of notice taken of him in contrast with the ovation given the entry of a famous bullfighter, which made the auditorium ring with applause.

Although it was customary for non-British ships to anchor in the open roads at Gibraltar, the Commander of the Home Fleet, Admiral Prince Battenberg[8], informed us that, on account of the persistent bad weather, we could anchor in a sheltered position to leeward of his flagship, the *Majestic*. When we called on him, he was kind enough to take us over his ship personally and show us every nook and corner.

After visits to Algiers, Palermo and Corfu, we made for Pola, where I was put in charge of the sailors' training. I cannot say that training recruits filled me with enthusiasm, but I had no complaint to make, as, a few months later, I was to my surprise given an appointment as captain of the *Artemisia*, a sailing ship of the venerable age of one hundred and fifty years. One of my predecessors as her captain had been Tegetthoff. She was a remarkably pleasant ship to manoeuvre, one of three training ships manned wholly by boys, the most suitable of whom were chosen for advanced training as petty officers. Those boys were resolute, agreeable lads, and it was plain that they had been submitted to a ruthless discipline at their school.

When I reported for duty to the head of the boys' school at Sebenico, the first officer told me that there was one boy on board with whom no progress could be made. The son of a wealthy Hungarian landowner, he had formed a most romantic picture of the Navy from reading. Reality having proved different from what he had expected, he was unhappy among people who did not speak his language and he was refusing to obey orders. During a rowing exercise, he had had his ears boxed for failing to take up his oar and had jumped into the water. As he could not swim, he was saved with difficulty. It was left to me to see what could be done with him.

On my arrival on board, I found the lad undergoing punishment: he had been standing in the rigging for six hours without food or water. I had him called before me and told him that he would be allowed to leave the school, and that

7   Charles I (1863-1908).

8   Admiral of the Fleet Prince Louis Alexander Battenberg (Mountbatten, from 1917) (1854-1921), grandfather of Prince Philip Royal Consort.

I was prepared to support the request his father would have to make. The procedure, however, would take time and until his departure he would have to behave himself and obey orders; otherwise he would find himself in very hot water. "Can't you see," I said to him, "that the whole Austro-Hungarian Navy cannot capitulate to the insubordination of one cabin boy?"

He did see that, and promised to obey orders; and he kept his promise. In the course of a few months, he had mastered German, Italian and a little Croat, had come top of his form and was generally considered a prodigy. By the time permission for him to leave came through, he did not wish to avail himself of it. I kept an eye on him then and later, and, after twelve years' service as a leading seaman, he became skipper of a Danube steamer.

On my return from the practice trip, I was surprised to find awaiting me at Sebenico instructions to take over the boys' school for a year. I was in despair. Sebenico was a picturesque little town, but a year's contemplation of the picturesque together with the necessity of teaching was a form of burial that had no appeal for me. Strangely enough, I found that I enjoyed the unaccustomed work of teaching, and I was none too pleased when, after four months, I received an unexpected order to report for duty at the naval section of the Ministry of Defence in Vienna. I left Trieste in a Lloyd steamer and the boys escorted the vessel in their boats for a fair distance.

My new work consisted of translating the budget of the Navy from German into Hungarian and of acting as interpreter at the joint deliberations of the Delegations of the Austrian and Hungarian parliaments. To interpret accurately is always a responsible and difficult task. Since Hungarian, like Finnish and Turkish, belongs to the Ural-Altaic family and not, like German, English, French and Italian, to the Indo-European, special difficulties tend to arise in translation. It is impossible to translate word for word, and in fact the interpreter must hear the last word of the sentence before he can even begin.

At the end of the dinner given by His Majesty to the delegates in the Marble Hall of the Royal Palace in Budapest, I found myself drinking coffee at the table of Count Tisza[9], the Prime Minister, who was an old friend of my family,

9   Count István Tisza (1861-1918) was a long time friend of Horthy's father and was instrumental in getting Horthy appointed to the position of aide-de-camp at the Court. (Sakmyster, Thomas: Hungary's Admiral on Horseback: Miklós Horthy, 1918-1944, Columbia Univ. Press, 1994.)

together with some of the leading Hungarian politicians. The conversation turned to Croatia, and as I knew that country and its people very well, I expressed some criticisms of our policy towards it. It would, I hazarded, be better if Croatia, Dalmatia, Bosnia and Herzegovina, a homogeneous language community, were to be united and if, above all, a stop were to be put to the ridiculous and vexatious minor provocations offered the Croats[10]. I pointed out, for instance, that their railway stations had notices in Hungarian only. In such ways, even generous government measures, especially in financial matters, were often lost to them. The others, however, were of the opinion that my suggestions would never find favour in Parliament. Later on, during the 1918 disturbances Count Tisza was requested by Emperor Charles to go and investigate conditions personally, he asked the Navy for a ship to take him from Zara to Cattaro. I sent him our fastest destroyer and my flag-captain, Vukovic, to act as his interpreter and aide-de-camp. To Vukovic I entrusted a letter addressed to Tisza in which I reminded him of that long past conversation and voiced my fears that years of pan-Serbian propaganda would defeat his efforts to bring the Croats round to a contrary view. Vukovic, who remained with him throughout the journey, brought me a long letter in reply, written from Budapest, in which Tisza gave his impressions and regretfully confirmed my views. He declared the position in Sarajevo to be particularly hopeless.

The sessions of the delegates, and with them my usefulness, came to an end, and I spent the leave I was given at home. I was then thirty-two years old. I had had thoughts of marriage, but had decided that a naval officer ought not to marry, a solemn theory that goes by the board as soon as one meets the right person.

I had intended to visit my sister at Miskolc, but on arriving at the railway station I was met by my brother-in-law, whose regiment of hussars was stationed there. My sister, it appeared, had gone to Budapest and he had accepted an invitation to visit some old friends of my elder brother and had been unable to postpone it. Why should I not go with him? Thinking it would be no more than an afternoon call, I agreed. I was, therefore, more than a little

---

10 Croatia-Slavonia had a very special status within the Lands of the Hungarian Holy Crown. According to the 1868 "Nagodba", Constitution, the Croats were entitled to the use of their own language even in the Hungarian Parliament, and in the Croatian units of the Hungarian national army. In fact, these regiments were commanded in Croatian.

surprised to be met at the station by a four-in-hand[11], which suggested that some distance lay between us and our destination. And, indeed, so it was. I had to resign myself to spending the night with an unknown host at Hejôbába[12]. It was, I thought, an awkward situation, and I had the impression that the master of the estate, his wife and her remarkably beautiful younger sister were, in spite of their cordiality, more than a little taken aback to see a completely strange naval officer step out of the carriage. I begged to be forgiven, but they would let me make no excuses, and the outcome was that I spent three extremely happy days with them at Hejôbába.

Chance or design? This visit proved the great turning point in my life. During the carnival, I went to a ball at Miskolc of which Mrs. Melczer[13], my charming hostess at Hejôbába, was the lady patroness. A yet more resplendent guest was her lovely sister, Magda Purgly[14], who was the best dancer I had ever met. The following year, I was asked to act as escort to the two ladies and my sister in a journey to Venice. Although I did not consider myself particularly equipped for the task, as I had never been there myself, I thought my knowledge of Italian might prove useful, and I had no hesitation in accepting the commission. After an unforgettably happy week, my mind was made up, and as I had the secret acquiescence of Miss Purgly, all that remained for me to do was to gain my father's consent, but his views on the marrying of naval officers were those I had held myself until that moment. He allowed himself to be won over, however, and Miss Purgly and I travelled to the estate of my future father-in-law for the celebration of the betrothal.

After I had been given the command of the torpedo-boat *Sperber* and had relinquished it again, I went with my staff to Arad. There, on July 22nd, 1901, with all the customary Hungarian pomp and ceremony, Magda and I were married. We chose Semmering for our honeymoon.

Even in those days it was not easy to find a house at Pola, the main Hungarian

---

11 A four horse landau carriage, 19th century equivalent of a stretch limousine.

12 Village near Arad, today in Rumania.

13 Mrs. László Melczer nee. Janka Purgly, future sister-in-law of Adm. Horthy.

14 Magda Purgly of Jószás (1881-1959).

naval base. After the birth of our first child, a daughter[15], we had a house built which had a garden and a fine view over the sea. This house saw the birth of our other children, another girl and two boys.

My chiefs were very considerate. As captain of the first-class torpedo-boat *Kranich*, which was used as a training ship for engine-room personnel, I used to return home each evening at six o'clock. After six months, I was put in charge of a destroyer flotilla and had to part from my wife for a few months. My next command took me to the *Habsburg*, the flagship of our Mediterranean squadron, in which we went on a cruise. Our first port of call was Smyrna, the present-day Izmir. The Vali and future Grand Vizier, Kiamil Pasha, returned our Admiral's visit dressed in a gold-embroidered frock coat, in which he looked most imposing. We found him a very likeable man.

In the wars with the Turks, from the fifteenth to the eighteenth centuries, the Magyars had often inflicted serious losses on them, but the fate of our country had been sealed for a hundred and fifty years by the catastrophe of Mohács. There, 25,000 Magyars had faced 200,000 Turks. The flower of our manhood was taken to Constantinople and trained for the Sultan's elite corps of janissaries. But by the beginning of the twentieth century, this ancient enmity had been forgotten. Magyars and Turks, speaking cognate languages, had learned to appreciate each other, and indeed the two nations have similar characteristics, both being courtly peoples. Nothing is further from the truth than to regard the Turks as 'Levantines', and to treat them as such is foolish. The German Ambassador, Franz von Papen, once told me that until the day he left Ankara, there was in the Embassy coffers one and a half million marks in gold and currency, sent him by Ribbentrop to use in winning over prominent Turkish politicians to Germany. But von Papen knew the Turks too well to use such dishonourable methods. He was aware that attempts at bribery would have seriously damaged the German cause, a fact apparently not known in Berlin.

15 Magdolna (1902-1918) died of scarlet fever, Paula (1903-1940) died of lung ailment, István (1904-1942) aircraft accident, Miklós (1907-1993).

Smyrna[16] at the time that I was there was a rich and flourishing commercial city, a centre for the export of tobacco, figs and mohair. Trading, however, as in so many other Mediterranean harbours, was carried on by the Greeks.

Perpetual shortage of money had compelled Turkey to borrow more and more from abroad, so that a special international administration had been set up in Paris, the "Dette Ottomane"[17]. Use was made of this by the Great Powers to exert political pressure on Turkey, and the Ottoman Empire had been placed under a kind of international receivership. When the financial pressure of the Great Powers proved unavailing, their demands were emphasized by naval demonstrations, as in 1903 when, after a meeting of Tsar Nicholas[18] first with Kaiser Wilhelm II[19] at Wiesbaden and later with Emperor Francis Joseph at Schloss Mürzsteg, the programme known as the Mürzsteg

Reform Programme was worked out providing for the creation of nationally limited areas of control in Macedonia. As Austria-Hungary, a neighbour of Turkey, was the party most interested in Balkan affairs, our armoured cruiser *St. Georg*, in which I was torpedo officer, became the flagship of the international fleet that was assembled in the Piraeus. Austria-Hungary, Great Britain, France and Italy each sent two warships; Russia contributed one gunboat. The German Empire remained aloof. Our Commander-in-Chief was Vice-Admiral Ripper[20], an energetic and circumspect naval officer. Although unaccustomed to maneuvering with foreign ships, he saw to it that the squadron became well integrated and he never overlooked the slightest dereliction of duty. Our first operation was directed against the island of Mitylene; once we had anchored, the order was given that we were to act as if we were at war. The landing party was led by the first officer of the British armoured cruiser *Lancaster*, I was beach-master and interpreter. There was no resistance; the Turks remained quiet and behaved as if we did not exist. Lemnos also was occupied. As the Sultan still made no move, Vice-Admiral Ripper decided to force the Dardanelles. The other commanders were of the opinion that this would be too dangerous an undertaking on account of that

16 Today Izmir.

17 Agency to handle the international indebtedness of Turkey.

18 Russia's Tsar Nicholas I of Romanov (1868-1918)

19 German Kaiser Wilhelm II of Hohenzollern (1859-1941).

20 Rear Admiral Julius von Ripper (1847-1914).

area's strong defences, and they declared that they would have to consult their respective Governments. The answers were in the negative. The matter was then again referred to our diplomats, who found a successful solution, and we were all able to return home. Our ships reached Pola just before Christmas.

It was written in the stars, however, that I should see Constantinople again. After a few shore assignments, and after having been in command of the *Lacroma*, the yacht of the naval commander Admiral Count Montecuccoli[21], I became captain of the *Taurus*, the Embassy yacht. I took over the ship at Tophane, seventeen years after my first sojourn in Constantinople, on June 8th, 1908.

At the next *selamlik*, as they called the Friday visit of the Sultan to the mosque, our Ambassador, Count Pallavicini[22], presented me to Sultan Abdul Hamid II[23]. The impression he made on me was of a thoroughly suspicious and narrow-minded autocrat who refused to admit, even to himself, that power had slipped from his hands. He adhered meticulously to the empty formulae of power. Even when an Embassy yacht went on a cruise, she had, before she could enter the Bosporus or the Dardanelles, to have a permit signed by the Sultan himself. It was singularly difficult to obtain such a permit. He was strangely afraid of electricity in any form: lights, trams or anything else. It was said that this was because he had once heard the word dynamo and it reminded him of dynamite, a substance he held in dread.

Even we could see that the country was seething beneath the surface. A few weeks after my arrival, the revolution of the *Young Turks* broke out. On July 23rd, 1908, at Salonika, Enver[24] Bey proclaimed afresh the 1876 constitution which Abdul Hamid had abolished soon after his accession to the throne. When Enver Bey and Nazim[25] Bey, together with their troops, mutinied, the Sultan gave orders for them to be hanged, and his Grand Vizier had the task of pointing out to him that his power was insufficient. Elections were proclaimed, which put Vienna in a difficult predicament. To prevent

21 Adm. Count Rudolph Montecuccoli (1843-1927),

22 Count János Pallavicini (1848-1945).

23 1842-1918.

24 Enver bey Turkish army commander (1881-1922).

25 Hussein Nazim (1848-1913), army commander, later pasha.

elections from being held in Bosnia-Herzegovina, which though actually occupied was still nominally part of the Ottoman Empire, the Dual Monarchy proclaimed on October 5th, 1908, that Bosnia and Herzegovina would be added to Austria-Hungary as a *corpus separatum*, while the Sandjak of Novibazar would be returned to Turkey.

The annexation of Bosnia-Herzegovina was diplomatically ill prepared. Great Britain protested, on the grounds that it was an infringement of the Berlin Treaty of 1878; Serbia and Montenegro threatened war. The Turks began a general boycott of our exports, which caused much hardship, as in those days Austria-Hungary was the main supplier and also the main customer of Turkey. Our steamers were left with unloaded cargoes; they were no longer bunkered; and the Austrian firms in Constantinople were either picketed or ostracized.

As the captain of our Embassy yacht, I found this damaging to our prestige, and I therefore called on our Ambassador to obtain his approval for forcing the transfer of the cargoes held in the warehouse of the Trieste Lloyd. Count Pallavicini asked me what I intended to do in face of the armed Kurds, who had hitherto prevented the transfer. I replied that I intended to make use of gunboats and an armed guard.

"And what if they fire on you?" he asked with an anxious air.

"Then we'll return their fire."

"But that might lead to war, and war must be avoided at all costs."

In the end, he agreed to my proposal, but requested me to be as careful as I could. Everything went smoothly; the Kurds preferred not to fight.

As Germany had emphatically declared that she would support Austria-Hungary if necessary, the Great Powers and finally Turkey herself gave way in February, 1909, on the annexation question. The victory was not wholly to our advantage, as was to be shown a few years later. But of that we had then no inkling.

The pleasant social life of Constantinople was not dimmed by these political events. I had taken a villa at Yenikeui on the Bosporus next to the summer residence of our Embassy, residing there with my wife and four children. Receptions, regattas, polo matches, dances and similar gaieties made our life pleasant and varied. I had had my sailing boat sent me from Pola, and I was able to participate in the yachting races; at the end of the season, I even won the first prize. Twice a week we played polo on the large meadow at Büyükdere, the site on which Godfrey of Bouillon and his crusaders had once pitched their tents. On the Atmeidan in Stamboul, I bought a fine Arab stallion, small but swift, which brought me victory in the Polo Scurry. I also gained the Grand Prix du Bosphore in the face of fierce competition in a field of twelve; the Krupp representative had asked me to ride his horse, and I had trained assiduously, following instructions given me by my brother Stephen in his letters. At that time, Stephen was our champion male horse-rider. In the obstacle race, the horse of Prince Colonna[26], a cousin of the wife of the Italian Ambassador, broke its neck and its rider was carried unconscious from the field. Fortunately, I had my steam launch at hand, so that we were able to transport him without loss of time to the Italian Embassy. After a few days, I heard to my great satisfaction that he was out of danger. Twenty-six years later, I met Prince Colonna again as Italian Ambassador to Hungary.

After such successes, I set my heart on winning the international tennis tournament for Hungary. When my first officer was recalled, I proposed Lieutenant Árvay[27] as his successor, for not only was he an excellent seaman but he had, that spring, come first in our Army and Navy tennis tournament. The captain of the British Embassy ship had, however, had the same idea; he too acquired as his first officer an Army and Navy tennis champion, a man we could not defeat in the singles. But Árvay and I were pleased enough when we carried off the victory in the men's doubles against the British team.

This catalogue of sports victories may have a boastful ring, but I do remember how proud we were at the time of these triumphs. Indeed, as I look back on them now I still feel the pleasure I felt then.

As usual, the Embassies moved back to town for the winter months and we weighed anchor and went to the artillery arsenal Tophane and moored alongside.

---

26 Ascanio Colonna, Prince of Paliano (1883- ?).

27 Capt. Frigyes Árvay (1875-1952).

After the opening of Parliament, relative peace descended on the political life of the country. Sultan Abdul Hamid, who had never hitherto ventured outside the Yildiz, apart from the few hundred yards to the mosque, now began to display an interest in his people. He even showed himself in Stamboul and was greeted with great respect by the inhabitants. Even so, he could not resign himself to the loss of absolute power. His wise Grand Vizier, Kiamil Pasha, who was in favour of retaining the Constitution and the Parliamentary system, had a difficult time. He was unable to prevent the Sultan himself from fomenting a mutiny, the preparation of which he entrusted, by the irony of fate, to the unworthy son of the worthy Kiamil Pasha.

With my father-in-law, my brother-in-law and his wife, all of whom were staying with us on a visit, we had planned an expedition into Stamboul one morning to see certain mosques and the bazaar. That day, however, we were woken by the sound of shots. Shops were closed and armed soldiers were walking singly or in groups through the streets. I made enquiries at our Embassy to find out what was going on. All they could tell me was that guns were being placed on the bridge across the Golden Horn between Galata and Stamboul. We decided to go out of town toward Ejub to the 'sweet waters', but near the palace of Dolmabagché the street was closed by cavalry. The commanding officer came up to our carriage and asked us to turn back. He was the son of Djemil Bey, who for years had been the Turkish Ambassador in Paris, and we knew him, having often met him at receptions. He knew no more than our Embassy did what exactly was happening. Apparently some troops had mutinied, and his regiment had received orders to close the roads leading to the Yildiz Kiosk. He instructed one of his officers to see us safely home.

In the afternoon, the officers were arrested by their own men; many were murdered. Djemil Bey succeeded in persuading his men to disarm, but preferred himself to seek safety in flight. The mutineers marched to the Parliament Buildings and demanded the resignation of the Government. The general in command, Mohammed Mukhtar[28] Pasha, asked the Sultan for permission to open fire, but received no reply. After the Minister of Justice and the Minister of Marine had been shot by the rebels, he telephoned again, declaring that his own loyal troops might begin to waver should he fail to act. He was then expressly forbidden to make use of his arms.

28 General Mohamed Mukhtar (1867-1919).

45

Mohammed Mukhtar wrote me a note asking me to save Djemil Bey and to let Mukhtar know where he was hiding. As night fell, I despatched a motor launch, the officer in charge of which succeeded in making contact with Djemil Bey and in bringing him to the *Taurus*, where we gave him the uniform of a naval inspector to wear. Two days later, he was able to leave for Trieste in one of our Lloyd steamers, together with his wife and child, whom I had also had brought on board.

Acting on the news that Constantinople was in the hands of the rebels, the commander of the troops at Salonika, Mohammed Shefket Pasha, rushed his troops to the city to clear it. He pitched camp outside the walls and waited for the situation to develop in order to shed as little blood as possible. I had, meanwhile, sent a detachment of sailors to guard the Embassy. One morning I received the information that a company of Turkish troops had marched upon the Embassy, whereupon I immediately hastened over, only to find that they were military cadets who had been sent by Mohammed Shefket Pasha also as a guard. In the company of our military attaché, I often rode out of town to visit the besiegers. The officers were naturally very anxious to know what was happening in town. We asked them when they were going to attack, but they did not know. Rumour had it that Mohammed Shefket Pasha was waiting for the selamlik, for which the entire garrison was wont to march out.

Opposite the mosque, to which the Sultan was accustomed to drive in the carriage of state accompanied by the Grand Vizier, who sat facing him, there is a building with large plate-glass windows, from which the representatives of foreign powers could watch the ceremony and the parade of troops. This time, I took part in the selamlik, but the expected attack was not made. In any case, not a single officer was present in the parade; whole regiments were commanded by old and bearded subalterns. As usual, the Sultan was driving the fine Lipizzaners which had been a present to him from our monarch, but this time the Pashas were not walking behind his carriage as was their custom.

At last the day of attack came. We were woken by the thunder of guns. I went at once to the Embassy. Count Pallavicini told me that a rifle bullet had struck the wall over his bed, had ricochetted and had fallen on his hand. Although the fighting was taking place round the arsenal, I succeeded in reaching the *Taurus*. Shortly afterwards, the ship's doctor arrived. As he was being rowed to the ship, rifle bullets were hitting the water all round the boat, and to the general merriment the doctor instinctively opened his umbrella.

By early afternoon, the outcome of the battle had been decided. General Hussein Hüssni was given the delicate task of informing the Sultan that he had been deposed. He did this with great skill, telling the Sultan that he had come to save his life and that the special court train was waiting to take him and his harem to Salonika. As the Sultan was in the habit of adding to his harem every year at the feast of Kurban Bairam, the new wife and her odalisques taking up their abode in the Yildiz Kiosk, it was estimated that there would be three hundred women to transport. There proved to be only thirty-three left.

On April 27th, 1909, Abdul Hamid's brother, Reshid Effendi, was proclaimed Sultan by the Parliament and given the appellation of Mohammed V. The storm had subsided and all was still again. Peace and order were restored. Conscription was introduced and General von der Goltz[29] was entrusted with the reorganization of the Turkish Army.

There was, therefore, no reason why the *Taurus* should not go on her customary spring cruise. We sailed, via Varna and Odessa, up the Danube along the Sulina branch as far as Galatz. On the return voyage we touched at Constantinople and, via Salonika, went to the Piraeus where our squadron lay. The *Taurus* was there inspected by the squadron commander.

On my return, I found an official letter awaiting me to say that if I would care to accept the post of aide-de-camp to His Majesty, Admiral Count Montecuccoli would like to nominate me. I replied by telegram that I should consider such an appointment a great honour, but at heart I regretted having to leave the Bosporus so soon. I was not, therefore, heartbroken to learn by telegram that the post was being provisionally filled by an officer of the Imperial Rifles. My stay would be prolonged by a few months, at any rate.

The good old *Taurus* was a paddle-steamer built originally for service on the Danube. Her fighting value was nil, and, moreover, she lacked suitable accommodation for the Ambassador when he had to undertake a tour of inspection in the Embassy yacht. For that reason, I had suggested that a suitable yacht should be procured and my suggestion was accepted. A French yacht was found that met the necessary requirements and was bought.

---

29 Baron Colmar von der Goltz, "Goltz Pasha" (1843-1916).

I was thus destined to be the last captain of the *Taurus*, and it was with a heavy heart that I left Constantinople, where, but for one break, I had spent two and a half years. I had come to know the Turks in a number of diverse circumstances, and had grown to like them. They are a people of strong character, a noble, reliable race, and excellent soldiers.

Nor was parting from Pallavicini, the Ambassador, easy. I respected him as a high-minded, wise and clearsighted diplomat to whom the other Ambassadors, in those difficult days of revolution bringing in their train many ambassadorial conferences, were only too glad to give the leading role. After the death of Aehrenthal, Pallavicini was offered the Ministry of Foreign Affairs, but he made conditions which did not prove acceptable to Vienna. Had it been he who was resident at the Ballhausplatz[30] at the time, it would not, in my opinion, have come to war. As it was, instead of Pallavicini, Count Berchtold[31] was appointed the successor of Aehrenthal.

Two months after I had entered on my duties as general co-ordinating officer on board the *Kaiser Karl VI* in the Bocche di Cattaro, my appointment as aide-de-camp to Emperor Francis Joseph came through. I said goodbye to the sea and exchanged sea breezes for the air of the court and the big city.

30 The site of the Foreign Ministry in Vienna.

31 Count Leopold Berchtold (1863-1942).

3. Aide-de-Camp to Emperor Francis Joseph I at the Court of Vienna 1909-1914

His Majesty had four aides-de-camp to represent the main branches of the armed services. The first aide-de-camp to have been drawn from the Navy was my captain of the *Saida*, the later Vice-Admiral Sachs von Hellenau. I was proud and happy to be in the immediate entourage of our King-Emperor, a man respected and beloved by all, but those who perceived only the outward glitter of my post were under a misapprehension. Service at Court, so profoundly different from life on board, brought me many difficulties. I began by reporting to my highest chief, His Majesty's first Adjutant-General, Count Paar. He had held this position for many years, and of all the members of His Majesty's staff was no doubt the one who stood closest to him. With the charm of the grand seigneur, he gave me several hints and much friendly advice, and referred to me to the senior aide-de-camp, Colonel of Dragoons Baron Bronn, who was the son of a Prince Hohenlohe by a morganatic marriage, so that, in accordance with the traditions of his family, he could not bear his father's name. Three years later, he was created a prince under the name of Weikersheim. With his wife, Countess Czernin, and their children, he lived a singularly happy and harmonious life. The second aide-de-camp was Count Heinrich Hoyos, at that time Lieutenant- Colonel in the Windischgrätz Dragoons. His mother was the sister of Count Paar. A man of imperturbable good temper, always ready for a joke, he was generally liked. As he was a passionately keen huntsman and a good shot, I was delighted when we chanced to be together in a hunting party. The third aide-de-camp was a Lieutenant-Colonel in the Imperial Rifles, Count Manzano.

I also had to report to the second Adjutant-General, Baron Arthur Bolfras, who for many years had been Head of His Majesty's Military Chancellery. His was an extremely responsible position, for it was his task to submit to His Majesty names for the more important military appointments. A profound knowledge of men, a clear judgment of character, made him eminently suitable for this task, especially as he was a man of high intelligence and sterling good nature. His unusually clear diction was much appreciated by His Majesty, who retained him in his service in spite of his great age. The Military Chancellery was situated within the Imperial Palace, and apart from Baron

Bolfras and his deputy nine or ten General Staff officers worked there. The adviser for Hungarian affairs was then Staff Captain Baron Láng.

During my years of service, Emperor Francis Joseph resided at Schönbrunn. Twice a week, accompanied by an aide-de-camp, he drove to the Hofburg, the Imperial Palace in Vienna, arriving there at seven o'clock in the morning, to grant audiences. He usually returned at half-past four in the afternoon.

As aides-de-camp, we had an official residence in the Hofburg, of which we made full use; there was a similar residence at Schönbrunn for the use of the aide-de-camp on duty.

It was arranged, soon after I had reported to Count Paar, that I should be received in audience by His Majesty, an interview I anticipated with tension and excitement. From my early youth, I had heard the King-Emperor spoken of as almighty, a being of a higher order, enthroned in regions beyond human aspiration. Now I was to meet him face to face, to be daily in his personal service. When I entered his study, His Majesty, wearing the uniform of a General, took a few steps forward to meet me. I have never known any other monarch who personified majesty as did Francis Joseph. This, my first impression, I have never had reason to modify. If the high dignity that radiated from him and which was entirely free from affectation demanded that visitors should keep their distance, I quickly observed that all embarrassment melted away before his kindness and affability. This was the greatest moment of my life as I stood before the grey-haired ruler. On beholding his frame, bent beneath the heavy cares of state and the tragic fate of his kin, I was filled with compassion and affection, feelings that I have always retained. From the questions he put to me, I realized that he had been fully informed of my origins and my career. Even now, it is as if I can see the glance of his kindly blue eyes, can hear the intonations of his voice. When he dismissed me, the audience lasted about ten minutes and was conducted standing, and I left the audience chamber walking backwards, I was in a state of ecstasy, determined to serve my King and Emperor faithfully, and if necessary gladly to give my life for him.

The duties of the aides-de-camp were so organized that two of them were, for a month, on duty on alternate days. On the last day of each month, a court equipage arrived to take an aide-de-camp to Schönbrunn, where he installed himself in the service apartments and took over the duties of his predecessor.

The aide-de-camp on duty was dismissed each day at six o'clock by His Majesty personally. The third aide-de-camp then began a month's leave, while the fourth was in reserve for special missions, to accompany His Majesty's guests, for instance.

I do not know how these matters are arranged in other courts, but in Vienna, at any rate, no written instructions were ever given the aides-de-camp. Their behaviour and functions were dictated by oral tradition, which meant that matters were neither simple nor straight-forward. If one enquired, one usually received the reply, "You'll see for yourself, there'll be no difficulty at all." That did not satisfy me. I therefore wrote down a series of questions as a guide to conduct for the day that my duties began: December 1st. Which uniform should I wear on duty? Should I wear the adjutant's lanyards? Were gloves *de rigueur*?

"No, no gloves."

"Why not? Gloves are worn on all other occasions when reporting for duty."

Was the aide-de-camp to knock? To my great surprise, the answer was again no.

I was still feeling extremely uncertain when, on the evening of November 30th, a guardsman came to inform me at what hour His Majesty would rise the next morning. He reported as follows: "The hour is four."

His Majesty sometimes got up at half past three; indeed, during my last two years of duty, that was the rule. We naval officers were in a more favourable position than our military colleagues, for on board ship we had been used to a four hours' watch at night and had become used to sleeping beforehand. If I remember correctly, even on that first night I slept well, having turned in early, and rose feeling fresh and energetic as I hastened down to the aides-de-camp room on the first floor, separated from the Emperor's study by a baroque reception hall.

On his desk the monarch would find the documents sent from the Chancelleries of the Cabinet and the Ministry of War, and his aide-de-camp was rarely in demand while he studied them. With the approach of half-past eight, the two Adjutants-General arrived. On the stroke of nine, the

51

aide-de-camp announced first Count Paar and after him Baron Bolfras. They might be followed by archdukes, cabinet ministers, chiefs of the general staff and other high dignitaries with important communications or reports to make. These audiences lasted until lunchtime. Then His Majesty, usually alone, went for a stroll in the conservatory, after which he resumed work, going on until dinnertime at half-past five, dinner usually being served to him at his desk. At six o'clock, he dismissed his aide-de-camp. During the whole of my period of service, no aide-de-camp was ever kept late or recalled in the evening or during the night. My first day passed happily and without misfortune. My colleagues had been right when they told me that in the main the rules consisted of tact and common sense. The Emperor was not a talkative man and preferred concise answers. Once, an aide-de-camp who was on duty for the first time felt, as they drove out of the palace, that he ought to make conversation. As they passed the tower, he pointed to the monument of Maria Theresa and remarked: "What a glorious work of art! A triumph of the human urge to create." On their arrival at Schönbrunn, the Emperor called for Count Paar and ordered him to have "that chatterbox" replaced immediately by someone else. Another aide-de-camp met with the same fate for clicking his heels loudly every time he made a statement. That sort of thing was not done at the Viennese Court.

General audiences were granted at the Imperial Palace. They began at ten o'clock and the list invariably ran to fifty names. In earlier days there had been a hundred. The order of precedence had to be worked out by the aide-de-camp on duty, though for what reason I do not know. It would have been more natural for that task to have been left to the protocol experts, who had, in the first place, dealt with the requests for an audience. It was no simple matter for an officer to find his way about the hierarchies that exist at Court and to know who ranked above whom when dealing with princely personages, high-ranking clergy, present and past cabinet ministers, foreign dignitaries and officers. We had general guiding rules, but each one seemed to have its exceptions. A princely privy councillor or chamberlain, for instance, went before all others; if, however, a prince, such as one of the Schwarzenbergs, had not applied for the chamberlain's status, he had no 'rank' and fell among the last.

Those who had been called gathered in a hall where an official would conduct them one by one, in accordance with the aide-de-camp's list, to the aide-de-camp whose duty it was to announce them. Two officers of the

Guards, one Austrian and one Hungarian, stood with drawn swords at the door of the audience chamber. Each of the fifty individual audiences, usually to express thanks for an appointment or a distinction, occasionally to make a personal request, was bound to be very short. In the afternoon, more visitors were received until, at half-past four, His Majesty drove back to Schönbrunn.

On one of these drives, it was a rainy November day and we were in a closed carriage, His Majesty looked out with great interest at the Palace Guard and expressed emphatic thanks for the honour they were showing him. "This regiment," he said, "is mounting guard at the Palace for the first time. It is the best regiment in Vienna and one of the best in the monarchy." I was proud to hear him say this, for the regiment in question was the 82nd Austro-Hungarian infantry regiment from Székelyudvarhely, Transylvania. During the First World War, that regiment performed marvels of bravery and suffered tremendous losses.

Before the audiences began, the aides-de-camp room was usually a hive of activity. Everyone present was drawn willy-nilly into discussions on a number of often delicate problems. I learned to view the 'nationalities problem' from a new angle. It filled me with anxious forebodings to observe in the course of discussions that foreign influences were at work and to note how, even indirectly, the theories of irredentism and separatism were infiltrating. At times, socialist ideas were also mentioned. The people who voiced these were plainly unaware how well off they were. They wanted to see the country governed on the basis of abstract theory and failed to allow for the immutable laws of nature. Their gaze went as far as the destruction of what was in existence. What the new state they were striving after would be like or what it would turn into, of that they had only the vaguest notion. If, therefore, we, that is to say those of us who lived in close contact with His Majesty, were not wholly without cares. The Bosnian crisis of 1908 had brought the dangers threatening the monarchy clearly before all eyes, we were obviously far from the spirit of defeatism that may have prevailed elsewhere. The strength of tradition and mutual interest, ensuring the stability of the Habsburg Empire, was shown at the outbreak of the First World War. Those who had argued that the monarchy would fall asunder on the first day of a major war were proved wrong by the facts. The military defeat which enabled the forces of revolution to carry out their destructive work was not the result of any inherent weakness in the monarchy but of the crushing superiority of an enemy coalition.

An officer, and in particular an aide-de-camp, was not in a position to make political comments nor give political advice. Only among his friends could he discuss the advisability of taking stronger measures to counteract pan-Slav propaganda or pan-Serbian activities or Italian irredentism. The question whether such measures could have diverted historical development must remain unanswered.

In the aides-de-camp room, we noticed also that between His Majesty and his nephew Archduke Francis Ferdinand, the heir to the throne, there were differences that went deeper than the usual divergence between generations. That, however, will be discussed in a later chapter.

In spite of his advanced age, His Majesty adhered to the traditional representative duties of the sovereign, among which were the gala dinners on the occasion of visits made by high-ranking guests, and in honour of the Diplomatic Corps in general. So large was the number of Ambassadors and Envoys that they had to be invited in groups. The diplomats assembled in the Pink Drawing-Room in Schönbrunn and engaged in conversation until the Lord Steward of the Household, Prince Montenuovo, gave three raps with his staff to announce the approach of His Majesty. All conversation ceased and all took position according to rank. Time and time again, I observed how profound an impression his appearance and personality made. I always admired the perfection with which he held court. Even when he talked with a hundred people in the course of an evening, and that in many languages, the Lord Steward murmuring the names and countries of the guests, he had some friendly, personal comment to make to each one and was never at a loss for a subject. It is utterly false that he asked the same question over and over again: "How do you like Vienna?" as Count Sforza, the Italian Foreign Minister after both the First and Second World Wars, averred in his book "Makers of Modern Europe", which he wrote while in exile. There he speaks of Francis Joseph as "a petrified eighteenth century autocrat" and talks of his "cold, proud and closed nature", disclosing how utterly he had misunderstood the personality of Emperor Francis Joseph.

His Majesty retired about eleven o'clock and was at his desk the next morning at his customary hour. That this is no legend I can vouch: with his proverbial sense of duty, Francis Joseph spent every working day, beginning at five o'clock in the morning, at his desk going through the documents submitted to him by his Ministers. Never did I see him idle or wasting time, and I can speak with authority on this point, for the aides-de-camp invariably entered his study without knocking. He never took a nap, even after meals, as do so many younger men, though they have not risen at half-past three or four o'clock in the morning. At the age of eighty, Emperor Francis Joseph always inspected his garrisons on horseback, whether in Vienna, Budapest or at Sarajevo.

His Majesty loved music and art. In my time, admittedly, he no longer went to the Opera or the theatre. Only once did I attend him, while at Ischl, to the premiere of a farce entitled *When the Capercaillie Capers*, in which Girardi's artistry made him laugh until the tears ran down his face. And, of course, the prima donna of the Court Opera, Frau Jeritza, who later became so famous, began her career in the summer theatre at Ischl.

His Majesty always opened the spring art exhibition in person. He did not hide the fact that the then modern art, of which the Viennese *secessionism* were the representatives, was not to his   taste. I remember the drive to the Künstlerhaus on the first occasion that I accompanied him, and the agonies I suffered on the way, for the day was chilly, we were in a closed carriage and had a fur rug across our knees. We were bound to moor on the port side, I had decided, which meant that I would have to jump out first. But what was I to do with the fur rug? Shortly before we arrived, as if aware of my dilemma, His Majesty threw the rug on to the carriage floor.

At the exhibition, he passed by most of the paintings in silence, listening to the explanations given by an eminent artist. He paused in front of a landscape with a hunting lodge in the woods and asked, "Is that meant to be a lake in front of the lodge?" The artist was summoned. His Majesty repeated his question and received the answer, "No, Your Majesty, that is a forest meadow." "But it's blue." The artist, who was one of the modern school, said proudly, "That is how I see it." At which, His Majesty smiled and remarked, "In that case, you oughtn't to have become a painter."

He never learned to appreciate faces depicted in shades of green and yellow; on one occasion, while viewing the art section of a hunting exhibition, he came upon a female nude, drawn entirely out of proportion, and, turning to the President of the exhibition, asked, "Tell me, are these gentlemen altogether in earnest, or are they pulling our legs?"

55

The reader may be surprised to find judgments on art in this narrative. But the seaman's eye can be used for purposes other than estimating distances at sea, and I have tried my hand with brush and palette. After the exacting service of the Navy, Vienna gave me the feeling that I had too much spare time on my hands. Not that the musical life of Vienna was lost on me; I first thought of having my voice trained, but decided that I was too old for that. I turned instead to painting. As, in view of my position, I could not attend a public academy, I took the advice of the daughter of the Steward of the Household of Archduchess Annunciata and joined the private class of professor Mayerhofer which she and other ladies attended every morning. The professor introduced me to the ladies and placed me in front of an easel with a sheet of carton, put a stick of charcoal in my hand, and set me to draw a Caesar who, clad in a toga and with a laurel wreath on his brow, was seated on the dais before us. I set to, but the laurel wreath which I drew was not one that I should have cared to aspire to. I seized a cloth, wiped out what I could and started afresh, only to rub it out again. At one moment, I was in such despair that I thought I might as well go home and give up the idea for good. But after the fifth or sixth attempt, the drawing was beginning to be recognizable, so much so that I ventured to begin working with brush and paint as the ladies were doing. The pleasure I took in the work helped me to make rapid progress. It may have been due to my nautical training that I was able to observe with great accuracy and precision. After a few months, the professor gave me high praise in saying that I could get a likeness better than any of his other pupils. As I was eager to advance to painting landscape, game and horses, I often went, on the Professor's advice, to the Art Museum to copy the works of the great masters. The drawback to that was that one tended to become a centre of public attraction.

For five years, I spent most of my spare mornings painting. In the end, at Ischl, I tried my hand at a portrait of His Majesty, without his knowledge, of course. I saw him every day at lunch, he lunched at half-past two; and as I sat opposite him I would closely study some particular detail of his face, impress it on my memory, and transfer that memory to canvas in my service apartment. The two Adjutants-General and the Emperor's valet, who knew him better than anyone else, declared that they had never before seen so striking a likeness.1 I do not say this in boastfulness; I succeeded because I was familiar with every wrinkle in his face after having painstakingly studied his features for weeks, whereas His Majesty did not sit to other portrait painters more than once and then only for a short time.

One day, the first valet, good old Ketteler, came to me to ask whether he could take the portrait as His Majesty wished to see it. The next time I was on duty, I was told how much he had liked it. To me, the painting was a happy memory of years of contentment. It accompanied me to our villa at Pola and, after the debacle, to my father's house at Kenderes; in each of these places it survived two looting raids, to fall a victim at last to the fifth and most thorough gang of looters.

During my period of service, His Imperial Majesty, twice came on a visit. On the first occasion, we drove to the railway station to meet him. Our Emperor wore his German Field Marshal's uniform, and as the imperial train drew in he automatically straightened himself, so that, from the back, he might have been taken for a subaltern in spite of his eighty years. We boarded the train, remaining on it as far as Hitzing. On arrival there, the German Emperor sprang to the window, then, stepping back, exclaimed, "This is a spectacle I shall never forget." Outside the station, twelve carriages could be seen, facing the station, all drawn by matching snow-white Lipizzaners, and as the engine entered, all the horses performed a perfect 'eyes left', turning their heads toward the engine and displaying the identical markings on their foreheads.

When King Nikita of Montenegro came on a visit to the Court of Vienna, I was sent to meet him in Trieste, to which our torpedo-boat depot ship, the *Pelikan*, often used as a yacht, had brought him. He was on that occasion presented with the command of an infantry regiment. The appropriate uniform, made for him by a skilled Viennese tailor in a day, was so much to his liking that he wore it constantly until he returned to the *Pelikan* at Trieste.

This visit was particularly harmonious. King Nikita was an intelligent man with a likeable personality. By means of a clever marriage, he was related not only to the Serbian but also to the Italian and Russian dynasties.

In 1910, King Peter of Serbia had had an enquiry made to ascertain whether or not a visit from him would be welcome. The negotations in this matter were protracted. Francis Joseph had no particular liking for the Karadjordjevich dynasty which had acceded to the throne as a result of the murder of King Alexander Obrenovich in 1903. When the latter's father, King Milan, was monarch, excellent relations had existed between Belgrade and Vienna. Since that time, Serbia had moved moved more and more into the Russian orbit. In the end, however, the Serbian envoy was informed that

His Majesty would receive King Peter on such and such a day in Budapest. Shortly before the date fixed, the reception was cancelled on the plea of indisposition. In my opinion, that was to be regretted. The visit might have improved relations, whereas the cancellation could only aggravate existing tensions.

Every year, early in July, His Majesty would go to Ischl in the Salzkammergut, the country in Upper Austria near Salzburg, for two or three months. Ischl was a friendly, clean little village with potent mineral springs; but the visitor had to accustom himself to the frequent rainfall. The Imperial Villa stood in a great park, consisting mainly of highland forest, with peaks rising to some two thousand five hundred feet, inhabited by chamois and other game. His Majesty's summer residence acted as a magnet to the aristocracy; they were followed by the rich manufacturers, who built elegant villas along the Traun. The mountain air and the springs were extremely beneficial to health, and there were many who became converts to the motto of the discoverer of the Ischl springs: "The greatest happiness on earth is not to be healthy, but to get healthy."

Here His Majesty's life was less constrained. After an early morning ride, he had breakfast; then he dealt with the documents that had arrived and received people in audience. After a walk in the garden, he was served with a meal at half-past two, at which his two daughters, the Archduchess Gisela with her husband Prince Leopold of Bavaria and their two children, and the Archduchess Marie Valerie with her husband Archduke Francis Salvator, would be present, and also Count Paar and the aide-de-camp on duty. If the weather was tolerably good, His Majesty would, in the afternoon, ride on a pony through his preserves to some covert near which a stag was known to break cover. The Emperor was a keen and skilful huntsman, and an excellent shot, advanced though he was in age. I once suggested the use of telescopic sights, which facilitate one's aim by making both game and horizon stand out better, but in vain. His Majesty would have none of such new-fangled gadgets; he was so conservative that he did not even use modern guns but remained faithful to his old carbine.

For centuries the Emperors had had the hunting rights in all Austrian state forests. In each region, an Imperial Master of the Hunt was appointed who organized excellent hunts in accordance with ancient traditions. I was told that in many of the drives, the area which the beaters had to cover had been handed down from father to son. Though, in mountainous country, the drive might take one man over a mountain and another through a valley, the chain of beaters would always emerge from the wood in a straight line.

Although I too was a keen hunter, I had to learn many things, even if it was mainly a matter of vocabulary. Special words were used for the stag's eyes, his feet, his ears. To use the wrong expression was to make oneself a butt for ridicule. We always went out in the regional costume, in chamois leather shorts, that is to say. I had to accustom myself to appearing before the Archduchesses at dinner with bare knees, although I knew no objection would be made.

At Ischl, we mainly shot chamois. His Majesty, whose eyesight was remarkable, was often the first to see a chamois on some distant rock while to the guests it was still invisible. At the Naval Academy, to which only candidates with first-class eyesight were admitted, I had been able to read the small No.7 print at the maximum distance at every eye test during my four years of training. Again I do not recount this in boastfulness, for, after all, it was a physical fact for which I could hardly be held responsible, but as the key to the following experience. His Majesty was once driving in an open carriage along an unfamiliar road leading to the palace of the Archduke Rainer, whom he was visiting to congratulate him and his wife on their diamond wedding. We passed within a fair distance of an exceptionally large building which was under construction. "I wonder what that place is," His Majesty remarked. I replied that it was the new premises of a municipal trades school.

"How do you know?"

"It says so on that notice attached to the central balcony."

His Majesty could not read the notice, and told the coachman to drive nearer to the building until he too was able to decipher the words. Then he ordered the man to turn and drive on. "What eyes you've got!" he said to me. I felt a certain regret at having outclassed him.

For the battues after chamois, which usually took place twice a week at Ischl, we would drive early in the morning to the hunting ground in a carriage drawn by two splendid Lipizzaners, and then mount ponies to reach the coverts. To the more distant hunting grounds we travelled by private train.

59

Over the centuries, records had been kept of what had been shot at the various coverts. By that means, a scale of values had been worked out: there was the Emperor's covert, a No. 1 covert, and so on. These were assigned to guests according to rank.

Most game, once raised, remains on the move until it has found good cover. Chamois, on the other hand, are uncertain in behaviour and the right moment to fire has to be carefully judged. His Majesty preferred to shoot them on the move. At the end of each shoot, he would interrogate the participants and ask them what they had seen and shot. Woe betide anyone who had not acquitted himself correctly.

At one chamois shoot, the first shot was fired from the covert next to Count Paar, and he guessed that it was his neighbour the Archduke of Tuscany. There was a ridge in the terrain immediately in front of him at a distance of just over a hundred yards, and after a few minutes the head of a chamois popped up above it, disappearing again at once. Count Paar decided that it was a buck and fired. After a few moments, during which the Archduke fired again, another chamois head appeared at approximately the same place, and again Count Paar fired. The same sequence was repeated for a third time. Count Paar had no idea what he had hit, if anything, and the gamekeeper who had been assigned to him offered to go and investigate. It was, of course, strictly forbidden to leave the covert, but curiosity proved too strong. After some time, the gamekeeper returned looking very upset and reported, "Three kids, Your Excellency."

Count Paar was in despair, but refused the offer of the well-meaning gamekeeper that he should quickly bury the kids. When the shoot was over, he went to make his report with a very guilty conscience, which was in no way relieved when he saw that His Majesty was considerably perturbed by something the Archduke was saying to him. As he drew nearer, he could hear the Archduke being rebuked for having shot three female chamois that had kids. When his turn came, Count Paar declared that he had disposed of the kids which had lost their mothers. This luckily won the Emperor's approval.

One afternoon, we went to shoot on the Jainsen peak in the park. While the Empress was alive, this had not been permitted. Even after her death His Majesty had never himself joined in these particular shoots. On this occasion, however, he gave permission as the game had been doing considerable damage in the park. As we set off in the carriage, after dinner, His Majesty accompanied us, ascertained the direction of the wind, and said to me, "You'll have a chance to get a stag today."

I was given a very awkward covert; beyond an open space I had facing me a rocky wall of some hundred feet high, and rising above it the forest where the beaters were. Nor was the light good. I was looking into the sun and had to aim into the dark wood. A few minutes after the chain of beaters had gone by above me, I heard a branch snap and two stags, which had broken through, followed each other rapidly. I fired one shot at each, but neither faltered and I thought my bullets must have struck trees.

After the battue, I went to the place where I had seen the stags and followed the trail of blood that I found. I soon came upon the body of one of the stags, but saw no trace of the other. On my return to the house in the park where we lived, I found my family and some of the gamekeepers standing round my second stag, which had managed to drag itself even further. It was the finest stag that I have ever shot in Austria.

At the end of April, the capercaillie season opened. His Majesty took part in a shoot for the last time when he was seventy-nine. Raising his gun for the first cock, he brought the bird down faultlessly, and then said, "This is no longer a sport for me." But although he had given up this pleasure which he had so much enjoyed in the past, he still had to know exactly how his guests had fared. Every morning, the Imperial Master of the Hunt had to report by telegram the tally of the birds that his guests had shot or missed. His Majesty was always annoyed to hear if game was wounded and lost. For this reason, I invariably used my 6.7 mm. Mannlicher-Schönauer with metal-cased bullets, even though the other sportsmen used shotguns.

Most of the guests went to Neuberg in the vicinity of Mürzsteg, capercaillie being plentiful there. I used to choose either the hunting lodge at Eisenerz or the one at Radmer, but the first time I shot capercaillie, I went to Hieflau. At the station, I was met by a bearded old gamekeeper called Loidl and with him went to the cabin near the mating place. This was the first time that I was shooting capercaillie, though I didn't tell Loidl that, as I did not wish him to take me for a tyro. Naturally I let him tell me what to do: at the first light of dawn, the cock begins his mating song in the highest branches of a larch or a pine-tree. His song consists of three phrases, and it is during the third phrase, when he can neither see nor hear, that you draw near. At four in the morning, we set out in the dark, Loidl going ahead with a lantern. After about ten minutes, we came to a halt, blew out the lantern, and waited. Soon Loidl began to nod, listened intently, and whispered to me, "Hear him?" I answered, "No." After a few minutes, he asked again, "You still don't hear him?" Again I had to say no, for I wasn't too certain what I was supposed to be listening for. Then Loidl said, "Now we're going after him," and at intervals he moved two, three paces forward. By that time, I could hear the cock and was able to distinguish the three phrases. But the pace of this "going after him" was too slow for me, and I thought I knew better than Loidl, who had been doing it for forty years. At the third phrase, I rushed forward past him. When a canary is singing in a room, I thought to myself, one often has to plug one's ears; considering the size of the bird we were after, I imagined it must still be a few hundred paces away, but I was very much in error. We were on the crest of the hill; the cock was in a tall larch growing below us on the hillside, so that suddenly, to my dismay, I saw the bird at eye level not a hundred feet away. I stopped short and stood as if rooted to the ground, but the bird had seen me and, stretching its neck like a bottle of hock, it took wing. In a reproachful tone, Loidl said, "Now he's off." felt very ashamed of myself, but, after a little while, Loidl said, "He's calling again," and once more we slowly advanced. This time I kept dutifully behind Loidl, and at last we spotted the bird. He was a long way away, and we could get no nearer as there was a clearing between us. Against Loidl's advice, I fired and fortunately brought the bird down, thus regaining Loidl's esteem.

Some time during the first half of September, we would return to Schönbrunn in readiness for the winter season with its receptions and balls, theatres and concerts. I particularly remember the occasion on which we heard Caruso sing the part of Don Jose in Carmen. Perhaps it was because we expected a mighty voice, whereas Caruso had a soft, beautifully lyrical tenor, but after the first aria he received hardly any applause. With the Song of the Rose in the second act, however, which he sang with a rare perfection and so beautifully that tears stood in one's eyes, he won storms of applause and cries of approval such as I had never heard before. For a quarter of an hour, Caruso could not be persuaded to rise from the kneeling position he had assumed to express his gratitude.

Vienna was not known as the city of song for nothing. We enjoyed the best music, classical and less classical. Among the latter, I think especially of the light operas of Franz Lehár, whose rise followed with considerable interest, for he had been a naval band leader for three years and, during my bachelor years, had often come to Pola to play me his own compositions or to accompany my singing. I remember very well the high hopes he had of his first opera *Kukuschka*, which he had composed at that time. He had suffered a sad disappointment, for this urge to compose had not won the approval of his chiefs, being regarded as unsuitable in a naval bandmaster, and he was dismissed. At its premiere, *Kukuschka* was a flop. Both that and his dismissal proved to be strokes of luck for the young musician in that he was left free to devote himself to his real talent: light opera, so many of which he has given the world. They have made him famous. We often met at Ischl, where he had bought an elegant villa on the bank of the Traun. There, again, he was lucky. He was able to pay the price of the villa from the proceeds of a sale of a lot of old prints and paintings that he had found in its attics, for he bought the villa complete as it stood, including furniture. In memory of the old days, Lehár later dedicated a spirited parade march to me.

Vienna was famous, not only for its opera and concert hall, but also for its theatre, all three competing with one another in quality. I saw Kainz and, of course, Frau Wilbrandt-Baudius, who later made her appearance at the Imperial Theatre at the age of ninety. In those days, moreover, we had the time and leisure to visit the world-famous museums of the city.

For a naval officer, it was rare to be able to enjoy family life for so long and in such pleasant circumstances. Our four children had a governess and were taught, in accordance with the Hungarian educational system, by the Augustine friars. These were plainly marked out as episcopal candidates. One of them, Mgr. Luttor, was later active for many years at our Legation to the Vatican; another, Czapik, became Archbishop of Eger. At the end of the school year, we took our children to Pressburg, where they entered for their examinations and obtained their school certificates.

Upon our return, I met the commanding officer of the Hungarian Guards, General Count Lónyay, who enquired charmingly after my family. With paternal pride and joy, I told him of the excellent results of the Pressburg examination. "Yes, I know," he said, "those first examinations make one wonder what this young genius is going to become in life. Minister of Foreign Affairs? Perhaps even greater? And then, a few years later, he goes to a grammar school and you go to the headmaster and you say, 'Tell me honestly, is the boy an idiot?' and you receive the reply, 'Oh, no, not quite...'

Count Paar was renowned for his ability to relate interesting occurrences and anecdotes. He used to make time seem fleeting when we came on duty in the early morning and had to wait for the clock to strike nine. He almost invariably began with "Have I told you this before?" and I invariably answered, "I don't think so," so that over the years, as is often the case with old gentlemen, I heard his stories time and time again. Many of them I got by heart and can retell them to this day, for instance, the story of the visit of His Majesty to Paris, a return visit to the Emperor Napoleon III. A big parade had been arranged and at the head of the column rode the comfortable figure of the commanding General. As the troops approached our Emperor, who stood beside the Empress Eugenie, they roared from thousands of throats, "Vive l'Empereur!" The General's horse reared at the noise, and its rider, sword in hand, flew, describing a perfect parabola, to the ground. Full of indignation and at the same time somewhat amused, Napoleon III turned to Count Paar and remarked: "And now the Empress will want to give him another horse, for she thinks it was the horse's fault. But you'll see, he'll go down again just the same next time."

In Hungary, we do not know this jubilant shout of the people. I had heard it before at the selamlik whenever the Sultan made his appearance: "Chokyasha Padishah!"

At other times, Count Paar would tell the story of the member of a South German ruling house who had been appointed to the command of the 12th Hussars at Klagenfurt. As soon as he had found a suitable villa, he sent for his wife and all his belongings. Shortly afterwards, the senior officer of the regiment sent a smart Hungarian lieutenant to the villa to enquire when it would be convenient for the officers' corps to be presented to the Duchess. In the hall of the villa were the mounds of luggage and bending over them near the door was a young woman busy unpacking. The lieutenant could not resist the temptation and gave the young woman, whom he believed to be a housemaid, a hearty smack on the bottom. As she sprang up, he took her tenderly by the chin and asked where he might find His Highness. Laughing at the young man's impudence, she told him to go up the stairs to the first floor and knock at the first door. The lieutenant carried out his mission, and the next morning, at eleven o'clock, the reception was held. As they all stood waiting in order of seniority, the Duchess and her husband entered the reception room and, to his horror, the lieutenant recognized the bewitching housemaid. One after the other, the officers were introduced, and for each one Her Highness had a few charming words. When the lieutenant's turn came, she said, "I believe we have met before," whereupon the lieutenant, completely losing his head, in his confusion blurted out in the broadest of Hungarian accents, "Alas, Your Majesty!"

Count Paar could tell stories of the great festivities that had taken place in Vienna in 1908, before my period of service began, on the occasion of His Majesty's Diamond Jubilee. What events had not those sixty years seen? "Nothing," His Majesty had said when the news of the murder of the Empress was broken to him, "nothing has been spared me." His brother, the Emperor Maximilian, had been court-martialled and shot by the Mexican revolutionaries. His only son, the very intelligent Crown Prince Rudolph, in whom lay all his hopes, lost his life under tragic circumstances. His wife, the Empress and Queen Elizabeth, so highly esteemed and gratefully honoured by the Hungarian people, was murdered by an Italian anarchist in Geneva. The same fate later befell his nephew Archduke Francis Ferdinand, the heir to the throne, at Sarajevo. He still carried the burden of the execution of the thirteen Hungarian Generals at Arad in 1849 at the end of the War of Liberation, though he was blameless in the matter, since he was then a youth of eighteen in the hands of the Camarilla. Even the losses at Königgraetz weighed heavily on his soul, and it was his most fervent wish never to have to experience another war. But not even that experience was spared him.

In all those dark hours, His Majesty sought and found solace in his strong religious faith. He saw his task, of ruler as one given him by God and he performed it with a sense of duty to which he subordinated his own personal desires. Painfully precise, even in the smallest details, he personally cleaned the red surface of his desk with a small brush every evening when the day's work was finished. Simple and unassuming in the conduct of his private life, he did not regard the strict Spanish Court etiquette as an end in itself but as the necessary outward form for a tradition, the maintenance of which among the diverse ethnic elements of the Habsburg monarchy was more important than in other countries. The fundamental traits of his character were kindliness and courtesy. In his wisdom, which long experience had refined, he aimed first of all at righteousness, which to him was the 'foundation of the realm'.

When His Majesty celebrated his eightieth birthday on August 15th, 1910, his physical and mental faculties still unimpaired, the huntsmen of Austria dedicated a statue in bronze to him. An excellent likeness, portraying him in the leather shorts of the traditional national hunting costume, his gun over his shoulder, his alpenstock in his hand, standing on a rock. At his feet lay a fine stag with a royal head, the antlers modelled after those of a stag that His Majesty had actually shot in the vicinity of the monument. In keeping, all the guests invited to the unveiling ceremony wore hunting costume. Count Wurmbrandt gave the address and the whole gathering was deeply moved when, following upon it, the Viennese male choir sang in the forest the national anthem: "Gott erhalte, Gott beschütze unsern Kaiser, unser Land" (God preserve, God protect our Emperor, our Land).

In 1912, His Majesty went for a relatively long visit to Budapest, where the joint delegations of the Austrian and the Hungarian Parliaments were meeting to vote on the annual budget. From the Western Railway Station, we drove on a sunny afternoon in open carriages to the Royal Palace. The 'new times' found their expression in the fact that masses of workers, organized by the Social Democrat Party, were demonstrating against the Hungarian Prime Minister, Count Tisza. It was a demonstration all the more reprehensible in that the Balkan War was raging at the time and dangerous incidents were yet again occurring on the borders of the Habsburg Empire. The delegations voting on the increased expenditure necessary for the strengthening of the armed forces made great difficulties in their inexplicable shortsightedness, an attitude they bitterly regretted having taken in years to come.

Upon our return to Vienna, the Navy was mobilized in readiness should the flames blazing behind our coast leap their confines. I was authorized to leave the Court and take over the command of the *Budapest*. To breathe the sea air again, to feel the deck of a ship under my feet once more, to be among my old friends, was a great delight to me. All went smoothly; action was not found to be necessary and before long the fleet was demobilized. I returned to Vienna.

As a result of the two Balkan Wars, Turkey had been practically driven out of Europe. All that she retained was a small region between Adrianople and the Narrows. Greece expanded considerably towards the north and acquired Salonika. The Kingdom of Serbia was enlarged, encouraging it to put forward further claims. The reckoning was paid by Bulgaria, which, in the second Balkan War, had tried to revise by force of arms what she considered the unjust territorial settlement dictated by the Powers. Montenegro remained independent, and a new state, Albania, was created, on the throne of which the Great Powers placed the Prince of Wied. Balkan affairs were regarded with a very different eye in Vienna and in Budapest. Premier Count Tisza upheld the view that the recognition of the changes brought about by the war was in keeping with the traditions and interests of Hungary, and that Hungary should help the peoples of the Balkans in their struggle for independence.

My period of service as an aide-de-camp was again extended, so that I spent the years immediately preceding the outbreak of the First World War in Vienna.

4. Archduke Francis Ferdinand

My intention is not to attempt to draw a picture of the life of the heir to the throne, but to limit myself to giving an account of him as I knew him during my years of service at Court and to relate what I then heard about him.

The Archduke Francis Ferdinand[1] of Austria-Este, at the age of twelve he had taken the name of Este upon inheriting the large fortune of the deceased Duke of Modena, was the eldest son of the Archduke Charles Louis, the only brother of the Emperor to have progeny. Archduke Maximilian, the Emperor of Mexico, had been killed; Archduke Louis Victor had remained a bachelor. The mother of the heir to the throne was Princess Maria Annunciata, daughter of Ferdinand II, the Bourbon King of the Two Sicilies. The marriage had been solemnized in 1862 in the chapel of the Imperial Palace in Venice. The Archduchess was a beautiful woman, but a sufferer from tuberculosis. Her lifelong invalidism merely lent wings to her soaring ambition. She longed for a son who, one day, should occupy the Imperial throne. When Francis Ferdinand was born in 1863, it was at first thought that he would not survive. Owing to careful nursing and to a prolonged stay at Schloss Wartholz at the foot of the Raxalpe in Austria, he grew up to healthy manhood, though for many years he was very delicate.

Against the advice of her doctors, the Archduchess bore three more children, two boys, Otto and Ferdinand, and one girl, before she died nine years after her marriage at the age of twenty-eight. She was aware of the nature of her malady and had her children kept away from her. The lack of motherly love, which was only partly compensated later by the affection lavished on the children by their stepmother, the eighteen-year-old daughter of the widowed Duchess of Braganza, Maria Theresa, showed itself in the later development of Francis Ferdinand. As a boy, he often displayed symptoms of the unreasoning jealousy of the sickly towards his robust younger brother Otto[2], a jolly, healthy child, generally beloved as the "beautiful Otto". The elder boy's relations with his stepmother were, however, very close.

1 Francis Ferdinand (1863-1914).

2 Archduke Otto Francis Joseph Habsburg (1865-1906), father of Emperor Charles IV.

At the age of fourteen, the Archduke was appointed a second lieutenant, though this involved no change in his way of life. Only when he was appointed a first lieutenant was he taken away from his home and sent to Enns to join the Dragoons. Conditions there were strange to him and he was not on good terms with his fellow officers; his promotion to the rank of major in 1888 and his transference to the 102nd Infantry Regiment in Prague came as a relief to him. He expected to lead a different life in the city from that of the dull little town of Enns. He lived in the Hradzhin[3], and he looked forward to enjoying music, life, company as did other officers. But again he did not succeed; his presence had a paralysing effect. On January 30th, 1889, on returning from duty to his house, he was met with the shattering news that Crown Prince Rudolph had died at Meyerling in mysterious circumstances. His mother's ambitions for him seemed likely to be realized, for Rudolph's death meant that Francis Ferdinand's father was next in succession to the throne of Austria-Hungary. However, in view of his advanced age, Francis Ferdinand himself could be regarded as the heir to the throne.

Francis Ferdinand was a young man of strong and energetic personality, intelligent, very religious, but by temperament he was excitable. He was self-contained, had few intimate friends, and was little known to the people. To prepare himself for his future high position, which among other things demanded a thorough grounding in political science and in the several languages of the dual monarchy, the Archduke thought that he should know something of the world. To that end decided to undertake a long sea voyage which would also be beneficial for his health. But such a journey needed thorough diplomatic preparation, even though the heir to the Austro-Hungarian throne travelled incognito as the Count of Hohenberg. Couriers, in those days, took a long time to reach distant parts of the world and return with answers. Moreover, His Majesty had to be persuaded to give his consent to the project; this was achieved through the mediation of the Empress Elizabeth. On December 15th, 1892, Francis Ferdinand left Trieste in the armoured cruiser *Kaiserin Elisabeth*.

The Archduke Leopold, a schoolmate of mine at the Naval Academy with whom I had remained on friendly terms, asked me to join the expedition, saying that he himself was going as a lieutenant. I rejected the proposal, and even went so far as to advise him against going. The two Archdukes were temperamentally so different that I could foresee nothing but trouble. Events

3   Prague's royal palace.

proved me right. They quarrelled, and at Sydney Archduke Leopold had to leave the ship and return to Europe on his own. He was dismissed from the Navy and transferred to an Infantry Regiment at Brunn. Later, as a result of his marriage to a woman not of equal birth, he lost his rank and emigrated to Switzerland, where he lived under the name of Leopold Wölfling, dying there after the First World War.

To members of the British Royal Family, world tours and visits to distant parts of their Empire are almost a matter of course. But what other country had ever sent its heir to the throne on a world tour? The return voyage from Yokohama was made in a luxury liner and a visit was paid to the United States. It was a sign that the Austro-Hungarian dynasty, in allowing the heir to the throne to acquaint himself with other parts of the world, was not so hidebound as it was sometimes declared to be.

The Archduke, by making his voyage out in one of the ships of the Austro-Hungarian Navy, had, of course, gained a liking for her; it also drew him closer to Kaiser Wilhelm II, who later insisted on Austria-Hungary expanding her fleet. This demand met with little understanding from the Austro-Hungarian Parliaments, an obstructionist and shortsighted attitude with which I myself was only too familiar.

When, after the return of Francis Ferdinand, the question of his marriage became paramount, His Majesty advised him to bring some fresh blood into the family. He was even prepared to consider an alliance with a non-Catholic dynasty. The Archduke, however, followed this advice in an unexpected fashion. He had secretly fallen in love with the Countess Sophie Chotek[4], whom he had met at a ball given by the *Statthalter*, the representative of the Crown in Prague. As Francis Ferdinand was a frequent guest of the Archduke Frederick at Pressburg, it was conjectured that his choice would fall on one of his host's seven daughters, until it was noticed that the magnet that drew him was the Archduchess's lady-in-waiting, the Countess Sophie Chotek. It was no passing infatuation. Nothing could move him from his determination to marry the Countess, although he knew that by the laws of his dynasty a marriage to a person not of equal birth would deprive him of all claim to the succession and that his wife could never be admitted to the Imperial family. The most powerful advocate of this ruling was the Lord Steward of the Household, Prince Montenuovo, who, himself a descendant of the Imperial

4   Sophie Chotek (1868-1914).

House, had considerable influence: he was a nephew of Archduchess Marie Louise, who, after her first marriage with Napoleon, had married Count Neipperg.

Vienna rang with talk, chiefly rumours of the Emperor's despair over his nephew's obstinacy. In Society, there were two parties, one of them criticizing the 'antiquated dynastic laws', the other the heir to the throne. But in actual fact, after all the sorrows he had experienced, the Emperor had mellowed, especially where matters of the heart were concerned. He merely asked for a year in which to come to a decision and he instructed the father confessor of the Archducal family, Bishop Marschall, to do what he could to influence the Archduke.

It was all in vain. Francis Ferdinand was ready to relinquish the throne rather than his life's happiness. In vain also was the attempt to compel the Countess, who had retired to a convent to await the final decision, to give up the Archduke and take the veil. She remained adamant and rejected Bishop Marschall's assurances that His Majesty, and the Pope, would be everlastingly grateful to her if she would make the sacrifice.

The year passed, and His Majesty had to pronounce judgment. After he had discussed the matter with the aged Archdukes, who agreed with his views, he called Francis Ferdinand before him. He informed him that he could enter into a morganatic marriage without endangering his own right to the succession; his wife and children, however, could not be admitted into the Imperial family. The heir apparent would thus be Archduke Charles, the first-born son of Francis Ferdinand's brother, Archduke Otto. Archduke Francis Ferdinand declared himself willing to agree to these conditions. In the year 1900, on June 28th, a fateful day: fourteen years later June 28th saw the murder at Sarajevo, he swore a solemn oath to that effect. In the Privy Council Chamber of the Imperial Palace, the Archdukes, the high dignitaries of the realm and the Speakers of the Lower and Upper Houses were called together. His Majesty stood before the throne; the Prince Cardinal the Archbishop of Vienna offered the Archduke the Book of the Gospels, upon which he placed his hand as he read out the form of oath handed him by the Hungarian Prince Primate, the concluding sentence of which ran, "That we shall never attempt to revoke our present declaration or to put our hand to anything aiming at weakening or lifting its binding power."

72

After His Majesty had left the Council Chamber, the two candles, between which stood the famous crucifix of Emperor Ferdinand II[5], were extinguished. For centuries, every oath sworn by a member of the Habsburg family had been witnessed by that crucifix. Shortly afterwards, in the chapel of the Reichstadt Castle in Bohemia, the marriage was solemnized. The consort of the Archduke was handed a congratulatory telegram from His Majesty, addressed to the Princess Hohenberg.

Even as a Princess, however, the position of the former Countess gave rise to many disagreements and difficulties. On all official occasions, a Court Ball, for instance, the order of precedence, as the couples went in under the supervision of the Lord Steward of the Household, separated her from her husband. The Princess, on a Chamberlain's arm, had to follow after the long line of the immediate Imperial families, followed by the ladies-in-waiting. Once a Court Ball had to be cancelled owing to uncertainty about the order of precedence, which impelled a number of ladies to declare their intention of staying away. In later years, the Archduke preferred, in general, to spend the pre-carnival days with his wife far from Vienna until His Majesty, in 1910, raised the Princess to the rank of Duchess of Hohenberg with the title 'Highness', which meant that she could henceforth make her entrance immediately after the youngest Archduchess at the Ball.

The Archduke, who held the rank of Admiral, had been appointed the Emperor's deputy as Commander-in-Chief of the armed forces. Advised by Conrad von Hötzendorf[6], the Chief of the General Staff, he wielded a strong influence over military affairs while finding it difficult to assert himself politically. His Majesty, in spite of his advanced age, was not the man to submit to external pressure, even if it were brought to bear by a close relative. He listened to the views of his advisers, but it was understandable that, after occupying the throne for more than six decades, he preferred making as few changes as possible in the affairs of state and government. That the heir to the throne had views entirely opposed to his uncle's on certain topics was well known. It was becoming increasingly clear that he disapproved of the Austro-Hungarian dualism. Francis Ferdinand had in mind a reorganization of the state in a threefold, federative form. In this matter, he came into progressive conflict with Hungary and this conflict found expression in his

5 Ferdinand I of Habsburg (1503-1564), first Habsburg king of Hungary.

6 Major General Conrad Francis von Hötzendorf (1852-1925).

personal dislike of the Magyar nobility. He was perhaps influenced in this by his wife's family and circle, as also by other considerations, the existence of which was widely rumoured.

Even as commanding officer of the 9th Hussars at Sopron (Ödenburg), the Archduke had been involved in a marked clash of opinions when he had complained to the Colonel that he had found his men all speaking Hungarian. The Colonel replied that officer would certainly not speak Hungarian in the presence of people ignorant of that language, but that among themselves they would certainly continue to use their mother tongue.

It was a known fact that the Archduke had frequent conferences with the leaders of the national minorities in the Budapest Parliament such as the Slovak, Hodza[7], and the Rumanians, Vajda Vojvod[8] and Julius Maniu[9].

In my official capacity, I rarely encountered Archduke Francis Ferdinand. At social functions, I frequently met both him and his wife. Our common interest in the Navy gave us much to discuss. We never touched on political questions.

The Archduke's plan to unite into a confederacy all the South Slav territory, i.e. Slovenia and Dalmatia, which belonged to Austria, Croatia, the land of the Crown of St. Stephen, and the State lands of Bosnia-Herzegovina, roused fierce antagonism in the Serbian nationalists, who were aiming at acquiring an outlet to the sea and a South-Slav realm with Belgrade as its capital. Had the plan of the heir to the throne materialized, this Yugo-Slavia would have exerted an irresistible attraction on the Serbs by reason of its great political and economic advantages. And this the shrewd Serbian Prime Minister Pasic[10] knew full well. So did St. Petersburg. The secret organization of the Serbian nationalists, the *Crna Ruka* or Black Hand, instigated the murder at Sarajevo,

---

7 Milan Hodæa (1878-1944), Slovak politician, MP in the Hungarian parliament.

8 Alexander Vajda-Voievod (1872-1950), politician, member of the Romanian Nationalist party, MP in the Hungarian parliament.

9 Julius Maniu (1873-1953) MP in the Hungarian Parliament, later became prime minister of Rumania.

10 Nikola Pasic (1846-1926).

thus setting in motion the avalanche that engulfed the heir to the throne as the first victim in its fatal path.

On Sunday, June 28th, 1914, we had taken our children in our car from Vienna to Székesfehérvár to visit my brother[11], who was the officer in command of the 13th Hussars in that town. We were met by my brother and his wife in the courtyard, both looking extremely preoccupied. On our enquiring what the matter was, they replied that a friend of theirs, a journalist, had just told them that the heir to the throne and his wife had been assassinated at Sarajevo.

At first we refused to believe the news. We could not credit that on the occasion of the official entry of the heir to the throne into Sarajevo the necessary security measures had not been taken to guard against an attempt at assassination. I had, admittedly, wondered why Archduke Francis Ferdinand had chosen for his visit to a town so near the border Vidovdan, St. Vitus's Day, the Serbian national day, on which the Battle of Kosovo in 1389 was commemorated and on which national passions were always liable to flare up.

We soon learned that the rumour was indeed true. We realized that this political murder was bound to have international repercussions. It seemed out of the question that it had been the unaided act of a single individual; it is now a historical fact that Belgrade had a hand in it and that the plotters had the assurance of Russian support.

The murder at Sarajevo has often been described in full detail. The Archduke was the victim of his noble and humane altruism, which caused him to disregard the customary safety precautions. As the cars had set out for the Town Hall, a bomb had been thrown at them, severely injuring the Archduke's aide-de-camp. On leaving the Town Hall, the Archduke had ordered his car to be driven to the hospital to which his aide-de-camp had been taken.

As the car turned slowly into a side street out of the well-guarded main street, the grammar school boy, Gavrilo Princip[12], took advantage of the confusion arising from the approach of the Archducal car to fire two pistol-shots. The

11 István Horthy.

12 Gavrilo Princip was a Bosnian Serb (1895-1918).

75

dying Duchess of Hohenberg sank on to the shoulder of her mortally wounded husband. Both were taken to the Konak, the residence of Potiorek[13], the general in command, and the Archduke expired shortly afterwards without regaining consciousness.

Those two shots fired by the young fanatic ended an era of which we, who lived in it, can say, as Talleyrand said after the French Revolution, that those who have not known it have not known life. Those two shots at Sarajevo were the first shots of the First World War, from which sprang the yet more murderous Second World War. The peace of which they robbed us has not yet returned.

Gavrilo Princip, being a minor, could not be condemned to death. He was sentenced to thirty years' imprisonment in a fortress, and there he died of tuberculosis after a few years. This reckless young murderer claimed a hecatomb of human sacrifice, the like of which the world had not known before. After 1919, a commemorative plaque was placed on the site of the murder.

To the Navy was assigned the sad task of conveying the coffins containing the bodies of the two victims to Trieste. They had been taken by train to Metkovic. Solemnly they were carried on board the flagship *Viribus Unitis*, surrounded by the ships of the squadron anchored at the mouth of the Narenta. In line ahead, the battleships proceeded along the coast, close inshore, and as they passed the people bared their heads; many fell on their knees to pray and the priests blessed the coffins as the ships steamed slowly by.

In Vienna, the final absolutions over the coffins were given in the Castle Chapel and then removed to Artstetten to be placed in the crypt built by the Archduke.

That Russia should give Serbia her active support was to be expected. The Russian Ambassador, von Hartwig, who was rumoured to know all the intrigues, had a fatal heart attack   during his visit of condolence to our Ambassador, Baron Giesl[14], so great was his agitation. That the murder at Sarajevo would have to be avenged was manifest. Indignation at the plot

13 General Oscar Potiorek (1852-1933).

14 General Wladimir Giesl von Gisslingen (1860-1936)

76

instigated by the Serbians was intense and unanimous throughout Europe. I am still of the opinion that this general reaction could have been utilized to avoid a world war without loss of prestige. Had the representatives of the Courts of the Great Powers, as was customary, been invited to Vienna for the appropriate obsequies, the work of the diplomats would have been made easier and might have met with success. The Prince of Wales[15] and the Russian Grand Duke Nikolai Nikolayevich[16] expressed their willingness to undertake the journey. Kaiser Wilhelm II had announced his intention and that of the Princes of the German States to be present. But owing to the influence of the Lord Steward of the Household, Prince Montenuovo, Spanish etiquette and dynastic rules were adhered to, because of the morganatic nature of the Archduke's marriage which forbade royal mourning ceremonies. The formal excuse given to the world was the advanced age of the sovereign, and every offer to attend the obsequies was met with refusal.

On July 23rd, Baron Giesl handed an ultimatum to the Belgrade Government. Two days later, Pasic gave his reply, which was considered unsatisfactory. When Baron Giesl telephoned Count Tisza in Budapest from Semlin, the then Hungarian frontier town facing Belgrade on the other bank of the Sava, to announce his departure, the Prime Minister exclaimed, "Did it have to be then?"

That question was one that we have put to Fate, and the answer has not yet been vouchsafed to us. After the breaking off of diplomatic relations between Austria-Hungary and Serbia, His Majesty ordered partial mobilization. In 1912, the last occasion on which partial mobilization had been ordered, it had not led to Russian mobilization. In 1914, it did, and this in turn caused Germany to mobilize.

On July 27th, 1914, while I was still at home on leave, I received my calling-up papers as captain of a ship of the line, a rank to which I had been raised on November 1st, 1913. That document brought to an end the five interesting and happy years of my service as aide-de-camp at Court.

---

15 Prince of Wales Eduard Albert, who later became King Eduard VIII (1894-1972).

16 Grand Duke Nikolai Nikolayevich (1856-1929), was the war-time Commander of the Russian Army.

I am grateful to Providence for having granted me those years in the immediate entourage of His Majesty Emperor Francis Joseph I. What I then learned and experienced enabled me to see my way clearly when I was called to the leadership of the Hungarian nation, a task that was not of my own seeking. The example of the most noble, courtly and kindly man I have ever met in my life was before me throughout my later years. The values that had been put to the test in Vienna throughout the centuries, and had proved their worth, I was able to take with me to Hungary.

Those five years were assuredly the finest of my life.

5. Naval Warfare in the Adriatic. The Coronation of King Charles IV

From Sofronya, my brother-in-law's estate where my calling-up papers had reached me, I travelled to Vienna to report at naval headquarters. There I was given instructions to go on a special mission to His Majesty at Ischl. The next morning I was received in audience. Shortly after dinner, Prince Lobkowitz[1], Steward of the Household to the young heir apparent, Archduke Charles, came to the Hotel Elisabeth to request me to visit his master. The Archduke greeted me with the question, "Well, what's it going to be?"

"World war," I replied.

The Archduke thought that improbable. That very morning, Count Berchthold[2], the Foreign Minister, had assured him that the war was unlikely to spread and would therefore be restricted to a conflict between Austria-Hungary and Serbia. When I put forward the contrary view, based on incontrovertible grounds, he remarked that a world war would be terrible, with which comment I agreed. If only England would remain neutral, I said, we could deal with our other enemies.

At Pola, I took over the command of the *Habsburg,* the flagship of the Third Battleship Division. I have to confess that I was not happy about this particular command; the *Habsburg* was old, slow, and poorly armed. My first task, however, was the organization of the defences of our major naval harbour, with mines, nets, booms and similar devices.

Archduke Francis Ferdinand, to the gratification of the Navy, had advocated naval expansion, insisting that our Navy should not only be strong enough to defend our coasts but also to attack. In actual fact, the Austro-Hungarian Navy, on the outbreak of war, had not achieved that standard, hostilities having interrupted the building program. Adding to our difficulties was the

1   General Prince Zdenko Lobkowitz (1858-1933), Charles IV's chief military aide.

2   Count Leopold Berchtold (1863-1942).

fact that the excellent, natural harbour of Cattaro could not be utilized until Montenegro had been conquered, as it lay within range of the Montenegrin batteries on the Lovcen heights.

After the First World War, it leaked out that a secret naval agreement had been concluded in November, 1913, between the members of the Triple Alliance, providing for a concentration of the Austro-Hungarian, Italian and German units in the Naples-Messina-Augusta naval sector. A similar agreement had been concluded a few months before between England and France.

Italy's declaration of neutrality upset the plans of the naval staffs. The escape of the two cruisers *Goeben* and and *Breslau* from the hostile British and French fleets was due only to a successful maneuvre carried out by the German Vice-Admiral Souchon[3], who had received timely warning from our naval attaché in Rome. The cruisers took refuge in the Dardanelles and, according to a British view, the appearance of these two ships was instrumental in winning the Turks over to the side of the Central Powers.

At Pola, we prepared ourselves for an attack by superior enemy forces, an attack that was never made. A French submarine that succeeded in penetrating our minefields was caught in a steel net and brought in undamaged; later we were able to use it ourselves. British and French naval units made sporadic appearances in the south Adriatic, but after a successful submarine attack on the French flagship, such expeditions were discontinued as being too hazardous.

As early as November, my family was plunged into mourning by the first of its war losses. My younger brother Szabolcs had refused to remain at his post as chief commissioner of our county[4]; in spite of protestations made to him by myself and by the Prime Minister, who considered his duties on the home front more important. He had volunteered as a lieutenant of Hussar reserves and had been killed in ambush on a reconnaissance mission in Poland.

Nothing frets the nerves more than forced inactivity at a time when everything calls for action. We at Pola were condemned for long periods to spend our

3   Wilhelm Anton Souchon (1864-?).

4   Jász-Nagykun-Szolnok County.

time carrying out normal harbour duties. Fortunately, in December, I was unexpectedly appointed captain of the armoured cruiser *Novara*, which had just been completed at Fiume and which, being the fastest ship of our fleet, was intended for special assignments. This command improved my temper considerably.

Unfortunately, the trial trips of the *Novara* brought delay owing to engine-room trouble, probably due to sabotage during construction. I lost the chance of taking her to Smyrna as a blockade breaker to carry munitions to the Turks. They were short of everything on account of the the mining of the Danube by the Rumanians[5], which would have been the conventional shipping line. This blocade lasted until the conquest of Rumania in 1917.

The British landing at Gallipoli[6] and the attempt to force the Dardanelles promised us action at last, and plans to assist our beleaguered allies were discussed. We were not prepared, of course, to risk our larger ships in the eastern Mediterranean, but what about submarines? Though, at that time, the penetration of the Straits of Gibraltar had not been attempted, the German Navy had been sending submarine parts to Pola by rail to be assembled there; we called them *ocarinas*. I was instructed to tow the *U 8*, commanded by Lieutenant von Voigt[7], if possible as far as Cape Matapan in order to save her using fuel in the Adriatic. I had the *Novara* metamorphosed in secret into a harmless-looking cargo-boat by means of wooden deck-houses, and on May 2nd we sailed from Pola. We passed successfully through the narrow Straits of Otranto but were sighted about a hundred nautical miles from Cape Matapan by a number of French battle-cruisers. I changed my course towards Patras to keep up the fiction that we were a cargo-boat. The French vessels came nearer and the *U 8* had to be given orders to cast off and proceed on her own. She

5 Submitting to growing French pressure, following a secret treaty signed in Bucharest on August 17 in which the French promised most of eastern Hungary to Rumania after the war, Rumania initiated a surprise attack Austria-Hungary on August 27, 1916, and occupied southern Transylvania. Counter-attacking Austro-Hungarian and German forces under general Falkenhayn cleared the country of Rumanian forces by October 13, and occupied Bucharest on December 6. Rumania was kept under occupation for two years.

6 The April, 1915, attack was planned by Winston Churchill, First Lord of Admiralty.

7 German Navy Lt. Ernst Voigt.

submerged. Meanwhile I had thrown off our camouflage and had hoisted the naval ensign. The French had forces concentrated at Corfu and these were given the alarm by wireless telegraphy so that it looked as if the Straits of Otranto would be closed from the opposite shore. However, we succeeded in breaking through to the north. The *U 8* reached the Dardanelles and I returned to my home port. For this action I was awarded the Iron Cross. Later I read with much gratification in an English account of the war in the Mediterranean, *The History of the Great War: Naval Operations (London, 1920),* by Sir Julian Corbett[8], that in breaking through the blockade of Otranto twice we had considerably perturbed the British Admiralty and caused a redisposition of available forces.

Hardly had I returned to Pola, the Italian entry into the war created a new situation. Grand-Admiral Haus, the Commander-in-Chief of the fleet, hoisted the signal 'Raise steam' from his flagship within half an hour of Italy's declaration of war. The plan of attack was prepared and all the captains had their orders in readiness. At 11 p.m., the whole Austro-Hungarian fleet sailed to launch an attack on the Italian east coast from Venice down to Brindisi. Our main task was to delay the Italian advance by disrupting the railway system along the Adriatic, thereby giving us time to move our troops to the frontier, where, at that moment, only a few battalions were stationed, leaving the road to Vienna open. As a result of our operation, the Italians, fearing a landing at Ancona and an attack on Rome in the rear of their armies, did halt their advance.

I was in command of the northernmost section of the fleet and, in the Novara, together with four torpedo-boats[9] and the destroyer *Scharfschütze,* attacked Porto Corsini. Suspecting the presence of submarines and motor-vessels in the canal linking Ravenna to the Adriatic, I sent the *Scharfsütze* in stern first. The Italian troops, who were, oddly enough, in trenches, made no move. About five in the morning, they showed themselves, full of curiosity, and an N.C.O. came and naively enquired, "Ma che cosa volete?" (What do you want?). Machine-guns soon made our wishes clear to him. After the *Scharfsütze* had performed her task of destroying the signal station, she steamed out of the canal, which is about three-quarters of a mile long, at a fair speed, running the gauntlet of a considerable fire, but the level of the canal was so low that she was

8   Sir Julian Stafford Corbett (1857-1922), British military historian.

9   WW1 version of the PT boat.

not hit. The Italian batteries did succeed in placing a few hits on the *Novara*, and my courageous torpedo-officer Lieutenant Persich[10] and several sailors were killed. One of the torpedo-boats was damaged. I ordered her to come alongside, out of the line of fire, and with tarpaulins we sealed off the hole in her side so successfully that the *Scharfsütze* was able to tow her back to Pola. After this operation, the ships under my command set course for Trieste. I had instructions to attack the Italian squadron which was thought to be returning there from Venice. As our reconnaissance planes reported that not a ship had left Venice, I was recalled to join the main fleet, and returned with it to Pola.

The north Adriatic remained quiet, but in the south there was considerable activity, for the enemy was occupied in sealing the Straits of Otranto to prevent more U-boats from entering the Mediterranean. We discussed the situation and the Commander of the fleet ordered the *Novara* to the Bocche del Cattaro. Though remaining under the orders of the flotilla-commander, I kept full freedom of movement and to act largely on my own initiative. On the day I set out, I informed the flotilla commander of my intentions and asked for his support should it prove necessary. Secrecy was essential as the enemy had a well-organized spy system with a number of transmitters at its disposal which we had been unable to trace. From the moment that I gave the order to get up steam, all communication with the shore was forbidden, and only then did I acquaint my officers and men with my plans.

To ensure a crew being at its best in action, it has to be well fed and well rested. I had alarm bells fitted in every part of the ship which could be set off from the bridge by pressing a button. This I pressed only when the enemy came in sight, so that the crew could rest until the last moment.

Often I went 'stalking' without any particular aim, and, generally, had the luck to come upon game that showed fight or trawlers hunting U-boats with trailing nets. Before we sank them, we gave the crews warning to abandon ship. My gunners were so skilled that with a single shot they could explode the boiler, and down went the ship.

In our wartime Navy, all sea cadets and naval lieutenants who showed no particular aptitude for the work were transferred to the reserve so that they could seek careers more suited to them. At the outbreak of the war the general manager of a large factory joined up again, having been in the past at the top of

10   Lt. Emil Persich von Köstenheim (1885-1915).

his year in the naval college, though he had left soon afterwards. As an officer he proved useless, until by chance we discovered his aptitude for decoding enemy signals.

One afternoon, he came running along the alleyway of the *Novara* and rushed into my cabin to announce breathlessly that King Peter of Serbia was embarking that evening in an Italian destroyer at Durazzo for Brindisi. This followed upon the successful termination of the Serbian campaign, when the remnants of the Serbian Army had been forced to fall back into Montenegro and Albania. I wasted no time on questions but ordered steam to be got up immediately. Escorted by three torpedo-boats, I set out. There was no possibility of reaching Durazzo in time, but there was a good chance of intercepting the Italian destroyer. A stiff sirocco was blowing, whipping up quite a sea. As the sky was practically cloudless and the moon nearly at the full, visibility was excellent. For some hours, we cruised about on the Durazzo-Brindisi route without sighting a ship. Two days later, our information service reported that the King had indeed gone on board very punctually but had been so sea-sick that he had cancelled his voyage.

On another occasion, this decoder informed me that enemy signals had been referring repeatedly to a fleet that was to transport ordnance to Lovcen to replace the batteries that had been put out of action, together with arms, munitions and supplies for the Montenegrin and Serbian armies. He had been unable to ascertain the date of sailing, nor had he been able to discover the place of embarcation or the destination. On reflection, I decided that Durazzo was too far from Montenegro, Antivari too near the Bocche di Cattaro, so that the transport would probably call at San Giovanni di Medua, the Albanian harbour occupied at that time by the Serbs.

I asked the flotilla commander for four destroyers to escort the *Novara* in case of a surprise attack by superior enemy forces. With these, I set out at eleven o'clock one night on the off-chance, my main objective being to arrive at the harbour mouth unseen in the dusk[11]. We knew that there was a battery of ten guns there. We hugged the rocky Albanian coast until we arrived at the breakwater. We could see a single-storied house, in which the gun-crews were probably asleep. One salvo sufficed to blow up the house and thereby put the

11 Astonishingly, Horthy's original battle report (Novara #796; Dec. 5, 1915) still exists. (Csonkaréti, K. : Horthy, the Seaman, Budapest: Zrinyi, 1993, in Hung.)

battery out of action. With a beating heart, I advanced. Were we going to find anything there or not? When the view was clear, we saw, to our intense joy, a harbour full of ships; later we learned that they had arrived the night before. It was sheer luck! Had we come a day earlier, we should have found an empty harbour; a day later, and much of the cargo would have already been unloaded. After giving the crews time to leave their ships, I gave the order to open fire. One ship blew up, a second caught fire, a third sank soundlessly. A sailing ship was burning with a weird yellow light, she may have had a cargo of salt. We even succeeded in making something out of these cargo-boats, for by sinking one that was on fire, we quenched the flames. She was loaded with preserves, which were later salvaged by our troops and despatched to our army in Albania.

By the time we had finished our task, the shore batteries were beginning to wake up, but they were so poorly served that it was a full quarter of an hour before shells began to drop anywhere near us. By manoeuvring, we avoided being hit more than once during an hour and a half. That one shell struck the sick bay and deprived us of our excellent chief petty officer, who had been the captain of our naval football team and a very fine violinist.

Altogether, we sank twenty-three steamers and sailing ships, and were able to return home, again keeping close inshore, fully satisfied with our work. Only after the occupation of San Giovanni did we learn that there had been a triple screen of mines outside the harbour, and that it was owing to our sailing so close inshore that we had avoided disaster. Our operation proved a useful preparation for the assault on Lovcen in 1916.

On the homeward voyage, the destroyer *Warasdiner* reported a stranded enemy submarine lying on a sandbank at the mouth of the Bojano. She turned out to be the French *Fresnel.* I sent one of my officers over to her in a launch to take the French crew off and to see what chance there was of refloating her. The latter proved impossible, as a torpedo had exploded in its tube and had torn the bows wide open. The crew refused to surrender until some shots had been fired. The French captain, Lieutenant R. Jouen, was very crestfallen. He had been lurking for weeks in those waters with no result, and he had at last run aground at the only point along the whole of that rocky coast where it was possible to do so. I consoled him as best I could.

Our prisoners were taken off in the Bocche di Cattaro and sent to camp. On the following day, our casualty and one of the Frenchmen who had died of injuries on board the *Novara* were buried with military honours, the French Tricolour on their coffins; the Frenchman had as many flowers as my own man. After the funeral, I gave Lieutenant Jouen my address and told him to write to me should there be anything he needed while he was a prisoner. I was able to provide him with French books later on.

After the First World War, I received two Paris journalists at the request of the French Ambassador. I was not in the habit of granting interviews to the press lightly, for journalists have a tendency to put words into one's mouth. The two Frenchmen, having agreed not to ask any catch-questions, asked for details about the loss of the *Fresnel.* A report was printed in Le Temps to which no objection could be taken other than that the *Monge* had been substituted for the *Fresnel.* The first officer of the *Monge* made a protest to Le Temps and ex-Lieutenant Jouen in reply pointed out that there had merely been a confusion of names in the first message. He took the trouble to stress the courteous treatment he and his men had received while in our hands. Alas, the Second World War failed to produce similar occurrences.

It was about this time that I had a job to do at Durazzo. As I was drawing near the harbour, I sighted clouds of smoke out at sea. I hugged the land and gave orders that our boilers should make as little smoke as possible, but we had already been observed and before long I could make out the approach of a British battleship and a fast cruiser. Though no larger than the *Novara*, they were more heavily armed, and I had no other course than to turn round. The cruiser, following a parallel course, opened fire from a distance so great that it would have been useless for us to reply in kind.

It was not pleasant to have to run away. But the slightest damage in the engine-room would have been enough to enable the battleship to overtake us and deal with us at her leisure, for a broadside from the *Novara* would have bounced off her like peas off a wall. I sent a wireless message with the short aerial, in English, to the cruiser, "If you want to fight, I am ready, but send away your big brother." She answered, "I would, but I can't." As the *Novara* was the swifter of the two, the battle was cut short. This exchange brought me a reprimand, even if smilingly given, on my return to Pola, for having parleyed with the enemy.

To my regret, I had to return to Pola to have my ship overhauled. This made an Allied 'Dunkirk' possible, for the defeated Serbian Army-some 134,000 men, according to the enemy, were evacuated from Durazzo to Corfu. I should not have cared to offer battle in a ship which had lost speed to the extent of four to five knots. But I had hoped to be back from Pola in time. The plan had been to join the probably numerous enemy ships during the hours of darkness as if I belonged to the convoy, place several torpedoes and then make off. Even had I been discovered, the risk would have been minimal, as the commanders of a unit consisting of ships of three nations would have hesitated to open fire for fear of hitting an ally.

Whenever I was at leisure in the mornings, I went ashore for exercise. On one of these walks, I saw to my surprise a regiment encamped in a clearing in the woods; hearing some words spoken in Hungarian, I made enquiries and was informed that it was a regiment from Szeged which had come over from the Isonzo front. Later I came upon two more Hungarian regiments. The Czech troops on the Bocche di Cattaro were being replaced[12], a sign that we were now in earnest.

Gun-sites were also being built for three mighty mortars which, on a January morning in 1916, began the bombardment of the Montenegrin batteries on the Lovcen heights. Our naval artillery was also brought into play. The battleships being heeled to gain higher aim for their heavy guns that thundered at the enemy fortifications. Our cruisers fired at the Montenegrin troops in the Zupa from out at sea and, after a few well-placed rounds, those troops were withdrawn.

Anyone who has climbed from Cattaro, or Kotor as the Yugoslavs call this town, following the splendid road which Austrian army engineers built, rising nearly to six thousand feet up the Lovcen heights to Cetinje, will be able to realize how difficult the conquest of that mountain was. It so happened that the attack was aided by heavy fog. Also, the most dangerous enemy batteries on the Kuck plateau had been silenced by our naval guns, their gun crews having been killed by exploding ammunition.

In the evening a fresh bora set in, scattering the mist. The mighty Lovcen stood there like a Christmas tree, camp-fires burning everywhere and our

12 Czech troop's lack of battle-worthiness was well established by that time.

battle flag flew on the peak[13].

The gateway to the land of the Black Mountains had been forced. Our victorious troops swarmed across Montenegro, deep into Albania.

During the night of November 22nd, 1916, I was woken by the first officer with the news that His Majesty Emperor Francis Joseph I had breathed his last a few hours earlier. Against the advice of his doctors, he had spent all day at his desk and, when at last he retired, he had given orders to be called at half-past three, "for," he had said to his personal servant, "I have not been able to get through all the work."

The next morning, flags were flown at half-mast. I asked the Commander of the fleet for leave to attend the obsequies, a request I felt justified in making as the *Novara* was still being overhauled. Permission was granted, and I was therefore able to be present at the moving, majestic and sad ceremony in the Cathedral of St. Stephen and to accompany the coffin on its last journey to the Capuchin crypt. We were very conscious that one of the last great figures of a bygone age was being carried to his rest.

His Majesty Emperor Charles took over the government at one of the darkest periods of Austro-Hungarian history. With him came new men and the old guard disappeared. The new ruler was twenty-nine years old. His intentions were good but circumstances were against him. He was not destined to hold on to the heritage Emperor Francis Joseph left him.

My first meeting with the new monarch was many years old. He had been fourteen when I was presented to him by my brother, to whom Archduke Otto, Charles's father, had entrusted his training in horsemanship. At that time, my brother was riding-master in the military riding academy in Vienna, commander of the hunting division, and he had been, for seven years, Master of the Hounds. During the steeplechasing season, the Archduke would always visit him at Holics. I had frequently encountered Archduke Charles during my period of service as aide-de-camp, as his mother, the Archduchess Maria Josepha, had graciously issued many invitations to my wife and myself.

13 On January 11, 1916, the Austro-Hungarian 47th Division, under General Ignaz von Trollman, stormed the heights. Two days later Montenegro capitulated. (H. H. Herwig: The First World War, Germany and Austria-Hungary, 1914-18. London: Arnold, 1997.)

Whenever Archduke Charles visited Pola, he sent for me. I was also in the company of Emperor Francis Joseph on the occasion of the Archduke's wedding to Princess Zita[14] of Bourbon-Parma. The Emperor had travelled to Schwarzau in order to tender his congratulations to the young couple personally. After the wedding breakfast, he had made Princess Zita Archduchess.

The coronation of the young ruler as King of Hungary in Budapest on December 30th, 1916, at which ceremony I was able to be present, was an unforgettable experience. The narrow streets of Buda, through which the procession wound, were decked with columns embellished with a variety of decorations, and from all flagstaffs flew the flags of Hungary, of the Houses of Habsburg and Parma, and of the city of Budapest.

Hungary was no doubt the only country in which the sovereign entered upon his full rights only after the coronation. This ceremony was a parliamentary procedure in which both Houses of Parliament participated. The coronation took place during the parliamentary session which was prorogued for the duration of the crowning. Hence, all members of the two Houses had to be present in the church. From early in the morning, the splendid equipages drove up to the Coronation Church of St. Matthias, the interior of which had been draped with red hangings. All the high dignitaries of the state were present as well as the Archdukes, the Papal Legate and King Ferdinand[15] of Bulgaria. The men wore uniform or Hungarian national costume, and the sunlight, falling on the stalls where the ladies sat, produced a sparkle and glitter as if the lid of a vast jewel casket had been raised.

From the Royal Palace the ceremonious procession drew near. A squadron of hussars rode ahead of the state carriages of the high dignitaries, which were followed in turn by the mounted Hungarian Guards, who presented a resplendent spectacle, the heron plumes in their shakos and their panther skins fluttering in the breeze. Then came the golden State Coach, in which were seated the King and Queen with their infant son and heir, Archduke Otto. After the religious ceremony, which closely followed the tradition of centuries, the actual crowning took place. First the King was anointed by the Prince Primate Csernoch; then the Prince Primate and the Lieutenant

14 Princess Zita Maria Adelgunda of Bourbon-Parma (1892-1989).

15 Tsar Ferdinand I of Koburg (1861-1948).

Palatine, the Premier Count Tisza, jointly placed the Holy Crown of St. Stephen on his head. The symbolic crowning of the Queen by touching her shoulder with the crown followed. The Queen and the heir to the throne then left the church to be driven back to the Palace in a glass coach drawn by eight Lipizzaners. The King remained to perform the first act of his kingship: conferring the accolade of Knighthood of the Order of the Golden Spur on twenty-four officers who had won distinction in the war.

With that act, the ceremony in the church was over, and the King mounted the steps of the Pillar of the Trinity outside the Church of St. Matthias, there to take the oath to the Hungarian constitution, wearing the ancient royal robe of Saint Stephen[16], on which the Queen, as tradition demanded, had sewn a few stitches the night before. After taking the oath, the King mounted his horse, his unsheathed sword in his right hand, his sceptre and bridle in the left. The coronation procession was formed anew, and the King was conducted to the Coronation Mound, composed of earth brought there from every county of Hungary. At the head were the hussars, then the mounted banner-carriers of all the counties of Hungary, that is to say, the dignitaries of the Hungarian realm, and, after them, the King. The Guard troops brought up the rear. On arriving at the Mound, the procession surrounded it as the King, alone and wearing the Holy Crown, galloped to the summit. There, while the grey stallion pranced on his hind-legs, the King swung his sword to south and west, to north and east, to signify that he would defend the land against enemies from every quarter. This symbolic act, which incidentally involved a fine feat of horsemanship, was accompanied by enthusiastic shouts of "Éljen!" ("Long Live") raised by the assembled multitude.

From the Coronation Mound, the King rode to the Palace, where the traditional coronation banquet was held at which Count Tisza proposed a toast to the prosperity of His Majesty, and the King to that of the Hungarian nation.

At this solemn moment, all hearts went out to the ruler. But all too soon the jubilation evaporated and cares weighed down the minds of the people. With anxious forebodings, I returned to the fleet in the Bocche di Cattaro.

16 This and the rest of the coronation regalia is presently on display in the Hungarian National Museum in Budapest.

The victories which the Central Powers were gaining on land and at sea, even after the coronation, were no longer sufficient to stem the tide of revolution and collapse.

6. The Naval Battle of Otranto

On February 1st, 1917, the unrestricted German submarine warfare began. From the point of view of naval strategy, the decision was defensible: the figures for enemy losses rose from a monthly average of 80,000 gross tonnage to 210,000 in April. Whether the decision was politically defensible is a much disputed question, to which a definite answer could be given only if it were absolutely certain that the United States would not have entered the war had the decision not been taken. That the intensified submarine warfare gave strength to the interventionists in the United States of America is not open to doubt. Could the Supreme Command of the German Army, which had, from August 29th, 1916, been taken over by Hindenburg[1] and Ludendorff,[2] have foreseen the collapse of the Russian front a few weeks later, the decision would no doubt have been deferred as it would then have been superfluous.

In Vienna, the agreement with the German proposal had been hesitant. The Emperor was vacillating. The Foreign Minister, Count Czernin[3], and the Hungarian Prime Minister, Count Tisza, were opposed to it. The scales were tipped by the vote of the Commander of the Fleet, Grand-Admiral Haus[4], who, in the decisive discussion held in the Imperial Palace, sided with Zimmermann[5], the German Foreign Minister, and Admiral von Holtzendorf, the German naval attaché in Vienna.

1   Paul von Beneckendorf und von Hindenburg (1847-1934), German chief of staff during the war, president of the Weimar Republic from 1925 until his death.

2   Gen. Erich Ludendorff (1865-1937), German quartermaster-general during the war.

3   Count Ottokar Czernin (1872-1932), was advisor to Emperor Franz-Joseph, and war-time foreign minister of Austria-Hungary between 1916 and 1918. He sought a negotiated peace, but was unwilling to give up war aims against Italy and the Balkans. He was dismissed after French Premier Clemenceau dramatically disclosed the private peace-making attempts of Emperor Charles IV through Prince Sixtus of Bourbon-Parma, brother-in-law of Charles.

4   Antal Haus (1851-1917).

5   Arthur von Zimmerman (1864-1940), Deputy Foreign Minister of Germany.

In the Mediterranean at that time there were thirty-two German and fourteen Austro-Hungarian submarines. At the outbreak of the war we had had only eight. Though we could now make full use of the Bocche di Cattaro, our operations were nevertheless considerably hampered by the bottleneck formed by the narrow exit from the Adriatic between Cape Santa Maria di Leuca and the islands Fano and Corfu; for the Allies were obviously making every effort to cork that bottleneck as tightly as possible. To this end, a stronger patrol service of torpedo-boats and destroyers had been instituted. The moment a U-boat showed its periscope above water, it was spotted by the destroyers and attacked with depth charges. If they evaded the destroyers, the U-boats were always in danger from the drifters, which trailed, at first to a depth of about seventy feet and later of a hundred and forty feet, which was the maximum diving capacity of the submarines, long nets fitted with explosives and warning devices.

I had talked at length with every U-boat commander who had entered the Bocche di Cattaro. They all agreed: it was becoming more and more difficult, if not impossible, to break through this blockade. I made up my mind that it was time to make a clearance.

The operation was carefully prepared. I asked the flotilla commander for the two cruisers *Helgoland* and *Saida*, which were of the same type as the *Novara*, and for the two destroyers *Csepel* and *Balaton*. To deceive the enemy, I again made use of camouflage and had the mainmasts of the three cruisers shortened to make the ships less easy to identify.

On the evening of May 14th, 1917, we set out; the two destroyers under the orders of Captain Prince Liechtenstein[6] sailed on reconnaissance an hour before the cruisers, which followed in line ahead. The time of departure had been calculated to allow us to arrive at a point near the Straits of Otranto as night was falling. The cruisers were then to fan out: the *Novara* eastward towards Fano, the Helgoland, in the centre, southward, and the *Saida* westward towards Cape Santa Maria di Leuca.

At three in the morning, we heard gunfire to the south. Our destroyers had intercepted a convoy sailing to Brindisi. They did a good job in sinking the two large steamers and their escorting destroyer.

6   Prince Johann Lichtenstein (1873-1929).

Meanwhile, we were drawing near the point at which we were to scatter and soon we came upon the net-trailing drifters. We gave their crews warning, but not all of them took to their boats. Some manned their automatic guns and fired until their boilers exploded or their ships capsized. Crews that had abandoned ship were taken on board by us.

Our task had been carried out. Between them, the cruisers destroyed twenty-one drifters and took seventy-two prisoners. Damage to our own ships was negligible. The *Novara* had been attacked by an Italian sea-plane without suffering harm. The three cruisers joined up again and turned for home in line ahead, with the destroyers in the van.

The drifters meanwhile had given the alarm with rockets and wireless signals. Several enemy destroyers set out from Valona. A gun battle was fought, after seven minutes of which the eight enemy destroyers turned back towards Valona. We could not, however, prevent them from keeping us under observation and from furnishing the enemy command with accurate details of our positions. At this point, we were informed by the Liechtenstein vessels and by our aeroplanes that strong enemy forces had been sighted in the Gulf of Drin, off Durazzo, which had obviously set out from Brindisi to attempt cutting off our retreat. The first report gave one Italian and two British cruisers and two destroyers.

As I knew their positions, it would have been simple to shape a course to avoid them, for I knew both their speeds and ours, but as I was considering the best plan, I received a wireless message from Prince Liechtenstein stating that his two destroyers had found their way to the Bocche barred and were being forced towards the coast. I therefore made for the enemy, who, as soon as we were sighted, called off the attack on our two destroyers and steamed towards us. After sinking an Italian destroyer, Liechtenstein's two destroyers reached home safely.

The flotilla commander, who had a clear view of the situation, sent a wireless message to ask whether he should come out. I replied that it would be a good manoeuvre to try and get the enemy between us.

When the enemy cruisers had reached their firing distance, they followed a course parallel to ours and at 9:28 a.m. opened fire. A British cruiser had meanwhile replaced the Italian in the lead.

The British cruiser's first volley fell within yards of the *Novara's* bows, directly on our course. Since the range of the enemy artillery was plainly superior to ours, I ordered the smoke-screen apparatus to be used, so that we should be able to draw in closer and thus be able to use our smaller-calibre guns and launch our torpedoes to greater effect. The enemy was certain to come nearer, as he would be convinced that we were refusing battle.

When I thought the enemy cruisers were within reasonable distance, I sailed out of the smoke screen and continued on a northerly course. The destroyers, which had approached on the port beam, were driven off with gunfire.

A violent battle now developed along parallel courses at a distance varying between 15,000 and 25,000 feet. In spite of the slow speed of the *Saida*, which did not exceed twenty-five knots, we were able to move our formation slowly and keep within our gun range. The fire of the British cruisers was accurate and scientific, the *Novara*, the leader of our formation, being the main target. At first, hits were negligible, but gradually the situation grew serious. The conning tower was hit and the chart-room was destroyed. One of our guns was put out of action and a number of fires broke out which we succeeded in extinguishing before they had any considerable hold. On the other hand, we could see that the enemy ships were not going unscathed either.

At 10:10 a.m., I was wounded by a shell that exploded near me, five shell splinters embedding themselves in my leg. A piece of shrapnel weighing a couple of pounds carried my cap off my head without injuring me, that piece of metal with singed shreds of my cap still adhering to it was later handed to me. I was wearing my overcoat over my uniform and although, except for shoes and socks, my clothes were singed right through to my chest, I did not have a single burn. But I felt as if I had been felled by a blow on the head with an axe. I was also overcome by the poisonous fumes and lost consciousness. I was quickly brought round, however, by the cold water that was poured over me to extinguish my smouldering garments.

I had myself put on a stretcher and taken to the fore-deck, knowing I should have a satisfactory view of affairs from there. I intended to hand over the command of the vessel to my excellent first officer, Lieutenant Szuborits[7], but received the sad news that he had been killed. I therefore delegated the

---

7   Robert Szuborits (1877-1917).

command to the officer next in rank, Lieutenant Witkowski[8], the artillery officer, who had stood on the open upper bridge throughout the engagement, leading the firing in a first-rate manner. I remained in charge of the flotilla, however.

At 10:35 a.m., we received a serious direct hit which exploded in the turbine chamber aft and destroyed the pipe-line of the condenser. The fires of eight of the sixteen boilers had to be extinguished. We could have gone on for a while on sea water, but I did not care to damage the remaining boilers and therefore informed my sister ships that the a *Novara* could proceed under her own steam only for another ten minutes. The fires were raked out and before long we were lying motionless. Meanwhile, the British fire had noticeably decreased; at 11 a.m., the enemy turned south-west and joined the destroyers approaching from the south.

At 11:20 a.m., the *Saida* came alongside the *Novara* to take her in tow, while the *Helgoland* sailed between the *Novara* and the enemy to cover the maneeuvre. While the hawser was got across, both sides were continuing to fire. A sharp attack by the Italian cruiser *Quarto* was beaten off as was that of a destroyer which shot forward to fire a torpedo at us Captain Ritter von Purschka[9] of the *Saida* carried out the difficult hawser manceuvre faultlessly in spite of a rain of shells. We were also attacked by enemy aircraft, one of which we brought down.

We were beginning to breathe more freely when more columns of smoke appeared on the southern horizon and soon an Italian cruiser and several destroyers came in sight. Joining forces, the whole enemy formation, about ten vessels in all, moved towards us along a wide front. These were critical moments. In view of the numerical superiority of the enemy and the lame condition of the *Novara*, the situation seemed hopeless.

As I was unable to see the enemy fleet from my stretcher, I asked Witkowski what they were doing. He studied them through his binoculars and, after a long pause, replied, "It looks to me as if they are turning around and leaving us the field."

.   .

8   Lt. Stanislaus Witkowski (1869-1935), later captain.

9   Rear Adm. Ritter Ferdinand von Purschka (1870-1940).

97

And, indeed, the enemy broke off the action and set course for Brindisi. That was at 12:07 a.m. Few columns of water marked the enemy's parting salute before they vanished in the mist of the southern horizon. Northward, the smoke of our *St. Georg* and a number of destroyers hastening from the Bocche di Cattaro had appeared.

The Italian Admiral Acton[10], who had been on board the leading British cruiser, had decided that the risk of an encounter with our battle cruiser *St. Georg*, supported by the coastal patrol vessel *Budapest*, was too great. He preferred to let the *Novara* slip from his grasp, though, on account of losing our mobility, we had been at his mercy. We had, therefore, won the battle.

At 12:20 p.m., the *Saida*, with the *Novara* in tow, turned towards the *St. Georg*. Before long, had joined her and our torpedo-boats, the crews of which gave us a rousing cheer. Twenty-four hours after leaving the Bocche di Cattaro, we returned victorious.

Together our three cruisers mustered twenty-seven 4.2 inch guns; against them had been arrayed one Italian and two British cruisers, apart from eleven Italian and three French destroyers, with thirty-three superior guns of 4.8 inch and 6 inch calibre and fifty-six guns of smaller calibre. Our tonnage was 12,200, the enemy's 25,932: twice as much as ours.

The enemy had lost twenty-three net-trailing drifters, two transports, two destroyers and one aeroplane. In addition, the enemy flagship *Dartmouth* was attacked by a German U-boat as she was entering the harbour of Brindisi and holed by two torpedoes. The French destroyer *Boutefeu*, going to the assistance of the *Dartmouth*, ran onto a mine released by the U-boat and sank. We had not lost a single vessel and the Straits of Otranto were once more open to U-boats. We had shown that the drifter blockade could be broken. The enemy, as can be gathered from statements made at a later date, recognized the danger and, for a long time, drifters operated only during the hours of daylight, so that U-boats were able to pass through the Straits of Otranto at night unhindered.

10 Adm. Alfredo Acton (1867-1934).

After the war, the wife of the British Admiral Mark Kerr[11] visited Budapest on the occasion of a Girl Scouts' Conference and brought me a letter from her husband, who had been in command of the British Adriatic Fleet. In this letter, Admiral Mark Kerr quoted from the despatch he had sent to the Admiralty after the battle of Otranto:

"Undoubtedly the Austro-Hungarian cruisers behaved most chivalrously. Whenever a drifter put up a fight and refused to surrender, it was noticeable that most of the guns of the broadside were directed not to hit the fishing-boat, and the shots went wide and they left their plucky little adversary afloat and passed on. It was keeping up the ancient tradition of chivalry at sea." (See: Admiral Mark Kerr: The Navy in My Time, 1933.)

After we had entered the Bocche di Cattaro, I was transferred to the hospital ship. It so happened that my wife had been granted leave to visit me. She had arrived the day before our sortie, so that she had followed the excitement of the battle, being kept in touch by the flotilla commander. She had learned that I was wounded and was waiting for me on board the hospital ship. The pleasure of our reunion made the pain seem negligible. I was fortunate in find-finding myself in the care of the best, ablest and most loving of nurses.

Some temporary repairs were made to the *Novara* and as soon as I could be moved, I took her to the naval arsenal at Pola, I lay on a stretcher on the bridge. This was no theatrical gesture on my part. At that time, the Adriatic was a dangerous area, riddled with submarines. Both enemy and our own mines made the passage difficult. I had the feeling that this would be my last trip on the good old *Novara*. I could not endure the thought of her being taken to Pola by other hands than mine. I had the most reliable and excellent officers on board, but I had had more experience than they.

I was taken to Vienna for an operation. On the advice of the famous surgeon, Professor Dr. Eiselsberg[12], I spent six weeks regaining my strength before the operation. Professor Eiselsberg took me to Baden, where we had rented a small house. The ear-specialist, Dr. Biel, joined us there, as the explosion had affected my ear-drums. He gave it as his opinion that nothing could be done, but natural regeneration saved me from deafness. After a while, my hearing

---

11 Adm. Mark Edward Frederick Kerr (1864-1944).

12 Baron Anton Eiselsberg (1860-1939), professor of surgery.

returned, and in time had improved so much that no one talking to me would have guessed that anything had ever been wrong with it. Only when several people are talking at once, or when there is an extraneous noise, do I fail to hear what is being said.

Professor Eiselsberg allowed me to be moved when my wounds had begun to heal on my insistence that the climate of Kenderes would do me good. I should have done better to be guided by his advice, for the doctor at Kenderes proved a little too zealous and another operation, this time in Budapest, had to be performed.

7. Appointment as Commander of the Fleet. The End

On April 2nd, 1917, the United States of America entered the war on the side of England, France and Italy. The already considerable superiority of the enemy coalition was thereby increased to such an extent that the outcome of the war could hardly be regarded as in doubt. Even the cessation of the pressure in the East, brought about by the Treaty of Brest-Litovsk, could not re-establish a balance of forces. One of the first American measures was to send Franklin D. Roosevelt, the then Deputy Secretary for Naval Affairs, to Rome to urge the Italians to more intensive naval activity. Thaon de Revel, the Italian Minister for Naval Affairs, admitted that the Austro-Hungarians were numerically inferior in ships and guns but added that they had excellent shelters among the Dalmatian islands and that they had some audacious commanders. My name was also mentioned and Roosevelt, in telling this story to J. F. Montgomery, the future American Minister in Budapest, commented, "That was my first diplomatic defeat, and I owed it to Admiral Horthy." (John Flournoy Montgomery: *Hungary the Unwilling Satellite*, New York, 1947)[1] I mention this as one of many testimonies showing that our Navy was never defeated at sea. The debacle was caused by defeats on land. The weakening of the home front through hunger and shortages, engendering an internal collapse that spread to the Navy. After my wounds had healed, I was appointed captain of a dreadnought, the *Prince Eugen*. At Pola, the battle fleet was not in good form. Since the day of the Italian declaration of war, for three years that is, the crews had been largely inactive. They had been condemned to a kind of barrack-room existence, which is fatal to the best type of men. Much the same conditions prevailed at Kiel and the same atmosphere developed, demoralizing the naval personnel there. In our case, difficulties were exacerbated by the fact that all nationalities[2] of the monarchy were represented in our ships, so that to the underground activities

---

1   p. 45-6. Republished: Morristown, NJ: Vista Books, 1993.

2   The distribution of nationalities among the crews of the navy in 1914 were as follows: Croats 31.0 percent; Hungarians 20.4; Germans/Austrians 16.3; Italians 14.1; Czechs/Slovaks/Ruthenes 11.8; Poles/Rumanians 3.0; Slovenes 2.8.

of the Socialists were added the political agitation of Yugoslav, Czech and Italian nationalists.

During my first evening on board the *Prince Eugen*, I kept hearing shouts of "Hurrah!" I sent for the first officer, who told me that the crew had refused to eat the evening meal without apparent reason and that a craze for irrational cheering had spread through the fleet.

I went on deck and my presence sufficed to re-establish order. As I was going down to the battery, I came upon a sailor in the stairway who, unaware of my approach, was shouting "Hurrah!" I thrust him back unceremoniously, and, calling the crew together, nationality by nationality in separate groups, issued a grave warning against listening to hate-mongers.

The Magyars were called to the half-deck, as they, I thought, were the smallest group. To my surprise, I found more than three hundred men assembled, and from that moment I knew that, whatever happened, I shall be master of the situation.

This particular command gave me no joy. Inactive, we were moored to a buoy, and had to watch cruisers, destroyers, torpedo-boats and U-boats sail away and return, happily engrossed in their heavy duties. Among those who were, day after day, endangering their lives, traitors were not found.

In the evenings, as I walked on deck, I could hear the gun-fire from the Isonzo front. Meanwhile, the gateway to the Adriatic, which we had forced the previous May, had been closed again. At a naval conference of the Allied Powers in Rome in February, 1918, it had been decided "to pay the greatest attention" to the Otranto blockade. The number of British destroyers was increased to forty and to them were added twelve French destroyers. Seventy-six drifters and a flotilla of American U-boat chasers kept guard over the blockade. Naval air force stations had gradually been strengthened and the speed and range of the planes were increasing.

Under these conditions, I was suddenly called, together with my two old academy-mates, Rear-Admirals Ritter von Keil[3] and Holub[4], to go to the

3   Rear Adm. Franz von Keil (1862-1945).

4   Rear Adm. Franz Holub (1865-1924).

Imperial Supreme Command, which had its headquarters at Baden. There I was taken to His Majesty Emperor Charles, who appointed me Commander-in-Chief of the Adriatic Fleet[5]. I was taken aback and begged His Majesty to change his mind. I put it to him that, in view of the number of able seniors there were above me in the Navy, many would consider themselves slighted and that my appointment would cause much controversy. It was without precedent. Moreover, a Commander of the Fleet could not be expected to perform miracles in this fourth year of hostilities.Certainly I could not hope to influence the course of the war. The Emperor refused to change his mind and adhered to his decision on the grounds that young blood was needed in the higher ranks of the Navy.

Rear-Admiral Holub was appointed Chief of the Naval Section of the Ministry of War. Rear-Admiral Keil was to remain at the disposal of the Supreme Command at Baden. I was appointed Rear-Admiral, of a fleet that was on the verge of mutiny.

Shortly after I took over, a plot was discovered on board a destroyer destined convoying transports to Albania. Two sailors, one a Czech and the other a Croat of the Orthodox faith, had tried to talk the rest of the crew into murdering the officers when out at sea and joining the enemy at Ancona. The plot, however, was reported and the two sailors were arrested and sentenced to death by the naval tribunal. I confirmed the judgment and ordered the execution to be carried out the next day in the presence of twenty men from each ship. For the time being, it sufficed to bring the men to their senses.

It was very clear to me, however, that the effect of such deterrents could not be permanent. Earlier in the year[6], a bad case of mutiny had broken out in the Bocche di Cattaro; the red flag had been hoisted in a number of ships on the calling of a general strike in Vienna, and other cities. The Third Battleship Division had had to be ordered to the Bocche and it had not been easy to suppress the mutiny[7].

5   March 1, 1918.

6   February 1, 1918.

7   This incident was the root of the fabricated Communist charge that Horthy, "The Butcher of Cattaro" has suppressed a major socialist uprising in the fleet, jailed some seven-hundred sailors and executed more than four. (Vas, Zoltán: Horthy, 3ed. Budapest: Szépirodalmi K., 1977.) Horthy was not in command at the time. The commander in charge of the Third Division at

It seemed to me that the best way to restore discipline in the Navy would be to put the ships into action, a view that I knew was shared by our colleagues of the German Navy. The men who had not yet heard a shot fired in anger must be shaken out of their lethargy.

I decided therefore to take the fleet out and once again try to break the blockade of Otranto. The whole fleet was to be engaged in this operation, for it was fairly certain that, after their experience of May 15th, 1917, the enemy would throw in battle cruisers at least in an attempt to intercept and destroy our returning warships. I hoped that our fleet would be able to surround and destroy them.

The attack was made on June 11th, 1918, after the consent of the High Command had been obtained. Two nights were needed for reaching the decisive area safely and unseen. At dusk, I ordered the first division out, and before dawn it had anchored at Slano, a well sheltered harbour north of Gravosa, not far from Ragusa. The second division under Captain Seitz[8] had only half the distance to cover to reach its anchorage off Isola Grossa, and therefore left twenty-four hours later.

For some unexplained reason, the harbour boom had not been removed and the departure of the second division was delayed, partly by this and partly because the *Tegetthoff* had engine trouble. It arrived late at the anchorage, and just before dawn the *Szent István* was holed by two torpedoes fired by an Italian torpedo-boat which had not been observed in the uncertain light. She sank in less than three hours and the Italian vessel escaped, which meant that the enemy could no longer be taken by surprise, for the Italian would have given the alarm. We would have to face enemy forces far superior in the neighbourhood of the Otranto barrage than we had contemplated. With heavy heart, I decided to call off the attack and gave the order for the ships to return to port.

In the autumn of 1918, Albania had to be evacuated and the coastal command removed from Durazzo to Alassio. The fleet provided cover for these operations, safeguarding the withdrawal of part of the Pfanzer-Baltin Army.

Pola was Vice-Admiral Seidensacher. The true story of the mutiny is described in detail by David Woodward: Mutiny at Cattaro, 1918 (*History Today* Vol. XXVI, No. 12, Dec. 1976, pp. 804-810).

8   Capt. (Later Rear Adm.) Heinrich Seitz-Treffen (1870-1940).

Italian, British and American warships made a sharp attack on the transports at Durazzo but were beaten off by the Austro-Hungarian fleet.

The situation was deteriorating. On September 29th, Bulgaria asked for an armistice, thereby making the Balkan front practically untenable. The supplies of the Army and of the hinterland were becoming increasingly deficient. Count Tisza, the former Prime Minister, was sent by the Emperor to Bosnia to survey conditions and gather information. His report left little hope of preventing a secession of the South Slavs.

On October 17th, His Majesty issued a manifesto, promising the transformation of Austria into a federal state, the union of the Polish parts of Austria with an independent Polish state, a special status for Trieste and self-determination for all nationalities within the monarchy. If this manifesto was intended to stem the dissolution of the monarchy. Events showed that this "call to the conscience of an old and venerable monarchy" merely served to strengthen the centrifugal forces. The dissolution of the Austro-Hungarian monarchy could no longer be stayed.

In the Budapest Parliament, Count Michael Károlyi[9] rose and demanded the recall of all Hungarian troops for the defence of the Hungarian homeland. On October 1st, the Southern Slav National Council met; by the formation of a South Slav (i.e. Yugo-Slav) state, embodying Dalmatia and the northern coastal area. The monarchy was to all intents and purposes cut off from the sea. As I heard it, His Majesty was persuaded by generals of Croat nationality to hand over the fleet to the Yugoslavs to prevent it from falling into the hands of the Italians. Perhaps this decision was made on the basis of promises that were never honoured.

On October 26th, 1918, Emperor Charles sent the following telegram to Emperor William II:

"Dear friend, it is my duty, however difficult, to inform you that my people are no longer either able or willing to prosecute the war. . . . Hence I inform you that I have taken the irrevocable decision to seek, within the course of the next twenty-four hours, a separate peace and and immediate armistice. . ."

9   Count Michael Károlyi (1875-1955), see later.

105

I knew nothing of this and, on October 17th, I sent in my report to the effect that I was prepared to attempt allaying the spreading mutiny on board the ships by personal appeals to the men. In fact, I went the round of the fleet and addressed the crews. At the same time, I took the precaution, lest matters should come to the worst, of seeing to it that all Imperial German secret instructions were destroyed. A large number of Germans had already left for their homeland, including the majority of the workers in the U-boat yard at Pola, after they had blown up all U-boats under construction.

On October 28th, 1918, I received the signal from His Majesty to hand over the fleet to the South Slav Council.

This order came as a crushing blow. Future prospects were grey and sorrowful, yet it was calamitous to have to relinquish our glorious undefeated fleet without a fight. No enemy lurked outside the harbour, the Adriatic was empty. Nothing was left but for me to receive the South Slav Committee. The meeting was arranged for nine o'clock in the morning of October 31st on board my flagship *Viribus Unitis*.

In the Admiral's cabin gathered Captain von Konek[10], my Chief of the Naval Staff; Captains Lauffer and Schmidt[11], the Commanders of the Second and Third Divisions; and the Commander of the Second Torpedo Flotilla. The Yugoslav National Council was represented by Dr. Tresic-Pavicic[12], Dr. Ivo Cok, Vilim Bukseg, and a few delegates[13] from the local Council, among

---

10 Capt. Emil Konek (1970-1944).

11 Rear Adm. Franz Lauffer (1969-1951); Capt. Felix Schmidt Bornemissza (1895-1969) who, in 1944, was later captured by the Gestapo and taken to Mauthausen together with Horthy's son Nicholas.

12 Ante Tresits-Pavicich (1867-1949) Croat writer, politician, diplomat.

13 Laczko Kriz, Dr. Lovro Skalier, Dr. Mirko Vratovich, and Dr. Mario Krmpotic.

whom to my surprise was our naval captain Method Koch[14].

The discussion was short and cool. I refused the request of the Yugoslavs to strike the Imperial red, white and red ensign and hoist the Yugoslav national flag. Until I left the ship at half-past four that afternoon, my pendant and the Imperial red, white and red ensign would be worn.

The following document was drawn up and signed:

"Minutes relative to the surrender of the Austro-Hungarian fleet to the accredited delegates of the National Council of Slovenes, Croats and Serbs in Zagreb, pursuant to the command of His Imperial and Royal Apostolic Majesty. The Austro-Hungarian fleet, together with all its equipment and stores, is hereby surrendered to the National Council of Slovenes, Croats and Serbs in Zagreb with the special proviso that claims to ownership shall be reserved also for the non-South Slav states, and the Nations hitherto comprising the Austro-Hungarian monarchy. Pola, October 31st, 1918."

Dr. Tresic-Pavic asked me to transmit to all naval officers serving in the fleet the request of his National Council that they should remain in active service, conditions of service to be unchanged. I did so, but, apart from the Croats and Slovenes, not one wished to stay.

I asked to whom I should deliver the command of my fleet. None of the delegates had considered that point. I therefore proposed my flag-captain, von Vukovic[15]; my proposal was accepted with some hesitation, though von Vukovic was of Croat nationality.

Half-past four struck. This was one of the saddest moments in a life hitherto singularly happy. As I appeared on the deck of the *Viribus Unitis*, the crew stood as one man to attention. I was so moved that for a few moments I stood speechless, unable to begin my short farewell address to the men. The portrait presented by His Majesty Emperor Francis Joseph to the flagship which bore his personal motto *Viribus Unitis* as her name, the silk ceremonial ensign and my own Admiral's flag I took with me.

14 Capt. Method Koch (1874-1952), later became Rear Admiral in the Yugo-slav navy.

15 Capt. Janko Vukovich of Podkapels (1871-1918).

As my flag was struck, all the flags on all the ships followed suit: a war flag that had never been struck to an enemy. The majority of the officers, including many Croats and Slovenes, left the ships after me to leave Pola next morning.

With this episode, regular service in the fleet had ceased. The chief posts remained unoccupied. The electric lights were extinguished. The harbour booms were no longer guarded. This made it possible for two Italian officers to enter Pola harbour on the following day with the help of a newly invented apparatus and to attach a mine with a time-fuse to the *Viribus Unitis*[16] below the waterline. As they were swimming away, they were observed by a petty officer who pursued them in a boat and had them brought on board. In a state of great excitement, they demanded to be taken before the Captain, to whom they related their exploit, explaining that the mine they had fixed to the hull would shortly explode. Captain von Vukovic, Commander-in-Chief of the fleet, ordered the crew to abandon ship immediately. He himself went up on the bridge and awaited the explosion. He went down with his ship. All honour to his memory.

Those of the officers and petty officers who had been unable to leave the ship in time succeeded in saving their lives by swimming to the shore, but they lost all their possessions. They came to my villa and from them I heard that the flagship of our fleet had not survived the change in her destiny. I shared out my wardrobe, uniforms and civilian clothes, among them. Then I shut up the house in which I had spent so many happy years, the house which had seen the birth of my children, and left never to return. All the household goods: silver, carpets, pictures, were left behind.

A special train conveyed the staff officers of the fleet, the majority of the officers of the flagship, and myself from Pola. It was sad to see all these young and energetic men journeying forth into a life of uncertainty.

My career also.seemed to be at an end. What could I look forward to in Hungary, a country in the throes of revolution?

16 The ship was renamed "Yugoslavia" by that time. (Holger H. Herwig: The First World War, Germany and Austria-Hungary, 1914-1918, London: Arnold, 1997, p.440.)

8. Revolution in Hungary: from Michael Károlyi to Béla Kun

The phenomena of disintegration in the Austro-Hungarian fleet described in the preceding chapter were only a part of the great upheaval. It radiated from the Empire of the Tsars since 1917, which gripped the Central Powers and led to the overthrow of the monarchy in Austria-Hungary, Germany and Turkey, and to the abdication of King Ferdinand in Bulgaria. The forces of nationalist and social revolution, nurtured by the tribulations, hunger and privations of the war years, had been working partly in the same and partly in opposed directions. Hungary, the target for underground propaganda levelled by the Allied Powers at the various nationalities, was heavily involved. I refer particularly to the report, already mentioned, drawn up by Count Tisza after his journey to Bosnia. The Rumanians and the Serbs also wished to break away and found a greater Rumania and a pan-South Slav state respectively. Meanwhile, the Czechs were planning to incorporate the Slovaks into a Czechoslovak state. The efforts of His Majesty, Emperor-and-King Charles to extricate his realm from the war as soon as possible must be considered against this background, as must also his proposed reforms in home politics.

For Hungary, His Majesty insisted that Count Tisza, the Prime Minister, should introduce a far-reaching extension of the parliamentary franchise. The difficulties which arose over that reform proved insurmountable. In consequence, in May, 1917, Tisza handed in his resignation and thereby introduced the era of short-lived Cabinets. After the fall of Tisza, first Count Moritz Esterházy[1] and then Alexander Wekerle[2], an experienced politician, became Premier. But though, in his manifesto of October 17th, 1918, His Majesty granted Hungary full political independence and empowered

---

1　Count Moritz Esterházy, 1881-1960. Later he returned to politics, elected MP in 1931 and 1939. One of the confidential advisors of Horthy during WW2.

2　Alexander Wekerle (1848-1921) was finance minister between 1889 and 1895. From 1892 to 1895 he was Hungary's first prime minister without aristocratic roots. He established modern, sound governmental fiscal policies, balanced budgets, introduction of gold standard in Hungary. Introduced liberal laws on matters of religion.

Premier Wekerle to announce that the union *de facto* of Austria and Hungary would be replaced by a union *in nomine* in which there would no longer be joint Ministries, the Wekerle Government could not withstand the pressure of events. After the resignation of Wekerle, His Majesty entrusted Count Hadik[3] with the formation of a coalition government. It never came into being, however, as power had already been seized by the 'National Council'.

This National Council was composed of Count Michael Károlyi[4], his adherents and a number of extra-parliamentary left-wing radicals. On bad advice, His Majesty decided to appoint Károlyi Prime Minister, not realizing that he had no intention of opposing the revolution but regarded himself as its protagonist.

By the time the old Emperor died, Károlyi had become the leader of the rapidly growing party of defeatists in Hungary whose aims he hoped, as Prime Minister, to realize.

Soon after his appointment to the Premiership, Count Károlyi, wishing to have a free hand, asked His Majesty to accept his resignation and that of his Cabinet. His request was granted and the revolution, led by unscrupulous left-wing radicals and socialists of every shade, hastened on its unchecked career. King Charles even went so far as to agree that the Hungarian troops should be released from their oath of loyalty. Károlyi immediately made them swear a new oath of fealty to the National Council. On the Russian model, they organized themselves into Soldiers' Councils, i.e. Soviets, furthering the forces of disorder and anarchy. One of the first victims of this rule of anarchy was Count Tisza. With complete distortion of the truth, for in July, 1914, he had emphatically pronounced against a declaration of war, he was now decried throughout the country as an instigator of the war. Loyal to his monarch, Count Tisza had remained silent; in silence he now submitted to the accusations made against him and fearlessly faced four revolutionary

3 Count János Hadik (1863-1933). Major landowner, politician, after 1919 he was active in agrarian organizations.

4 Count Mihály Károlyi, 1875-1955, was member of parliament from 1905 on behalf of the Indepencence Party. In the Summer of 1919 he emigrated to France. In July, 1944, he offered his services to the Soviet embassy in London to organize a Hungarian brigade from prisoners of war to fight the Nazis. He was refused. (Gosztonyi, P.: Air Raid, Budapest!, Budapest: Népszava, 1989. P. 37, in Hung.) Incongruously, his statue still stands in front of Hungary's Parliament building.

soldiers who, on October 31st, entered his villa. Though fully aware of his danger, he confronted his murderers unarmed. His wife and Countess Almássy[5] were spectators of the scene and later wrote down what was said, words that a dramatist could use unchanged for the overpowering climax of a tragedy. Count Tisza's death was the symbol of defeat.

Michael Károlyi, however, continued to follow the path he had chosen, or rather to slide down the slope to Bolshevist chaos, a process that was impossible to halt.

To demonstrate the independence of Hungary from Austria, Károlyi, after he had seized power, wished to conclude a separate Hungarian armistice, though, in North Italy, an armistice, leaving the Hungarian territorial position unchanged, had been negotiated for all the parts of the monarchy[6]. It was a fateful step for Károlyi to take. Accompanied by fellow members of the National Council, he travelled to Belgrade to meet General Franchet d'Esperey, the Commander-in-Chief of the Allied troops in the Balkans, who had hurried there from Constantinople. When Károlyi presented his request for an armistice, the General asked him in whose name he was speaking. Károlyi replied that there had been a total revolution in Hungary, that he was the spokesman of the National Council and Soldiers' Councils which had taken over the command of the Army. Franchet d'Esperey's contemptuous response to this has become famous: "Vous êtes, déjà tombés si bas?" (Have you sank that low already?)

The terms of the armistice opened the way for the entry of the Serbs into the Bácska district and of the Rumanians into Transylvania. The dismemberment of Hungary had begun. General Field Marshal von Mackensen[7], under whose command German, Austrian and Hungarian troops had defeated Rumania in

5   Tisza's niece, Countess Denise Almássy, 1890-1950.

6   On November 3, 1918, representatives of the High-Command of the Allied Forces in Italy and the Austro-Hungarian Army Command signed a cease-fire agreement in Padua. This defined a line of demarcation only along the south-western front, and allowed the entente forces to cross or occupy any part of the Monarchy.

7   August von Mackensen, 1849-1945.

1916 by a series of brilliant victories[8], was interned upon the orders of Károlyi, and the return of his army to Germany was prevented. Similarly, Károlyi had the Hungarian troops which had returned from the front disarmed and disbanded. Instead, however, of gaining the goodwill of the victors by these measures and by his protestation of strongly democratic and pacifist views, Károlyi merely succeeded in strengthening the arrogance of Hungary's neighbours, from which his country was before long to feel the bitter effects.

Turning to domestic policy, Károlyi, to win over the returning soldiery, had Barna Búza[9], the Minister of Agriculture, announce a radical policy of agrarian reform, which was destined never to be carried out, for the second wave of the revolution swept Károlyi himself away.

The first to march into our country were the Czechs. In December, the Hungarian Government was informed by the military representatives of the Allies in Budapest that the claims of Masaryk[10] on Pozsony, the Slovak region, Kassa and Upper Hungary had been allowed. Simultaneously, the Rumanian minority of Transylvania declared their allegiance to Rumania, and Rumanian troops occupied the country as far as Kolozsvár[11], which was formally annexed to Rumania on December 27th. On the strength of the Belgrade Convention which Károlyi had signed, the Serbs entered the Banat and the Bácska, while Croatia joined the newly created Kingdom of Serbs, Croats and Slovenes.

---

8   Horthy is too sparse with details. On August 27, 1916, Rumania attacked Austria-Hungary on the day when Rumanian Premier Bratianu (1864-1927) assured Ambassador Count Czernin of Rumania's neutrality. A Rumanian force of 440 thousand entered deep into Transylvania that night. Axis forces counter-attacked on October 4th, under the command of German general Mackensen. By December 6 Bucharest was taken. An armistice was signed at Focsani on December 9, 1917. The Peace Treaty of Bucharest was signed on May 7, 1918. Secretly encouraged by the French who promised Transylvania and Eastern Hungary to the Tisza River after the war, Rumania reentered the war on November 9, 1918. As part of the Allied Forces, she occupied, and thoroughly looted, eastern Hungary.

9   Barna Buza, politician, 1873-1944.

10 Tomás Garrigue Masaryk (1850-1937), Czech Nationalist writer, philosopher, and politician, founder and first president of Czechoslovakia.

11 Cluj, in Romanian.

The Károlyi Government[12] supinely watched this vivisection of their country. They even forbade the troops to oppose the Rumanian advance. Politically, the Government was moving further and further to the left. In January, a new Cabinet was formed, the Social Democrat members of which were in sympathy with the radical-wing, Austro-Marxist views of Otto Bauer[13] and Viktor Adler. On January 11th, 1919, King Charles IV and Queen Zita in their coronation robes as King and Queen of Hungary, Károlyi was proclaimed President of the Republic of Hungary. In the newspapers, however, the name of Béla Kun[14] was appearing with increasing frequency. Béla Kun (Kohn) was a Hungarian Jew who, while serving in an Austrian regiment, had been convicted of theft from his comrades and had deserted to the Russians, returning from Moscow to Hungary in November, 1918. He and his friends were inciting the masses and in their Vörös Ujság ('Red Paper') the armed intervention of the proletariat was threatened. On Match 19th, 1919, the French Colonel Vyx[15] demanded, in the name of the Allies, that the Hungarian troops be withdrawn to the line of the Tisza. Rightly or wrongly the Hungarians understood that the line was to constitute the definite frontier between Hungary and Rumania, the price, it was rumoured, for their renunciation of the Tripartite alliance. The Hungarian Social-Democrats fused with the Communists. Károlyi, in a proclamation dated March 21st, 1919, turned 'to the world proletariat for justice and help', resigned from office, and relinquished power 'to the proletariat of the Hungarian peoples'. The Paris Peace Conference, which opened on February 16th, 1919, and by which it was decided that almost all Hungarian territory should be occupied by the troops of Hungary's neighbours, paved the way for the Bolshevik

12 One of the ministers of this government was Oscar Jászi. Horthy did not mention his name specifically. Nevertheless, Jászi's corrosive propaganda against Hungary is pervasive even today. After the revolution Jászi immigrated to the USA and became a professor at Oberlin College. His books, particularly his *Revolution-Counterrevolution*, are still quoted quite often.

13 Otto Bauer (1881-1938), Viktor Adler (1852-1918);Austrian socialist politicians.

14 Béla Kun (1886-1939) in 1914 he worked for the Laborer's Insurance Company in Kolozsvár. Charged with misappropriating some funds, he returned the money and the case was dropped. Serving on the Russian front in the spring of 1916 he became a prisoner of war. He was Lenin's emissary to Hungary. After the 1919 revolution he spent his life in the Soviet Union. He was ordered shot by Stalin in 1939.

15 Fernand Vix (1876-1941), Mission head of the Allied Forces.

113

Revolution, in the name of which Béla Kun launched his bloodthirsty regime of terror.

"*Hungary,*" writes the English author, Owen Rutter, "*would never have gone Bolshevik if the Allies had restrained the Succession States from pre-empting their rights under the coming peace treaty. Much of the mischief was caused by the extraordinary influence secured in Paris by the Czech leaders, who not only obtained the reversion of Slovakia, but also permission to occupy it before the treaty which was to regulate the cession was either published or signed, while the*

Rumanians and Yugoslavs secured similar advantages at Hungary's expense." (Regent of Hungary, London, 1939, p. 160)

The atrocities of the Bolshevists filled the land with horror. Their agitators penetrated even into our hitherto peaceful district. The peasants were terrorized by groups of men who went from village to village, held courts martial, and with sadistic pleasure hanged all those who in the war had been awarded the gold medal for bravery.[16] "Terror is the principal weapon of our regime," boasted Tibor Szamuely[17], a close collaborator of Béla Kun, whose main function was that of an executioner. The Jews who had long been settled among us were the first to reprobate the crimes of their co-religionists, in whose hands the new regime almost exclusively[18] rested.

Béla Kun attempted to raise an army. From resentment at the advance of the Czechs, Rumanians and Serbs, or from sheer distress, a number of demobilized officers joined it, and these troops fought some successful actions against the Czechs, not so much because they were activated by loyalty to the

16 There were several peasant rebellions against the Communist regime during its 133 days. One of the ministers of the 1949 - 1956 Communist reign of terror, Zoltán Vas, who himself sat in Horthy's prisons for over 16 years, reports that anti-Communist peasant rebellions had to be suppressed in Trans-Danubia, also in twenty villages in the Kalocsa region, as well as in Budapest. These counter-revolutionary rebellions took Szamuely's "Lenin Boys" several days to suppress. (Vas, Zoltán: Horthy, 3rd ed., Budapest: Szépirodalmi, 1977.)

17 Tibor Szamuely (1890-1919), Communist newspaperman, chairman of the roving martial law enforcer "Lenin Boys" behind the front.

18 Of the 34 member Hungarian Supreme Soviet, 23 were Jewish.

Béla Kun regime but because they were fired by their ancient Hungarian patriotism.

The Rumanians made the Bolshevization of Hungary an excuse to advance yet further with their well-armed forces, plundering as they went; train-loads of loot rolled eastward. Our finest breeding cattle were driven off, among them the best stock on my estate. We were deeply moved a month after this pillage to find three of the brood mares standing outside the stable door, one with the saddle hanging under her belly, another with a harness dangling round her neck and the third without even a halter. Where they had come from, how they had escaped, they could not tell us, but they must have covered at least three hundred miles to return to their home.

Pressure was bound to set up counter-pressure. The best elements in the land could be counted on to gather around those determined men who had made up their minds to free the country from the Bolshevist reign of terror and to appeal to the Great Powers to restrain the conquering ardour of our victorious neighbours. Soon after the Commune had been proclaimed in Hungary, Count Stephen Bethlen[19] gathered around him in Vienna a number of expatriate politicians. At the same time and independently of Bethlen, for travel was virtually impossible and news spread slowly and uncertainly, Count Julius Károlyi[20] in the second half of April was forming an opposition government in Arad, then occupied by French troops, whose Commander, General de Gondrecourt, promised Károlyi help and support. The Rumanians, fearing that the excuse for their occupation of Hungary would vanish with the overthrow of the Communist regime, were perturbed by this development. They advanced on Arad and Károlyi decided to move to Szeged, whereupon the Rumanians, disregarding the passes issued by General de Gondrecourt[21], arrested him and his colleagues as they passed through Rumanian-occupied territory. They were held prisoners for several days.

---

19 Count István Bethlen (1874-1946), organized the Anti-Bolshevik Committee in Vienna, he was to became prime minister later, arrested by the KGB in 1945 and died in a Soviet prison.

20 Count Gyula Károlyi (1871-1947), landowner, politician. One of Horthy's close confidant during the whole period.

21 French general, commander of Allied forces in Hungary in 1919.

9. Counter-Revolution. I am Appointed Minister of War And Commander-in-Chief

I had witnessed the sad effects of the revolution from the seclusion of Kenderes, to which I had returned with my family in November, 1918. It was no easy task to see one's way clearly in these changing circumstances. Budapest, as we saw it on our journey from Vienna to my father's estate, was unrecognizable. The reins of order were trailing; hooligan bands roamed the streets, led by men in filthy uniforms flourishing red banners. The citizens were terrorized; shops and offices, with few exceptions, were closed. The people were in despair, fearing that a bad today heralded a worse tomorrow. We were relieved when the city lay behind us. But even Kenderes was no longer the comfortable home[1] it had been; though it had never been luxurious, there had never in the past been want. War service had denuded the estate of servants and horses; barns and store-room were empty. Since the death of my father[2], the estate had been run by a bailiff, and in recent years I had had less and less time and opportunity to supervise his management. This, I thought to myself, should be my first task and I exchanged my uniform for the garb of the estate-owner. It was consoling to find the peasants on the estate still so faithful to their master[3]. Making a common effort, we set to work to repair buildings, machines and tools, and to prepare for the spring, in so far as that was possible. I occasionally visited Budapest to see my friends and call on those whose political views I shared, knowing that they too were longing to put an end to the intolerable conditions then prevailing. But though many of

---

1   A forty room baroque mansion surrounded by a fifty acre park. Currently it houses an agricultural technology school.

2   1904.

3   Horthy enjoyed enormous popularity in Kenderes (still is). According to the commander of the detachment of gendarmes assigned to guard him (Major András Pallós; personal communication) the most difficult job at guarding was to hide the gendarmes lest Horthy might notice them as he did not believe he needs protection. He freely walked the town, talking to people like old friends. One typical anecdote: Horthy went riding and fallen off his horse. When he went to the doctor's office to have his bruises treated, he waited at the end of the queue of patients till his turn came.

their plans were bold, they were also often impracticable, and it was a long time before action could be taken.

My delight and gratification can be imagined when a messenger from Count Julius Károlyi arrived at Kenderes with the request that I should raise a new national army on behalf of the opposition government Almost simultaneously; a courier arrived from Vienna from Count Bethlen with a similar petition; for Bethlen and Károlyi have agreed that the liberation of the country from the terror of the Bolshevists and the encroachments of our neighbours would never be achieved by diplomatic means alone.

I was eager to answer the call at once, but it was not in practice a simple matter. Kenderes, where I was living with my wife and children, lay between the two danger zones of Red supremacy and Rumanian occupation. On receiving the news that Count Károlyi had succeeded in entering Szeged and had there held his first Cabinet meeting, which was attended by Count Paul Teleki[4] from Vienna, my determination was set. I travelled by car as far as Mezőtúr, and thence by rail to Szeged, arriving there on June 6th, 1919.

My short civilian interlude had come to an end. My career entered a new phase. At the request of Károlyi, I took the portfolio of war and issued a proclamation for the formation of a Hungarian national army.

To issue the proclamation, I needed the assent of the French, who were at that time occupying Szeged. Only after laborious negotiations did I succeed in obtaining it. Unlike General de Gondrecourt, Colonel Betrix, the French town commander, and General de Lobit, the Commander-in-Chief of the French troops of occupation, were not at first inclined either to permit or to support a Hungarian national movement. Not that they were in sympathy with the Bolshevists, far from it. They were on the side of the Rumanians and were therefore prepared to recognize only the Béla Kun regime.

When diplomacy is deficient and power lacking, stratagem must be resorted to. From our only aeroplane, I had leaflets strewn over the Red troops and I had the satisfaction of seeing a fully equipped squadron of hussars draw up before my house the following day. From all corners of the land, officers arrived, from among whom Colonel Prónay

4 Count Paul (Pál, in Hung.) Teleki (1979-1941) professor of geography, statesman.

118

[5] and Major Ostenburg[6] formed officers' companies. Ex-servicemen rallied from the Szeged region, and before long we had the nucleus of a well-disciplined, reliable troops. Couriers from Vienna had brought us money, appropriated from the Communist Hungarian Legation in a bold *coup de main* by a group of Hungarian officers under the blind eye of the friendly Viennese Chief of Police Schober, and with the aid of the Vienna correspondent of the Daily Telegraph, Ashmead Bartlett. Several millions had been deposited there for propaganda purposes.

Our freedom of movement was curtailed, and not only because of the hesitant attitude of the French and the pressure of the Rumanians. To launch a military attack on the Red Army, we had to secure the railway to Transdanubia, which was in Serbian hands. We knew that Belgrade was strongly anti-Bolshevist. King Peter was related to the Tsar's family through his Montenegrin wife; their son, the then Regent Alexander[7], had been trained in St. Petersburg as a cadet. In Belgrade the Imperial Russian Embassy still enjoyed all diplomatic privileges and had become a centre for White Russian refugees. With Count Teleki, I travelled to Belgrade to open negotiations with the Serbian Prime Minister Protic.[8] He gave me the desired assurances, with the proviso that the French raised no objections, and consented to accredit a representative of our government in Belgrade. This was the first diplomatic recognition of our Counter-revolutionary Government. Our mission, therefore, had some success, though we were unable to avail ourselves of his good will without the agreement of the French.

Count Bethlen was also sending us encouraging reports from Vienna concerning the British attitude; the passes with which Hungarian officers and couriers had travelled to Szeged had been personally signed by the British representative, Sir Thomas Cunningham, who, moreover, had sent Colonel

5   Cavalry Col. Baron Paul Prónay (1875-1945), commanded a detachment of officers who later committed atrocities against suspected Communists. Prónay and other rogue officers, such as Iván Héjjas, Mihály Francia-Kiss, Jenő Ranzenberger were responsible for what was later called: White Terror.

6   Lt. Colonel Gyula Ostenburg-Moravek (1884-1944?).

7   Alexander Karadjodjevich (1888-1934), later he became King of Yugoslavia.

8   Stojan Protich (1857-1923) Serbian politician.

119

Alexander Fitzgerald as a liaison officer to our Counter-revolutionary Government. We also received support from Admiral Troubridge[9], who was in Belgrade. I had known him in the past when he was naval attaché at the Court of Vienna. The attitude of the French remained exceedingly reserved. Their ostensible neutrality could only be to the advantage of the Bolshevists. The French at Szeged were bound by their instructions from Paris. Clemenceau[10] was known to be an avowed enemy of the Austro-Hungarian monarchy.

Unfortunately, the conflicting policies of the two main partners of the Allied Powers had their repercussions also within the Hungarian Cabinet. The Minister of Trade and Commerce, Varjassy[11], an adherent of the left-liberal element, used the French attitude as cover. It was never made clear what part he played in the removal from Szeged by the French of my Deputy Secretary, Staff-Captain Julius Gömbös[12]. The French insisted on the formation of a 'democratic' government, a government, that is, consisting of all parties and colours. Against my emphatic advice, Károlyi submitted to this demand. Under the leadership of the former parliamentary representative Dezsô Ábrahám-Pattantyus[13], a new government was formed on July 12th, 1919. I refused to take office as Minister of War in this Cabinet, though I remained Commander-in-Chief of our new National Army, on receiving assurances that it would on no account be used for political party battles. I had but one wish: to free Hungary from the Communist terror, for the atrocities and crimes of the Communists were daily augmenting and I felt that the cleansing should be done by ourselves and not by a foreign power.

9   Sir Ernest Charles Troubridge, British Admiral, 1862-1926.

10 Georges Clemenceau (1841-1929) French Premier between 1906 and 1909, and between 1917 and 1920. In 1920 he lost in the presidential elections and retired from politics. Hungarians considered him to be the prime mover behind the unfavorable Trianon peace treaty. Official French documents released in 1994 absolved him from some of the blame.

11 Lajos Varjasy, mayor of the city of Arad.

12 Gyula Gömbös (1886-1936) captain, Nationalist politician. One of the leaders of the Anti-Bolshevik Committee in Vienna.

13 Dezsô Ábrahám-Pattantyús (1875-1973). Politician, member of Parliament since 1909.

This was by no means in agreement with the French, and even less with the Czech, point of view. Though the troops at my disposal at Szeged were ready for action, I dared not as yet march to Budapest, in spite of the fact that Béla Kun's Government was forced to resign under the pressure of the Rumanian Army and the ultimatum of the Supreme Allied Council in Paris. Béla Kun himself fled to Vienna, taking with him the country's finances; the mass-murderer Szamuely was shot by a gendarme while attempting to cross the border[14]. A new, Social-Democrat Government under Peidl[15] was overthrown by a coup d'etat on August 6th, 1919. The new Prime Minister, Stephen Friedrich[16], formed a provisional Cabinet, declared the Republic abolished and proclaimed Archduke Joseph[17], who during the break-up of the monarchy had been made *Homo Regius*, i.e., the King's representative in Hungary, as Head of the Hungarian State.

There were thus two governments in existence, both with their hands tied, and with the Allies still insisting that a Hungarian government must consist of representatives of all parties. The Rumanians, meanwhile, had entered Budapest the day after Friedrich had assumed control, and refused to withdraw in spite of orders sent by the Supreme Council in Paris. There is no need for me to describe the activities of the Rumanians in detail. General H. H. Bandholtz[18], the American representative of the quadripartite Allied Military Mission in Budapest, has given an account of the looting and dismantling of factories in his memoirs, 'An Undiplomatic Diary' (New York, 1933[19]). If he had not appeared in person at the Royal Palace, his riding crop[20] under his arm, the Palace would have been sacked. He also saved the National Museum by sealing its doors in the name of the Allies in the nick of time, as

14   He was detained by Austrian gendarmes and may have committed suicide.

15   Gyula Peidl (1873-1943), printer, one of the leaders of the Social Demo-
     cratic Party. In emigration between 1919 and 1921. Elected to parliament in
     1922.

16   István Friedrich (1883-1951) Christian - Liberal politician, first elected MP in
     1912, served until 1939, parliamentary critic of the extreme right politicians.

17   Archduke Marshal of the Army Joseph August Habsburg (1872-1962). In
     October 16, 1944, he has warmly greeted the Nazi takeover by Szálasi.

18   (1867-1925).

19   Available on the Internet at http://www.hungary.com/corvinus/

20   It is now displayed in the National Museum in Budapest.

lorries were already waiting outside to carry off the booty. Archduke Joseph confirmed my appointment as Commander-in-Chief of the Hungarian Army and I used my position to demand that Prime Minister Ábrahám should make this command independent of the Ministry of War. At the same time, I planned the movements of the units at my disposal. I was faced with a difficult problem, as a narrow strip lying between Serbs and Rumanians had to be crossed. When I was sent a message on August 12th by the Archduke that the President of the Interallied Military Mission had demanded that the entire operation should immediately be countermanded and the troops be withdrawn to Szeged. I realized that he was not identifying himself with these orders which, were we to obey them, would retain us in the power of the French and would make all action impossible. On the excuse that there was no means of communicating with the troops already on the march other than by dropping a message from an aeroplane, I offered to undertake the task myself. I flew from Szeged in the sole company of my aide-de-camp, Major Magasházy[21]. He came by the ruse of leaving the government and turning in his resignation, and the French was left in the belief that I would return. Once in the air, however, I turned the plane towards Lake Balaton, where we landed on a stubble-field near the bathing resort of Siófok, which then was the headquarters of the Bolshevist forces. The mere sight of the eagle-feather on the cap of my aide-de-camp, indicating his status as an officer of the National Army, sufficed to make the Bolshevists take to their heels. Within two days, the last Red sympathizers had fled. The Chief of their General Staff and several other officers were glad to be able to show their true colours and put their services at our disposal. When I called at the General's headquarters, an order given by Major Magasházy brought the Red Guard to attention and impelled them to present arms to the representative of the National Army. On the third day, we were joined by Colonel Prónay's company of officers.

I aimed at creating a barrier from Lake Balaton in the south to the Danube in the north, and to move this to Budapest, but as things were then, this was a diplomatic rather than a military task. Sir George Clerk, the representative sent by the Allies to Hungary, dispatched a British officer to Siófok to inform me that he intended to visit me there. As I was eager to go to Budapest to make contact with the government of Friedrich and meet the Allied representatives and the Rumanian Commander-in-Chief, I proposed that I should call on the chargé d'affaires. Within a few days, I received an invitation from him and travelled by car unmolested straight to Budapest. I asked   Sir George Clerk

21 Major László Magasházy (1879-1959), later became general.

to have the Rumanian advance halted; I told the Rumanian General Mardarescu[22] my intentions and showed him, on the map, the line my troops would occupy.

"And what if we cross that line?" he asked.

"Then we fire," I replied.

There were a few minor skirmishes but nothing more serious In Budapest, I was staying at the town house of my brother who, before the war, had been in command of a regiment of hussars at Székesfehérvár. After a discussion with Friedrich, the Prime Minister, and supper with Sir George Clerk at the Zichy Palace, I returned home about midnight, and had the delightful surprise of finding my wife there. The happiness of our reunion was enhanced by the fact that since I had left Kenderes we had had no word of each other. I had heard that there had been some fighting in that region. My wife told me that she had fled with the children in a cart to Debrecen as the thunder of guns and the rattle of machine-guns drew near.

She had at any rate been spared the sight of the second looting of our property, this time by the Rumanians, the first having been by the Bolshevists. All the furniture was smashed, mattresses and feather beds were ripped open in the search for money and valuables. My wife had given our three children, we had lost our eldest sixteen-year-old daughter that spring, into the care of the Catholic priest and had herself travelled on to Budapest in the hope of obtaining some news of me there. After an adventurous journey, she had arrived on my first day in the capital. I was now able to offer her a new home at Siófok.

I myself, however, had frequently to go to Budapest to beg the Military Mission over and over again to persuade the Supreme Council in Paris to agree that the Rumanians should actually withdraw to the line along the Tisza river agreed to by Clemenceau. In these negotiations, I gratefully remember not only the help given me by Sir George Clerk but also the support of Admiral Troubridge, who, as Chairman of the Danube Commission, had moved from Belgrade to Budapest. The Rumanians made difficulties whenever they could in order to have as good a bargaining position as possible at the coming peace conference. Not before mid-November did they evacuate

22 Gen. G. D. Mardarescu (1866-1938).

the Hungarian areas west of the Tisza. On November 16th, I made my entry into Budapest at the head of my troops.

It was a rainy morning, but all the streets were packed with excited, jubilant people who hailed us with enthusiasm, happy in the knowledge that their sufferings under the Red terror were ended. The official welcome to the troops by the Mayor of Budapest took place outside the Hotel Gellért. My reply, which still strikes me today as the expression of the general sentiments of the time, ran as follows:

"Mr. Mayor! In the name of the Hungarian National Army, I offer you my sincere thanks for your warm words of welcome. Today, on the threshold of this city, I am not prepared to speak in conventional phrases. My sense of justice compels me to tell you plainly what is uppermost in my mind at this moment. When we were still far distant, when our hope of returning to this poor, Il-fated city, arms in hand, was the merest glimmer, we cursed and hated her, for from afar we saw only the mire into which she had sunk and not the persecution and martyrdom which our Hungarian brethren were suffering. The Hungarian nation has ever loved and admired Budapest, this city which, in recent months, has been its degradation. Here, on the banks of the Danube, I arraign her. This city has disowned her thousand years of tradition, she has dragged the Holy Crown and the national colours in the dust, she has clothed herself in red rags. The finest of the nation she threw into dungeons or drove into exile. She laid in ruin our property and wasted our wealth. Yet the nearer we approached to this city, the more rapidly did the ice in our hearts melt. We are now ready to forgive her. We shall forgive this misguided city if she will turn from her false gods to the service of the Fatherland, if with all her heart and soul and strength she will return to her love of our land in which the ashes of our ancestors rest and which our brethren till with the sweat of their brows, if she will revere once more the Holy Crown, the Double Cross, the Three Hills and the Four Rivers, in short, our Hungarian Fatherland and our Hungarian people. My soldiers, after they had gathered in the harvest, took up arms to restore order in the Fatherland. Now their hands are held out unencumbered to you in friendly greeting; but these hands remain ready to mete out punishment and to strike blows should need arise. May God grant that this need shall not arise, that the guilty, having seen the error of their ways, may strive to play their part in rebuilding a Budapest that shall embody the best of Hungarian virtues. We extend to our fellow sufferers, who have endured so much tribulation and who yet gave us their sympathy, our heartfelt salutation."

We then marched across the Elisabeth Bridge and along the Ring to the Parliament Building. On Freedom Square Prime Minister Friedrich expressed his thanks to the Army. After my reply, I dismounted and ascended the steps of the building. An altar had been set up, at which Prince-Primate Csernoch celebrated Mass and blessed the splendidly embroidered banner of the National Army presented by the eminent authoress, Cecile Tormay, as President of the League of Hungarian Women.

A year had had to pass before Hungary, though not yet at peace, for the armistice was still in force, could feel secure in having once again a national army within the walls of her capital. A year of revolution, of Red Terror and, as certain historians will have it, of the reprisals of the White Terror. I have no reason to gloss over deeds of injustice and atrocities committed when an iron broom alone could sweep the country clean[23]. A German officer who, during the Second World War, had fought against the Communist partisans in Serbia, once told me of the hatred he and his men had felt on seeing, along a country road, rows of their comrades hanging from trees, their eyes gouged out their bodies bestially mutilated: at such moments, the most ardent lovers of peace are transmuted into bitter avengers. I considered the disbanding of units which had been spontaneously formed throughout Hungary to combat the Red Terror, and the transforming of them into well-disciplined units of the new National Army, one of my main tasks. The headquarters of this army never issued a bloodthirsty order[24]. But I do not hesitate to endorse what Edgar von Schmidt-Pauli wrote about this period in the book he has written about me:

23 According to Communist sources, there were 626 documented executions: 329 of these were on formal convictions. Of the latter victims 32 were of Jewish origin. In a post-Communist review of this era by a pre-eminent historian in Hungary (Nemeskürty, István: *Glance of Farewell*, Budapest: Szabad Tér, 1995, in Hung.) the expression "White Terror isn't even applicable for what happened". There was general lawlessness, a major crime wave, the suppression of which, and the reestablishment of law and order, took considerable time.

24 This was proven by the fact that during forty years of Communism not one trace of such order was found either in the archives or by recollection of witnesses. However, according to the biography of Horthy by Thomas Sakmyster, he has 'tacitly supported the right wing officer detachments' who committed these atrocities. (Sakmyster, T.: *Hungary's Admiral on Horseback: Miklós Horthy, 1918-1944*, Columbia Univ. Press, 1993.) No proof was offered by Sakmyster.

"A troop of soldiery, hurling itself forward to create order at the risk of life, the fighting spirit and will to sacrifice having to be maintained at all costs if the leader is to achieve the great task he has set himself, cannot be reprimanded for every trifle; the officers who exceed their competence cannot always be shot or even disciplined, not, that is to say, if the danger of mutiny, or worse, is to be avoided. In times of disturbance, the military cannot be too softhearted. Hell let loose on earth cannot be subjugated by the beating of angels' wings." (Schmidt-Pauli: Nikolas von Horthy. Hamburg, 1942. p. 10.)

And the Communists in Hungary, willing disciples of the Russian Bolshevists, had indeed let hell loose[25]. It took time for the stormy waves to subside, and for law and order once more to prevail throughout our land, in keeping with our ancient traditions.

25 According to the official report by assistant state prosecutor Albert Váry, during the four and a half month long proletarian dictatorship there were 590 politically motivated executions in Hungary. This number does not include summary executions by the Hungary's Red Army on the fronts. (Váry, A: *Victims of the Red Regime in Hungary,* Budapest, 1922.) After the demise of the Communists, rogue detachments of the Nationalists army carried out pogroms against former participants of the Communist regime in several towns. The Social Democratic Party's human rights commission surveyed the country in the 1920. They found that the so called White Terror resulted about 600 - 800 missing persons. The uncertainty of this number is based on the fact, that those missing included persons killed by the invading Romanian army as well as persons emigrated from the country during the time of troubles. Hungarian historian Ignác Romsics admits that the victims of the Red Terror probably exceeds those of the White Terror "by one order of magnitude" (*HVG,* Jul. 31, 1999).While there is no doubt that several hundred Communist activists and sympathizers were unlawfully executed by the Nationalist "free detachments", American general H. H. Bandholtz who was stationed in Hungary during the months is question and British roving ambassador Repington who visited Hungary for a week in 1921 made no reference to political reprisals or oppression at all. (Repington, Lt. Col. Charles à Court: *After the War,* New York: Houghton - Miffin, 1922.) However, Communist propaganda abroad since 1920 undertaken by exiled Communists, as well as the official party propaganda of Communist Hungary between 1945 and 1989 has decreed that "5,000 were killed and 70,000 imprisoned by the "Horthy Regime" after the 1919 Communist reign. This stunt of propaganda was so successful that even the official American publication: *Hungary, a Country Study,* (Library of Congress Research Division, 1989) repeats the same numbers. The lie lives on.

126

10. Regent of Hungary

The very thing I had tried so hard to avoid had happened: I found myself caught in the maelstrom of politics. In a country which at first was only half freed from occupation, its sovereignty restricted by the Supreme Allied Council in Paris and the Interallied Military Mission in Budapest, its government without a parliamentary mandate, and which was still suffering from the ravages of revolution and counter-revolution, the Army was more than the military defender of the nation. It embodied the power of the state. Even at Siófok, it had been my task to bring about the re-establishment of the civil authority in the liberated areas by appointing men suited to civic office. I had called men who were specialists in constitutional law to my headquarters to prepare the transition to a new order, for it was not enough merely to repeal the measures introduced by the Communists. To further these preparations, I had aimed at turning the Allied Mission in Budapest from an antagonist into an ally, insofar as that was possible. My new, unsolicited and, in many ways, unwelcome role in politics, therefore, sprang largely from the fact that excellent working relations existed between myself and the Mission. I was on particularly good terms with Sir George Clerk, the British representative, who found it preferable to come to me with the political instructions he received.

As yet, the Friedrich Government had not been recognized by the Allies. Archduke Joseph's abdication from his position as Regent at the end of August had been due to direct Allied intervention; upon the insistence of Benes[1]. He had stated in a letter to the Paris Peace Conference that a Habsburg as Regent was bound ultimately to lead to a restoration of the monarchy, which would be regarded by the Czechoslovak Republic as a direct menace to its existence. Corresponding instructions had been drawn up which had to be implemented by the Military Mission.

---

1   Eduard Benes (1884-1948) Czech politician and statesman. Together with Thomas G. Masaryk (1850-1937), he established the Czechoslovak Foreign Committee on November 14, 1915, and began a vigorous propaganda activity to influence the politicians and public opinion in France toward in favor of destroying the Monarchy. Interestingly, earlier in his doctoral dissertation (Univ. Dijon, 1908) he wrote that "one can not think seriously of an independent Czech state since the third of the population (the Sudeten Germans) would determinedly resist it and would not consider it legal." (Miksche, F.O.: *Danubian Federation*, London: Kenion Press, 1952.) Q. E. D.

The slogan of the First World War had been to make the world safe for democracy. From this sprang the insistence that Hungary should institute a government supported by representatives of all parties, oblivious of the fact that Social Democrats and Communists had merged so that, after the downfall of the Kun regime, the people held all representatives of the Workers' Party responsible for the terror. At the request of Sir George Clerk, on November 5th, 1919, I declared myself willing to enter into discussions with the representatives of the Left. I gave the men who assembled at the Zichy Palace the assurance that I was not planning a military dictatorship and that I would not countenance any anti-Semitic persecution.

A second similar discussion, again at the insistence of Sir George Clerk, was held on November 22nd, after the Army's entry into Budapest. The British representative issued an ultimatum in the most courteous form: Hungary was to form a parliamentary government, the elections for which could not be held under the Premiership of Stephen Friedrich (who was regarded in Allied circles as representative of 'feudalistic traditions'). If this wish of the Supreme Council was not met, he, Sir George, would have to leave Budapest and with his departure all foreign supplies of coal and raw materials would cease. After Count Albert Apponyi[2] had given a faultless translation of this speech, Sir George Clerk left the room to allow free discussion. Differences of opinion were violent. Even those who had not forgiven Friedrich for having originally collaborated with Count Michael Károlyi could hardly agree to the Premier yielding to foreign pressure. But what would a gesture of pride have availed us? That I, a military man, should advocate moderation and prudence made its impression. My proposal that Stephen Friedrich should resign from his present office and take over the Ministry of War was readily accepted. Huszár[3], the Minister of Education, was elected Premier in his place. Furthermore, a representative of the Social Democrats was co-opted into the Cabinet in which Count Somssich[4] remained Foreign Minister. On the following day, this Cabinet was recognized by Sir George Clerk on behalf of the Allied Powers. Hungary at last had an accredited government which could begin to combat misery and want and to hold elections at home, and could

2 Count Albert Apponyi (1846-1933) politician, was the Chairman of the Hungarian Peace Delegation in Paris. Later, he represented Hungary in the League of Nations. His speaking knowledge of foreign languages was truly amazing.

3 Károly Huszár (1882-1941).

4 Count Joseph Somssich (1864-1941), diplomat.

128

wage the battle of the Peace Treaty abroad. Now that a Second World War lies behind us, even those who have not experienced the economic collapse and the years of famine following upon the First World War should be able to form some idea of the conditions prevailing at that time. Even the refugee problem is familiar to us today[5]. I need therefore only say that of the forty thousand people who had fled to Budapest from territories occupied by the Czechs, Rumanians and Serbs, thousands had to camp in railway trucks during the bitter cold of winter. But even worse than the physical destitution was the demoralization of the people. Four years of war, ending in the debacle of defeat, followed by a Communist regime, had undermined the will to work and the sense of community. Party struggle was waged with hitherto unknown ferocity. Right-wing radical circles laid all blame on Jews and Communists. Admittedly this coincided in many cases. Meanwhile, the Communists refused to accept defeat. In December, 1919, a few Communists, who had been sent by the Viennese central organization to blow up the Royal Palace in which were the headquarters of the International Military Mission, the Ministries and my headquarters in the Hotel Gellért, were arrested. There were frequent outbreaks against Communists and Jews, which was regrettable[6].

I should never have dreamed that I might one day take up a role resembling that of an itinerant preacher. But as the people knew that I was not speaking to them as a party politician, that I had no dictatorial ambitions and that I was averse to radicalism in any form, left or right, they listened to me, and from all quarters I received invitations and requests to speak. One of my tours took me to Kaposvár; there a delegation insisted on my meeting Nagyatádi-Szabó[7], the leader of the recently founded Smallholders' Party, a man who had been described to me as a rabid revolutionary. Contrary to my expectation, I found him to be not only an intelligent man but a true representative of the patriotic, upright and conservative Hungarian peasantry.

5   These memoirs were completed in 1952.

6   Zoltán Vas, one of the Muscowite ministers during the Communist Reign of Terror in the 1950's described the intensive covert subversive activities of the suppressed Communists in this period. He also laments the lack of popular support of the Communists, and blames this on their caste-like behavior. Vas, Z.:*Horthy*. Op. Cit.)

7   István Nagyatádi-Szabó (1863-1924).

129

In the field of domestic politics, it was soon clear that the former Premier could not reconcile himself to his diminished status. He was making things difficult for his successor, who was demanding the conclusion of the Peace Treaty so that Hungary might know where she stood and could devote herself wholeheartedly to reconstruction. Friedrich was of the opinion that the states upon our borders would rapidly crumble into their component parts and that we had therefore only to wait. The terms of the peace treaty that had been handed to our delegation, headed by Count Apponyi, in Paris on January 15th, 1920, seemed utterly fantastic to me. I was convinced that the day would come when our neighbours would regret having made such inordinate claims. Yet I did not suffer from the illusion that the near future would bring a collapse of Czechoslovakia or of the federation of Serbs, Croats and Slovenes[8].

The first task of the Parliament which met on February 16th, 1920, was to clarify certain points of constitutional law. The crowned King had not relinquished his rights. He could be deposed only by a revolutionary measure. He had been so deposed, but to every constitutionally minded Hungarian, the proclamation of the Hungarian Republic was invalid, and the Friedrich Government had always considered it so. On the other hand, Archduke Joseph, not for personal reasons but because he was a member of the House of Habsburg, had been forced to resign by the Allies.

The National Assembly, being the guardian of national sovereignty, solved the problem by taking a decision that accorded with the facts: that the Union with Austria and the 1867 Compromise should be dissolved and that the King's rule should be considered to have been dormant since November, 1918. Until such time as it could once more be openly exercised, a Regent of the State was to be appointed.

On grounds of foreign policy, neither Archduke Joseph nor Archduke Albrecht was eligible for the Regency; Archduke Joseph withdrew on February 2nd, 1920; the Allies had issued yet another formal declaration that the return of the Habsburgs would not be tolerated. It was now that my name began to receive public mention as a candidate for the Regency. Neither the Prime Minister nor any of the leading politicians discussed this idea with me. I hardly need to say that it was not a subject I was likely to broach myself. I was hoping that Count Apponyi, one of the worthiest and most brilliant figures in our public life, would be chosen. Instead, I was unexpectedly elected Regent

8   Indeed, it took some 75 years to happen.

130

of the Realm on March 1st, 1920, by 131 votes out of 141. A delegation, headed by Bishop Proházka[9], called on me to tell me the result of the voting, and to ask me to go at once to the Parliament Building, there to take the oath.

I thanked my visitors for the great confidence that had been shown in me, but declared that I was not in a position to accept the high office to which I had been elected. Out of deference, however, to the National Assembly, I was prepared to acquaint its members with my decision in person. But before I appeared in front of the Assembly, I was implored to change my mind. The members of the government, the party leaders and other prominent political figures gathered in a large room of the Parliament Building. They used every argument to persuade me to reconsider my decision. When I persisted in my refusal, the government was censured for not having ascertained my willingness before electing me. The assembly then broke up into small groups for discussion. As an officer, I had sworn an oath of loyalty to His Majesty. As Regent I would have to swear a new oath to the constitution and to the nation. Was there not a danger of a conflict of loyalties? Such considerations I could not easily voice and I was well aware that, at this grave stage in the peace negotiations, appeals were bound to be made to my patriotism. I put forward the objection that the rights of the future head of the state, as they had been given in the press, were inadequate. He would not even have the right to prorogue Parliament, and certainly not to dissolve it.

Another short discussion followed my statement. Then the President of the National Assembly, Stephen Rakovszky[10], sat down at a desk, took up a pen and said: "Please dictate your demands. Parliament will agree to them."

I composed another subterfuge. A matter as serious as this could not be decided without mature reflection nor without the advice of experienced legal minds, I declared. Thereupon, the proposal was made that the Regent should be given the general prerogatives of the King, with the exception of the right to name titles of nobility and of the patronage of the Church. What objection could be made to that? I was cornered. I accepted the election and we entered the vaulted hall where the representatives had been waiting over an hour. In the presence of these elected representatives of the Hungarian people, who

9 Catholic Bishop Ottokár Proházka (1858-1927).

10 István Rakovszky (1858-1931), Legitimist Party politician. Legitimists supported the reinstatement of the Habsburg dynasty.

had chosen me in the name of the sovereignty of the people whom they represented, I swore the oath as Regent.

The Regency was no new phenomenon in Hungarian constitutional life. As far back as 1446, John Hunyadi[11] had been Regent until 1452 while the son of Albert I, Ladislaus Posthumus was a minor. To the office was attached the title 'Fôméltóságú', meaning literally 'High Dignitary', corresponding to the English 'Serene Highness', the French 'Altesse Serenissime' and the German 'Durchlaucht'. The Regent is head of the state and exercises the prerogatives pertaining to the sovereign. In accordance with the law of 1920, he is Supreme Commander and therefore Commander-in-Chief of the *Honvédség*, the National Defence Force. Declaration of war and conclusion of peace need the sanction of Parliament. The Regent represents the country in international relations; he sends out ambassadors and receives the ambassadors of foreign states. He exercises his executive powers through the Ministry appointed by him. He has the right to convene Parliament, to prorogue it, (the prescribed maximum period fixed originally at thirty days was abolished in 1933), and to dissolve it. He does not possess the right of veto, but has the right of initiative and the right to submit an accepted Bill twice for renewed consideration; if it is again accepted, he has to promulgate it. The person of the Regent is inviolable. The original clause stipulating that he could be called to account should he infringe the constitution was rescinded in 1937.

The law of 1920, which was passed in the expectation of an early return of the King, contained no enactment for a successor to the Regent. Not before 1937 was this law modified by an enactment which empowered the Regent to hand a sealed letter to the two Keepers of the Crown containing the names of three candidates in the event of his death or abdication. Parliament was not, however, to be bound by his nominations.

That the Regent should not have the right to create nobility was a welcome restriction to me. Less welcome was the restriction concerning the patronage of the Church, a privilege which had belonged to the Crown for a thousand

11 John (János) Hunyadi (1385-1456), Hungarian national hero, leader of the resistance against the Turks. He won numerous victories against them. His fight was a Christian crusade aided by Pope Calixtus III. With John Capistran, who was sainted later, Hunyadi in 1456 defeated the Turks at Belgrade (then a Hungarian border fort) and thus staved off the Turkish conquest of Hungary by 70 years. His younger son became king as Matthias Corvinus. (Quoted from Columbia Encyclopedia, 1950).

years and which now was ceded to the Pope. A solution which gave the Regent this right should have been found, for the appointment of bishops includes not only their membership of the Upper House but also considerable transfers of property. A ruling could have been made that a Protestant Regent must consult the Catholic Prince-Primate.

The government instructed me to take up residence in the Royal Palace. This was a necessary step, as the Regent's Cabinet and Military Chancelleries would require space for the incessant political, civil and military traffic that passed through them, and the Guards attached to the Regent would have the duty of mounting guard over the Palace and its many treasures. Naturally, I did not install myself in His Majesty's former apartments. For my residence, chancelleries and audience chambers, I occupied what were known as the visitors' quarters in the new wing of the Palace.

The choice of a Regent had been made, as I pointed out, during the 1919 course of the peace negotiations. There was nothing particularly attractive about assuming office in these circumstances. Not even the boldest ambition would aim at presiding over the partition of a thousand-year-old state. And yet, the country was in dire need of a head whose patriotism stood above reproach. I considered my task that of a pilot who had to steer his ship in the teeth of a violent typhoon.

In consideration of the Paris negotiations, on March 15th I entrusted Alexander Simonyi-Semadam[12] with the formation of a small and powerful Cabinet.

"The peoples of Austria-Hungary, whose place among the nations we wish to see safeguarded and assured, should be accorded the freest opportunity of autonomous development." This was the text of the tenth of the Fourteen Points announced by President Wilson in his speech to the American Congress on January 8th, 1918. On the basis of which the Austro-Hungarian Government had offered, on October 7th, 1918, in a Note to the American President, to conclude an armistice and to enter into negotiations for peace. It is a well known fact that President Wilson confirmed and restated the validity of his Fourteen Points as a basis for negotiation (compare his Note of May, 1919, to the German Peace Treaty Delegation), and that the Peace Treaties disgracefully ignored them. A line of demarcation was drawn separating the

12 Alexander Simonyi-Semadam (1864-1946).

peoples of Austro-Hungary into Austrians and Hungarians on the one side, and Czechs, Slovaks, Poles, Italians, Rumanians, Serbs, Croats and Slovenes on the other. A line separating the conquered from the conquerors, the disinherited from the favoured sharers in the fruits of victory. The Hungarians suffered the greatest humiliation. It is not my task, in this book, to write the history of the Treaty of Trianon. Skilled pens have done so already. There were no negotiations. Our government had formulated objections, point by point, to the draft submitted to it on January 13th, 1920, indicating the political and economic injustices and follies it embodied, but in vain. Count Apponyi had made his masterly speeches before the Supreme Allied Council in Paris in French, English and Italian, defending the Hungarian point of view, to no avail. The fate of Hungary had long been decided, on the basis of falsified statistics and maps drawn up by Benes and of political accusations of 'Hungarian war guilt', accusations that have long since been discredited by historians and students of international law. Though Lloyd George[13] and President Wilson had repeatedly asserted, even while the war was still being fought, that the Austro-Hungarian monarchy should remain in being, the secret treaties, understandings concluded with Italians, Rumanians and Czechs had already dismembered Hungary. Even the Treaty of Versailles foresaw plebiscites in some of the areas that were to be taken from Germany. The Hungarian proposal that the peoples who had until then belonged to the realm of St. Stephen's Crown should be given the right of self-determination was not accepted in a single case. (The plebiscite that was held in 1921 in western Hungary, in Burgenland, was the outcome of a later decision.) Only the Croats and the Rumanians had left Hungary of their own free will; the Slovaks, Ruthenians, Transylvanian Saxons and the Germans of the Banat and the Bácska would have pronounced by an overwhelming majority in favour of remaining within Hungary, as later the German-speaking population of Sopron (Ödenburg) did.

On May 5th, the Hungarian Government received the final text of the Treaty. It contained the identical terms of the draft of January 15th, except for two minor alterations in the question of optants, and with regard to the Danube catchment area, points that I had discussed in detail with Sir George Clerk. On June 4th, 1920, the Treaty was signed at the Trianon. Hungary, which, before the war (excluding the crown lands of Croatia-Slavonia), had extended over an area of 203,000 square miles and had counted 18.3 million inhabitants, lost by this Treaty more than two thirds of its land, and 58

13 David Lloyd-George (1863-1945), British Prime Minister.

percent of its inhabitants, 10.6 millions. Not only were the nationalities, which over the centuries had entered and become part of the Hungarian kingdom, united to their countries of origin, but, as Lord Newton[14] wrote, "what is worse, more than 3,000,000 Magyars were handed over to nations of different race and lower cultural level with an utter disregard of the sacred principle of self-determination". The Czechs were allotted Slovakia, together with large tracts of upper and western Hungary, including the ancient coronation city of Pozsony (Bratislava). The Danube became the southern frontier of Czechoslovakia and the walled city of Komárom (Komorno), with its purely Hungarian population, was therefore partitioned into a Czech and a Hungarian town[15]. In total, an area of 40,000 square miles and a population of 3,517,000 was incorporated in Czechoslovakia.

Rumania, whose army had been utterly routed during the First World War, received the major portion of the booty. The whole of Transylvania with its neighbouring territories and part of the Banat with Temesvár (Timisoara), altogether 64,000 square miles and a population of 1,509,000. Serbia was given the rest of the Banat together with the rich granary of Hungary, the Bácska, which included the important towns of Szabadka (Subotica), Ujvidék (Novi Sad), and Versecz: 12,500 square miles with 1,509,000 inhabitants. This area was combined with Croatia-Slavonia, Dalmatia, Slovenia, Bosnia, Herzegovina, Montenegro and the one-time Kingdom of Serbia to form a large South Slav state: Yugoslavia. Austria, which had made no territorial claims, was given Western Hungary, called the Burgenland, with an area of 2,000 square miles. To Poland, 390 square miles were allotted. By D'Annunzio's[16] *coup de main*, Italy helped herself to the old Hungarian harbour city of Fiume (Rijeka).

"The central Danube basin," so it was once put by our foremost geographer, the future Prime Minister Count Paul Teleki, in a lecture given at the University of Berlin, "is a geographical unit in that it has in the main a clearly demarcated boundary and a clearly marked centre, while the component parts within its confines complement each other in their harmonious economic

14 Lord Newton, Thomas Wodehouse Legh (1857-1942), British politician.

15 This is like placing an international boundary between Minneapolis and St. Paul.

16 Gabriele D'Annunzio, Prince of Montenevoso (1863-1938), Italian writer, poet, and politician. With his armed band he prevented the opening of Fiume as a free port in 1920, and succeeded in annexing it to Italy.

functions[17]." But in Paris no one bothered about the ethnic problems that are raised when a state loses fifty-nine per cent of its population and sixty-eight per cent of its area. No one considered the structural modifications of agrarian and sylvan economy. Hungary lost eighty-eight per cent of her forests and more than ninety-seven per cent of her fir-woods. These are timbered areas which were of importance not only as sources of building material and fuel but were also vital for the regulation of the irrigation of the Hungarian plains, for which reason Hungary had always exercised great vigilance over her deforestation. The neighbouring states to whom these forest areas were given did not adhere to the conditions laid down by the Peace Treaty. They recklessly cut down timber, so that in spring Hungary endured floods and in summer droughts. Hungary also lost eighty-three per cent of her iron ore and nearly fifty percent of her ironworks.

Hungary, like Germany and Austria, had to pay reparations. Like Germany and Austria, she had to sign a declaration of *war guilt*, even though the Hungarian Prime Minister Count Tisza had vehemently opposed the ultimatum to Serbia. A military restriction was laid on Hungary by which she could maintain a standing army of only 35,000 men[18]; her thorough demilitarization was carried out by a deservedly unpopular Allied Control Commission.

Admittedly, Millerand[19], the successor as Chairman of the Peace Conference to Clemenceau, signed a letter of May 6th, 1920, known as the *Lettre d'Envoi*, in which hopes of a revision of the Treaty were held out. But beyond this gesture, nothing was ever done; the letter lay as dead as Article XIX of the League of Nations Covenant.

From June 4th, 1920, all flags in Hungary were flown at half-mast. Eighteen years were to pass before once more they could be fully hoisted.

17 For example, in the past Slovak mountaineers earned their whole year's wheat supply by assisting in the harvest on the Hungarian plains (Ed.).

18 In contrast, the combined military strength of the successor states exceeded 600 thousand men, a twenty-fold superiority.

19 Alexandre Millerand (1859-1943).He was France's minister of war during WW1. Later, he was the president of France from 1920 to 1920.

Count Apponyi had resigned when he saw the futility of his efforts in Paris. The Simonyi-Semadam Government also resigned after it had submitted the Treaty to Parliament on July 26th.

On July 19th, 1920, I appointed as Prime Minister Count Paul Teleki, who had been Foreign Minister at Szeged. The fragment of Hungary that remained endeavoured as best it could to resuscitate its mangled body. Slowly, slowly, apathy and work-shyness receded. The harvest had to be brought in, the fields tilled afresh. Hungary was still an agricultural country and the rhythm of peasant life penetrated the whole nation as it derived strength from its soil. Plans were put in hand for financial reconstruction, for new industries to combat the problem of unemployment. It looked as if we were following the right course.

And then came the surprising news of the return of His Majesty King Charles.

11. Attempts at the Restoration of King Charles in 1921

Easter Sunday, which fell on March 27th, was a day of brilliant sunshine. The trees were in blossom and amid burgeoning nature the whole of Hungary. Town and country was celebrating the resurrection of Our Lord, grateful that the signs of better times were visibly multiplying. On the insistence of my wife, I had at last decided to take a day's holiday with my family, the first for a considerable time. In the morning, we had given the children their Easter eggs and small gifts had been handed out to the members of the household. We were sitting down to our midday meal when my aide-de-camp, Major Magasházy, entered with the message that Count Sigray[1] had arrived and was waiting for me with an important communication. I rose from the table and went to receive Count Sigray, the Government Commissioner for western Hungary.

We had hardly finished exchanging greetings before he disclosed to me that His Majesty King Charles was in Budapest and was awaiting me in the Prime Minister's residence. It was plain to me that His Majesty's return must have the worst consequences for Hungary, and I asked Sigray if he were in any way responsible for it. He denied this.

The King, he told me, had arrived late the previous night and totally unexpectedly at the palace of Bishop Count Mikes[2] at Szombathely after having called on Count Thomas Erdôdy[3] in Vienna on Good Friday in the company of his brother-in-law, Prince Sixtus of Parma[4]. Count Erdôdy had put his car at the King's disposal for the journey to the frontier. He had not known that His Majesty had left Switzerland, nor had he heard the slightest

1   Count Antal Sigray (1879-1947). He died under torture in a Communist prison.

2   Bishop Count János Mikes (1876-1945).

3   Count Tamás Erdôdy (1886-1931), landowner, legitimist (pro-Habsburg) politician.

4   Prince Sixtus of Bourbon-Parma (1886-1934), brother of Queen Zita.

139

rumour of his intention to do so. He had been overcome by surprise when an unnamed visitor had been announced who, on removing his motoring goggles, had disclosed himself as the King. Not even Count Joseph Hunyady[5], the Steward of the Household and confidant of His Majesty, had been consulted or even informed. At Szombathely, Sigray went on, His Majesty had received the homage of the Bishop and of the leading churchmen who had assembled there for the Easter festival. He had, moreover, conferred with the Prime Minister, Count Paul Teleki, who chanced to be in the neighbourhood as he was staying as a guest at the castle of Count Sigray. Sigray himself had been present at that interview, and Teleki told me later, when he had accepted full responsibility for the course that events took and had handed in his resignation, that he had done what he could to dissuade the King from taking the step he was contemplating, expressing his opinion by the simple statement, "Too soon." But his words had no effect. He had been instructed to go to Budapest in advance and inform me that the King was arriving. As he had travelled by a different route and his car had broken down on the way, he had not reached Budapest before the King.

I told Count Sigray to go at once, with my aide-de-camp, to the Cabinet Chamber and ask His Majesty to come to the Palace. I did not have to reflect very long what I should say to him. This self-sought situation had only one solution: the King must return to Switzerland without delay.   Six months before, on the occasion of the unveiling of a commemorative plaque at Sopron, I had made my attitude towards the Crown and the monarch very clear.

"We all," I had said, "would like to see the Crown of St. Stephen resplendent in its former glory. But before this restoration can be achieved, immense tasks of external and internal   consolidation must be performed. Anyone who at the present juncture brings the question of the restoration of the monarchy to the fore will be doing a disservice to the peace of the country, will be hampering reconstruction and will be putting obstacles in the way of our resumption of relations with foreign powers."

This meant, and in those days I frequently stressed this point when discussing affairs with foreign diplomats, that I and the members of the government considered a return of His Majesty to the Hungarian throne the concern of Hungary alone. In any case, the Habsburg question had not been touched

5 Count Joseph Hunyadi (1873-1942).

upon in the Treaty of Trianon. To have a certain right and to possess the means of exercising that right are, however, two different matters. In Paris, there was still an Ambassadorial Conference of the victorious powers claiming full competence in dealing with all questions concerning Hungary, Austria and Germany, the question of German reparations, for instance, and having the coercive means at its disposal with which to enforce its decisions. Its representatives in Budapest were the British and French High Commissioners and the Italian chargé d'affaires as well as a Military Mission. On February 2nd, 1920, this Ambassadorial Conference had issued a formal veto against a restoration of the Habsburgs in Hungary, as such a restoration would in its view "rock peace to its foundations" and it could therefore "neither be recognized nor tolerated" by the Allies.

This attitude, far from being modified at a later date, was instead confirmed. On January 3rd, 1921, Count Sforza, the Italian Foreign Minister, in the course of a long discussion with our diplomatic representative in Rome, Count Nemes[6], on the question of Italy's attitude should a Habsburg return to the throne, had exclaimed, "L'Empereur Charles, jamais!" For Italy feared that the return of a Habsburg would menace her possession of Trieste and the South Tirol and she had therefore undertaken, in the Treaty of Rapallo (November 3rd, 1920) with the Kingdom of Serbs, Croats and Slovenes, to do everything within her power "to oppose the return of the House of Habsburg to the Hungarian throne". In the course of a visit made by Edvard Benes, the Prime Minister of Czechoslovakia, to Rome in the early days of February, 1921, this had been further emphasized when he declared that a return of the Habsburgs would be considered a *casus belli*. Finally, the Ambassadorial Conference itself had reiterated its declaration of February 2nd, 1920, on February 16th of the following year, a few weeks before the return of His Majesty to Hungary.

I had all this clearly in mind as I awaited the King. Had these facts not been put before him by his advisers? Our discussion soon gave me the answer to that question.

I did not have to wait long before His Majesty was announced. He had walked the short distance to the Palace. We had not met since the fateful day, two and a half years previously, when I had had the painful duty of informing His Majesty at Schönbrunn of the surrender of the fleet in accordance with my

6   Count Albert Nemes (1866-1940).

instructions and of asking him to accept my resignation as Commander-in-Chief. On that occasion, as on all others, His Majesty had displayed his kindly disposition towards me; now as I prepared to conduct him from the aides-de-camp room to my study, he flung his arms round me.

King Charles, wearing a Hungarian officer's uniform, expressed the hope that he could once more take his place as head of the state. He gave me a graphic account of his life in exile.

I assured His Majesty that, were I able to recall him, our crowned King, whose legitimate claims I recognized and was prepared to defend, it would be the happiest termination of my present office.

In Hungary, I told him, his estates had been left unsequestrated and the income deriving from them was at his disposal. Although my petition to the heads of the victorious states asking that the Succession States should contribute to the grant to His Majesty in proportion to their size and population had borne no fruit. I begged him to believe that I still felt myself bound by the oath I had sworn to the Emperor and that I had no wish whatsoever to retain my office as Regent. "But Your Majesty should consider," I continued, "that the very moment I hand the reins of state over to the King, the armies of the neighbouring states will cross our frontiers. We have nothing with which to oppose them in the field. Your Majesty will then be forced to return to Switzerland, Hungary will be occupied by foreign troops and the evil resulting from renewed occupation will be incalculable."

The effects of the Rumanian occupation were still fresh in my memory. I wished to convince His Majesty that the menace of a renewed occupation was not imaginary. At the time I am writing this[7], the world has an aspect very different from the one it wore in 1921, and the peoples of Austria-Hungary would no doubt prefer the two-headed eagle to the hammer and sickle. But at that Easter time of 1921, the tide of nationalism was running high in our neighbour states. Their governments would not have permitted a restoration of the Habsburg symbols. These were considerations that the Great Powers had to bear in mind. For it must be remembered, that they themselves caused the partition of the Austro-Hungarian empire on purpose, to the subsequent misfortune of Europe and the world.

7   1952.

142

As I was explaining the attitude of the Great Powers, the King interrupted me to tell me that he had come with the knowledge and approval of the Entente. To my courteous request for more details, he mentioned the name of Briand[8], who at that time was the French Prime Minister and Minister for Foreign Affairs.

"Has Your Majesty had a personal conversation with Briand?"

"No. I have been in touch with him only through intermediaries."

The intermediary turned out to be the brother of the Empress Zita, Prince Sixtus of Parma, who had close contact with French royalist circles, but these did not represent the French Government.

I could not doubt for one moment that His Majesty was speaking in good faith when he declared that his return had the approval of France at any rate. I do not consider that it was out of the question that a certain encouragement may have been given him from Paris. I had a vivid memory of some half-promises and vague assurances concerning the relaxation of the terms of the Treaty of Trianon which were made when it was likely that Hungary would have to lend support to Poland when that country had been invaded during the summer of the previous year by the Bolshevist Russian armies. After the Battle of the Vistula, in which Hungarian munitions played an important part, the threat to Poland receded, and Paris promptly lost interest in Hungary. That Colonel Strutt, the British confidant of King Charles and his companion at Eckartsau, had sent him a telegram in code in mid-March to advise him against an attempt at regaining his throne, was a detail that I was to hear a few days later from Masirevic[9], our diplomatic representative in Vienna.

To clarify the situation, I proposed to His Majesty that Briand should be asked, through the French High Commissioner in Budapest, whether he would be prepared to guarantee Hungary French support in the name of the Allies should the Succession States turn on what was left of our country. His

8   Aristide Briand (1862-1932) in 1909 became prime minister of France, a position he occupied ten times. In 1917 he attempted to make peace with Germany, and, after opposition by Clemanceau, he resigned. Later he became a leading advocate of international peace.

9   Szilárd Masirevich (1879-1944), Hungarian diplomat.

Majesty agreed to this proposal and also acceded to my request that he should return to the Bishop's palace at Szombathely to await the reply from Paris.

"Should Briand accept the responsibility, I shall gladly restore your hereditary rights to Your Majesty," I declared. "Should the answer be unfavourable, I shall have to beg Your Majesty to leave the country immediately before your presence here becomes generally known."

Attempts have since been made to place this two-hour discussion between His Majesty and myself in a false light. As I held then and still hold today, it was a discussion on the outcome of which depended the very existence of our Fatherland. I must add that, before he departed, His Majesty expressed his profound thanks to me and invested me with the Grand Cross of the Military Order of Maria Theresa, creating me Duke of Otranto and Szeged. And I must add further that I have neither worn the Grand Cross nor used the ducal title. This gesture of His Majesty, however, shows better than words that he, at any rate, was convinced of my good faith and that my attitude sprang from my sense of responsibility and duty.

I begged King Charles to retain his confidence in me and, with regard to Hungary, to undertake nothing without consulting me lest he should create new difficulties for our country or endanger his own return to the throne at some future time.

While King Charles, accompanied by Major Magasházy, returned by car to Szombathely, the Ministers assembled, and to them I gave a succinct report of the situation. All who had seen the King were sworn to secrecy.

Meanwhile, I had called M. Maurice Fouchet, the French diplomatic representative, to the Palace to transmit through him His Majesty's request to Briand. The answer was a definite denial. Briand emphatically declared that at no time had he expressed his agreement to the return of King Charles to the throne of Hungary. Whether or not this was true, and later I learned that Prince Sixtus had conferred with several French Generals, including Lyautey,[10] and that M. Berthélot[11], the General Secretary of the Quai d'Orsay, perturbed about a possible union of Germany and Austria, had played an

10 Marshal Louis Hubert Gonzalve Lyautey (1854-1934).

11 Philippe Berthelot (1866-1945), French diplomat.

144

ambiguous part. Briand's answer, publicized later in the press, did at any rate represent the official attitude of the French Government. I informed His Majesty over the Hughes apparatus, a special telephone on which conversations cannot be overheard, and asked him to leave the country as quickly as possible. Koloman Kánya[12], the Foreign Minister's deputy, informed him in person of the content of the Paris answer and of the various protests of the Great Powers and of our neighbours. As King Charles had caught a cold which necessitated his staying in bed for a few days, his departure was delayed until April 5th. We had obtained from Berne permission for his re-entry into Switzerland, and Vienna had given us the assurance that his journey through Austria would be smooth and in keeping with his dignity. However, though His Majesty was escorted by Allied officers and Austrian security personnel, there were regrettable Socialist-Communist demonstrations at Bruck-an-der-Mur.

That my attitude was justified was soon made clear. My first callers on Easter Monday were the High Commissioners of England and France, who came to stress the "categorical opposition" of their governments to any attempt at a restoration. Shortly afterwards, the Italian chargé d'affaires arrived to declare that the prevention of a Habsburg restoration was "a cardinal point of Italy's foreign policy". On the Tuesday morning, I received the Yugoslav representative, who declared that the return of His Majesty would be regarded as a definite *casus belli*. The protest of the Rumanian representative was not quite so violent, as Queen Marie[13] of Rumania had not been altogether a stranger to King Charles's plan. Benes, as he told our diplomat Count László Szapáry[14], put the attempted restoration to good use, for shortly afterwards, on April 23rd, 1921, he was able to conclude a military anti-Hungarian alliance between Czechoslovakia and Rumania.

Benes's representative in Budapest made almost daily appearances at the Ministry for Foreign Affairs to threaten reprisals should the King prolong his stay on Hungarian territory. The final demarche was made collectively by the Great Powers. Their representatives, upon instructions of the Allied

---

12 Kálmán Kánya (1869-1945) former Austro-Hungarian diplomat, later foreign minister.

13 Queen Marie, Princess of Saxon-Koburg-Gotha (1875-1938), wife of King Ferdinand.

14 Count László Szapáry (1864-1939).

Ambassadorial Conference in Paris, delivered a joint Note which referred to the declaration of February 2nd, 1920, and called attention to the "serious consequences" that would follow should the Hungarian Government not take active measures to prevent any attempts at restoration.

I hope that this statement will counterbalance the many incorrect versions of the incidents of those memorable Easter days.

The royal question was once more to cause excitement in Hungary and abroad in that same year, 1921. Again I received no warning, though I was in regular communication with His Majesty. From his despatches, I augured that his information, particularly on personal matters, was inadequate and that he was therefore insufficiently aware of the true state of affairs. I decided at last to send a confidential envoy known personally to His Majesty to Hertenstein Castle, to which King Charles had moved in April. Unfortunately, my choice turned out to be an unsuitable one. From what motives I do not know, Boroviczény[15], married to one of the ladies-in-waiting of the Queen, gave the King bad advice instead of giving him a true picture of actual conditions. I could not have foreseen this, for in his former capacity of secretary to my friend General Sarkotic[16], the government's representative in Bosnia and Herzegovina, I had come to look upon him as an intelligent young man. Later, he had become the assistant of the liaison officer of the Austro-Hungarian Ministry for Foreign Affairs at Court. Boroviczény, Count Sigray, who in March had informed me of the King's arrival, and Colonel Baron Lehár[17], a brother of the world-famous composer, played an important part, as far as my knowledge goes, in the inauspicious second attempt at restoration[18]. The leaders of the Legitimists, to use a term that makes a fundamentally false distinction between their attitude and mine. Whereas we differed only in the method by which the restoration was to be brought about,

15 Baron Aladár Boroviczény (1890-1963) legitimist politician.

16 Gen. István Sarkotich (1888-1939) former provincial commissioner of Bosnia-Herzegovina.

17 Lt. Gen. Baron Antal Lehár (1876-1962). In retirement, he traveled all over Hungary recruiting Legitimist army officers to the cause.

18 Throughout the summer of 1921 the Legitimists, have made extensive preparations for the return of the king the planned *coup d'etat* was almost an open secret. (Dombrády L. & Sándor Toth: The royal Hungarian army: 1919-45; Budapest: Zrinyi, 1987, in Hung.)

in my opinion men such as Count Julius Andrássy[19], the last of the Austro-Hungarian Foreign Ministers, Gustav Gratz[20], the former Hungarian Foreign Minister, and others were not involved in the preparations. It had been made very clear on August 22nd, at a conference held under my chairmanship, that a return of the King could occur only in conditions of domestic and foreign security. The crowned King is the King of all Hungarians; he could only be recalled by representatives of all Hungarians and not by a minority group. Above all, the person of the King could not be made the centre of a hazardous *coup de main*.

The first information reached me on October 21st: telephone and telegraph communications with Sopron were found to be cut. The reason for this appeared later when I heard that His Majesty and the Queen had arrived by plane the day before at Count Cziráky's[21] estate at Dénesfa. This place had been chosen apparently because there was, on account of coming elections, a relatively strong party of state police there who were under the orders of Colonel Lehár and of Major Ostenburg at Sopron itself. Ostenburg obeyed the orders of Lehár, his men swore an oath of loyalty to the King, and joined His Majesty on the train which was to take him to Budapest. Their idea that the King's presence in the country could be kept secret until he entered the capital was a mistaken one. The Kingdom of Serbs, Croats and Slovenes had been informed of his movements by an agent stationed at Hertenstein. The other powers heard of his arrival at Dénesfa from their military missions then located at Sopron. Simultaneously with the first news of the King's presence came the first protests of the Great Powers and the Little Entente. Belgrade had immediately called up three classes of reservists, and Rumania was preparing partial mobilization. Benes sent telegrams to the various Czech legations declaring that the presence of the ex-Emperor on Hungarian soil was a *casus belli*. Great Britain informed our Prime Minister, Count Bethlen, through the High Commissioner, Thomas Hohler[22], that the British Government set its face against any attempt at a *coup d'etat* and would therefore do nothing to exert a restraining influence on the Little Entente. If the Hungarian Government was not in a position to keep order within its own frontiers, energetic measures would have to be taken from abroad. The joint

19 Count Gyula Andrássy Jr. (1860-1929), son of the former prime minister.

20 Gusztáv Gratz (1875-1946), economist, politician.

21 Count József Cziráky (1883-1960).

22 Sir Thomas Beaumont Hohler (1871-1946), British diplomat.

Note presented by the British, French and Italian diplomats reiterated the text of the Note of April 3rd and also demanded an unambiguous statement from the Hungarian Government that it should "without delay take the necessary measures once more to remove the King from Hungarian territory".

To emphasize the seriousness of the Note, the three Ministers called not only on the Prime Minister, but also on me. Hardly had they left before the Ministers of the Little Entente called to inform me that their troops would cross the frontier should His Majesty resume power.

Count Bethlen, who, by a remarkable coincidence, had chanced to make an important speech at Pécs on the very day His Majesty had, unknown to the Prime Minister, set foot on Hungarian soil. In this he emphasized the legitimistic views of the government and, while condemned every attempt at dethronement, yet insisted on the Hungarian right to determine the day on which the King should return to his country. Bethlen considered the situation to be as serious as I did. It was not because Stephen Rakovszky, the President of the Hungarian Parliament, the man appointed by the King as chief of the Counter-Government, threatened him, during a telephone conversation, with the gallows if the King were not well received in Budapest. "This is terrible!" Bethlen exclaimed as he replaced the receiver. It was because he realized that the advisers of the King were aiming at an armed conflict to achieve their ends. Indeed that is what developed.

Caught in this tragic situation, I tried to persuade the King to relinquish his scheme. I wrote him the following letter, to which I appended the Anglo-Franco-Italian Note.

"*Budapest, October 22nd, 1921.*

Your Majesty!

In the utmost distress of mind, but moved by the oppressive weight of my anxiety, I must beg Your Majesty to abandon your advance to the capital at the head of armed forces. The situation has in no way altered since the spring when Your Majesty left the country.

The conditions which then prompted me and Your Majesty's trusted advisers, who, like myself, have the welfare of Hungary at heart, to beg you to leave the country, still prevail in a yet more aggravated form. The position at the moment is even more precarious. In the spring, the arrival of Your Majesty took not only this country but also the foreign powers by surprise. Since then, it is seen that preparations have been made against such a possibility. This is evident from the fact that the protests we received in the spring came only after a lapse of days, whereas on this occasion they have been handed to the government immediately and are couched in far stronger terms, the Little Entente openly threatening invasion. From our point of view, power relations have deteriorated. We are threatened on three sides by an enemy we cannot possibly subdue. But even should we attempt the impossible, even should our nations succeed in holding up the enemy, it would be at the cost of the devastation of large tracts of our land. The distress arising from such devastation would be exacerbated by the hardships of winter, and together these would be the sure ally of Bolshevism. An earnest survey of the situation assures us that such a menace would arise even sooner, for it is certain that an enemy advance would foster bitterness and anarchy.

The temper of the majority of the people is such that Your Majesty would not have the country behind him, and the prevention of civil war would not be within my power.

Should Your Majesty proceed towards Budapest with armed forces, our fate is certain and within a few days our country would be under foreign domination.

Should Your Majesty wish to verify the facts with the representatives of the Allies, with me or with my Ministers, no difficulties will be put in your way. Your Majesty can, with a small retinue, cover the short distance that separates us in complete safety. I have always tried to carry out my duty with selflessness. Today it is my duty to inform you that, should Your Majesty enter Budapest with armed forces, Hungary will cease to exist forever.

> *With profound respect,*

> *Horthy."*

I gave this letter to Bishop Vass[23], the Minister of Social Welfare, who was in His Majesty's favour on account of his behaviour at Easter. I sent with him Lieutenant-Colonel Ottrubay[24], a former attaché at the Austro-Hungarian Military Chancellery. These two men met the royal train at Komárom, but

---

23 József Vass (1877-1930), Catholic priest, politician.

were not admitted to His Majesty's presence. For reasons for which he alone was responsible, the King's Prime Minister designate, Rakovszky, omitted to deliver my letter to His Majesty. A few days later, Rakovszky drew it unopened from his pocket in the presence of Count Julius Andrássy, Count Francis Esterházy[25] and Baroness Fiath, the President of the Hungarian Red Cross. Whether His Majesty would have acted differently had he received my letter, none can say.

That night, I issued the necessary military orders to prevent by force of arms that which force of arms sought to achieve. I need not go into my feelings. Naturally I wondered whether I ought to withdraw from the whole ghastly conflict by resigning office. But, faced by the destruction of the Fatherland, it would have been cowardice on my part to evade the issue. Bethlen, the Prime Minister, emphatically supported my views.

Meanwhile, the train bearing the royal pair, which had been repeatedly delayed by torn-up tracks, had reached Biatorbágy, not far from Budapest. His Majesty's demand that the government should submit unconditionally to him and the determination of the government to resist a *coup d'etat* were in conflict. To my profound grief, the order to open fire had to be given. The miserable gendarmes, simple Magyar peasants' sons, who had been trained all their lives to passive obedience, were the victims.[26]

I sent Colonel Shvoy[27] to parley and to request the King to come to Budapest for negotiations under guarantee of personal safety. Upon the insistence of his advisers, the King rejected this proposal. My second proposal, that government representatives and responsible advisers of the King should meet the following morning and that until then there should be a truce, was accepted.

These discussions between the Minister Kánya and General E. Sárkány[28] on the one side and Colonel Lehár and Gratz on the other proved fruitless.

24 Staff-Colonel Károly Ottrubay.

25 Count Ferenc Esterházy (1896-1939), composer, politician.

26 Some of the forces resisting the King's return were the armed students of the Technical University, who were raised by Gyula Gömbös.

27 Kálmán Shvoy (1881-1971), his memoirs was one of the first published on this era.

150

Though the government troops had meanwhile been reinforced, and though the officers who had sworn allegiance to the King at Györ and Komárom begged to be released from their oath on the grounds that they had been deceived, the King was urged to press on, regardless of consequences.

Yet His Majesty came to a different decision. He turned westward. The sight of the killed and injured must have brought him to his senses and made him realize that a civil war was starting. His Majesty was averse to the thought of bloodshed, for he was a man of a kindly and noble disposition. He and the Queen accepted the invitation of Count Esterházy to stay at his castle at Tata.

My Ministers and I were left with the task of ensuring the personal safety of His Majesty. We thought the safest place for his temporary sojourn would be the Benedictine Abbey of Tihany, situated on a peninsula of Lake Balaton. A number of political negotiations were held there and it was proposed to the King, in order to circumvent the probability that he would be deposed by foreign powers. Indeed, Hungary was forced to pass a law enacting the dethronement of the King, that he should abdicate in favour of his nine-year-old son, Archduke Otto. Though this proposal was advocated in person by the Prince Primate Cardinal Csernoch, it was rejected.

In the end, the decision of the Allies was received: His Majesty was to leave Hungary in the British monitor *Glow-worm*. So it came to pass. In the Black Sea, the King and his retinue were transferred to another ship which took them to Funchal in Madeira. There His Majesty, surrounded by his mourning family, died on April 1st, 1922.

My attitude during the two attempts at restoration has been the subject of frequent attack. Critics have invariably ignored the fact that on neither occasion did I act as a tyrannical rebel. Both attempts were doomed to failure on account of our unfavourable international position, which was determined by the anti-Habsburg policy of both the Great Powers and the Little Entente. In the face of that policy, Hungary was powerless. Our dependence on the Allies was most plainly manifested in the demand made to us that an Act of Dethronement be passed, an extreme example of foreign interference in the domestic concerns of a state.

28 Maj. Gen. Jenô Sárkány (1869- ?), commander of the Budapest military district.

151

To depict the variance of feelings and opinions concerning the monarchic question, I shall narrate an incident which had never hitherto been mentioned, all participants in it having been sworn to secrecy.

In August, 1922, a group of politicians and other leading figures of Hungary, among them a Catholic bishop, came to see me at the castle in the Crown domain of Gödöllô, where we always spent the months of August and September. They had an important proposal to lay before me, they declared, a question about which they had hesitated to approach me. I soon gathered from their spokesman, Count Gedeon Ráday[29], a former Chief Comissioner of a county and Minister for Home Affairs, and, now, Deputy, that after mature consideration they had come to offer me the Crown in the name of all classes of the people. To ensure the country's peace, they said, the struggle for the chief office of state must cease. Some wanted an independent Hungary with the legitimate King, others were for electing Archduke Joseph or Archduke Albert. Elements of the Left were aiming at a republic. "But the majority of the Magyars," Count Ráday declared, "want to live, as Hungarians have done for a thousand years, under the Crown of St. Stephen and a Hungarian dynasty. Accept the crown, your Serene Highness, and at one blow the whole dangerous situation will be resolved."

I was, naturally, extremely astonished and I replied that I fully recognized the difficulties that they had expounded. I thanked them for the confidence in me that their proposal showed, but said that I did not feel able to accede to their request. For what was it that gave me courage and strength to work at the reconstruction of our shattered Fatherland? Only the feeling that, in my status as Regent of the Realm, I could count on the confidence shown a trustworthy and honourable man. Were I to stretch my hand towards the crown, I should cease to be selfless and worthy of respect, and my own brothers would turn against me. Never, not even should a plebiscite be unanimous, would I accept the royal crown.

29 Count Gedeon Ráday (1872-1937).

12. The Road to Freedom

The attitude of the Successor States during the two attempts made by King Charles to restore the monarchy had drastically shown Hungary how powerful were the walls of the prison that Trianon had built round the country and how eagerly her neighbours constituted themselves her gaolers. Benes had gone so far as to demand monetary reparations for the expense Czechoslovakia had incurred by her partial mobilization in October, 1921. Plainly, my task, therefore, was the consolidation of domestic politics and the economy of the country in order to clear the road to freedom. A kindly Providence had given me a colleague in whom I could put full trust, confident that he would put into practice the projects I had in mind: Count Stephen Bethlen, a man of outstanding mental power and of fine character. Upon the retirement of Count Teleki in April, 1921, I had appointed him Prime Minister. The Bethlens belonged to the old Protestant nobility of Transylvania. Throughout the centuries, many men of eminence in Hungary have borne that name. Bethlen possessed that happy combination of a conservative background with liberal ideas of reform. His knowledge of the world and his innate political talent made him able to seize and even create those opportunities in foreign politics which aided Hungary in gradually regaining her independence.

The first opportunity arose when the west-Hungarian or Burgenland question became acute. In the Treaty of Trianon, western Hungary had been promised to Austria with the primary intention, it was thought, of providing Austria and Hungary with a bone of contention. The secondary intention was, allegedly, of laying the foundation for a future Slav corridor between Czechoslovakia and the Kingdom of Serbs, Croats and Slovenes. The date by which this region, the population of which was largely German-speaking, was to be ceded had not been stated in the Treaty. Just like in eastern Upper Silesia, where German partisans were active, partisan bands had sprung up in Hungary under the leadership of Prónay, Colonel of Hussars. They were fired with the determination to prevent their fatherland from being whittled away any further. The Czechs were insisting on partition and offered Austria military support. This offer, made at the meeting of Hallstadt on August 10th, 1921, by the Czechoslovak President to the Austrian President, was confirmed on December 16th by the Treaty of Lana. I have already mentioned the fact that the presence of Hungarian units influenced the choice of landing ground for the aeroplane in which King Charles had arrived to make his second attempt to regain the Hungarian crown. When the Prague Government sent us a Note demanding that we hand Burgenland over to Austria. This Note roused great indignation. A conflict seemed inevitable. In the then existing circumstances, it could only have had results disastrous to us. But Count Bethlen succeeded in securing the support of Marchese della Torretta[1], the Italian Foreign Minister, who, for obvious reasons, was opposed to the formation of a Slav corridor. With his consent, an international conference was held in Venice at which, on October 11th, the region in question was divided into two zones, A and B. A plebiscite arranged for Zone A, to which belonged the town of Sopron and fourteen villages. The result of the plebiscite was that seventy-five per cent of the population elected to remain Hungarian. A yet more important outcome was that Hungary had shown her willingness to revise her frontiers by peaceful means. Thus the Venice Conference made the first breach in the wall that had been thrown up round the country.

At my request, Count Bethlen had again assumed office, after having handed in the resignation of his whole Cabinet when Parliament, on December 3rd, 1921, had been forced by Allied pressure to pass the Bill enacting the dethronement of the Habsburgs and the annulment of the Pragmatic Sanction[2]. His action had been a demonstration against this blatant interference in the internal affairs of our country, an interference that could scarcely redound to the credit of the democratic powers, and which impelled the Hungarian Parliament to emphasize in the preamble to the Bill that the law would not have been passed had it not been for external pressure.

Problems of domestic politics were coming more and more to the fore. While still a Member of Parliament, Bethlen had succeeded, on July 13th, 1920, in bringing about the amalgamation of the chief political parliamentary parties: the United Christian National Party, and the Smallholders' and Agricultural Labourers' Party. The name of the new party thus formed was changed repeatedly and even its component elements varied greatly at times, but, until 1944, it remained the political backbone of the country. At the elections of May, 1922, which were held after an electoral reform, there were already in Parliament not only representatives of the bourgeois opposition but also of the Socialists. Upon Bethlen's decision, taken in order to obliterate all internal

1   Count Pietro Paolo Tomasi della Torretta (1873-1962).

2   A law, dating back to 1713, assuring Habsburg hereditary succession in Hungary in the female and not only the male line.

dissensions remaining from the days of revolution and counter-revolution, to allow trade union organization, to assure the liberty of the press, of speech and of political meetings, and to effect a general political amnesty. This conciliatory course, which had my fullest approval, was followed also in the treatment of those who, in October, 1921, had supported the attempted restoration. Even those who had taken part in it under arms, were not indicted.

As neither the Upper House, the House of Magnates, which in its old form corresponded more or less to the British House of Lords, nor the unicameral system was to be recommended for our domestic conditions, the Bethlen Government, in 1926, introduced legislation for the creation of a reformed Upper House. The old Upper House had consisted of the senior members of the higher nobility who paid a certain minimum land tax. The new Upper House consisted of four groups of mainly elected members: members of the House of Habsburg Lorraine, provided they were able to speak the Hungarian language, and the representatives of the higher nobility, these families electing their own representatives, numbering half as many as the representatives from towns and counties; the holders of certain functions and offices, among whom were the Catholic bishops, the representatives of the three Protestant Church communities, the Chief Rabbi, and the President of the High Court; representatives of the rural and municipal councils, universities, academies of art and music, and the professional representatives of trade, industry, agriculture and the free professions; and finally forty-four members whom the Regent had the right to nominate.

The Upper House with 244 members and the Lower House with 245 members, who were elected anew every five years by universal suffrage, open ballot in rural districts and secret ballot in towns, together formed the Parliament[3] which exercised the legislative powers. Even declarations of war and the conclusion of peace needed the assent of Parliament in conformity with the provisions of the Constitution. As Regent of the Realm, I had, as I have already explained, the right to object to any Bill twice, but a third passing of a Bill with a simple majority set aside my objection. The Prime Minister and the Ministers were appointed by me, but were responsible to Parliament.

---

3 In contrast, no more than a third of the British Parliament is composed of elected members.

155

We Hungarians are as proud of the antiquity of our unwritten Constitution as the British are of theirs. This Constitution goes back to the Golden Bull of 1222. In no Continental country has constitutional and parliamentary thought played so prominent a part as in Hungary and Poland. Also, nothing is further from the truth than to call Hungary a 'feudal' country. The part played by the nobility, which was represented in the Upper House *ipso jure* by thirty-eight members chosen from the highest families, was comparatively less important than it is in England, where the King has the right to create new titles of nobility, a right, which as I have already stated, I did not possess. Nor is it true that the major part of the land was in the hands of a small class of great landowners. Seventy-five per cent of all arable land, according to the 1935 statistics, belonged to small farmers and owners of medium-sized properties of 2000 *holds*' or under. (One Hungarian cadastral *hold* equals 1.43 acres.)

This does not mean to say that either I or the governments in power during my Regency regarded the agrarian problem as solved. Legislation for the breaking up of certain large estates had to be drawn up with great circumspection. The great density of the population and the relation between the number of people and the area of arable land rendered it impossible to solve the agrarian problem by simply dividing up the land, especially as for a country such as Hungary, which bases its economy on the export of agricultural produce, efficiently run large estates are a necessity. It must not be forgotten that our country has been greatly impoverished by the loss of its most valuable mines and forests, by the cost of warfare and the subsequent payment of reparations. Expropriation without compensation similar to that which was carried out in certain neighbouring states, mainly at the expense of national minorities, would have run counter to our traditions and to our sense of justice. Our task was, therefore, to bring a policy which was necessary from social considerations into agreement with economic and financial conditions and with the dictates of justice. And that is what was actually done. After the Land Reform Act of 1920 had shared out more than a million holds, the Settlement Act of 1936, to anticipate later developments here, and the Land Reform Acts of 1940 and 1941 divided up another nine hundred and thirty thousand holds. This apportioning of landed property to the extent of two million holds amounted to two-thirds of the large estates of more than a thousand holds in private possession. In total, there were created, by 1940, 412,537 new small holdings, 251 model farms and 55 estates of medium size.

As by origin I belong to the land, I was familiar with the disastrous results of the liberal right of inheritance. An equal division of a farmer's estate among his heirs leads not only to the creation of increasingly smaller holdings but also to the limitation of families. I had long borne in mind a statement made by Lord Castlereagh at the Congress of Vienna; in agreeing to peace terms for France. These, in his opinion were too favourable. He remarked that the laws of inheritance under the Napoleonic Civil Code would render France harmless from the military point of view within a hundred years.

It was not, however, feasible to introduce sufficiently radical changes in long-existing rights of inheritance. As a solution, I created a military Order of Merit: all Magyars and those also of other origin who had displayed great military bravery and were of unblemished character became entitled to a 'hero's estate' of approximately sixteen holds, including house, stable, two horses and a cow. Members of the Order who already possessed land could have it registered in total or in part as a hero's estate. The right to inherit such an estate belonged solely to the eldest son. For the first three years of ownership, an estate of this kind was altogether tax free; after that period of time, amortization had to be paid, payment to be spread over thirty years or more. In total, some three thousand such estates were set up, the necessary means of tilling the soil being provided by the state, by voluntary endowments and from the fees collected from those who were given commemorative war medals.

I need hardly say that the raising and training of an army was a subject close to my heart. We studied the work of German General von Seeckt[4] to advantage, for the peace treaty had limited us to keeping a regular army of not more than 30,000 men.

My efforts to improve the standard of education were implemented most ably by the Minister of Education, Count Klebelsberg[5], whose fame had spread far beyond our national frontiers. In 1920, 12 percent of the population over the age of six was illiterate; by 1930, this figure had been reduced to 9.6 percent. By 1941, in the same area (excluding, that is, the territory that had meanwhile returned to us), it shrank to 4 percent. During the twenty years from 1918 to 1938, the number of primary schools was increased from 5,584 to 6,899, the

4 Gen. Hans von Seeckt (1866-1936), organizer of the German armed forces.

5 Count Kuno Klebelsberg (1875-1932). He has established Hungarian cultural centers abroad, and strengthened provincial universities.

number of primary school teachers from 14,400 to 20,149. In country districts, special aptitude tests were given so that the gifted children of poor parents could be selected to receive the assistance necessary to enable them to go to secondary school and university. Attending our universities were 10,000 students in 1918; in 1938, the number of students had risen to 18,000. In 1937, the government established the Nicholas Horthy Scholarships in my honour, which annually enabled several hundred students of limited means to go to the university. The former universities of Kolozsvár and Pozsony were transferred to Szeged and Pécs respectively.

Like many other countries, we also had suffered from inflation in the years after the First World War. The partition of Hungary, the payment of reparations, and the burdens of the aftermath of war made it impossible for us to stabilize our currency unaided, for our most valuable assets were in pawn to our creditors. Before we could obtain a loan from abroad, it was necessary to reclaim these securities. To this end, we joined the League of Nations on September 18th, 1922, thereby laying ourselves under the supervision of the League of Nations Finance Commission. The loan of two hundred and fifty million[6] gold crowns we used to such good purpose that the Finance Commissioner, Mr. Jeremiah Smith[7], on the eve of his departure to Geneva on June 30th, 1926, after a two-year sojourn with us, was able to declare that we had carried out our obligations and had balanced our budget. The following year, our currency was changed from crowns to pengôs, the Hungarian word for 'clinking', a pleasing appellation reminiscent of the ringing sound of coins[8].

Mr. Smith, an American and a reliable friend of our country, placed the whole amount of his fees at the disposal of Hungarian students in America. He also gave us much good advice later. Only once did he put me in an awkward position. When the time came for him to leave us, we wished to show our appreciation in the shape of the present that would give him the most

6   The estimated value of goods looted by Rumanian occupation forces from Hungary was over four times this amount.

7   Jeremiah Smith, Jr. (1870-1935), American financier, law counsellor of the J.P. Morgan banking house's Boston office.

8   János Bud (1880-195?), Bethlen's financial advisor, economics professor, was Minister of Finance between 1924 - 1928. The Hungarian National Bank was created under his direction. He deserves credit for Hungary's economic reconstruction.

pleasure. On my enquiry, he asked for both more and less than I had expected: he said he would like to see St. Stephen's Crown. To us the holy relic is not a showpiece, as the Papal Secretary of State Pacelli[9] felt when he was Papal Legate at the Eucharistic Congress of 1938 and, kneeling, prayed before it. The three keys of the chest in which it was kept were in the trusteeship of the Prime Minister and the two Keepers of the Crown. The key to the vault in which the chest was housed was in the keeping of the Commander of the Crown Guards, with the rank of colonel. The Crown Guards, all ex-NCO's, wore special uniforms: a white cape and helmets with heron feathers.

To comply with Mr. Smith's request, I had to lay the proposal before the Privy Council. A solemn procession to the vault was ordered and there the chest was opened. Mr. Smith stood speechless before this product of a Byzantine goldsmith's art, its cross bent as it was when it was dug out of the ground after being buried during disturbances in the Middle Ages. Mr. Smith called on me again and declared: "I understand now. That wasn't the crown. Saint Stephen's Crown is Hungary herself."

I have already stated that my aim was to achieve the revision of the Treaty of Trianon by peaceful means. The friendship with Germany, of which Field Marshal von Hindenburg, whom I held in great respect, had been elected President, was to us, during the early years after the First World War, largely a matter of sentiment. Our slogan "Nem, nem soha!" ("No, no never!") with which our nation had answered Trianon found a strong echo in Germany. But at the time, the German Reich had its own cares and, in the councils of the nations, its voice went unheeded time and time again. Wise statesmanship, with an eye to the future, would have paid attention to the German proposals concerning a revision of the peace treaty. A small country, encircled by a hostile outer world, Hungary had to seek friendship with all the leading powers.

Our friendship with Poland after the Polish-Soviet war, discussed earlier, meantime had little effect. The close relations between Warsaw and Paris relieved the Polish-Czech tension which had been potentially useful to us. The first treaty of alliance concluded by Hungary was with Turkey in 1923; our relations with that country had rapidly developed since the creation of a Turkish national state under Kemal Atatürk. As the Little Entente had expressly joined forces by treaty against Hungary (and only secondarily

9   Cardinal Eugenio Pacelli (1876-1958), became Pope Pius XII in 1939.

159

against Bulgaria), my main concern was with our southern neighbours. In the past, I had learned to know and appreciate the Croats as fine sailors and naval officers. I was fluent in their language. The military gallantry displayed by the Serbs during the war led me to think that a frank talk as soldier to soldier might well meet with understanding. Therefore, I availed myself of the opportunity offered by the celebration of the quatrocentenary of the Battle of Mohács. This battle that had brought, for a century and a half, the Hungarians and Serbs the same fate, a yoke that the Serbs had had to bear yet longer after the Battle of Kosovo. I referred, in my speech made on August 26th, 1926, to "the ancient friendship and the ancient confidence" that had existed between us. Turning to the Turkish Ambassador, who was present at the celebrations, I said that we Magyars had taken the lessons of history to heart and that "the enemy of the past has become the friend of the present". And I continued: "Unfortunately, we are at this moment separated by a deep-rooted difference from those with whom we, in the past, jointly defended the southern frontiers of these lands. I hope and believe that it may not be long before we shall be reconciled."

Yet it was not Belgrade that drew practical conclusions from these words but Italy, to which a Hungarian-Yugoslav reconciliation would have been most unwelcome while the cries of "Mare nostro" and "Nase more" resounded from the opposite shores of the Adriatic. A few months after my speech, Bethlen was invited to Rome to sign a pact of friendship with Italy. This implied the resumption of historic relations and assured us of the support of one of the victorious nations in combating the stubborn anti-revision policy of the Little Entente and of France. The effects of this pact, signed by Mussolini and Bethlen on April 5th, 1927, were soon made manifest: five months later the Control Commission was terminated.

During the following years, Count Bethlen went on missions to Berlin, Paris, London and Madrid. Economic factors, proceeding from the great south-east European agrarian crisis after 1928, led to the strengthening of our relations, especially economic, with Germany. She was the only country offering us a large market for our wheat and corn.

Another sign that the road to freedom was opening lay in the fact that Budapest was once again being visited by eminent foreign statesmen. Thus, in 1929, we welcomed Grandi[10], the Italian Foreign Minister, and Zaleski[11], the

10 Count Dino Grandi (1895-1988).

Polish Foreign Minister, and in 1931 Ismet Inönü[12], the Turkish Premier and his Foreign Minister, Rüstü Aras[13]. Our thoughts go out in gratitude to Lord Rothermere[14], who was the first person in England to insist in his newspapers in 1927 on justice for Hungary, after Lord Newton had exposed in the House of Lords the follies and injustices perpetrated by the Treaty of Trianon upon its ratification. Lord Newton, Sir Robert Gowert and Lord George Sydenham[15] were presented with honorary doctorates in the University of Budapest in recognition of their services to the cause of justice.

The intervention of Lord Rothermere and his clarion call for justice came at a moment of national despair and found a spontaneous response throughout the land. Immediately after it had been proclaimed that an address of gratitude was to be sent to Lord Rothermere, crowds of people assembled to append their signatures to the document. Within a few days, 1,200,000 people had signed it and the sheets of names were bound in twenty-six volumes. If a date had not been fixed for dispatch, it is certain that the whole nation would have signed their names.

The inclusion in these memoirs of an account of the festivities held in connection with the tenth anniversary of my election as Regent of the Realm is made in order that I may express my gratitude to my friend and collaborator, Count Bethlen, (who was taken as prisoner to Russia in 1945), and to the Hungarian Parliament, which unanimously passed a Bill bestowing a number of honours on me. It is impossible for me to forget the vast procession that marched to the Palace in February, 1930, and the chanting of

11 August Zaleski (1883-1972), historian and diplomat.

12 Pasha Ismet Inönü (1884-1973), Turkish statesman.

13 Rüstü Aras (1881- ?), Turkish physician, politician.

14 Lord Rothemere, Harold Sidney Harmsworth (1868-1940), publisher of the Daily Mail, politician. His article, "Hungary's Place under the Sun" was published on June 21, 1926. One of the consequences of this article was the establishment of the Revisionist League (July 27, 1926) in Budapest, under the chairmanship of Ferenc Herczeg, a renowned writer and a confidant of Horthy. It was a covert international public relations organization that paralleled Hungary's diplomatic service. Under the direction of Dr. Endre Fall, vice president of the national insurance organization OTI, the League maintained 'secretariates' in several major western countries. During the war, the League's major effort was to seek an armistice with the Allied powers.

15 Lord George Sydenham (1848-1933), British politician.

our national anthem by a choir of eighteen hundred singers. My greatest pleasure on that day was the fact that the pacification of the country, that had gone forward in the ten years of my Regency, enabled me to pardon a number of political prisoners.

After Count Bethlen had borne the burden of the Premiership for ten years, he asked me to relieve him of his office. It was with the utmost regret that I parted with him. His retirement gave rise, at the time, to considerable speculation. People refused to recognize the plain fact that his resignation was a normal step to take. In view of the difficulties arising from the agrarian crisis and the widespread world depression, Bethlen himself thought the time ripe for a change in the political leadership of the country.

On August 24th, 1931, I appointed Count Julius Károlyi, the former chief of the Szeged opposition government, Prime Minister. Károlyi concentrated his attention on financial and economic measures. In his economy drive, he even went so far as to take their official cars away from Ministers of State, himself setting an example by walking from his home to his office. From the beginning, we were in full agreement that he was to remain in office only during the transition period. Differences with the Government Party, which threatened to culminate in a split, induced Count Károlyi to resign on September 21st, 1932. Our close friendship survived; with his fine, reliable character, he remained one of my most valued advisers.

A new man was now at the threshold, Julius Gömbös. With him a new period opened, not so much due to his own activities as because conditions within Germany had by this time changed fundamentally, taking a turn that was to have the most far-reaching effects on our country and eventually on the whole of Europe and the rest of the world.

13. The Rome Protocols and the Rome-Berlin Axis

When I look back, after the passing of two decades and with the understanding brought us by the terrible events of the Second World War, upon the part played by my country during the thirties, it is the inevitability of the historic process that has left the most profound impression on me. By this phrase, I do not mean merely the self-evident necessity of judging events and incidents in their contemporary setting. It is of greater importance to realize and admit that the freedom of action of a small country such as Hungary, wedged between the formidable might of Germany and that of the Russian colossus, was extremely circumscribed. Time and time again, we tried, and with greater energy and tenacity than did others, to retain what freedom of action we could while pursuing a course in the interests of keeping the peace. We had every reason to aim at a change in the so-called 'order' of which we were the innocent victims, since we had opposed the Viennese ultimatum to Serbia in 1914. We could have availed ourselves of many opportunities to exploit the internal difficulties of our neighbours. This we never did. We tried instead to be a stabilizing force in the Danube Basin, the key to which, as I have always contended, is to be found in Budapest. But even our circumspect policy could not wipe out the now generally lamented folly of the dismemberment of the old Austro-Hungarian monarchy. It was inevitable that the Great Powers should try to turn to account the dissensions of the states in the Balkans and south-east Europe, some of which were newly created, others considerably enlarged or correspondingly reduced. If the other states had shown at least as much wisdom as we had in making the influence of the various Great Powers cancel out, had they come to an agreement with us, history might have taken a different course.

Hungary has always known that, in Italian policies, she was intended to play an anti-Yugoslav and anti-French part in the first place and in the second to serve as an obstacle to German southeastern penetration. We knew the Germans well enough to be chary of too close a friendly embrace, though we gave due recognition to their military, economic and scientific achievements. Nor were we oblivious of the third factor, the menace of which, after our experience of Communist revolution, we Magyars knew more than most: Soviet Russia. Diplomatic relations with Russia were not resumed until April 12th, 1934, after the United States of America, the last of the Great Powers to recognize Soviet Russia, had preceded us in taking this course on November 16th, 1933. What surprise, then, can be felt or what offence can be taken at the fact that we, cautiously and circumspectly, should have adapted ourselves to the changes in the European political constellation of 1933? The first treaties with Hitler were concluded by the Vatican and Poland. With mounting concern we watched the attempts of the National Socialists to undermine from within the independence of our neighbour Austria, attempts which led to the murder of Chancellor Dollfuss. Our relief was great when the energetic action taken by Mussolini in 1934 foiled the attempt at annexation. We watched with bewilderment as the Western democracies, with surprising weakness and lack of unity, permitted the re-arming of Germany and the re-militarization of the Rhineland, while practically driving Germany and Italy into each other's arms by opposing with sanctions the Italian East African colonization plans. Had their intention really been to halt Mussolini, his oil supplies should have been cut and the Suez Canal closed to him. While that was not done, it would have been better to avoid taking measures that did not help the Negus and merely pointed the contrasts between the haves and the have-nots, as they were called at the time. His discussions with Laval, in January, 1935, justified Mussolini in his belief that France approved of Italy's expansionist energies being directed at the distant, scarcely civilized Abyssinians. Even at the Stresa Conference, which dealt with the German entry into the Rhineland, the British had refrained from raising their voice against the unmistakable trend of Mussolini's claims, so that he believed he could at any rate count on British neutrality. Since, meanwhile, the relations between Hungary and Italy had been placed on a yet firmer footing by new treaties. Hungary had no reason to join in imposing sanctions. This put us in the black books of Mr. Eden, who ignored the fact that several of those nations who had agreed to apply sanctions continued to trade with Italy as before. When the 'Rome-Berlin Axis', a phrase first used by our Premier Gömbös, came into being and Mussolini found himself agreeing willy-nilly to the Anschluss. The situation was again very different, from the Hungarian point of view. Not only had we as our neighbour the Greater German Reich, but we had lost the possibility of playing Berlin off against Rome by referring political requests from either to the possible objection of the other. But I have gone ahead of my story in pursuing this point and shall therefore pick up the thread where I dropped it, at the change from the Károlyi to the Gömbös Government.

Julius Gömbös had been Assistant Secretary in the Ministry of Defence when I took over the Ministry at Szeged. Our first meeting was in the year 1919. Count Francis Hunyadi had stopped me in the street to tell me a mysterious story of a conspiracy fomenting against the Michael Károlyi Government. As this was plainly not a topic to be discussed in the open street, I suggested we should adjourn to a hotel. There, some twenty people gathered, all displaying great patriotic fervour but showing singularly little insight into the real factors governing such an undertaking. I was struck at the time by Staff-Captain Gömbös, whose answers to questions of a practical nature were precise and who was as free from false illusions as I was. From the earliest days of our collaboration, I was aware of the good qualities of Gömbös, and also of those qualities in him which were not so good. He was an excellent officer; as a politician he was inclined to be flamboyant. A gifted orator, he indubitably gave a new impetus to our domestic politics. That, under his predecessors had shown a tendency to 'stagnate', as critics put it, though this supposed stagnation had more advantages than those critics were prepared to admit.

For all his undoubtedly well-intentioned efforts, Gömbös often overshot the mark. I had always held that nobody should be prevented from expressing his patriotism by giving his name its Magyar form, but I opposed compulsion. Gömbös occasionally acted arbitrarily in this matter in the cases of officers and civil servants. As a professional soldier, Gömbös was naturally more interested in the German than in the Italian Army. However, by promoting very many and often very young people who shared his political views, he encouraged tendencies which I found difficult to reconcile with my own policy. In the long run, he did himself a disservice. His friends did him more harm than his enemies. Gömbös's nature was fundamentally autocratic and the example set by Hitler and Mussolini made a profound impression on him.

It was, therefore, with a certain hesitation that I decided on October 1st, 1932, to invite him to assume the Premiership, but Count Bethlen and a number of other leading politicians throughout the country had strongly recommended him to me. The scales were tipped in his favour by his undeniable achievements as Minister of Defence. He retained this Ministry when he became Premier. Another factor favouring his choice was his ninety-five-point programme, including a plan to change the national defence from a costly regular army to an army based on general conscription, which contained many excellent ideas. In the next two and a half years, Gömbös manifested certain dictatorial tendencies in home politics. In his foreign policy he sought increasingly closer contact with Germany, a policy which met with resistance on account of its one-sided bias. On both counts, he roused the opposition of the re-formed independent Smallholders' Party and of Count Bethlen.

Loyalty towards the new Premier led me to agree to his request that Parliament should be dissolved after Count Bethlen, the leader of the Government Party, and Tibor Eckhardt, the leader of the Smallholders' Party, had gone over to the opposition. A Premier must have his majority and Gömbös secured this when, at the next elections, a number of valuable politicians, to my regret, lost their seats. The victory struck me as being more of a quantitative nature than of a qualitative one.

Relations between the Premier and Koloman Kánya, the Foreign Minister, could not be called cordial. Kánya, cautious and fundamentally sceptical, did not at times take kindly to the sweeping plans and views of the somewhat cynical Gömbös. The strengthening of relations with Italy and Germany was, however, their joint achievement, even if the one acted with great enthusiasm and the other with a certain resignation, aware of the consequences such alliances might bring. It was certainly due to the initiative of Gömbös himself that he was the first foreign Premier to call on Hitler after visiting his counterparts in Ankara, Rome and Warsaw.

On March 17th, 1934, the Hungarian Premier Gömbös, the Austrian Chancellor Dollfuss, and Mussolini signed the Rome Protocols, which in a sense represented the answer to the Pact of Organization recently concluded by the Little Entente, and to the equally anti-revisionist Balkan League that had been signed on February 9th of that year. Apart from economic clauses, these protocols also contained arrangements for consultation on all questions of a general nature, especially those touching the interests of the three states concerned. There were, however, no secret clauses of a military nature. Rome and Vienna would have liked to have amplified the Protocols in this way, but we declined military commitments. In view of the tension between Germany and Italy at that time, the Germans commended our restraint.

The annals of that dark year which saw the murder of Dollfuss and the bloodstained days of the thwarting of the Röhm Putsch contain also the assassination of King Alexander of Yugoslavia. He, together with the French Foreign Minister, Louis Barthou, fell victim to a Macedonian terrorist on the

Marseilles Cannebiere on October 9th. I had met King Alexander once, and that only in passing during the period of his Regency. He was in the ante-room when I left the council chamber in which the discussion with Premier Protic, to which I have already referred, took place. Later we were in personal communication through his Adjutant-General, Admiral Prica, a Croat of the orthodox faith, with whom I had been friendly ever since my naval apprenticeship. Prica called on me twice on the King's behalf. Although the initiative I had taken in 1926 had had no tangible results, yet I had adhered to Hungary's publicly expressed readiness to come to an understanding with our southern neighbour. Questions referred to me by the Yugoslavs I invariably dealt with sympathetically. I had every reason to believe that King Alexander would, as soon as circumstances permitted, accept the proffered hand of friendship. His tragic death I therefore deeply regretted as much on political grounds as from personal sympathy. The same can be said of all responsible Hungarian statesmen, however critical their attitude was of conditions in the one-time Hungarian territories of the Bácska and the Banat, and of the oppression of the Croats by the pan-Serbian policy of Belgrade. Hungary's intense anger at being accused of having had a hand in the organization of that assassination can easily be understood, especially as its protagonists were Croat emigrés.

The accusations levelled against us were concentrated on Jankapuszta, an agricultural estate in south-west Hungary near Nagykanizsa. The Hungarian authorities set this place aside for those Croats who had fled to Hungary for asylum as political refugees with neither means nor identity papers. A Yugoslav memorandum, handed in at Geneva on November 2nd, demanded, on the strength of Paragraph II:2 of the League of Nations Covenant, that the question of support given to Croat terrorists in Hungary should be placed on the agenda of the League's Council. For, as the memorandum stated, "it is a case of the training, on the territory of a foreign country, of professional criminals whose task it is to carry out a series of assassinations and murders for certain definite political ends". The answer of our government to these fantastic accusations was to demand that the Council should at once convene to discuss the matter. At the same time the British and American Ministers in Budapest were invited to go to Jankapuszta to personally inspect conditions there.

I do not wish to describe at length the discussions that were held at Geneva, the report of which was drawn up by the British Foreign Secretary, Mr. Eden.

167

All those who had taken part in the investigation were agreed that Belgrade, in accusing Hungary, was beside the mark. The man who later boasted of the murder, Dr. A. Pavelic, was arrested at Turin shortly afterwards, but Italy refused his extradition. Our League of Nations representative, Tibor Eckhardt, moreover, noticed that a photograph, included by Belgrade as part of its documentation for the accusation and purporting to be one of shooting practice at Jankapuszta, had mountains in the background. This meant that the photograph could not possibly have been taken in the south-west regions of Hungary.

Laval at that time was preparing for his journey to Rome; Italy had therefore to be placated. When Laval showed the Hungarian Foreign Minister a draft of the final report, Kánya rejected it forthwith as it set forth that the Hungarian Government had had knowledge of the plans for the assassination. An hour later, Laval returned with a new text, admittedly toned down but still unacceptable. When Kánya thereupon declared that he would leave Geneva that evening, Laval brought forth a third formulation. As Kánya told me later, he handed it back to Laval after reading it with the utmost care, saying, "I find it utterly incomprehensible," whereupon Laval smiled and exclaimed, "Excellent!" He had purposefully drawn up the new text in such a way that no one could make head or tail of it. On May 25th, 1935, Eden proposed that the proceedings before the Council should be suspended.

The politicians who shared my views were becoming increasingly estranged from Gömbös. Kidney trouble was sapping the Premier's energy, and it was becoming more and more difficult for us to work together. The day came when I invited him to Gödöllô in order to advise him, in a friendly way, to hand in his resignation. As he entered the room, I realized that here was a man whose days were numbered. I could not bring myself to speak of his resignation but advised him to go straight to a hospital for treatment, which he did. But though he consulted a famous kidney specialist in the vicinity of Munich, his life could not be saved. Julius Gömbös died on October 6th. Hitler, who held him in high regard, travelled to Munich to follow his bier to the railway station and sent Göring to the funeral in Budapest as his representative.

The successor of Gömbös was the Minister of Agriculture, Koloman Darányi, an intelligent and reliable if not brilliant man. He retained his former portfolio so that the measures I had initiated for raising the efficiency of our agriculture could be carried out with no break in continuity.

Our soil is, as is well known, extremely fertile, and its products are famed for their particular excellence. This applies especially to our wheat, which on one occasion was awarded first prize in New York in competition with American and Canadian varieties. Hungary's major problem is the shortage of precipitation, and for this reason I directed the attention of the government to irrigation and canal-building projects.

In spite of limited finances, a series of pumping stations was built and the water supply was regulated. In the County of Békés alone the cheaper transport by water led to the saving of approximately a million pengôs a year. Rice-growing also became possible over a much larger area. I am familiar with Chinese, Japanese, Indian and Italian rice, but I find Hungarian rice has more flavour. Apart from that, its financial yield was a multiple of that of wheat. The outbreak of war in 1939 prevented the completion of my plan to link the Danube and the Tisza by a canal. Even our horse- and cattle-breeding made great progress during these inter-war years, as I was able to judge by the developments on my own estate. To rejuvenate the stock, we imported blood stallions and mares from England and from the studs of the Aga Khan in France; from Switzerland came Simmental bulls and cows. Kállay, the later Premier, did much to improve the country's agriculture when Minister of Agriculture.

I have mentioned elsewhere the measures taken in the matter of land reform. To that I must here add that, during the agrarian crisis of 1931, the Károlyi Government, by prohibiting compulsory sale by auction and by arranging the easier conversion of debts, must have saved some half a million people from ruin. As early as 1923, a law on minimum wages for agricultural labourers had been passed, though it applied only to casual labour; in 1940, wages were legally fixed for all categories of labour in agriculture. Between 1936 and 1939, laws were passed providing for old-age insurance for estate managers, for old-age pensions for agricultural labourers and for the insurance of employees' widows.

Peculiar to Hungary was the Health Service, founded in 1940 by Keresztes-Fischer, the then Minister for Home Affairs, under the name of the Green Cross, for the purpose of serving distant and sparsely populated areas.

Special attention was paid to marriage guidance, advice on careers, instruction on hygiene, pre natal and infant care, and the supervision of infants and primary school children, and to the fight against contagious diseases. In 800 health districts, there were 2,100 advisory bodies and 1,200 Green Cross nurses, who had passed through a course of training lasting several years.

Important as was the part taken by the rural population and by agriculture in Hungary's progress, yet in the inter-war years the contribution made by industry and trade came to constitute the larger part of the national income. The development of industry had proceeded apace, for owing to the restrictions imposed on our economy by the Treaty of Trianon, new sources of national income had had to be devised. From 1913 to 1938-39, the share of industry in production rose from thirty-three to forty-seven percent. As a result, we were confronted by many new problems. In their solution, we were helped by the fact that Hungary had always been particularly enlightened in these matters. Child labour had been strictly regulated since 1840. From 1872, the employment of children under twelve had been altogether prohibited. From 1911, night work for women had been abolished. Compulsory health insurance of labourers was introduced in 1891, only seven years after similar legislation had been passed in Germany and three years after in Austria. During my Regency, a law of 1927 introduced compulsory insurance for illness and accident; that of 1928 the compulsory insurance of invalids, widows and orphans. Other laws were concerned with the limitation of working hours, minimum wages in industry, holidays with pay, family allowances, the necessity to register large-scale dismissals and the regulation of the length of notice required to terminate employment. The income-tax legislation provided for a steeply rising scale of contributions, up to eighty-four per cent. Considerable attention was paid, in this respect, to the care of dependent relatives.

In connection with transport, the creation of an international free harbour on the Danube, which I had proposed, proved extremely valuable. We had seaworthy ships built on the model of the German mine-sweepers in our yards to ply between Budapest and Alexandria. These gave me my first experience of a broadside launch, for had the ships been launched stern first, as is customary, they would merely have run aground on the opposite bank.

I must refrain from going into detail to show the extent of cultural life in Hungary. I shall limit myself to a few indications, for it is common knowledge that numbers of Hungarian plays and books have been translated and produced and read abroad. Hungarian singers have been called to the world's most famous Opera Houses. Our own Budapest State Opera House and State Theatre, as well as other theatres, have won considerable fame; we had an excellent Philharmonic Orchestra and Academy of Music. Whatever repute modern music may have, it cannot be denied that such Hungarian composers as Hubay, Bartók, Dohnányi and Kodály have contributed much to its development. Our painters and sculptors also have given proof of Hungary's high position in art, and the labours of our scientists have been rewarded by two Nobel prizes.

We can say with a clear conscience that the injuries done to Hungary released the inner strength of her race. In all fields of culture, economics and politics, a noble competition sprang up. Even in sport, we had fine achievements to record. At the Berlin Olympic Games held in 1936, we gained third place among all the nations. We seemed then to be on the road that would bring Hungary, by peaceful labour and prudent foreign policy, not only to a established but also respected place in the world, and enhance the general welfare of the country.

14. Travels and Visitors

The Chancellor of the German Reich, Adolf Hitler, had repeatedly asked me to visit him. However, while the tension between our neighbour Austria and the German Reich continued, I did not feel that such a visit would be expedient. With the German-Austrian agreement of July 11th, 1936, this objection ceased to exist. I could then visit both Hitler and the Austrian President Miklas[1] without giving offence to either.

There can hardly have been a single person in the length and breadth of Europe who took no interest in the rise of the man whose origins and upbringing had been assiduously shrouded in mystery, who had just managed to rise to NCO in the First World War and was now achieving the most remarkable successes in every field. This interest, and it must be admitted a certain curiosity, were in conflict with my misgivings. The Budapest newspapers had incurred the displeasure of the German Ministry of Propaganda by having openly expressed their doubts of the story that the Communists had set fire to the Reichstag. In spite of the bloody June 30th[2], 1934, which had been sanctioned by the venerable President of the German Reich, von Hindenburg. This justice of vengeance with neither judge nor tribunal had profoundly shocked me. Though times had changed considerably since I had been aide-de-camp to His Majesty Emperor Francis Joseph, my concepts of honour, law and justice, fashioned after his noble example, had not altered. Yet, after all, it was not my task to stand in judgment upon the man who, since he had come to power, had shown nothing but goodwill towards Hungary and who had sent me an extremely friendly telegram on the fifteenth anniversary of my entry into Budapest. I decided, therefore, to avail myself of an Austrian invitation to a chamois shoot in August 1936 to seize the opportunity of paying a personal visit to Herr Hitler. The Austrian Chancellor Schuschnigg[3] had offered me the choice between three hunting preserves; I chose Hinterriss, which is famous for its chamois and to which Bavaria affords the only access.

1   Wilhelm Miklas (1872-1956).

2   The Nazi "night of the long knives" blood purges. It was executed under the direction of Joseph Dietrich (1892-1966) a close friend of Hitler, who has risen to be one of the top SS generals by the end of the war, without the benefit of formal military education.

3   Kurt von Schuschnigg (1897-1977).

173

At Berchtesgaden, I was met by one of Hitler's aides-de-camp who conducted me to the Obersalzberg. Hitler received me at the top of the stairs. We went first to his study, where he proceeded to expound his programme in sweeping terms. He began, of course, with Versailles, and as the Treaty of Trianon had committed the same injustices against Hungary as Versailles had against Germany. I had no grounds for contradicting him. I was struck by his remarkable memory, by means of which he, an uneducated man, had succeeded in amassing considerable knowledge. Hitler proved a delightful host. Contrary to his later habits, he asked a great many questions, displaying considerable interest in relations outside the German borders. Suddenly he asked, "What would you do, Your Highness, if you had to set Germany's course?"

"That question comes as a surprise to me, Your Excellency," I replied. "But if you really wish to know my views, I should do all I could to achieve a close friendship between Germany and England."

To a former naval officer like myself, such an alliance did not appear impossible of achievement, so long as Germany avoided making the mistake of a von Tirpitz[4] or of an Emperor Wilhelm II by entering into naval competition with Great Britain. For the new Germany, I added, that would not be difficult, as she could not possibly raise a mighty army and at the same time build a fleet equal to the British fleet. "Were you to conclude an offensive and defensive alliance with England, Germany would be in no need of a fleet."

Upon my saying that England, owing to her great experience, was the one power able to maintain order in the world, and that with relatively small armed forces, Hitler responded with the question why Germany should not, in my opinion, be in a position to do the same.

"It is quite simple," I rejoined. "The British have always known the art of gaining the confidence of the people they rule. They bring prosperity, put an end to internecine strife and introduce an incorruptible rule without burdening the people with police regulations and other vexations after an alien model."

---

4 German Admiral Alfred von Tirpitz (1849-1930) builder of the Imperial German fleet, advocate of the unlimited submarine warfare during WW1.

This theme was pursued no further, but I had an impression that Hitler agreed with my arguments. Even today, I believe that he was sincere in his admiration of the British Commonwealth of Nations, an admiration which he voiced not only in his *Mein Kampf* but also on several occasions during the war. Unfortunately, he never understood that the British insist that their partner in an alliance should at least be true to his given word. And this meant that any offensive-defensive alliance such as he did propose to Great Britain later would have been doomed to failure from the outset.

Tea was served by an S.S. orderly in the room that has so often been described, one wall of which consisted of a huge pane of glass which gave a view of the Alps that resembled a vast painting. My visit lasted about three hours altogether. We parted on friendly terms and I was left with the impression that in Hitler I had met a moderate and wise statesman. I was not the only one to make that mistake.

Towards nightfall, I arrived, after a delightful drive, at the hunting lodge of Hinterriss. As His Majesty had never made use of this particular hunting ground since it could not be reached by rail, it had always been let by the state, so that this was my first visit to it. In the morning, accompanied by a gamekeeper, I shot two fine chamois bucks.

On the journey home through the Tirol and Carinthia, I visited Miklas, the President of the Austrian Republic, at Velden on Lake Wörther. Politics were not discussed, and we had tea in the family circle.

The visit to the Obersalzberg was unofficial. The invitation transmitted to me in the same year, 1936, in the course of his visit to Budapest, by Count Ciano[5], the Italian Foreign Minister, on behalf of his sovereign, was for a state visit. Accompanied by Darányi, the Hungarian Premier, Kánya, the Foreign Minister, the Chief of the General Staff and the Chief of the Military and Cabinet Chancelleries[6], my wife and I travelled to Rome in November. We

---

5 Galeazzo Ciano (1903-1944) Count of Cortelazzo, son-in-law of Mussolini. In 1943, in the Grand Council of the Fascists he voted against Mussolini, for which he was executed.

6 Maj. Gen. Jenô Rátz, Gen. Lajos Keresztes-Fischer, and Sándor Vértesy.

were met most cordially at the railway station by the Italian King[7] and Queen and Mussolini. In open horse-drawn carriages, with an escort of cuirassiers, we drove through the flag-decorated streets, lined with welcoming crowds. The Governor of Rome, Prince Piero Colonna[8], an eminent and impressive personality, with the mien of an ancient Roman, received us in the Piazza Esedra in the name of the City. It gave me a feeling of elation to set foot for the first time in the Eternal City. We stayed at the Quirinal and Mussolini came there to take tea with us. In the evening, we were the guests of the King and Queen at dinner in the limited family circle at the Villa Savoia, a pleasant prelude to the memorable days that were to follow.

The following morning, I returned Mussolini's visit at the Palazzo Venezia, which, until 1915, had been the Austro-Hungarian Embassy. A new era had now set in. The former members of the Triple Alliance, after a period of hostility, were together again. Moreover, Benito Mussolini was particularly popular in Hungary as he had been the first responsible statesman openly to demand that the injustice done to Hungary should be amended. Of the posing of which he has been so generally accused, I saw no trace. I did notice that Count Ciano, his son-in-law and Foreign Minister, remained standing during our conversation, though I twice signed to him to sit down. Not even on this occasion did the Duce depart from his custom of keeping his Ministers standing by the side of his desk in the huge Sala del Mappamondo.

Mussolini impressed me considerably during that first visit. He plunged straight into a discussion of the problems that were of moment to both our countries after giving a shrewd and exact survey of the contemporary political world. We both knew that our discussion was regarded with the utmost suspicion by the Chancelleries of the Little Entente. I had, however, no intention of entering into negotiations for an alliance while I was in Rome. However, the conclusion that such was my intention had been drawn from the fact that I was accompanied by my Chiefs of Staff. The only matter of that kind discussed was a delivery of aeroplanes and arms, to which Mussolini agreed.

Throughout our visit, in the course of which I met His Majesty and Mussolini both separately and together, and heard the views of their entourages,

7   Victor Emanuel III (1869-1947), Queen Elena (1873- ?) Princess of Montenegro.

8   Prince Ascanio Colonna (1883- ?), diplomat, ambassador to Hungary.

discreetly expressed, I received the impression that the relations between the Crown and the Duce were excellent. I certainly could not tell whether His Majesty considered the new Imperial Crown an added prestige or a burden. However, in public at any rate, he displayed gratitude to Mussolini for the order he had established in the land. On his part, Mussolini seemed to appreciate the fact that the King gave him an entirely free hand in the running of the state.

From the Palazzo Venezia, I went to the Tomb of the Unknown Soldier, on which I laid a wreath. In the impressive military parade that was held, I rode with the King as he inspected the many branches of the armed forces which lined the Via dell' Impero. Afterwards, from a tribune we watched the march past, including the Bersaglieri[9], the fast-moving light troops.

In the afternoon, we visited the Capitol at the invitation of the City of Rome. We admired not only the brilliant social gathering but also the glorious view over the Eternal City with its buildings and monuments, among them the magnificent equestrian statue of Emperor Marcus Aurelius.

During the banquet at the Quirinal, the King said in giving his toast, "The memory of the courteous way in which our two countries waged war on the Adriatic has lived in our hearts and has rendered possible this new bond of deep friendship uniting Italy with the noble Hungarian nation." As an earnest of his words, the King bestowed on me the highest Italian decoration, the Order of the Santa Annunziata.

As a special mark of honour, a naval review was held, a hundred and fifty warships having assembled in the Bay of Naples for a grand parade. We were met by Crown Prince Umberto[10] and Crown Princess Maria José at Naples station. Their handsome, dignified presence deeply impressed us. Their small daughter, Princess Maria Pia, added a gay note to the reception, since she refused to part with the bouquet given her for presentation to my wife. With the Crown Princess and the other ladies, my wife went on board a yacht, while I was taken, with His Majesty and the Crown Prince, to the flagship, where I was welcomed on deck by Mussolini, as Minister of Marine, and Admiral Bucci.

9   Elite units of the Italian army, established in 1836, with a characteristic floppy felt hat with feathers.

10 Prince Umberto (1904-1983), King of Italy in May and June of 1946.

177

I find it difficult to describe the emotions which welled up in my heart as I gazed once more upon the sea, upon the ships and the ensigns fluttering in the breeze. When, obeying the supreme command of Emperor Charles, I surrendered our magnificent fleet in October of the year of misfortune, 1918, to the Yugoslav representatives, and our glorious, undefeated ensign had to be struck for ever, I decided in my despair to take my final leave of the sea. Now I found myself standing once more on the bridge of a proud battleship, my standard at her peak. But the battleship was named after the Dalmatian capital, Zara, which was now under another sway. The maneuvres of the first and second squadrons, steaming at full speed in line ahead from Gaeta, fascinated me. Ships, officers and men made an excellent impression. During luncheon, which was served in the Admiral's cabin, I made a short speech in Italian:

"Your Royal and Imperial Majesty, Your Royal Highness, Comrades of the sea! With these words, I enter once more the unique and glorious community which links the seamen of th world. Simple fishermen and mighty admirals all belong to one the same family; instinctively they understand one another, whatever race they be.

Our struggle with the elements unites us. When the storm the World War broke over our heads and we were forced by politics to face each other as foes, our actions were never dictated by hatred. The accuracy and range of our guns, the strength and speed of our vessels alone decided our judgment of chances and our actions. Our warfare was free from bitterness. We fought in the spirit of fair play. And now, eighteen years later, I once again behold the sea, breathe the sea air, feel a deck under my feet. You will understand what this means to me."

After the luncheon, we left the battleship and returned to Rome in a special train through a landscape that resembled a well-tended garden. For that evening, His Majesty had invited the Diplomatic Corps to a second gala dinner.

Among Mussolini's undeniable achievements must be reckoned the Lateran Treaties with which he put an end to the conflict which had raged since 1870 between the Italian State and the Papacy. Hungary looks back with pride to Abbot Astrik, who was sent to Rome in the year 1000, and who received from the hands of Pope Sylvester II the Holy Crown and the Apostolic Cross. By this act, our country was spared from homage to either the German or the Byzantine Emperor as their feudal lord. With the crown which graced the brow of the first King of Hungary, later to be canonized as Saint Stephen, Hungary became the easternmost of the Western community of nations. These thoughts moved me as we greeted the "gentiluomini di cappa e spada". It was, as it happened, the first time that representatives of His Holiness had entered the Quirinal. Until September 20th, 1870, It has been the residence of the Popes. The Swiss Guard, in its mediaeval garb, was drawn up in the inner courtyard of the Vatican. After a ceremonial, every detail of which was exactly prescribed, we were conducted up a gigantic flight of stairs, through many halls in which were hanging paintings famous throughout the world, to the Chamberlain on duty. He announced our presence to Pope Pius XI. His Holiness received my wife and I seated on a throne. He displayed a lively interest in the general political situation and in Hungary's foreign relations. The audience lasted over half an hour. The only concern in our appreciation of what, even to a non-Catholic like myself was a great and noble episode, was the realization that we saw before us a gravely ill man. As the Vatican protocol demanded, we went on to visit the Vatican Secretary of State, Cardinal Eugenio Pacelli, the future Pope Pius XII. He joined us at the luncheon which was given by Barcza[11], the Hungarian Ambassador to the Vatican.

Many Maltese Knights were among the guests of Prince Chigi[12], the Grand Master of the Sovereign Order of the Knights of Malta, whom we had met when he had visited Budapest. I was the only Protestant other than Emperor Wilhelm II to possess the Grand Cross of that Order.

After a dinner given at the residence of Baron Villani[13], our Ambassador to the Quirinal, we attended a gala performance at the Opera in the company of Their Majesties, during which the King, who was apparently not enamoured of that particular opera, made several witty criticisms. The conversational tone became agreeably informal.

---

11 György Barcza (1888-1961) former Austro-Hungarian diplomat, he was ambassador to London between 1938 and 1941. His last assignment was to seek contact in Switzerland with western powers concerning an armistice. His approach was rejected.

12 Prince Ludovico Chigi della Rovera Albani (1866-1951).

13 Baron Frigyes Villani (1882-1964), Hungarian ambassador to Italy.

The happiness of our visit made us reluctant to depart. We left Rome with an abundance of happy memories and with gratitude in our hearts. Wherever we had been, to whomsoever we had talked, we had invariably encountered sympathy with our homeland. We had learned to know a wise monarch and a queen who was a kind mother to her country. Rome itself, that unique city, the very stones of which speak to the beholder of the unbroken sequence of three thousand years of history, had afforded us a spectacle that was engraved on our memories.

We went from Rome to Vienna. President Miklas had given us a charming invitation to pay him a state visit. I had no desire to have to visit the Hofburg or the Palace at Schönbrunn, places that rouse in me so many sad memories. My reluctance had been understood though it proved impossible to respect my wish with regard to Schönbrunn. We were taken straight to the Imperial Hotel, and my first with the President and with the Chancellor, Schuschnigg, came after the luncheon at the Ministry for Foreign Affairs on the Ballhausplatz. We were in full agreement that the independence of Austria must be safeguarded in spite of what Schuschnigg called the 'economic Anschluss' that had recently been concluded. Mussolini, who had not touched upon this topic in his discussions with me, had promised Austria his full support in this matter, so the Austrian Chancellor informed me. This I was prepared to believe, but I doubted whether this promise or the firm will of the Austrian Government would be sufficient to withstand the pressure of National-Socialist propaganda or the pressure due to the great difference in size between the two German countries.

After some pleasant hours spent in the circle of my old comrades at the Naval League that afternoon, we drove in the evening along the Mariahilfer Strasse to Schönbrunn, the very road that I had covered many hundreds of times in the company of the old Emperor. The floodlit Palace and Pavilion made an overpowering impression. We were taken up the familiar blue staircase to the pink drawing-room before going into the great gallery where, as in the past, dinner was served, with all the same china and plates. Only, in His Majesty's now sat the President of the Austrian Republic. Throughout the evening, the ghosts of the past thronged at my elbow.

On the following day, after the military parade outside the gates, I went, as my heart dictated, to the Habsburg crypt under the Capuchin Church, to lay a wreath at the foot of the sepulchre of the old Emperor; the ribbon binding the wreath bore the inscription: "In reverent and grateful memory". I knelt before the tomb and offered up a prayer. His Majesty had been my great teacher, to whom I knew that I owed much. How often had I not, in performing my task as Regent, asked myself, "What would His Majesty Francis Joseph have done in a case like this?" Even after his death, I continued to trust in his wisdom. I have never regretted that I retained so many of his arrangements, tested by centuries of use, in dealing with Hungarian problems.

The Austrian President paid a return visit to Budapest on May 3rd, 1937, where he was received, as had been his Chancellor, Kurt Schuschnigg, a few weeks earlier, with great cordiality.

In diplomatic etiquette, special significance is attached to the shorter or longer time that is allowed to elapse before a visit is returned. The suggestion had been made that King Victor Emmanuel should be spared the fatigue of a long journey, but the King had scuttled it with the reply, "No, no, I am going myself." We were, therefore, extremely gratified when the date for his return visit was fixed as early as May, 1937, the season of the year during which Budapest is most beautiful. We did our utmost to render the visit of the King, who was accompanied by Her Majesty and the Princess Maria, as pleasant as possible. The centre block of the Royal Palace, which had been built in the reign of Maria Theresa[14] and which Emperor Francis Joseph had occupied, was prepared for the royal visit, some modernizations having to be made. The Arab horses requisite for the King's entry were brought from the state ranch of Bábolna; they were familiarized not only with the route but also with the music and the noise of cheering; they proved apt pupils. Only one item was overlooked, the gun salute. We had greeted Their Majesties and were about to enter the carriages when the batteries fired the salute, and up reared the three foremost horses, wildly pawing the air. Fortunately, no mishap occurred. In the experienced hands of our coachmen, they quickly became docile.

In three five-in-hands, ahead of which rode the Commander of the Guards, Colonel Lázár, with drawn sword, and six four-in-hands, we met our guests. The weather was kind and these perfectly matched carriages, all drawn by snow-white Arabs in gala harness, so alike that they were indistinguishable, and driven by coachmen in gold-green liveries, were a magnificent sight. His Majesty spoke from the heart when, entranced by the spectacle, he remarked

14 Maria Theresa of Habsburg (1717-1780), German-Roman Empress and Queen of Hungary. Mother of the French Queen Marie-Antoinette.

that it was a pity that these noble animals were being driven from the roads by cars. Many people in the crowd must have had the same thought as, amazed, they watched the unusual spectacle. Only the older people among the spectators could ever have seen a cortege like this before.

On the evening of May 20th, 1937, more than a hundred guests, members of the government, officers and civil servants, were present at the state banquet held in the Marble Hall of the Palace. In the toast, which I gave in Italian, I described Their Majesties' Visit as "a feast to Hungarian hearts" and referred to the aid Italy had given us, aid "which had, to a considerable extent, made it possible for Hungary to become once more a factor in international politics". In his reply, it should be noted that toasts of this kind are always carefully prepared beforehand, and their sentiments brought into accord, His Majesty took up my reference to Germany and spoke of the "policy which through cordial collaboration with Germany grows increasingly successful day by day, as, free from all exclusive tendencies, it offers opportunities for further developments in the interests of European stability and a friendly concourse of nations".

These speeches were intended for the ears of those who rejoiced at the newly won position of Hungary and also of those who still believed that by refusing amicable revision of treaties, they could halt the progress of history. The official political discussions were left to Darányi, our Premier, Count Ciano, the Italian Foreign Minister, and Kánya, our Foreign Minister. I had given instructions that the entertainments for the five days of Their Majesties' visit should be arranged in such a way that Their Majesties would have time to rest. One expedition made by the King was to the excavations of the Roman remains at Aquincum, the only site in Europe on which a Roman water-organ has been found. Together we also went to the races. The racecourse had been built on the outskirts of the town and is considered by many to be the finest of its kind in Europe. I mention this race-meeting to introduce another incident of the royal visit. It so happened that a horse belonging to my brother had been entered in the main race; its name happened to be Duce. This horse had already won a number of races, but on this occasion I had no idea what its chances were, as I had not had an opportunity of consulting my brother. Nevertheless, the Queen and her retinue all placed bets on Duce, and were naturally eager to see the horse come in first. Just as it looked as if Duce were certain of victory, two other horses drew dangerously near. Suddenly the crowd began to shout as the Italians had shouted in the Piazza Venezia:

"Du-ce! Du-ce!" Fortunately, the jockey had the horse well under control and it passed the winning post first. The excitement and jubilation in our enclosure was delightful to watch, and His Majesty presented the jockey with a handsome reward.

At the gala luncheon to which the Diplomatic Corps had also been invited, the gay Hungarian costumes were in colourful contrast to the uniforms and morning coats, which our royal guests appreciated fully. The garden party on the terraces of the towering Palace, attended by three thousand people, made the same impression on them. The view across the Danube and the beauty of Budapest are magnificent from that vantage-point, or should I say were, since death and destruction have now passed over the ancient city[15].

As in Rome, a dinner was held at the Embassy. The Italian Ambassador at this time was Vinci[16], a polished and entertaining raconteur, whose table-talk and speeches were invariably a delight.

The departure of the royal guests was as ceremonious as their arrival. The visit had been so enjoyable to our guests that parting was sad. Her Majesty turned to my wife and said: "Je suis si triste. J'ai envie de pleurer." (I am very sad. I could cry.)

These accounts of state visits will have indicated that in spite of the attendant gaieties, they are actually part and parcel of the professional duties of heads of states. They invariably have an underlying political purpose, and need considerable preparation, much tact and a modicum of luck to make them productive of political friendship either by creating it or confirming it, and to avoid endangering what progress has already been made in that line. History affords enough examples of consequences of either kind.

The friendship between Poland and Hungary, as I have already mentioned, is

15 It has since largely recovered. The destruction allowed extensive archeo-
    logical excavations revealing the medieval royal palace.
16 Count Luigi Orazio Vinci-Gigliucci.

centuries old. Stephen Báthory[17], Prince of Transylvania, ruled over Poland, and, before the Habsburgs became Kings of Hungary, members of the Jagiello dynasty[18] ruled over us. Polish volunteers hastened to the aid of Kossuth[19] in his fight[20] against the Habsburgs. Hungary and Poland have never been at war with each other. Though, at this time, we were not neighbours of Russia, the Carpathian Ukraine had been adjudicated to Czechoslovakia by the Treaty of Trianon and was by her 'voluntarily' relinquished to the Soviet Union in 1944, yet the situations of Poland and Hungary had much in common. I had therefore nursed for years the plan of paying a visit to Marshal Pilsudski[21], but his ill-health and death brought the project to naught. An occasion to visit Poland did not present itself until February, 1938, when I and my eldest son Stephen received a welcome invitation from President Moscicki[22] to join a hunting party. At Cracow, we were received by the President, and the Mayor of the City presented us with the traditional gift of bread and salt as the guilds paraded in a colourful procession in the castle. In the splendid rooms of the efficiently modernized castle, a banquet was held that same evening and we were given a cordial welcome in a toast by the President. The hunt over Europe's greatest hunting preserves, the Forest of Bialowieza, with its

17 Transylvanian Prince István Báthory (1533-1586)

18 Rulers of Poland and Lithuania from 1386 to 1572; Hungary from 1440 to 1444, and from 1490 until the Battle of Mohács in 1526.

19 Louis Kossuth (1802-1894) Hungarian statesman. Although Czech and Rumanian propaganda painted him as a rabid nationalist and propagator of "Magyarization", his voluminous writings confirm him as an early promoter of the Danubian Federation. His international stature as a champion for freedom is characterized by the fact that he was the second foreigner, after the Marquis de Lafayette to address the Joint Meeting of the U.S. Congress on January 7, 1852.

20 The Hungarian War of Liberation 1848-49, led by Kossuth, which was put down by Russian Imperial forces at the request of the faltering Austrian side.

21 Marshal Jozef Pilsudski (1867-1935), autocratic leader of Poland after a 1927 military coup.

22 Ignacy Moscicki (1867-1946). After the German invasion that began on September 1, 1939, Moscicki, marshal Edward Rydz-Smigly, and foreign minister Jozef Beck entered Romania on September 17, where they were promptly interned, inspite an earlier accord guaranteeing free passage to the Polish Government through Romania in case of war. Moscicki then resigned and, conforming to the Polish Constitution, passed the presidency to general Sosnkowski. However, since he did not known if Sosnkowski was

184

abundance of noble game-stags, wild boars, lynxes and wolves, lasted for three days. My bag of a few fine wild boars and a lynx was not as large as I had expected, but this was due to the fact that there had been scarcely any snowfall that winter, a phenomenon that had never occurred before in living memory. During the days of the hunt and later, while we were in Warsaw, I had opportunities of private discussions not only with the President but also with the leading personalities of the country, among whom were Marshal Rydz-Smigly[23], the Commander-in-Chief of the Army, Colonel Beck[24], the Foreign Minister, and General Sosnkowski[25]. They all knew that I was in sympathy with the Polish position not only through tradition and upbringing, but also through my realization of our mutual interests. I was therefore able to broach various topics, among them the delicate one of the Corridor. I pointed out that in spite of the fact that the creation of the Corridor and the separation of Danzig from the German Empire in 1919 had set up a permanent cause of friction between Poland and Germany. Yet Poland, with the increasingly powerful Communist Soviet Union on her borders, should more than ever try to come to an agreement with Germany. They listened to me attentively, but declared that Poland could not relinquish her claims to access to the sea and to the mouth of the Vistula, since that river was Poland's main artery.

"Is not the Danube Hungary's main artery?" I countered, "yet we do not control its mouth." And I went on to stress the need for a closer relation between Lithuania and Poland, which would be happier solution, since these

still alive, he appointed General Wieniawe-Dlugoszowski, Poland's ambassador to Italy, as temporary president until Sosnkovski was found. Moscicki was allowed later to move to Switzerland, where he died.

23 Marshal Edward Rydz-Smigly (1886-1941). He escaped from Romania in 1941 and returned to occupied Poland under the fictitous name: Adam Zawisza. Soon he died of pneunomia and bured under his assumed name. In 1992 his real name was put on his burial place.

24 Col. Jozef Beck (1894-1944).

25 Gen. Kazimierz Sosnkowski (1885-1969). In 1939 he managed to slip through Romania and reached France. He joined the struggle to organize the Polish Army and government in the free world. Meanwhile the French government ignored his lawful appointment to the exiled Polish Presidency and supported General Sikorski instead. Soon after Sikorski blamed the Katyn massacre on the Soviets, he died in a mysterious accident in a British plane over Gibraltar on July 4, 1943. After that, Sosnkowski became president and supreme commander of the Free Polish Army. He died in Great Britain.

countries had been linked for centuries. But this plea did not meet with approval, nor my contention that the military might of Germany was growing rapidly. It may have been that the Poles, as I was given to understand, anticipated victory should they be involved in a war with Germany. My visit ended with expressions of our traditional, sincere friendship, and I returned home with many delightful memories of a week of varied activities. I had, however, uneasy forebodings, for my sojourn in Poland had shown me clearly the dangers that were looming on the horizon.

An invitation to a hunting party such as I had received from President Moscicki often plays a greater part in politics than an official state visit. When the guest is a keen huntsman, the atmosphere is bound to be relaxed, so that even political topics can be discussed in a lighter and freer mood than in a conference chamber. Whether such meetings bear fruit or not, the pretence of the non-political character of the visit be upheld to the outside world, which is often an advantage. Hence, all states maintain domains which can be used for this purpose by the Premier or other political leaders. Hungary was particularly fortunate in her possession of hunting grounds, though the Treaty of Trianon had reft from her some excellent preserves, Görgény in Transylvania, for instance.

The Castle of Gödöllô and the hunting rights of sixty thousand acres of fields and forest-land had been given to His Majesty Emperor Francis Joseph at his coronation as King of Hungary in 1867; the domain itself had remained state property. It was famed for its profusion of deer, wild boars, pheasants, woodcock and snipe. Considerable damage had been done during the revolution years of 1918 and 1919. The noble red deer had been mown down with machine-guns. The remaining herds had fled northward to the Carpathians, which later proved to be a gain, as the stock improved out of recognition. Stags so fine as those that returned later to Gödöllô had never been seen there before. I remember a trophy of my own that weighed twenty-four pounds twelve ounces. Huntsmen will know what that signifies. I could fill a book with accounts of the hunting and shooting at Gödöllô, in which foreign visitors frequently took part. The Duke of Windsor[26], while still Prince of Wales, shot woodcock there. The King of Italy brought down a wild boar. The Italian Foreign Minister, Count Ciano, invited to hunt wild boar, shot a young stag; it was the close season for deer but he was satisfied, which was all we wanted. A master shot was the Maharaja of Patiala. During a wild

26 King Edward VIII, Abdicated on December 10, 1936.

boar hunt in winter, he was ahead of me along a narrow road. Two fine boars suddenly came bounding through the dense undergrowth in his vicinity, and the Maharaja threw off his fur cape and fired twice. I expected that the wild boars would be none the worse for this, but at the end of the day, when we left our coverts, there were the two boars, laid low by accurate hits over the shoulder-blade.

To another Indian Prince, the Maharaja of Kapurthala, we owed the reintroduction of falconry. He sent two of his men to teach our huntsmen to train falcons. When, in turn, I introduced this sport to the King of Italy, one of the falcons caught two pheasants and two rabbits.

There was scarcely one accredited head of a mission to Hungary who did not avail himself of an invitation to Gödöllô. Even those who did not hunt liked to come as spectators to this huntsman's paradise. The German Minister, Count Welczek, liked hunting in Hungary so well that he rented a hunting ground. When he was Ambassador in Spain he used to come from Madrid every year for the rutting season of the stags. Similarly, Franz von Papen[27], who in his younger days had often raced with my younger brother Eugen and had remained friends with him, was frequently my guest when he was Ambassador in Vienna and later in Ankara. When Admiral Canaris[28] came on an official journey to Budapest, he never failed to call on me. On one occasion he came when I was at Gödöllô for the rutting season. I asked him whether he was keen on shooting. "Most decidedly," he replied, whereupon I suggested that we go to the hunting preserves towards nightfall. I promised him a fine fourteen-tiner I had observed, and he was cheered at the thought. First we went to an observation covert from which we watched the mating battle of two stags in the centre of two herds of deer. The whole vicinity was vibrating to the bellowing of the two animals. From a second covert, we saw no fewer than three additional herds, but the fourteen-tiner which was normally to be found there was not to be seen. It was getting late and rapidly becoming darker. At last, he appeared, a magnificent creature. I quickly handed my gun to Canaris. He took aim, lowered the gun, took aim again. Then he put down the gun, saying: "It's too dark. To injure so fine a creature or to miss it

27 Franz von Papen (1879-1969) German diplomat. He was prime minister of Germany between June 1 and November 17, 1932. Acquitted at the Nuremberg Trials.

28 Admiral Wilhelm Canaris (1887-1945), head of German naval intelligence, executed by the Nazis.

altogether would turn this wonderful afternoon into a painful memory." That was the classic decision of a true sportsman, and to me this incident is typical of the man who was executed by Hitler after the fateful July 20th, 1944[29].

I must end this chapter with a word of thanks to His Holiness Pope Pius XII. He, while still Cardinal Secretary of State, attended the Eucharistic Congress in Budapest as Papal Legate in the summer of 1938. His presence was a high honour which we appreciated to the full. The Cardinal Secretary of State even went to the trouble of learning our language, adding yet another to the many languages in which he could so fluently express himself. All who were present at the Pontifical Mass before the Millenium Monument on the Heroes' Square, and who saw the Blessed Sacrament pass slowly up and down the Danube or a floodlit steamer, will never forget the honour which was bestowed on Hungary. The American Minister, Mr. Montgomery, wrote in his journal at the time that he had made the acquaintance of a truly great man. There was certainly no one in Budapest, Catholic, non-Catholic, who would not have held the same opinion after having met Cardinal Pacelli.

29 Date of the attempt by German officers to kill Hitler.

15. Friction with Hitler

The year of the Austrian Anschluss, of the Sudeten crisis, of the Munich Agreement, and finally of the Vienna Award arbitrating between Hungary and Czechoslovakia, put Hungarian politics to a severe test. As a former sailor, I was used to relying not on sunshine alone but also on the readings of barometers and weather charts. In 1938, I could see the storm approaching while not only the masses but also eminent statesmen still believed in "peace in our time". I knew, the helm would have to be firmly grasped to keep the small Hungarian ship of state on her set course through the mounting waves. We desired revision, yes, but revision by peaceful means. I am not writing this with the wisdom gained after the event. To my great satisfaction, I find in the memoirs of Ernst von Weizsäcker[1], the Permanent Secretary of the German Ministry for Foreign Affairs, a sentence which shows clearly how my thoughts were running at the time. "We must avoid becoming involved in a new war at all costs." These were the words with which, in August, 1938, I greeted Frau von Weizsäcker, who had come to accompany my wife on our travels through Germany. I am now going to record expressing these self-same sentiments, not to a lady, though she was the wife of a Permanent Secretary, but to Hitler himself.

In a state of extreme tension, we had watched, from Budapest, the dramatic struggle waged by the Austrian Chancellor, Schuschnigg, for the retention of the independence of his country. The unification of the two German states was the logical consequence of the violent disintegration of the Austro-Hungarian monarchy. Hungary was neither called upon nor was she in a position to guarantee Peace Treaties after the Western democracies, suffering from a fresh defeat in the Spanish Civil War, together with Mussolini had withdrawn their support from Austria. I learned later that even Yugoslavia, a member of the Little Entente, had strengthened Hitler in his resolve. When we, together with Italy and Yugoslavia, had become the neighbours of Germany on March 11th, 1938, it had entirely changed the balance of power in Central Europe. I realized that Czechoslovakia's hour had struck now that she was hemmed in by Germany on three sides. For Benes and Masaryk the time of reckoning had come for having procured the creation of

---

1   Baron Ernst von Weizsäcker (1882-1951), deputy to German Foreign Minister Ribbentrop. He was a secret participant of the anti-Hitler resistance movement. (See: Joachim Fest: *Plotting Hitler's Death*, New York: Henry Holt Co., 1994.)

their artificial state at the Peace Conference by means of falsified maps and fictitious[2] data. By such ruse they gained regions in which the Czechs, the State-nation, were a minority that ruled over incensed Slovaks and other despoiled nationalities: Germans, Magyars, Ruthenes and Poles. We, at any rate, felt no surprise when, a few weeks after the Anschluss, the Sudeten Germans came forward with their claims. Our Premier, Béla Imrédy[3], who had taken over[4] from Darányi on May 14th, and Kánya, our Foreign Minister, returned from their journey to Rome in July with Mussolini's assurance, after Hitler's Italian visit[5], that he, Mussolini, would 'unreservedly support' the German claims against Czechoslovakia. London sent Lord Runciman[6] to Prague. Was Hungary expected to go arm-in-arm with Litvinov[7] to the defence of the Czechs? Particularly, as three years earlier we had voiced our worry even to the American Government concerning the re-entry of the Soviet Union into the affairs of Central Europe by reason of her treaties with France and Czechoslovakia. However, it is important to establish this point, we had in no way bound ourselves politically or militarily to Germany during my visit to that country.

Hitler, in issuing an invitation to me to visit Germany in the summer of 1938, had bethought himself of a signal honour to pay me. In my distinction as the

2   Indeed, for example, they proposed for boundaries "navigable rivers" that were creeks so small that a child could wade through them.

3   Béla Imrédy (1891-1946), well respected economist and former Governor of the National Bank was originally known to be Anglophile. However, after visiting Hitler he became a Nazi supporter. He was tried and executed after the war.

4   "When it became obvious that M. Darányi was losing grip, was not stemming the onrush of the Hungarian Fascists and their foreign associates towards complete control of Hungary's destinies, there was a revolt inside the Darányi Cabinet. The Regent is said to have intervened and stated the alternatives very bluntly to M. Darányi; and the latter resigned." (Hutton, Graham: *Danubian Destiny*, London: Harrap & Co. 1939. pp. 193 - 194.)

5   On May 3, 1938.

6   Lord Walter Runciman of Doxford (1870-1949). He was sent to Prague on July 25, 1938 to mediate between the Czechoslovak government and the Sudeten Germans. On his return, he reported favorably on Nazi claims. The unsuccessful mission was a prelude to the Munich Pact.

7   Maxim Maximovich Litvinov (1876-1951), Soviet diplomat, Foreign Commissar.

last Commander-in-Chief of the Austro-Hungarian fleet, the traditions of which were now proclaimed by the German Navy, I was to attend the launch of a heavy cruiser and my wife was to christen the vessel. However much I enjoyed meeting my German friends of the sea, I was always inclined to be suspicious when my natural and understandable fondness for my former avocation was too blatantly invoked. In this matter of Hitler's invitation, the purpose was clear and it displeased me. And events were soon to prove how well founded my forebodings had been.

The journey, on which I set out with a considerable retinue in my special train on August 21st, had been arranged with all possible circumspection from the German side. The heavy cruiser was originally going to be named *Tegetthoff* apparently to stress the Austro-Hungarian traditon. After glancing through the proposed programme, I pointed out that to name the ship after the victor of the naval battle of Lissa might well be taken amiss by Germany's Italian friends, whereupon the name of the Prince of Savoy, *Prince Eugen*[8], was chosen. On the other hand, the Germans feared that I might take offence at the words of the bass singer in Lohengrin, the opera I had selected for the gala performance: "Oh Lord, protect us from the wrath of the Magyars!"

I put Baron Dörnberg's[9] mind at rest, he being the master of ceremonies. I knew the passage in question. As a sincere lover of Wagner, if I had not chosen Lohengrin on that account, I could not pretend to myself that I would be sorry to hear of a time when Hungary's might was greater than it was at that moment.

When our special train, which Baron Dörnberg had joined in Vienna, arrived at Kiel in the morning of August 22nd, Hitler received us. He handed my wife a large bouquet of lilies of the valley, a remarkable attention as these were my wife's favourite flowers and a rarity at that time of the year. Our rooms and the banquet tables were adorned at all times with a profusion of flowers. In Berlin, my wife, who is a Roman Catholic, was given a prayer-stool and a crucifix in her room.

The weather was glorious as we entered the open cars at Kiel and drove to the

8   Liberator of Hungary from the Turks. He recaptured the fort of Buda in 1686.

9   Baron Alexander von Dörnberg (1901-1983), Chief of Protocol of the German Foreign Ministry.

Germania yard, my wife in the car of Grand-Admiral Raeder[10], I in Hitler's. High above us towered the proud ship, elegant and strong, a fine example of modern shipbuilding, which owed much in ingenuity to the limitations imposed by the Allies on the German Navy. We mounted the tribune, my wife pronounced the words, "I christen you Prince Eugen," and pressed the electric switch, releasing the bottle of champagne which shattered against the bows. With well-directed hammer-blows, workmen knocked away the last supports, the last ropes were severed. Majestically, the *Prinz Eugen* moved down the ways, slowly at first, then gathering speed through the foaming water[11].

After the christening ceremony, Hitler showed me over the Germania yard, which was alive with activity. He laid particular stress on the fact that we two heads of states were mingling so peacefully with the workers. He seemed to think this remarkable, perhaps because dictators have special reasons for distrusting people. I am, however, only too ready to affirm that these north-German workers, strong and tall, gave us the most friendly greetings.

My wife, meanwhile, accompanied by a party of ladies and several other guests, had gone on board the elegant Hapag liner *Patria*. Hitler and I went on board the control vessel *Grille,* which Hitler used for his sea trips. At luncheon, Grand-Admiral Raeder made a short speech in which he referred very flatteringly to my career as a commanding Admiral and gave the assurance "that the German Navy would at all times safeguard and follow the great traditions of the Austro- Hungarian Navy". In the sense of this tradition, the German Navy has certainly proved its bravery.

10 Grand Adm. Erich Raeder (1876-1960).Appointed to command the German navy in 1928, he secretly rebuilt it in violation of the Treaty of Versailles. During the war he disagreed with Hitler's policies and was replaced by Admiral Dönitz. He was sentenced to life in prison in Nuremberg but was released in 1955.

11 The ship's timorous military career ended when on February 21, 1942, -off Trondheim, on her way to raid the Murmansk convoys-, the British submarine *Trident* (Capt. G. M. Sladen) torpedoed her, blowing off her rudder and thirthy feet of her stern. The ship limped back to Germany for eight months of repairs, after which she was converted into a training ship and did not again leave the Baltic. (Clay Blair: *Hitler's U-Boat War,* New York: Random House, 1996, pp.487.)

During the torpedo-boat and artillery manoeuvres on the Baltic, use was made of the target-vessel *Zähringen*, steered by remote control. The naval review that was held displayed the surprising number of vessels possessed by Germany, considering the short space of time she had had to build up her fleet.

On the return voyage to Kiel, Hitler asked me for a private conversation. Two years had passed since our talk at the Obersalzberg, and those two years had wrought a great change in Hitler. He was behaving as the master of Europe as he explained with few preliminaries his plan to absorb Czechoslovakia, which later became known by its code name: Plan Green. His aim was to smash the Czechs, as he put it, destroying Prague if necessary, and to make Czechoslovakia a German protectorate. He was fully resolved on war, and he tried to persuade me to pledge the Hungarians to march into Slovakia from the south as the Germans entered Czechoslovakia[12]. He gave me to understand that as a reward we should be allowed to keep the territory we had invaded. This project was put in the form of a request, and I replied with all courtesy but with great firmness that there could be no possibility of Hungarian participation. Hungary had, of course, revisionist claims on Czechoslovakia, I added, but it was our wish and intention to press those claims by peaceful means. I pointed out that, in any case, our restricted forces were not strong enough to overrun the fortifications that had been erected along our borders[13]. "We'll provide you with the arms," Hitler interrupted. But I adhered to my refusal and even warned him against the risk of a major war, as, in my opinion, the chances were that neither England nor France, nor even Soviet Russia, would passively watch a German entry into Czechoslovakia.

The friendly mood of the morning had evaporated; our conversation ended on a rather unpleasant note. A conversation, similar to that between myself and Hitler, was held between Ribbentrop, Imrédy and Kánya, during which the significant words, "If you want to join in the meal, you must help with the

12 Contemporaries' memoirs claim that Hitler suggested that Hungary attack Czechoslovakia first, and than ask Germany for military assistance. Hitler hoped that this would not have drawn the ire of the Western Powers. Horthy's resolute refusal irked Hitler. (Bokor, P.: *Endplay by the Danube*, Budapest: RTV-Minerva, 1982. p. 253: TV interview with general Kálmán Hardy (1892-1980) relative of Mrs. Horthy. In Hung.)

13 Both Rumania and Czechoslovakia constructed a line of concrete bunkers and other fortifications along Hungary's borders by this time.

cooking," were spoken. Herr von Weizsäcker, who was present at this conversation, made a note at the time that the answer of the Hungarians had "raised objections". Indeed, our Premier and our Foreign Minister refused, just as I had, to consider military co-operation. The Germans were also annoyed about certain discussions that were being held at the time between Hungary and the states of the Little Entente[14]. The provisional results of these had been simultaneously published in Budapest and in a communiqué concerning the Council meeting of the Little Entente held at Bled on August 21st and 22nd under the chairmanship of the Yugoslav Prime Minister, Dr. Milan Stojadinovic[15]. In this statement, both sides had declared themselves averse to violence in their mutual relations, while Hungary's right to re-arm had been fully recognized. Ribbentrop regarded this as an act of withdrawal on Hungary's part from the German policy towards Czechoslovakia. In a sense this was true, for we had no desire whatever to engage in warfare. Kánya had considerable difficulty in calming the extremely excited German Foreign Minister.

I took pains, while I was on board the *Grille,* to make my attitude clear to General Field Marshal von Brauchitsch[16], who gave me the impression that he fully understood my position. What I did not know, and what von Brauchitsch naturally did not tell me, was that the German military leaders, headed by Major-General Beck[17], were conspiring to arrest Hitler and his immediate collaborators if the Fuehrer allowed the Sudeten question to lead to war. The British, as far as I have been able to learn since, were aware of this in September.

14 As Foreign Minister Kánya has just before signed an agreement of non-belligerence with the Little Entente (Czechoslovakia, Rumania, and Yugoslavia), after very long negotiations at Bled, Horthy was in firm position to reject the proposal. (P. Pritz: Conditional Bridge Party in Dachau, Népszabadság, Nov. 25, 1995.)

15 Milan Stojadinovich (1888-1961).

16 Walther von Brauchitsch (1881-1948), Commander of the German Land Forces.

17 General Ludwig Beck (1880-1944). He was a highly cultivated career soldier who opposed Hitler's aggressive policies, and his attempts to destroy the independence of the army. In 1938 he retired in protest against the planned attack of Czechoslovakia. Implicated as one of the leaders of the failed attempt to kill Hitler, he was executed by the Nazis in 1944.

We spent that night aboard the *Grille*; the next day we went over to the *Patria*, which sailed through the Kaiser Wilhelm Canal to Helgoland, where Admiral Tegetthoff had fought a superior Danish fleet in the war of 1864. Inscribed on the base of the monument erected to his memory that was transported from Pola to Graz after the First World War are the words:

> *By battle bravely joined off Helgoland,*
>
> *By glorious victory at Lissa,*
>
> *He won immortal fame*
>
> *For himself and Austria's Navy.*

We inspected the island's new fortifications and also visited its famous aquarium. The Helgolanders in their gay costume entertained us with folk dances. As lobster-culture is an important part of the island economy, my wife was offered a gigantic specimen on a silver dish.

During the cruise to Hamburg, the entertainment provided for us was magnificent. The pianist, Elly Ney[18], and the cello-player, Hoelscher[19], gave two excellent recitals. The band of the former Hungarian officer, Barnabás von Géczy, played dance music on board. According to the original programme, it was not intended that we should go over to the *Patria* before the evening. Apparently, my "no" to Hitler had effected the change in arrangements, to the consternation of the wretched master of ceremonies. I noticed, however, that Hitler, contrary to his usual practice, spent the whole evening amid the merrymaking throng, after having had dinner with my wife and myself at a special table. He, of course, was served with vegetarian dishes. Our conversation ran mainly on music. Hitler said that the days of the Wagner Festival were his only time of relaxation, and he invited us to visit Bayreuth. As nearly all the members of the German Government, the leading military figures and several of the diplomats, including the Italian Ambassador Attolico[20], were on board the *Patria,* there were many easy opportunites for discussion.

18 Noted German pianist Elly Ney (1882-1968).

19 Celloist Ludwig Hölscher (1907- ?)

20 Bernardo Attolico (1880-1942).

The old Hanseatic city of Hamburg, which we toured before the luncheon held at the Town Hall, delighted us with its combination of rustic beauty, natural elegance and industrial activity. On the journey to Berlin, Hitler repeated the manoeuvre he had employed on the occasion of Mussolini's visit. He saw us off at the railway station in Hamburg, and, by some clever shunting, contrived to reach Berlin some three minutes before our train drew in, so that there he was on the platform, welcoming us on our arrival. I was fascinated by the mobile chancellery coach and the news-van attached to his private train which I saw as it overtook us. To Hitler's considerable annoyance, the Czech and Rumanian Ministers had also come to meet us as a result of the rapprochement induced by the recent statement of Bled. This caused the Fuehrer to give the innocent master of ceremonies, Baron Dörnberg, a ferocious dressing down.

In Berlin, we were the last guests to be received in the old Palace of the Reich's President in the Wilhelmstrasse, one wing of which was then occupied by Meissner[21], the Minister of State. The building was earmarked for Ribbentrop, who contended that it was 'naturally' too cramped for him and had two new wings added. In his toast at the banquet given in the new Chancellery, Hitler declared that the Hungarian and the German peoples are at last near to reach "their final historical frontiers". He declared, similarly, shortly afterwards at Munich that Germany's last territorial claims had been satisfied by the acquisition of the Sudetenland. I had expressed my thanks for our reception while on board the *Grille*. I had added the civil warning that the destructive activity of a typhoon could not be stayed by calling it "an abnormal atmospheric depression". In Berlin, I emphasized our wish "to continue our work of peaceful reconstruction". Hitler's behaviour on that evening led the guests to understand that he was anything but satisfied with the results of our visit.

The military parade in my honour in Berlin on August 25th was the largest that had hitherto been held. The number of armoured cars, and they were not made of *papier mache*, the tanks and motorized artillery taking part, which lasted two and a half hours, seemed endless. Troops and armaments were amazingly impressive. As my eye fell on the tribune on which stood diplomats and military attachés, I had a feeling that the grandiose spectacle Hitler had orgarized was not failing in its objective.

21 Otto Meissner (1880-1953).

In the afternoon, I had my second private talk with Hitler. It not only failed to dispel the tension created by our first talk, it aggravated it. In a manner that I considered quite unwarranted, he asserted that I should not have discussed his plan, and my definite refusal to cooperate, with General Field Marshal Brauchitsch. I emphatically refused to accept his rebuke and declared that it was my custom to decide for myself to whom I spoke and of what I spoke. Moderating his tone, Hitler then insisted that the Generals had no say in any matter; he alone made decisions. I replied that I considered that a truly dangerous policy. Hitler than changed the subject, but our conversation remained uncomfortable.

I do not know whether Hitler noticed the line about "the wrath of the Magyars" in the opera that night. We, for our part, thoroughly enjoyed the performance of Lohengrin. The following day, we visited Potsdam and the tomb of the great King of Prussia, whose name Hitler so frequently invoked, though he had very little of the self-control and strategic genius of the philosopher of Sans-Souci.

To emphasize his exceptional position, Hermann Göring[22] had not put in an appearance before we arrived in Berlin. when he invited us to be his guests at Karinhall. Hitler had already told us about the breeding of aurochs[23] and wild horses on the Schorf Heath. He had added with a laugh that he would not be surprised if 'Hermann' were not one day to set about breeding a strain of Ancient Germans there. The Ancient German idea seemed to have captivated Göring. Not only did he himself receive us clad in an 'Ancient German' hunting costume complete except for the bearskin, but even his menservants and his maids were garbed similarly. Our host changed his attire at least twice, down to bangles and jewellery. As he welcomed us to his 'home', he added in the same breath, "and all you can see belongs to me".

We wondered why he should have to tell us that.

In spite of his many eccentricities, and the blatant luxury with which he surrounded himself, Göring had several conciliatory characteristics; I remember him lifting his little daughter Edda out of her cradle and swinging her proudly over his head. He also knew something about hunting and game,

22 Field Marshal Hermann Wilhelm Goering (1893-1946), commander of the German Luftwaffe.

23 Extinct European wild ox.

which was why I was pleased to accept his invitation to an elk-hunt to be held in September in East Prussia. An ardent huntsman, I was enthusiastic about the hunting laws he had inspired. The last leader of the Richthofen fighter squadron, wearer of the *Pour le Merite*, he was of all Hitler's immediate entourage the one whom foreigners would find most accessible. I am reminded of von Weizsäcker's remark, "the official world of the Third Reich remained utterly alien to me and I disliked all contact with it".

This alien quality was very much to the fore during our visit to Nuremberg, where, on the last day of our stay, we were shown the Party Conference Grounds. The ancient city, with its memories of Dürer and Hans Sachs, and the splendid castle of the Hohenzollerns, pleased us very much. But we felt out of sympathy with the mountain of stone which constituted the Party Buildings. We were told that more stone was used in their construction than for the Pyramids. We were taken over the Hall of the Fifty Thousand, which was then under construction, and Herr Himmler[24] explained that this was where the leading party members gathered annually to hear the Fuehrer's great speech. My wife could not resist asking, "I suppose this then is where they make their reports and put their requests?" "Certainly not," Himmler replied. "Only one person speaks here: the Fuehrer." My wife went on to voice her surprise that so vast and costly a building should have been built for a single annual event. Himmler, plainly disgusted by her failure to appreciate the greatness of the Fuehrer, expressed his opinion by giving her a contemptuous glance.

That night we boarded our private train and went home. If Hitler's intention was to impress us by so lavish a display of entertainments and festivities, tours and presents, he had certainly succeeded, but in a way that he could not have envisaged. The incredible achievements of the few years since 1933, the industry, discipline and ability displayed by the German people could only be admired. Factory chimneys were smoking, shipbuilding yards were ringing with the sound of multitudinous hammers, and in the fields the farmers were toiling at gathering in the harvest. But the overall picture was too feverish, the total impression filled the beholder with forebodings. He could not refrain from asking himself, "To what is all this leading?" It strengthened my determination to prevent Hungary from being engulfed in the vortex of

24 Heinrich Himmler (1900-1945), German Minister of the Interior, SS leader. Under his personal direction the Nazi death camps were built. He committed suicide in a British prison in 1945.

National-Socialist dynamism. Hitler might want Lebensraum, but we Hungarians were not prepared to render up our country as part of it.

Yet Hungary, I hear the critics murmur, has had her share of the spoils of the Munich Agreement and even, in the wake of the Germans, of the partition of Czechoslovakia. John Wheeler-Bennett[25] has gone so far as to accuse us, and Poland, of playing the part of a jackal. Sir Winston Churchill, in the first volume of his '*The Second World War*', gives an account of my talks with Hitler which is contrary to fact. He gives the reader to understand that it was I who insisted and Hitler who hesitated. Also, he puts forward the view that we were prepared to help with the cooking in order to share the meal.

The truth, however, was very different. I will make a long story of negotiations as brief as possible. Our agreements with the Little Entente states had, as I have said, been contingent on their giving us satisfactory guarantees for our minorities in their territories. To this effect, we then, at the same time as the Poles, demanded through our Minister in Prague, on September 21st, rights for the Magyars within Czechoslovakia equivalent to the rights granted the Sudeten Germans. Earlier we had been forced to protest, on the 16th of that month, against the military measures being taken along the Hungarian frontier. We had received no replies to our Notes. On the contrary. Since my return from Germany, conditions in the Hungarian areas of Czechoslovakia had deteriorated. Clashes and incidents were becoming more frequent. A suspicious aeroplane with Hungarian markings which was flying over a prohibited military area was forced down by our artillery and proved to be manned by Czechs. Thereupon, just before the Munich Conference, we immediately approached the two nations who were friendly to us, Italy and Germany, with the request that the discussions should also review the well-known claims made by Hungary at Trianon. We did this, not to gain a prize, but to assert our rights. The truth of this has been endorsed by Hugh Seton-Watson, the son of the well-known Slavophile Robert Seton-Watson[26].

25 British historian John Wheeler-Bennett (1902-1975)

26 Writing under the pen-name of *Scotus Viator,* Robert William Seton-Watson (1879-1951), a British journalist and historian, carried on a one-man crusade in the British press before and during World War 1 toward the dissolution of the Austro-Hungarian empire. He had a significant role in influencing the British public opinion in favor of dissolving the Monarch and partitioning Hungary. The anti-Hungarian propaganda emanating from the Successor States still, in the 1990's, rely on his books as references. Horthy's restraint of showing any rancor is quite admirable.

Count Csáky[27], the Chief of the Cabinet of our Foreign Minister, Kánya, was sent to Munich; he was received neither by Hitler nor by Ribbentrop. This was clearly the result of my attitude at Kiel. He was, however, able to talk with Count Ciano. As a result of that Mussolini demanded and achieved at the conference of the four powers that the Hungarian question should be dealt with and that the Prague Government should be instructed to come to terms with the Hungarian Government. Should no agreement be reached by direct negotiations, the Big Four would again take up the matter.

The latter alternative proved necessary. The negotiations which opened early in October soon reached deadlock although we proposed a plebiscite to solve the problem of allegiance. We should have preferred a question of this nature to be solved by amicable means as it ought to be between neighbours, but when Father Tiso[28] insisted, in the name of the Prague Government, in submitting the dispute to Germany and Italy, we agreed. We should, after the Munich decisions, have preferred to adhere to the original proposal that the four signatory powers should solve the problem. However, after the Slovak proposal had been made, this would have seemed a slight to Germany, a contingency that our Premier, Imrédy, wished to avoid at all costs.

A point that cannot be proven is whether Hitler would have awarded us the whole of Slovakia had we agreed to the proposal he made at Kiel. It seems likely, however, that the thought of an independent Slovak state occurred to him only after our talks. In Vienna, Kánya, our Foreign Minister, with Paul Teleki, our most eminent geographer, who had previously been Prime Minister and was to be Prime Minister again, watched our interests. The Czech interests were looked after by Chavalkovsky[29], the Czech Foreign Minister. On the ethnographical maps that had been prepared, new frontiers were drawn by Ribbentrop and Ciano, and on November 2nd their arbitration, by which part of the former Upper Hungary was re-united to its fatherland, was made known. In the official text of this arbitration statement, which was agreed to in the minutes signed by the four Foreign Ministers, the

27 Count István Csáky (1894-1941), to be prime minister later.

28 Roman Catholic priest, Jozef Tiso (1887-1947) became president of Nazi Slovakia. He was executed after the war. Apparently he was rehabilitated after the break-up of Czechoslovakia, his picture is prominently displayed on Slovak official functions.

29 Frantisek Chavalkovsky (1875- ?).

words Czechoslovakia and Czechoslovak were hyphenated, which cannot have been accidental.

Here it must also be recorded that, after the conclusion of the Munich settlement, the German Government claimed from Czechoslovakia the bridgehead at Pozsony (Bratislava; Pressburg), i.e. the village of Ligetfalu (Engerau) and its environs, south of the Danube. Regardless of the fact that this area belonged to Hungary prior to 1920 and that its population was purely Hungarian, Ligetfalu and the surrounding district were incorporated into the Third Reich even before the Vienna Accord. This action on the part of the German Government very understandably caused Hitler to lose much of his popularity in Hungary.

Even though Pozsony, with its large population of Hungarian inhabitants, was lost, still November 2nd was a great and significant day to the Hungarian nation. The average Hungarian was ignorant of the prehistory and background of the settlement. They were ignorant too of the appalling bad taste with which a day that decided the fate of so many thousands ended: the uproarious feasting on the Coblenz above Vienna and the pheasant shoot in the Wiener Wald.

I issued a proclamation addressed to the people who were again united to their fatherland:

"You are once more free. The days of sorrow and tribulation are past. Your sufferings, your unshakable determination and our common struggle have brought victory in a just cause. Once again the light of glory shines upon you from the Holy Crown. Once again you are sharers of our common fate of a thousand bygone years. The Hungarian fatherland has awaited your return with confidence. The Royal Hungarian Army is the first to set foot on the national soil that has now been freed from subjection. With deep affection we welcome all national groups in these areas, that they may rejoice with us and participate in the feast of liberation. May order, peace and honest endeavour prevail. Make no mistake: the eyes of the whole world are fixed upon you. May God bless our Fatherland!"

On November 6th, at the head of my troops, I crossed the Danube bridge at Komárom. On November 11th, I made my entry into Kassa. It was my experience to see the joy, often awkwardly expressed, of those two towns. As I passed along the roads, people embraced one another, fell upon their knees,

201

weeped with joy because liberation had come to them at last, without war, without bloodshed.

At Kassa, a huge triumphal arch had been erected, and our hussars, who were at the head of the procession, were carried away by their excitement. At gallop they rode across the frontier which was no longer a frontier. The old historic town had probably never before seen so vast a concourse of people. From near and far, even from Budapest, thousands of people had come together. It truly was the "laughing happiness of a nation which hitherto had been treated unfairly and had been plunged into despair", as Lord Rothermere declared. He had hastened over from London to see with his own eyes the outcome of the policy he had been so insistently advocating in his Daily Mail since 1927. Of the many orators, I shall name only Count John Esterházy[30], the leader of the Magyars in Czechoslovakia, who had courageously and selflessly defended the rights of his fellow countrymen. I replied to his speech first in Hungarian and then in Slovak, assuring our new Slovak-speaking citizens[31] that they would have no reason to regret the change of rulership. After the parade, in which former Czechoslovak soldiers in their old uniforms took part, a solemn Te Deum was sung in the ancient Cathedral. After that, I laid a wreath on the tomb of the hero of liberty, Francis Rákóczi[32].

A few months after the entry into Kassa, the Czechoslovak 'appendix', as Mussolini had called sub-Carpathian Ruthenia, was surgically removed. This narrow strip of land, inhabited preponderantly by Ruthenes of the Greek Catholic faith infiltrating from the northern slopes of the Carpathians, had been given to the newly created Czechoslovak state by the Treaty of Trianon in 1920 to make possible a direct railway link between Czechoslovakia and Rumania. It completed the encirclement of Hungary, thereby preventing her from having a common frontier with Poland. The Peace Conference had instructed the Prague Government to create an autonomous region with a

30 Count János Esterházy (1901-1957), spent many years in a Soviet prison, then returned to Czechoslovakia, died in prison there.

31 Traditionally, there was no enmity between Slovaks and Magyars. During the 1848-49 Revolution tens of thousands of Slovak miners and students fought valiantly in the Hungarian army. Austrian attempts to recruit Slovaks against Hungary were utter failures.

32 Prince Ferenc Rákóczi II (1676-1735) leader of the last major anti-Habsburg rebellion in Hungary. He died in Turkish exile and was reburied in Kassa, his favorite town, in 1906.

Parliament of its own, but Prague had ignored this charge. After the Second World War[33], Prague 'presented' Ruthenia to its Communist ally, although that territory had never belonged to Russia and the Soviet Union had declared itself in the Atlantic Charter averse to territorial expansion. The population was given no opportunity to express its own preference. When, earlier, we had announced our claim to Ruthenia as territory that had at one time belonged to the Crown of St. Stephen, we met with scant sympathy in Berlin. The possibility of a common Hungarian-Polish frontier conjured up unpleasant visions before the politicians and the German General Staff. After the Munich Agreement, conditions became increasingly anarchic in Ruthenia. The Prague Government found itself under the necessity of sending General Prchala[34] there, in January, 1939, to re-establish order. He did not succeed in doing so. On January 6th, a well-organized attack was made on the border town of Munkács, which had been returned to Hungary by the Vienna Accord. On February 28th, the town of Ungvár was attacked. Hungary could not remain inactive while irresponsible elements such as the Szics Guard[35] endangered the safety of her borders. The problem became acute when Hitler marched into Prague and Slovakia was declared an independent state. If the Prague Government had been unable to keep order, then the government of an independent Slovakia would certainly be in no position to do so. Since part of the area had for some months been re-united to Hungary, Ruthenia no longer had railway links with Slovakia and Prague, and even by road it was difficult to reach from Slovakia. It was no longer possible to submit the question to the arbitration of the signatories of the Munich Agreement, as that agreement had been torn up by Hitler. Our government, therefore, presented the government at Pozsony (Bratislava) with a twelve-hour ultimatum on March 14th, the day of the proclamation of Slovak independence, demanding that Ruthenia be forthwith evacuated. Pozsony submitted to the ultimatum and our troops occupied Ruthenia. Berlin had by now lifted its veto. It was of the utmost importance to us to avoid German encirclement by establishing a common Hungarian-Polish frontier.

33 June 29, 1945.

34 Czech general Lev Prchala (1892- ?).

35 Armed contingent of the Ruthene nationalist 'Ukranian National Party' in autonomous Ruthenia. Fr. Voloshin, Ruthenian leader's Sic Guard "made
trouble for anyone or anything considered Czech, Polish, Jewish or Magyar
in origin." Quote from: Alan Palmer: The Lands Between, a History of East
Central Europe since the Congress of Vienna, New York: Macmillan, 1970.

Looking back on that chequered year of 1938, we can clearly see the main lines of future events. Neither Munich nor the creation of a protectorate of Bohemia-Moravia had been the last of Hitler's claims. On the contrary, the Anschluss, the seizure of the Sudeten areas, and the occupation of Prague were well-planned preparations for the next and again the next step. The smaller states could but wait for the next blow to fall: either on Poland or on the Soviet Union, both being Hitler's eventual targets.

They had to wait, possessed of only one conviction: that it was in no way possible to halt the course of events.

16. The Second World War; Hungary's Non-Belligerence

The politics and attitude of Hungary in the Second World War can be understood only if sufficient weight is given to the fact that conditions differed fundamentally from those existing in 1914. In the earlier war, the anger roused by the infamous assassination of the heir to the throne, Archduke Francis Ferdinand, and the Russian inspired conspiracies aiming at the destruction of the Austro-Hungarian Monarchy was so great that it left no room for doubt that the Austro-Hungarian Monarchy was justified in taking energetic defensive measures. Recalled from my position as aide-de-camp, I had rejoined the fleet, fully convinced that war was inevitable, and that it was a defensive war, as we had been challenged without provocation. Our alliance with Germany had come into being decades before 1914, so that a strong comradeship existed between the Austro-Hungarian and German armies and navies.

Hitler's entry into Poland could, from no point of view, be called 'defensive', even if the frontiers established by Versailles were admitted to be unjust and in need of revision. I had clearly stated this during my visit to Cracow and Warsaw. The Russian threat which had played so great a part in 1914 was admittedly even more menacing in 1939. However, Hitler was not waging war against the Soviet Union. On the contrary, in August, 1939, he had concluded his notorious pact with Stalin, that caused utmost consternation in Hungary.

Yet perhaps more important was the change that affected political and psychological relations between Hungary and Germany. The First World War, which they had both lost, the Treaties of Versailles and Trianon, had admittedly engendered certain similarities in the views of both countries. But Hungary and Germany had reacted differently to defeat. Opposition in Hungary was directed against the countries of the Little Entente, not against the Great Powers, from whom Hungary was hoping to obtain rectification of injustices. The Germans, on the other hand, saw in the Great Powers their oppressors.

Apart from this, the friends of Germany in Hungary, among whom I counted myself, even though I refused to relinquish the right to maintain friendly relations with other countries, had to distinguish between 'Germany' and the 'Third Reich'. The pseudo-philosophy of the National Socialists and the methods of Hitler were profoundly repugnant to me. This feeling was enhanced by the infiltration of Nazi ideology into Hungarian politics, leading to the formation of a political party[1] which aimed at the overthrow of our traditional political structure.

The Germany of Bismarck and the Germany of Emperor Wilhelm II had never attempted to assail our liberty and our independence. Hitler and his followers never hid their opinion that Hungary constituted part of the German *Lebensraum*. That we adhered strictly to constitutional and parliamentary institutions, that we did not indulge in the madness of racial theory, that we did not wish to leave our Polish friends in the lurch when they were in trouble, and that we had many friendly ties, even family ties, binding us to the British and the Americans, all these were heinous crimes in Hitler's eyes. The matter was all the more complicated by the policy of the Western powers, which, by saddling us with the Treaty of Trianon had placed us in an untenable position, nationally, economically and politically. Even after the first Vienna Accord, millions of our countrymen were still living in territories outside our borders. Our concern with their fate was a matter of self-preservation. Without our intervention, the conditions under which they lived would have become more and more restricted.

Also, I must stress that there never was an alliance between Hungary and the German Reich comparable to the Triple Alliance[2] between Germany, Austria-Hungary and Italy, or to the German-Italian Steel Pact[3]. The Three Power Pact which Hungary joined on November 20th, 1940, obliged her only to render assistance if one of the signatories were attacked by a power not belligerent at the time of signing.

1   The Arrow Cross Party, established on October 16, 1937. There were several other Nazi parties in Hungary. To limit their influence, Interior Minister Ferenc Keresztes-Fisher issued an executive order (No. 3844/1938) on June 24, 1938 forbidding civil servants, and employees of state owned companies, to hold membership in eleven Nazi organizations.

2   The Rome Pact, signed on March 23, 1936.

3   "Pact of Steel", German-Italian Friendship Treaty, May 22, 1939.

Last, but not least, the following points must be taken into account. For geo-political and economic reasons, Hungary was a necessary factor in Hitler's warfare. The manner in which Hitler dealt with countries whose railways or raw materials he needed, or whose territories he wanted, not necessarily for immediate military purposes but to prevent them falling into other hands, was shown in the cases of Denmark, Norway, Holland and Belgium. On the other hand, we had also seen that the guarantees given by Great Britain to Poland, Rumania and Greece were of no practical value. We lacked a fulcrum on which to rest a policy other than a purely realistic one.

It is easily said that we should have preferred to engage in a hopeless struggle rather than to submit to Hitler's demands, and such a view reads well on paper. In fact, it is total nonsense. An individual can commit suicide, a whole nation cannot. For Hungary's tragedy was that, for the first time in her history, she saw herself simultaneously threatened on all sides. And the fate that overtook the Hungarians, who, as has been confirmed by subsequent events, made a correct estimate of the Communist peril, was the same as that which overtook those who allowed themselves to be misled into sharing Roosevelt's illusion that the Soviet Union was developing into a "peace-loving democracy" and would, after the war, collaborate loyally and peacefully with the Western powers[4].

I have pondered a great deal upon the policy we followed during the war. I have not lacked opportunities for meditation, first while under German arrest, then while in an American camp and finally while in exile. I cannot see how fundamentally we could have acted differently. No one in his senses can deny that our fate would in any case have been the same; Poles and Czechs have fared no differently from Hungarians, Rumanians and Bulgarians, whichever side they chose in Hitler's war.

The 'misunderstanding', to call it that, between Hungary and Germany became apparent in the early days of 1939.

The dissolution of Czechoslovakia had been made inevitable when Hitler neutralized the external forces supporting the Prague Government. The root of the matter is to be found in the false idea of Czechoslovakia as a national

4   Horthy's view on this matter was fully corroborated forty years later in *"FDR & Stalin, a Not So Grand Alliance, 1943-1945"* by Amos Perlmutter (Univ. of Missouri Press, 1993.)

state. She was, rather, a state of several nationalities in which all non-Czechs (with the exception of the Slovaks) had fewer rights than the same nationalities had had in the Austro-Hungarian monarchy. The Hungarian question had been dealt with at the Munich Conference and a solution found that was the logical outcome of the exposure of the fallacy. We could therefore not accept the view that we had 'a bill to pay' for the Vienna Accord, as was the unabashed suggestion of the semi-official German 'Diplomatic-Political Information Service'. In a statement made on January 20th, 1939, it made an attack on "supporters of the Volksfront, Jews, reactionaries, and other malcontents" in Hungary, which was an unjustified interference in our domestic politics. The fact that this occurred after the visit to Berlin of Csáky, our Foreign Minister, to sign the Anti-Comintern Pact, was a bad omen.

The express mention of Jews in the '*Korrespondenz*' issuing from the Wilhelmstrasse leads me to make some comments on the Jewish question, which was becoming the touchstone of friendship in Hitler's foreign relations. The relatively strong Jewish element in Hungary was a particular thorn in his flesh, especially as many Jews were eminent in Hungarian finance, commerce and industry, in the press and in the professions. Of course, the bourgeois middle classes cherished a feeling of resentment that the executive posts and the offices in the liberal professions most in demand were in Jewish hands. The Jews supported each other with the solidarity of their race and earned more than twenty-five percent of the national income. After the First World War, there had been a wave of open anti-Semitism in Hungary. Even writers with left-wing sympathies have pointed out that nine-tenths of the higher positions of Béla Kun's regime were filled by Jews. It was, therefore, humanly understandable that the crimes of the Communists were attributed to the Jews. But the innate Hungarian sense of fairness and justice, strengthened by the efforts of both Catholic and Protestant Churches to suppress all forms of racial prejudice, soon re-established good relations between Jews and non-Jews.

After the Austrian Anschluss, German pressure was brought to bear yet more heavily on us. The government decided to allay German insistence. The preparation of legislation circumscribing the civic rights of Jewish citizens, in itself a protection, was put into the hands of Dr. Béla Imrédy, former Minister of Finance and later President of the National Bank. On account of his work in the economic section of the League of Nations, he was on particularly good terms with the British and the Americans. Moreover, as a financier, had close connections with Jewish circles. This law, which was passed by Parliament in April, 1938, while the Darányi Government was still in power, differed fundamentally from the Nuremberg laws in that it was based on religion and not on racial origin. Jews who had been baptized before 1919 or who had fought in the First World War were not affected by the law. The law introduced a *numerus clausus* (quota) of twenty per cent for the employment of Jews in certain occupations[5]. This was not to take immediate effect; the purpose of the law was that banks, limited companies, etc., should be given five years in which to comply with the terms of the law, the authors of which, with Darányi, the Prime Minister, reckoning that general conditions were likely to be radically altered before 1943. The *numerus clausus* put no restrictions on the independent activities of Jews in commercial life.

To my regret, premier Darányi, whose health was failing, had to ask to be relieved of his office. For reasons for which to this day I have no satisfactory explanation, after becoming Premier in 1938, his successor Imrédy, hitherto Anglophile and by no means anti-Semitic, changed into a rabid anti-Semite and became an advocate of the German political theories. Did he think he could only retain his position if he made sure of German support? The violence of the German reaction to the interview he gave to the *Daily Telegraph*, in which he proudly stressed the fact that we had not yielded to Hitler's wishes on the occasion of my visit to Germany, must have made a deep impression on him.

Imrédy's appointment was generally welcomed. Congratulatory telegrams poured in, even from England. His predecessor, Darányi, had been a rather colourless personality. Much was expected of the new man whom Sir Montagu Norman[6], the Governor of the Bank of England, had called one of the ablest of European financiers. My visit to Germany and the first Vienna Accord, by which areas inhabited by Hungarians had been returned to

5   "Despite the fact that Jews represented only 6 % of the population of Hungary, by the early twentieth century they had achieved a dominant position in Hungarian banking and industry and a leading role in such fields as medicine (59.9 % of doctors), law (50.6 %), journalism (34.3 %), engineering (39.2 %), and music (26.6 %)." (Ezra Mendelsohn: *The Jews of East Central Europe between the World Wars*, Bloomington: Univ. of Indiana, 1983, pp. 100-102.)

6   Sir Montagu Collet Norman (1871-1950) was governor of the Bank of England for an unprecedented twenty-four years. He was a strong proponent of the gold standard.

Hungary, seemed to justify these expectations in the eyes of the world. In reality, however, it was soon apparent that our views often differed. When, therefore, in December, without having previously consulted me, he introduced new legislation concerning the Jews, in which not only was the *numerus clausus* reduced from twenty per cent to six per cent but the race[7] principle replaced the criterion of religion. His propose roused strong opposition, and I began to seek a suitable opportunity for dismissing Imrédy[8].

I did not have to wait long. In February, 1939, Count Bethlen informed me that a Budapest newspaper was about to publish proofs that a great-grandfather of Imrédy was of Jewish descent. Wishing to avoid a scandal, I called Imrédy to the Palace and showed him the document, which had been procured in Czechoslovakia. I asked him whether the information contained in it was true. He was upset to the point of collapse and immediately asked me to accept his resignation. It is more than likely that he himself was uncertain about his ancestry; since the publication of the original edition of this book, documents have been submitted to me which cast considerable doubt on the Jewish descent of even this one great-grandfather. In any case, neither the choice of Imrédy as Prime Minister nor later his dismissal was based on his ancestry. It was, I repeat, not his hypothetical Jewish strain that led me to accept his resignation but his rabid anti-Semitism.[9]

Our interview took place on February 12th, 1939. On the 16th, Count Paul Teleki was appointed his successor; he was one of the noblest and most outstanding personalities in Hungarian politics.

The elections, which were held in May, 1939, during his term of office, gave the Government Party, then known as the Hungarian Life Party, 183 out of 260 seats; twelve more, that is, than in the 1935 elections. But, for the first time the Arrow-Cross Party gained seats to the number of thirty-one, and representatives of other smaller National-Socialist parties were also elected.

8   Imrédy would have approved affirmative action programs and quotas on overqualified Asian-American students at some of America's elite campuses.

9   "Horthy, who disliked Imrédy personally and who always insisted that there were good Hungarians who happened to be Jewish, seized the opportunity to force Imrédy's resignation" page 237 of Alan Palmer: *The Lands Between - A History of East Central Europe since the Congress of Vienna*, New York: Macmillan, 1970.

The Arrow-Cross men were later to play a fateful part in Hungarian politics. Their leader, Ferenc Szálasi[9], of mixed Armenian, Slovak and German descent, he had one Magyar grandparent, was a man given to mystical fanaticism. A certain intelligence and strength of will power cannot be denied; from simple origins he had passed through the military academy and risen to the ranks of the General Staff. On account of his political activities, however, he had been dismissed from the Army and later had been sentenced by a properly constituted tribunal to several years' imprisonment. This was to have an effect on him as significant as Hitler's Landsberg[10] period had on the Fuehrer. It was him who introduced National-Socialist propaganda methods into Hungary. Szálasi's ambition was unbounded, as was his belief in his own infallibility, qualities which often embroiled him with members of his own party.

In a speech of January 30th, 1939, in which two very cool references were made to Hungary, Hitler termed the German-Polish friendship "one of the more reassuring phenomena of European political life." Today, we know that he genuinely hoped to achieve a peaceful conciliation with Poland in the face of the Soviet danger. In the anticipation of a lasting period of peace, we were also comforted by a statement made by Mussolini, who, in Rome on April 20th, 1939, had said to Teleki, our Prime Minister, and to Csáky, our Foreign Minister, that "all Germany and Italy want is a few years of peace and we shall do all we can to achieve it". Teleki and Csáky received similar impressions during their official visit to Berlin subsequent to their visit to Rome. I myself, after the return of Ruthenia, which had been torn from Hungary by the Treaty of Trianon, had sent a telegram to Moscicki, the Polish President, to declare that our new common frontier "would be the basis of friendly collaboration in the spirit of ancient traditions and would assure a happy future to both our countries."

The dismay that was felt throughout Hungary when the first signs of Hitler's warlike intentions towards Poland were discerned can be understood. We had been prepared in some important respects to fall in line with Axis policy. We had signed the Anti-Comintern Pact (which had caused Russia to break off diplomatic relations with Hungary), we had recognized Manchukuo, and we

9   Staff-Lt. Col. Ferenc Szálasi (1897-1946), Hungarian Nazi leader. His original family name was Salosjan. He was born in Kassa, his father, Karl Salosjan was born in Vienna.

10 Landsberg prison.

had left the League of Nations[11]. But our main interest was nevertheless to avoid war and to keep out of it should it break out after all. Obviously, Hungary, as a small state, could not take the initiative in advocating a peace move, a fact on which I laid emphasis in my speech on the occasion of the opening of the new Parliament on June 14th. The happiest solution, I said at the time, would be for the highest and most selfless forum in the world, the Pope, to lay a proposal before the Great Powers. The Holy Father, then Cardinal Pacelli, at the Eucharistic Congress in Budapest 1938, as Legate of Pope Pius XI suggested a discussion of explicit questions. When this suggestion passed unheeded, and the signs of impending war were multiplying, Count Teleki informed Berlin and Rome, in the early days of August, that Hungary, despite its fundamental agreement with the Axis policy, made reservations in the case of an attack on Poland. Or, in clearer language, that Hungary was not going to march against Poland. Later in that month, an unsuccessful attempt was made at Salzburg to persuade Csáky to change his mind.

It is worth recalling the fact that at this moment, August, 1939, Arthur Henderson, the prominent Labour M.P., arrived in Budapest. It was arranged that I should receive him on the 26th. That morning the announcement came of Ribbentrop's flight to Moscow. Subsequently, we had an enquiry from Henderson whether I was going to see him notwithstanding the dramatic new development. I naturally saw no grounds for changing the arrangements, and received him with pleasure and interest.

On September 7th, our Foreign Minister was again summoned before Ribbentrop, who asked him whether Hungary had any territorial claims against Poland. To this question Csáky naturally gave a reply in the negative. He had hardly returned to Budapest by air before Ribbentrop telephoned him to demand the use of the Kassa (now Kosice, Slovakia) railway for an attack on Poland from the south. With Mussolini's concurrence, this demand was refused.

I would sooner have died on the scaffold than have permitted Hungarian territory to be put to such a use. I issued orders that, should the march through be attempted, all bridges were to be blown up. Showing his clear estimate of the relations then existing, Count Ciano, referring to Csáky's reply to

11 April 11, 1939.

Ribbentrop in his diary, had added, that the Germans were not likely to forget this refusal and were certain to inflict retribution one day.

As it happened, no necessity for action on our part arose. The Blitzkrieg on Poland came to a speedy end owing to the Russian support of the Germans and the lack of effective help from Great Britain, terminating in the complete and tragic defeat of poor unfortunate Poland. The British then withdrew the guarantee they had given Rumania. (See: Grigore Gafencu: *Prelude to the Russian Campaign, 1945.*)

The readiness with which Hungary admitted civilian and military refugees from Poland was indicative of her mood. Large-scale assistance had to be organized. Many of these refugees later joined the Polish Army in exile. Equally indicative of Hungary's attitude was her eagerness to lend assistance in the form of an auxiliary brigade to the racially cognate Finns, who had been attacked by Soviet Russia.

Hungary's mood underwent a rapid change with the Blitz campaigns in Norway and in the West, campaigns in which Hitler, to the amazement or dismay of the whole world, obtained military sway on a scale never previously reached by Germany. This would have been the last possible moment to stop the war before its extension in space and time turned it into a general catastrophe. In fact, Hitler, on June 30th, 1940, had a Note drawn up by General Jodl[12] in which, objectively considered, some very sound proposals were made to England. When this Note was transmitted by the Papal Nuncio in Berne to the British Government, Churchill, as he himself has stated, sent the Note to Lord Halifax[13], the Foreign Secretary, with the comment that he hoped it would be made clear to the Nuncio that the British had no questions to ask about Hitler's peace terms and that their representatives abroad had been strictly warned against accepting proposals of this nature. Hitler had lost all credit in the West. The attempts of the German opposition to establish contact with the Western powers similarly failed. Meanwhile Roosevelt, as has been disclosed in published documents and journals, was preparing to enter a war with the purpose to annihilate of Hitler.

12 Gen. Alfred Jodl (1890-1946).

13 Edward Frederick Lindley Wood (1881-1959).

In Hungary, at this time, many voices demanded that we should follow Italy's example. Throw off our non-belligerence and enter openly into alliance with Germany. Chief among those advocating this policy were the officers whom Gömbös, while Minister of War and Prime Minister, had placed in leading positions. These demands could not be lightly set aside. To the Hungarian heart, all territories taken from Hungary by the Treaty of Trianon were equally dear. But one of them, Transylvania, was in a special position, for, according to our statistics, it was the home of 1.7 million Magyars, and, according to Rumanian statistics, of 1.4 million Magyars[14]. Transylvania, during the hundred and fifty years of Turkish domination, had been the hearth where the sacred flame of the national spirit had been kept alight. The leading men of Transylvania, the Bocskays, the Bethlens and George Rákóczi, had succeeded in neutralizing the power of the Turkish overlords by their shrewd policy. On the other hand, Transylvania had been the mainstay of the struggle for self-assertion against the Habsburgs. In the picturesque language of the time, Cardinal Pázmány[15], a leading figure in the Counter-Reformation, had declared, "We need Transylvania to prevent the Germans from spitting down our necks." Towards the end of the seventeenth century, the Principality of Transylvania had ceased to exist, but the Székelys[16] in south-east Transylvania had continued to be reckoned among the finest of the nation. The share taken by the Transylvanian Magyar nobility[17] in the affairs of the state was a large one. The historical and especially the social and economic development of this region had unfortunately caused the territory occupied by a purely Magyar people to be overrun by Rumanian shepherds[18] and agricultural labourers, so that an area of predominantly Rumanian settlement lay between the compact area of Magyar settlement in Hungary proper and the equally compact Magyar settlement in Transylvania.

14 In 1995 there were 2 million Magyars in Transylvania.

15 Cardinal Péter Pázmány (1570-1637) managed to re-convert most of Western Hungary to Catholicism.

16 Seklers, Hungarian speaking Transylvanians claiming independent heritage.

17 Bethlen, Teleki, Bánffy, and other aristocratic families.

18 Contrary to claims of Rumanians being the original inhabitants of Transylvania, the earliest written document reporting the appearance of Vlach shepherds in Transylvania is dated 1206. (Haraszti, E.: Origin of the Romanians, Astor, FL: Danubia Press, 1977.)

In the disturbed times of 1939 to 1940, with on the one hand our fellow countrymen under Rumanian rule impatiently pounding on their prison bars and demanding for themselves the liberation that the Magyars of Slovakia had achieved.   On the other hand Rumania opposing these demands with increasing ruthlessness. Incidents of all kinds multiplied, and it was rapidly becoming imperative to find a solution. On either side of the frontier, troops were being concentrated; a spark would have ignited a military flare-up. But that conflict would have been as little to the advantage of Germany and Italy as it would have been to the Hungarians themselves. Hence, as has been stated in Ciano's diaries, Teleki emphatically declared in Rome, on March 25th, 1940, that he did not wish to take responsibility, either directly or indirectly, for launching operations against Rumania which would bring the Soviet Union in and throw open the gates of Europe to her.

When Moscow issued its ultimatum to Rumania on June 26th, 1940, by which the cession of Bessarabia and Bukovina was demanded within twenty-four hours. Germany had no other course than to advise Rumania to accede to the Russian demands. She now began sending her troops across Hungarian territory into Rumania, as had been agreed in the previous spring. The troops were mainly sent at night, as inconspicuously as possible, in sealed wagons.

To prevent an armed conflict, the Axis powers informed us and the Rumanians that the Transylvanian question was to be settled by negotiation. In fact, that question could have been settled peacefully only by the formation of a Hungarian-Rumanian federation. Berlin was well aware of that. Later events were to show that the Transylvanian settlement was used as a bait held out alternately to the Hungarians and the Rumanians. When the direct negotiations which were opened with Rumania in August led to the anticipated deadlock, Rumania was induced to ask the Axis powers for their arbitration. The scene was once more set in the castle of Prince Eugen in Vienna. To here on August 30th, 1940, Ribbentrop and Ciano invited, or should I say summoned, Teleki and Csáky, our Foreign Minister, Manoilescu[19], the Rumanian Foreign Minister, and Valeriu Pop, the Rumanian Ambassador. Ribbentrop's attitude to our representatives was aggressive to the point of insult. He tried to nonplus them with a long list of Hungarian misdemeanours, including even our denial, in May 1940, of the existence of a Hungarian-German military alliance. Teleki was highly

19 Mihai Manoilescu (1891-1950).

incensed when the German Foreign Minister suddenly alleged that his request of September 9th, had referred only to hospital trains, whereas he had in fact demanded facilities for a military march on Poland. Count Ciano, on the other hand, was more conciliatory and defended the Hungarian interest at the Conference[20]. The Rumanians were to be persuaded to accept the decision of the arbitrators by a German-Italian guarantee of the integrity and inviolability of the remainder of the Rumanian State. As the map showing the new frontier was put before him, Manoilescu fainted. For that matter, neither were the new frontiers bringing about a partition of Transylvania any more satisfactory from our point of view[21]. The only members of that conference who were satisfied, apparently, were Messrs. Ribbentrop and Ciano, who, the day after they had announced their arbitration decree, went off hunting together.

In conformity with the arbitration, the towns of Máramarossziget, Szatmárnémeti, Nagyvárad, Kolozsvár, and Marosvásárhely[22] were re-united with Hungary, altogether 17,000 square miles with approximately 2.5 million inhabitants. On the other hand, the towns of Brassó, Nagyszeben, Segesvár, Arad and Temesvár were retained by Rumania. The second arbitration decree included the clauses of the first. The jubilation on either side of the old frontiers was great. The people could not know what odious intentions were behind this plan. Even the obvious absurdity of frontiers which cut across roads and railways, separating towns from their ancillary services, could not worsen the joy of the first moments. When I entered the liberated towns in September at the head of my troops, I did not foresee that we should again lose this part of Transylvania nor in what tragic circumstances.

Was it necessary for Ribbentrop to offer an arbitration decree with one hand and a treaty with the other, practically compelling us to set up a state within a state? How great a lack of tact and political psychology was patent in the German demand that the German national group in Hungary should be allowed an autonomous organization which, though this was not expressly stated, was clearly to follow instructions from Berlin.

20 It is referred to as the Second Vienna Accord.

21 However, the fact was that the new frontier separated the two nations in such manner that equal number of Hungarians ended up under Rumanian rule as Rumanians under Hungarian rule. In 1996, there are two million Hungarians living in Rumania, while only 9 thousand Rumanians live in Hungary.

22 Sighet, Satu-Mare, Oradea, Cluj, Tirgu-Mures, in Rumanian.

Two and a half months later, we received an 'invitation' to join the existing Three Power Pact. Considerable efforts were made to make it appear that a signal honour was being paid us in allowing us to join Germany, Italy and Japan as a fourth partner, but a hint was also dropped that should we hesitate to accept it, Rumania would be given this 'place of honour'. The Three Powers Pact of September 27th, 1940, was, as I have already stated, by no means an unconditional alliance. The signatories undertook, according to Section 3, to support each other with all political, economic and military means, should one of the signatories be attacked by a foreign power which was not at that moment involved either in the European war or in the Sino-Japanese conflict. Judged by its phraseology, this pact's chief aim was world peace, and an attempt to prevent the spread of the war. Ribbentrop stressed this in his greeting to Hungary as a new member of the pact on November 20th. In the declaration which Csáky read on behalf of the Hungarian Government, this very idea was brought to the fore: "Germany, Italy and Japan have entered into an alliance to restrict the spread of war and to bring to the world as speedily as possible a lasting and just peace." Csáky stressed the fact that Hungary had brought about the revision of the Treaty of Trianon "without shedding blood and in a peaceful way" and that she was filled with the desire "to maintain good relations with all her neighbours". In his report on his return from Vienna, Csáky stated, he is, alas, no longer alive to confirm this, that Ribbentrop had given him the express and official assurance that the signatories retained full freedom to decide what form the support they gave their partners in the pact should take should the necessity arise. In the event, this turned out very differently[23].

In the Foreign Affairs Committees of the Upper and the Lower Houses, the agreement of Hungary to join the Three Power Pact was sharply attacked by the leader of the Smallholders' Party, Tibor Eckhardt. Count Bethlen was in agreement, though he was fair enough to grant that the government, faced with a choice between two evils, had, humanly judged, chosen the least of them. It is very probable that refusal on our part would have entailed an immediate German invasion of Hungary. By joining the pact we postponed that invasion for three and a half years. To gain time seemed our wisest course. Rumania[24] and Slovakia joined the Three Power Pact three months after us.

---

23 German views on this may be portrayed by Goebbels' note in his diary on
    November 22, 1940: "We will never get anywhere with Hungary. One day
    we will have to crush it." (Page 163, Ranki, G: In the Shadow of the Third
    Reich, Budapest: Magvetô, 1988, in Hung.)

217

Section 5 declared that the agreement "in no way touched the political status existing between any signatory and Soviet Russia", but I had my doubts on the permanence of this point. Our military intelligence kept us informed of disturbing Soviet military preparations, and this information was passed on to Berlin.

The fateful infiltration of German influence into our internal politics was made manifest in July, 1940, when a plot hatched by the Arrow-Cross movement was discovered. Their plan was to free by force of arms the leader of their party, Ferenc Szálasi; who was at that time in prison, to assassinate Keresztes-Fischer, the Minister for Home Affairs, and to force me to resign in favour of Szálasi. In the course of the trial that was held in December, after the parliamentary immunity of those of the plotters who were Members of Parliament had been suspended, the Arrow-Cross man Wirth[25] and fifteen of the twenty-three accused were convicted of high treason and sentenced to terms of imprisonment with hard labour.

With Italy's attack on Greece on October 28th, the danger of the war spreading through south-east Europe became acute. We bent our heads to the storm and concluded a pact of friendship with the Belgrade Government in an attempt to avoid finding ourselves in a position towards Yugoslavia comparable to the one we had been in with Rumania. Even under Premier Cvetkovic[26], the successor of Dr. Stojadinovic[27], and Cincar-Markovic[28], the Foreign Minister, Yugoslavia pursued its policy of maintaining friendly relations with Germany. Our pact with Belgrade was, therefore, in keeping with the general trend. It had the added advantage, in the opinion of its originators, Count Teleki and Count Csáky, that there would be no possibility of one country being played against the other, once Hungary and Yugoslavia had come to an understanding. The pact, which was the somewhat

---

24 Horthy errs here. Rumania joined on November 23, only three days after Hungary.

25 Károly Wirth (1909- ?) Member of Parliament.

26 Dragisa Cvetkovic (1893-1969).

27 Milan Stojadinovic (1888-1961) Yugoslav prime minister between June 23, 1935 and February 3, 1939.

28 Aleksandar Cincar-Markovic.

tardy outcome of my speech of August 26th, 1926, was signed in Belgrade on December 12th, 1940.

The Italian campaign in Greece put Yugoslavia in a difficult position. Whether it would have been possible to keep Yugoslav politics in line with the Axis powers if Berlin had not stiffened its attitude in demanding that Yugoslavia too should sign the Three Power Pact, I cannot judge. In retrospect, it does not seem probable, since Roosevelt, by freezing Yugoslav assets in the United States of America on March 24th, that is, before Yugoslavia had signed the pact, and by other means, exerted a considerable pressure on Yugoslavia. This has been stated by Cordell Hull, the American Secretary of State, in his memoirs, and likewise by K. Fotic, the Yugoslav Ambassador in Washington, in his book, 'The War We Lost.' In any case, American support was undoubtedly a contributing factor in the *coup d'etat* that was carried out by Air Force General Simovic[29] on March 26th, 1941, three days after the Three Power Pact had been signed by Cvetkovic[30]. This, though hailed with great jubilation, was the starting point of irreparable tragedy. In no other sector of the vast front of the Second World War was the war fought with such primitive hatred and savagery as in Yugoslavia. Not only was the war waged with a foreign enemy: a fratricidal war developed between Serbs and Croats. Meanwhile a murderous conflict sprang up between the royalist adherents of General Mihailovic[31] and the Communist partisans of the future Marshal Tito[32].

Hitler's information concerning conditions in Yugoslavia must have been singularly poor, for, as he himself told the Ambassador, Count Schulenburg[33], the *coup d'etat* took him by surprise. At first, he had thought the news was a joke in bad taste. His fury, when he realized that it was true, knew no bounds,

29 Gen. Dusan Simovic (1882-1962), chief of staff of the Yugoslav army. After the coup, he led the Yugoslav government in place of King Peter who was yet a minor.

30 On March 27 Prince Paul of Yugoslavia was deposed by this *coup d'etat*.

31 Gen. Draæa Mihajlovic (1893-1946) the emigrant Yugoslav government's Minister of War in London. He turned against Tito's Communists and was executed in 1946 upon the dubious charge of cooperating with the Germans.

32 Josip Broz Tito (1892-1980), Communist President for Life of Yugoslavia.

33 Count Friedrich Werner von der Schulenburg (1875-1944).

for it upset his plans at a particularly sensitive point. Plan Barbarossa, the attack on the Soviet Union, was to have been launched in May. He gave orders, therefore, that Yugoslavia should be "wiped out as a military and national unit" with the utmost despatch. General Sztójay[34], our Ambassador in Berlin, was sent by air to demand of me "an immediate aflirmative answer" in my own hand to the demand not only to allow German troops to pass through Hungary but also to throw Hungarian troops into the onslaught on Yugoslavia. The German attack was to be made, not from Hungary, but from the Rumanian-Serbian Banat. Hitler proposed that we should take back all the Magyar areas which Hungary had, in 1919, lost to the Kingdom of Serbs, Croats and Slovenes.

This letter, which I at once put before the Privy Council[35], forced a particularly difficult decision upon us. We had refused to allow the passage of German troops to attack Poland; we had allowed the passage of German troops to Rumania, which we had regarded as a defensive measure. Now we were asked not only to allow offensive preparations to be made on our soil but were also asked to take an active part in the attack on a country with which we had concluded a pact of peace and friendship, the pact having been ratified four weeks previously on February 27th. Hitler was convinced that we would eagerly seize the opportunity to recapture southern Hungary. This war, he had told Count Schulenburg, "will be very popular in Italy, Bulgaria and Hungary". But with these words, Hitler showed how mistakenly he read the situation. The same error was no doubt made by all Germans. There were, of course, certain groups in Hungary, and not only the National Socialists, who had long since openly adopted the German line of policy. To these people Hitler's words might have applied. But the responsible leaders of the state had

34 Major Gen. Döme Sztójay (1833-1946,), prime minister during the German occupation. Executed after the war.

35 There is a detailed description of this in the memoirs of Gen. Antal Náray (1893-1973), who took the minutes on the Privy Council meeting on April 1, 1941. Náray wrote his memoirs in the spring of 1945. It was hidden in the archives of the bishop of Passau under seal for 38 years. (Memoirs of Antal Náray, 1945; Budapest: Zrinyi, 1988, in Hung.) The four hour Council meeting was attended by Horthy, Teleki, Bartha, Werth, Bánffy, Reményi-Schneller, Keresztes-Fischer, Laky, Bárdossy, and Radocsay. The pro-German proposal lost by a vote of seven to four. Horthy in his closing words emphasized that no military measures are to be taken before Yugoslavia, as a legal entity, breaks up, and that Hungarian military occupation should not extend beyond Hungary's former borders (i.e. North of the Danube and Drava rivers).

220

to weigh the consequences of Hungary's entry into the war. Teleki, our Prime Minister, had, soon after the outbreak of war between Germany and Poland, given me a message he had received from his sister-in-law, who had visited England and France in August, 1939. Owing to her excellent connections, she had heard the views of the leading men in those countries. Germany, she had been told, will gain victory upon victory during the first two years, then she will meet with the same fate that befell her in the First World War. Hungary was no longer Austria-Hungary; she now had the opportunity of acting independently, and her choice should be neutrality. This information strengthened Teleki's own views. Even among those who desired the victory of German arms, there were many who, taking into account British determination and the anticipated intervention of the United States of America, doubted the probability of such a victory. What widened the rift still further was the uncomfortable feeling that we ourselves had little to look forward to in the event of a German triumph. The bitter words which, so I was told, went the rounds in Italy, "If England wins, we lose; if Germany wins, we are lost," could be applied to Hungary. That other nations might be thinking along these lines was impossible for the Germans to believe or comprehend.

On April 3rd, 1941 Premier Teleki, unable to see any other way out, took his own life. He saw that to refuse Hitler's demand would bring about the immediate occupation of Hungary. He had little hope of success deriving from some 'exiled government' such as Tibor Eckhardt, who had gone to America, envisaged in founding a "Committee for an Independent Hungary". When he heard that our Chief of the General Staff had already come to an agreement of a technical nature with the German General Staff behind his own government's back. When London threatened Hungary with a declaration of war, he decided to end his life rather than pronounce a "Yes" which would have defied the dictates of his own conscience in view of the pact we had so recently concluded with Yugoslavia.

Teleki once made his expectations from the Nazis clear in a conversation with Ciano. In March, 1940, he had asked the Italian Foreign Minister if he could play bridge. "Why?" "So that we may have something to do when we are together in Dachau."

That Teleki intended his suicide as a protest against the pressure being brought to bear upon us is beyond doubt. The farewell letter that he wrote to me as his friend and leader would have proved this today had it not been lost with the rest of my private papers. I can no longer recollect the exact wording[36] We have allied ourselves to scroundels, - since not a single word is true about the alleged atrocities. Not against Hungarians, not even against Germans. We will become body-snatchers! A nation of trash. I did not hold you back. I am guilty". Signed: Paul Teleki[37], but I remember that he wrote, "We have allied ourselves to scoundrels." As Premier, he felt responsible for permitting this alliance to have been made, and thus for having allowed his country's honour to be lost. "With my death," these words I remember very well, "I may be able to render my Fatherland one last service." It was in that spirit that the Anglo-Saxon world regarded his death at the time. A few days later, Sir Winston Churchill declared in a broadcast that this sacrifice should not be forgotten in the peace negotiations of the future. "At the Conference table we shall place a chair for Count Paul Teleki. That empty chair will remind all who are there that the Hungarian nation had a Prime Minister who sacrificed himself for that very truth for which we too are fighting."[38] In the third volume of his memoirs, Churchill again speaks of the sacrifice of Teleki in words that must acquit him and his people of guilt in the German attack on Yugoslavia, and he adds: "It clears his name before history. It could not stop the march of the German armies nor the consequences." Of the 'empty chair' no more was heard, though, when that third volume went to press, the 1947 Paris Peace Conference had already been held.

Friends who saw and spoke with Count Teleki a few hours before his death had the impression that the telegram from our Ambassador in London[39] was

36 Teleki's letter to Horthy:

"Your Serene Highness:

We broke our word, - out of cowardice - , with respect to the Treaty of Permanent Peace outlined in your Mohács speech. The nation feels it, and we have thrown away its honor."

37 Gosztonyi, Peter: *Air Raid, Budapest!* Op. Cit. p. 17. In Hung.

38 This has been reported in the Hungarian language newscast of the BBC World Service at the time.

39 Britain threatened with withdrawal of diplomatic recognition if Hungary got involved against Yugoslavia.Teleki received the news from Ambassador György Barcza (Barcza, G.: *Diplomatic Memoirs,* Budapest: Europa Historia, 1993, in Hung.). Interestingly, Hungary and Britain had just signed a Pact of Friendship on February 27, 1941.

the final blow that drove him to his decision. He was already in a state of depression owing to the steady accumulation of bad news and to the fact that his beloved wife was ailing. To receive a threat in place of a message of understanding from his English friends at the very moment that he found himself faced with insuperable difficulties was more than he could bear. The threat was obviously intended only as a warning, for it was not until December, and then only at Stalin's urgent request, that Churchill decided to declare war.

With the death of Count Teleki, Hungary lost one of her foremost statesmen and I personally one of my most valued friends. It may well have been Count Teleki's tragedy that he was born too late. His sensitive, scholarly nature, his vast knowledge and his outstanding ability to foresee political developments would have enabled him to play a leading part at the Table of the 1878 Berlin Congress. He was not a man who could combat the ruthless totalitarian forces that were shaping the destinies of nations in his lifetime.

The suicide of the Premier, which, in spite of a vaguely worded communiqué, was soon known in Budapest, caused great excitement. The question of a successor was urgent and, therefore, on April 4th, 1941, I appointed Ladislas Bárdossy[40], hitherto Foreign Minister, to the Premiership. My decision was based not only on his former diplomatic career, he had been our Minister in Bucharest. On Teleki's advice, I had appointed him Foreign Minister upon the death of Count Csáky on January 27th, 1941, but on the more important fact that he was not allied to any party in internal politics. I knew him only slightly, but he was extremely popular among his fellow members of the Cabinet, also in Parliament, and in political circles generally. It is not easy to judge his achievements, and many of his actions remain inexplicable to me to this day. After the war, Ladislas Bárdossy was tried as a 'war criminal'. The Americans, after imprisoning him in Austria, delivered him into the hands of the Hungarian Communists. Before he was shot, he exclaimed, "God preserve Hungary from this rabble." Only he who thinks that, throughout his life, he has never made a political blunder, is in the position to cast the first stone at Ladislas Bárdossy. By his brave death, he has joined the ranks of Hungarian martyrs and his name will live in the hearts of the Hungarian people.

40 László Bárdossy (1890-1946) escaped with his family to Switzerland at the end of the war. Rather than staying quietly in a protected refugee camp, he claimed diplomatic status and insisted on his freedom. By calling attention of the highest authorities to his case, he was handed over to the Allieds on May 4, 1945. He was executed in Hungary on January 24, 1946.

With the death of Count Teleki, Hungary's period of non-belligerence was ended. The war now engulfed her.

17. Hungary Enters the Second World War

As the German troops were passing through our country to their offensive bases in the Banat even before we had given an official answer to Hitler's demand, we were faced by a *fait accompli*. If we had not marched, a vacuum would have been created in the area of the Bácska, which had been by-passed by the Germans. The ethnic Hungarian groups in that region[1] would have been defenceless against the attacks of the Cetniks, the Serb partisans. After the First World War, the Serbs had settled large numbers of their demobilized volunteers in this region, 'Dobrovolci', mainly Montenegrins and Macedonians. These were unlikely to wait for orders to attack minorities[2].

On the other hand, we had to take into account that had we refused to comply with Hitler's request, refused, that is, to occupy the Bácska, the German Army would have felt justified in occupying that region with its own troops to safeguard its own supply routes through the 'recalcitrant' hinterland. This would have meant that the Germans would have occupied the area around Budapest lying between the Danube and the Tisza. That, we all realized, would have meant the end of Hungarian independence. It was therefore necessary for us to take energetic measures to prevent such a calamity.

Moreover, the protection of our fellow countrymen south of the frontier established by the Treaty of Trianon was to us a matter of self-preservation. But I was in favour of limiting Hungary's belligerence to advancing our troops as far as Hungary's erstwhile borders and not a step beyond.

The collapse of Yugoslavia was very rapid. On April 6th, 1941, German troops crossed the Yugoslav border. On the 8th, a series of Yugoslav air-raids was made on Hungarian towns, including Szeged, Pécs and Körmend. On

---

[1] Some 600 thousand strong at the time.

[2] This, in fact happened in 1944-45. Some 20 to 30 thousand Hungarians were summarily executed by Titoist partizans in Voivodina in 1945. (Cseres, T.: *Titoist Atrocities in Voivodina, 1944/45*, Hamilton, Ont.:Hunyadi Press, 1993)

April 10th, the independent state of Croatia was proclaimed. At the same time we received a growing number of reports of acts of violence perpetrated by local partisans on the Hungarian people on Yugoslav soil. Wishing to end the ravages of anarchy, I only then gave orders to my troops to occupy the Bácska and to protect life and property of the large number of Hungarians living in this area, which had been torn away from the Fatherland in 1918.

On the same day, I issued a proclamation, in which I could not, of course, state what the fate of Hungary would have been had we refused to meet Hitler's demands. From the moment that war had flared up in Europe, my one desire had been to protect Hungary from more bloodshed and suffering, after her grievous loss of blood in the First World War. I was convinced that the injustices imposed by the Treaty of Trianon could and would be amended without war and bloodshed along lines of justice and negotiation. It was in this spirit, I said in my proclamation, that the pact of friendship had been concluded in December, 1940, with the Belgrade Government, which was then desirous of peace, solely in order to fortify peace in the Danube basin. It is the duty of every government to protect all minorities living within its frontiers from the assaults of its own national majority. This was, throughout, the criterion of friendly relations between Hungary and Yugoslavia. After the Government of General Simovic had come to power in Belgrade, Yugoslavia had, alas, lamentably failed in protecting the Hungarian minority.

On April 24th, I was received for a short interview by Hitler at his headquarters. We discussed the military and political situation in the south-east[3]. Our Minister in Moscow had recently given us unmistakable evidence of the growing tension between the German Reich and the Soviet Union. He had taken up his duties in September, 1939, upon the re-establishment of our diplomatic relations with Russia, which had been broken off when we joined the Anti-Comintern Pact. Vyshinsky[4], the acting

3 Answering Horthy's direct question concerning Soviet-German relations, Hitler flatly stated that there is no German threat against the Soviet Union. Six days later, the day of the German attack was decided upon. (Gosztonyi: Air Raid... op. cit.)

4 Andrej Januarjevich Vyshinsky (1883-1954), Soviet chief state prosecutor, later foreign minister.

Commissar for Foreign Affairs, had on April 12th declared to Kristóffy[5], our Minister, that the Soviet Union "could see no justification for the action of Hungary against Yugoslavia". Threatening words had been uttered to the effect that Hungary also might be in trouble one day and find herself "torn to shreds".

But Hitler too was dissatisfied with us[6]. He would have liked us to take part in the Balkan War. I refused to comply with his demand by referring to the attitude of the Soviet Union. On all sides our political horizon was darkening.

In his memoirs, (*Erinnerungen*, Munich, 1950) Ernst von Weizsäcker refers in a charming passage to the day that he and his wife spent with us at Kenderes, early in June, 1941. In the open, peaceful setting of the Hungarian countryside, it would have been easy to surrender to an illusion of universal peace; but we shared our guest's anxious mood. I can still see Herr von Weizsäcker standing at the edge of our swimming pool; the rest of us had already dressed, and his wife urged him to hurry. He replied, "I don't think I ever want to dress again." However banal these words sound, they were a sincere expression of his profound depression, comparable with Count Caulincourt's[7] state of mind as he pleaded with Napoleon on the eve of the Russian campaign of 1812.

For we were at this time approximately in the same position as was Rumania. Grigore Gafencu[8], the Rumanian Ambassador in Moscow, aptly summed up our situation:

5   József Kristóffy (1890-1960), Hungarian diplomat.

6   In Hitler's recorded monologues, published in 1980, his antipathy in regard to Hungarians is repeatedly displayed. (*Monologues in the Fuehrer's Headquarters, 1941-1944,* Munich, 1980. In German.)

7   General Count Armand Augustin Louis, marquis de Caulaincourt (1773-1827), French diplomat. He was Napoleon's aide de camp, then ambassador to Russia, then foreign minister of France after Napoleon's reign.

8   Grigore Gafencu (1892-1957), Rumanian journalist, politician, foreign minister.

"The rupture between the Reich and the U.S.S.R. drew Italy, Rumania, Hungary, Slovakia and Finland into the war against the Soviet. . . . Germany had succeeded in imposing her will on the peoples she held in her power; she had driven some into the war and forced others to make a gesture of solidarity.... Their participation in the war by the side of Germany had an entirely different significance. In the first place, it was the expression of a necessity from which they could not escape. The occupied countries paid their tribute of blood to the new master of Europe. This participation was also, in one sense, a precautionary measure, because the 'allies' had no wish to disappear in the storm unleashed by Hitler, as had Poland, Czechoslovakia and Yugoslavia. Going to war alongside Germany was paying an insurance premium to preserve the right to live. Fear and resignation were the motives animating the auxiliary troops. The 'crusaders' ranged under Hitler's orders were scarcely more enthusiastic than were the little German princes who followed Napoleon to Russia: like them, they realized that the victory was not their victory, and that the only privilege they would share with the elite troops of the Grande Armee was the honour of dying in battle." (Grigore Gafencu: Prelude to the Russian Campaign, 1945, pp. 215-214.)

Save Europe from Communism? We might have believed that, we would readily have believed it had Hitler entered Russia as a liberator[9]. But the annexation programme decreed in *Mein Kampf* had demonstrated the falsity of that illusion. The first measures taken in Russia left no possibility of doubt concerning Hitler's real intentions.

We had avoided, until now, entering into full alliance with Hitler. Even after June 22nd, 1941, we tried to follow rather than co-operate. Immediately after the German attack had been launched, I received another of those hand-written notes from Hitler, which I opened as usual with a sinking heart. This one demanded that we should declare war on the Soviet Union. At the next Cabinet meeting, the Prime Minister, Bárdossy, would not even assent to

---

9   Regardless, on June 28, Horthy wrote to Hitler: "For the great struggle that Your Excellency started against Bolshevism, this Asian danger, not only Hungary but the whole Europe will forever be indebted to you. ... I am happy that our weapons, shoulder to shoulder with the glorious and victorious German army, take part in the destruction of the Communist den of danger and in the Crusade for the defense of our culture..." (Gosztonyi: Air Raid..., op. cit.)

the breaking off of diplomatic relations with Moscow. He has put forward the argument that we could justify this attitude in German eyes by pointing out that our Moscow Legation would provide us with an excellent source of information. When this came to the knowledge of the German Minister, through the Press Service of the Ministry for Foreign Affairs, he at once called on Bárdossy and told him that breaking off diplomatic relations was the least that Berlin expected of the Hungarian Government.

On June 23rd, another Cabinet meeting was held to consider a letter from Werth[10], the Chief of the General Staff, to the Prime Minister in which an immediate declaration of war was demanded. Rumania had already entered the war, so that Hungary risked being left behind in the race should she hesitate any longer, and, instead of securing the whole of Transylvania, would perhaps lose even those parts of it that had been returned to her by the Vienna Accord. Bárdossy refused to be moved by this argument. He voted against a declaration of war and was supported by the other members of the Cabinet with the exception of General Gyôrffy-Bengyel[11], who was standing in for Bartha[12], the Minister of War, and spoke in his chief's name. It was decided that we should break off diplomatic relations with the Soviet Union; but beyond that we would not go[13].

I sent Hitler an answer, acquainting him with our decision and pointing out that Hungary was not in a position to declare war unprovoked on the Soviet Union. Considering the weakness of the forces at our disposal and the disparity in size between the two countries, such a declaration of war would have been ludicrous.

10 Henrik Werth (1881-1952) was imprisoned by the Nazis in 1944. In 1948 he was sentenced to death by the Communists *in absentia*. He died in the Soviet Gulag in 1952.

11 Gen. Sándor Gyôrffy-Bengyel (1886-1942), politician, later minister in the Bardossy government.

12 Gen. Károly Bartha (1884-1964). Minister of Defence between Nov. 15, 1938 and Sept. 24, 1942.

13 According to reports, Bartha and Werth threatened Horthy with a rebellion of the officer corps if Hungary does not enter the war, saying that "the honor of the army is at stake". (Gosztonyi: *Air Raid...*, op. cit. p. 46.)

On June 26th, I received the startling news that Kassa and Munkács had been bombed. The investigation that had been immediately set on foot showed that the attack had been made by Russian planes, according to the message sent me by Werth. Marks of a Leningrad factory had been found on bomb fragments. This constituted provocation. On June 27th an official announcement was made: "Hungary, as a result of repeated air attacks made, contrary to international law, by the Russians upon Hungarian sovereign territory, considers herself in a state of war with the Soviet Union[14]."

I cannot, however, exculpate Bárdossy from having suppressed a telegram from our Minister in Moscow, which he received during these critical days. I heard of it for the first time three years later. On being charged with the suppression, Bárdossy reluctantly admitted it. That telegram contained a message from our Minister Kristóffy that Molotov[15] had promised us Russian support in the Transylvanian question, on condition that Hungary remained neutral. To give weight to this offer, our Legation had received permission to continue sending out coded telegrams to Budapest in the usual way for eight days after June 23rd. Moscow, moreover, energetically denied that the 'provocation' raids on Hungarian towns had been carried out by Russian planes. The promise made by Molotov to Kristóffy was, in any case, of problematical value. The Great Powers are always very generous when they are trying to involve smaller countries in their quarrels or to induce them to stay neutral, especially if the reward promised is to be made at someone else's expense.

The Moscow denial, however, was true enough. Also, the message from our Chief of the General Staff was not in accordance with the facts. I find myself forced to this bitter conclusion by information given me in 1944 by the Prime Minister's parliamentary secretary, Bárczy[16], who revealed to me the details of a plot that I could not have believed possible. From his own knowledge of events, Bárczy told me that Air Force Colonel Ádám Krúdy[17], who was in

---

14 This, however, was never submitted to the Hungarian parliament, as required by the constitution.

15 Vyacheslav Mihailovich Molotov (1890-1986) Soviet foreign minister.

16 István Bárczy (1882-1952), deputy minister, Chief of Protocol in the Foreign Ministry at the time.

command of the Kassa airfield, had written to Premier Bárdossy to say that he, Krúdy, with his own eyes had seen the German planes dropping the bombs. But by the time Bárdossy received this letter, Hungary had already declared war on Russia. Bádossy had therefore replied to Krúdy, asking him to keep silent on the matter if he wished to avoid personal unpleasantness. He also imposed silence on his staff. Colonel Krúdy repeated his original statement under oath in 1946 during the trial of Bádossy in Budapest.

It is, theoretically speaking, within the bounds of possibility that Colonel Krúdy was mistaken in what he thought he saw on June 26th, 1941. However, for two reasons this is unlikely. Our Chief of the General Staff had, as I have stated, urged us to take an active part in the war against Soviet Russia in compliance with Hitler's wishes. He was, as was Hitler, an interested party. Therefore both had interest in causing the 'provocation', on the absence of which I had based my refusal to declare war on Russia, in my reply to Hitler. In the second place, the weakness of the Russian Air Force, especially in those days of rapid Russian retreat, is well known. The few planes at the disposal of the Russians at that particular time would more probably have been used to halt an enemy advance than to bomb the cities of a state whose continued neutrality was undoubtedly to Russia's advantage.

This, therefore, is the story behind our entry into the war against the Soviet Union. I have not recounted this story to belittle the bravery of those men who, in the belief that they were defending their Fatherland, gave their lives in battle. Nor can anyone contend with certainty that Hungary, even without the existence of the plot, could have followed the same course as Bulgaria, which did not declare war on the Soviet Union. That course, in the long run availed Bulgaria little, as Moscow, during the armistice negotiations of September, 1944, suddenly presented Sofia with a declaration of war. But the facts should be laid out, if only to make clear, yet again, the nature of the 'alliance' in the name of which Hitler made ever heavier demands on us.

In his book, *Hungary: The Unwilling Satellite*[18], the former American Minister in Budapest, John F. Montgomery [1878 - 1954], whom I have mentioned

17 Colonel Ádám Krúdy (1907-1973).

18 Op. Cit.

before, makes the perceptive comment that, in wars of alliances, any belligerent nation may be at one and the same time on the 'right' and on the 'wrong' side:

"As Soviet imperialistic designs are now revealed, it is apparent whether or not we wish to admit it that, by sending a few troops against Russia, Hungary fought on the wrong side as Hitler's ally, but on the right side as an opponent of Soviet Russia."

Montgomery portrays the position we were in at the time remarkably accurately. We had reason to desire neither a German defeat nor a Russian victory, and he goes on:

"Woodrow Wilson's postulate in 1917 that the war should lead to a peace 'without victors and vanquished' was one of the wisest of his utterances. When Russia entered the war, that was the desire of most Europeans. Today Americans might well ask themselves whether our own country would not be safer now if our victory had been just sufficient to establish German democracy and reliable control of German and Japanese research and production, without depriving twenty nations of the four freedoms for which we supposedly fought the war. The catchwords 'unconditional surrender' put Stalin on Hitler's throne and have prevented us from devoting constructive thought to the future."

These are singularly astute admissions. If I add that Montgomery's book was published as early as 1947, while the dismantling policy was still in process in Germany and Japan, and the peace treaties with Germany's former allies were playing into the hands of Soviet domination, the American's comments will be seen to be even more clear-sighted.

Sir Winston Churchill was the only statesman on the other side who, if not always consistent and above all not always stressing the most cogent point, tried to bring a touch of realism into Roosevelt's policy of unlimited appeasement towards Stalin. Let me remind the reader of his efforts to avoid a British declaration of war on Finland, Rumania and Hungary in spite of Russian insistence. On November 4th, 1941, he wrote to Stalin that these countries had been overwhelmed by Hitler and that in them were many good friends of England. Nor did he think Hitler should be encouraged by creating what had the semblance of a solid continental coalition. But Stalin would not give way, beyond agreeing that the declaration of war on Hungary and Rumania could be postponed for a time[19].

The exiled Czech Government under Benes, having been recognized by Great Britain on July 18th, informed us that the frontiers decreed by the Treaty of Trianon would again be imposed on us. On December 7th, 1941, the British declaration of war on Hungary was finally published as being effective from December 6th.

In July, 1941, Hungary had sent approximately 30,000 men to the Eastern front, of which Hitler, at my personal request, permitted part to be sent home in October. During the first months of the war, Hitler had gained a series of resounding victories over the Red Army. However, he made a blatant strategic mistake in ordering an attack on Moscow in defiance of the advice given by his General Staff to form a defensive line. The severe check he received before Moscow shook the general faith in the invincibility of German arms.

The attack on Pearl Harbour on December 7th, whatever its precoursors may have been and however great were the losses inflicted upon the Americans, must be counted a serious mistake on the part of Japan, by drawing the coalition facing the Axis more firmly together. Prime Minister Bárdossy decided to forestall the inevitable German demand. I had just entered a clinic to be treated for a stomach infection, and without consulting me and without asking Parliament for its assent, broke off diplomatic relations with the United States of America. Berlin, and Rome, declared this insufficient. Hence Bárdossy thereupon did what was required of him. He summoned the American Ambassador and on December 12th informed him that Hungary considered herself at war with the United States of America. In his conversation with Mr. Pell[20], who tried to offer a golden opportunity for Hungarian neutrality, Bárdossy pretended that Hungary was acting of her own free will. It was a serious error of judgment. As Hungary was acting under

---

19 Eventually Britain declared war on Hungary, Rumania, and Finland on their refusal to withdraw from the war on the USSR on December 5, 1941.

20 Herbert Claiborne Pell (1884-1961) was U. S. ambassador to Hungary in 1941. Father of the former U. S. Senator.

pressure, it would have been wiser to admit it openly. Bárdossy, apparently, found it inconceivable even to suggest it.

The departure of the American Ambassador and his wife caused a political demonstration, from which the representatives of Germany and Italy could have learned much concerning the true feelings of at least some prominent Hungarian circles. Since the Berlin Government held the view that it was no more than Hungary's plain duty to wage war by Germany's side, the flowers and presents that were lavished on Mr. and Mrs. Pell must have been ascribed to Hungarian unreliability.

As Cordell Hull[21], the American Secretary of State, records, Roosevelt decided, on December 13th, that he would not ask Congress to declare war on Germany's allies, "for it was obvious that these governments were Hitler's puppets and had to dance when Hitler pulled the strings."

In April, 1942, Washington made one more unsuccessful effort to try to persuade us, together with Rumania and Bulgaria, to limit the assistance we were prepared to give Germany, but no reference was made to the Allied war plans. Then, on June 5th, Roosevelt signed the American declaration of war on us.

In spite of the traditional forms with which the Foreign Minister, von Ribbentrop, was welcomed on January 6th, 1942, on the occasion of his first visit to Budapest, it was clear to those behind the scenes that there was a considerable gap between the contribution Hitler demanded of us and that which we were prepared to make. He who relies too much on propaganda tends to take for propaganda the truth that is put before him. We were not fully convinced that the Allies, as Ribbentrop declared, "had gone so far in their reckless indifference as to promise the Communists a free hand in Europe in order to encourage the Soviets to make greater sacrifices". When Field Marshal Keitel came on a visit to our Minister of War, Bartha, towards the end of January, he received the promise that a second army of 150,000 men under the command of General Jány[22] would be raised after Keitel himself had promised to equip it with the necessary transport and armoured

21 Cordell Hull (1871-1955).

234

vehicles. This material was given us neither before our troops set out nor, in spite of renewed assurances, upon their arrival at the Eastern front. As a direct result our troops suffered exceedingly heavy losses in the autumn fighting in the Voronezh sector. When the facts of Keitel's visit leaked out, a macabre joke went the rounds. "What has Keitel brought us, do you know?" "A film." "Yes, Deadly Spring." This was the name of a Hungarian film then being shown in Budapest.

It must be recorded here that, with our occupation of the Bácska in January, 1942, several regrettable excesses were perpetrated. The town of Ujvidék (Novi Sad) in particular suffered, hundreds of innocent people being killed and thrown into the Danube. The number of victims[23] was later estimated to be about 1,300: Jews, Serbs and a few Magyars. The military commander, Feketehalmi-Czeidner[24], succeeded in suppressing all news of this holocaust. However, as soon as the first rumour reached Hungary, questions were asked in Parliament[25] and the Prime Minister, Bárdossy, agreed to an enquiry. He had as yet received no official information. I had heard even less than what he about it. The first investigation proved fruitless as both investigator and investigated did their utmost to hush the matter up. The Serbian partisans were blamed on the grounds that it had been necessary to take "exemplary action". Public opinion refused to accept this explanation. The next Premier, Nicholas Kállay, vigorously urged a new investigation by the military

22 Gen. Gusztáv Jány (1883-1947, born Hautzinger) At the end of WW1 he served in the famous Sekler Division trying to push the Romanians out of Hungary. He commanded the Hungarian Second Army that was completely destroyed on the Soviet front. He willingly returned to Hungary after the war, tried and convicted to death. He did not appeal the verdict, and was executed by the Communists on January 26, 1947.

23 Official figures give 3,309, including 147 children.

24 Gen. Ferenc Feketehalmy-Czeidner (1890-1946, original name was Zeidner) was appointed by Szombathelyi, after the interior minister, Keresztes-Fischer reported to Horthy that the police is powerless in face of the mounting partizan actions. Others responsible for the atrocities were Col. József Grassy, Col. László Deák, and Gendarmerie Colonel Dr. Márton Zöldi (1912-1946). They were tried and executed by the Yugoslavs in 1946.

25 Endre Bajcsy-Zsilinszky, MP, who was later executed by the Nazis, informed Horthy about the matter.

authorities. By this time, I was convinced that the reports sent in by the military were, to put it mildly, somewhat one-sided. I instructed Szombathelyi, the new Chief of the General Staff[26], successor to Werth, to hold an enquiry, and to make full use of the penalties prescribed by law. As a result of this second enquiry, four of the accused were condemned to death, twenty got prison sentences ranging from eight to fifteen years. The death sentences could not be carried out as the culprits were abducted by the Germans and taken out of the country. These men later joined the S.S., and when the Arrow-Cross Party seized power in 1944 they were placed in high positions.

No one could more deeply regret the crimes of Ujvidék than I, who had invariably done my utmost to keep the name of the Hungarian Army undefiled. Immediately after the war, during the days of the Nuremberg trials, my attitude was vindicated by the Americans. They, after a full investigation, refused to comply with Tito's demand for my extradition as a war criminal for complicity in the Ujvidék atrocities.

26 General Ferenc Szombathelyi (1887-1946) was one of Horthy's most trusted man. He was instrumental in the attempts to arrange Hungary's surrender to the West. After the war he was put to trial and received the relatively light sentence of ten years in prison. The 'people's court' intended to dismiss all charges but they were advised that "Gábor Péter" (Muscovite Secret Police chief) "would not like it". In an illegal manner he was extradited soon after by Hungary's Minister of Justice István Riesz to the Yugoslavs. Fittingly, Riesz himself was beaten to death in Vác Prison by the Communist secret police in 1950. After a show trial, Szombathelyi was executed in Ujvidék (Novi Sad) on November 4, 1946.

18. Appointment of a Deputy Regent

During the war years, with their doubled and trebled burdens, I began to feel the weight of my advancing years more heavily than would have been the case in times of peace, when 'ruling' and 'governing' are so much more clearly defined in a strictly constitutional sense. Nor could I eliminate the possibility of a protracted illness. The 1920 law on the Regency contained no provisions for such a contingency. The 1937 law, with my retirement or death in view, provided that I could deposit a sealed letter with the two Keepers of the Crown in which I could nominate three candidates for the Regency, though Parliament would not be limited to my nominations. That, however, was not the consideration that worried me, although the problem of succession had been in my thoughts. I was constantly being advised that I should delegate at least part of the burden of running the state, and that a law should be passed creating the post of Deputy Regent. This way, should I be prevented from carrying out all or part of my duties for any cause, there would be a responsible person to whom I could entrust certain of my functions. After exhaustive discussions with the various officers of state, a suitable Bill was framed which was put before Parliament by Bárdossy early in February, 1942. It was passed with large majorities by both Houses on February 10th and 14th respectively. By this law, as the Premier phrased it to the parliamentary committee for constitutional affairs, "an institution *sui generis*" was created. The law empowered the Regent to propose three candidates for the office of Deputy. Parliament could appoint another candidate only if I approved their choice. Section II emphatically stated that the former arrangements for the appointment of a successor to the Regent remained unchanged. The function of the Deputy Regent would cease to exist immediately after a new Regent had taken the oath. The powers of the Deputy Regent were to be formulated in detail by the Regent in consultation with the Prime Minister; the law itself merely decreed that in the absence, illness or other incapacity of the Regent, the Deputy Regent should be empowered to act with the full powers of the Regent. If this law is compared with similar ones in canon law, one great difference emerges: the Deputy did not have the the right of succession.

This law had been passed in conformity with my express desire. The discussion concerning the Deputy Regent began with a survey of possible candidates. I wished the choice to fall on a man of strong character, a man who could make a stand against the ever increasing German pressure. The name of my eldest son Stephen was put forward. After giving the matter considerable thought, and having ascertained that all the former Prime Ministers, the Prince Primate Serédy and the President of the Curia, our Supreme Court, Dr. Géza Töreky, considered my son a suitable choice, I agreed.

My hesitation had been twofold. I had no wish to lay myself open to the accusation that I was trying to found a dynasty; and I had to think of my son's own life, a consideration that in a father cannot be taken amiss. Stephen was thirty-eight, and I wondered whether so young a man ought to be asked to give up his personal freedom, especially as he had recently embarked on a harmonious married life with Ilona, Countess of Edelsheim-Gyulai. At heart, I was convinced that my son was the only one who could really assist me and lighten my burdens. The legislators of 1920 had plainly had no wish for dualism in the Regency. However, the element of danger that such a dualism entailed would be minimal in the appointment of a man so closely in accord with me as was my elder son. I could assure myself without undue parental pride that with regard to character, training and political views, he would contribute all that so high an office would demand of him.

The tragic ending of the First World War had cut short his career, for Stephen had chosen to follow my profession, and the Austro-Hungarian Navy had been lost. He finished his schooling in Budapest and then studied engineering at the Technical University of Budapest. After some practical work and after his military training, he had become a first lieutenant in the Air Force Reserve in 1929, he went to the United States of America and worked as a labourer in the Ford works at Detroit. Returning to Hungary, he entered the state railways' iron, steel and construction works, which at that time was a subsidized concern. Specializing on the export side, he visited a number of countries, making use of his excellent knowledge of English, French and German. It was due largely to his activities that the factory was able to enlarge its staff from 5,000 to 22,000 and before long had become a paying concern. To give an example of his methods: when the possibility arose of considerable export to India, knowing that to go by sea would take too long, my son immediately set off for Bombay in his small Arado-79 sports plane. It was a bold undertaking, for it meant flying four thousand miles solo. The Chief of our Air Force begged me to forbid him to make the 'suicide trip', but I felt that my son knew his own capabilities well enough. We did, however, keep his flight a secret from his mother.

238

When the directors of the state railways asked for a large subsidy to repair damage sustained in the First World War, the Minister of Finance agreed to give it to them on condition that my son was made President. After long hesitation, he accepted the position, and then set to work in earnest. His achievements were to the entire satisfaction of the management, the investors, the staff and even to the Minister of Finance himself.

On February 19th, 1942, the Speaker of the Upper House, Count Bartholomew Széchenyi, chaired a joint session of the two Houses, 203 members of the Upper House and 280 of the Lower House being in attendance, many more, that is, than was required by law. Before he had even explained the method by which the candidate had been nominated, the name of my son was called out. In conformity with tradition and law, Stephen Horthy was elected Deputy Regent of the Realm by acclamation. The session was then interrupted while my written consent was obtained. After another pause, my son was called before the members. Wearing his Air Force uniform, he took the oath with solemnly raised hand.

Congratulations flowed in from all parts of the country and also from friendly states, especially Italy. Only German officialdom remained aloof. On February 4th, Goebbels had already noted in his diary that the choice of my son was a great misfortune, as "this son is even more friendly to the Jews than Horthy himself". A similar, even more malicious entry was made on February 20th, the end of which reads: "But we are keeping hands off. . . this isn't the time to bother about such delicate questions. . . . After all, we must have something left to do after the war!" As evidence, that is clear enough. My son, those who elected him were aware of it, was of the opinion that the superiority in men and materials of the Allies had been so great from the outset that Germany had no chance of success. To the Nazis my son appeared as their determined antagonist. His file in the Reichssicherheits-hauptamt, to which a friend once chanced to gain access, was exceedingly voluminous.

My son was not a man to be swayed by the opinions of others. He wished to see for himself how matters stood at the front. A few weeks after his election, during which time he had already relieved me of much work by receiving diplomats and politicians, and by going on inspections and performing a number of representative duties, he went to the front as a fighter pilot. The government did not approve of this step, but Stephen found he could not endure the thought that his position should be regarded as one that released him from his obligations. In this I agreed with him. On August 22nd, 1942, on St. Stephen's Day, he crashed shortly after takeoff.

Years have gone by, but the grief of the parents who had now lost their third child, and of his young widow who was left with her eighteen-month-old son, is undimmed. Nor have those years brought us the answer to the riddle of his death. I should like, however, to contradict the vicious and slanderous rumours that were spread by the Hungarian and German Nazis. Nor can I confirm the rumour which was current in Hungary that only sabotage could have caused so experienced an airman to crash. The secret transmitter, Radio Kossuth, declared that Gestapo agents had placed a time-bomb in the plane. I shall confine myself to inserting a statement written by my daughter-in-law, who was with her husband two days before his fatal accident:

"After my training as an surgical nurse, I was directed to a Hungarian military hospital at Kiev and arrived there on a hospital train. My husband was given three days' leave, which we spent together in the house of a German General who happened to be away The natural joy at our reunion after so long a separation was somewhat marred by my husband's dark, almost despairing mood. He was fully convinced that the war was lost, and his experiences at the front had strengthened this belief. He was harassed by the problem of how Hungary, situated as she was between two enemies, as he put it, could possibly be saved. He had made up his mind to discuss the matter thoroughly with his father as soon as he returned home. We openly talked on this subject without thinking that our conversation might be overheard. Later I was told that microphones had been installed in our rooms. My husband also complained about the Italian fighter planes he had to use, saying that they were inclined to slip in rapid turns. That had once happened to him, but fortunately at a height of 13,000 feet so that he had had time to regain control of the machine. He promised me that after that experience he would guard against a repeat performance most carefully. On August 18th, I accompanied my husband to the Kiev airfield, from which he and his orderly flew back to the front. This same man told me later that my husband and the other officers of his squadron went to bed early on the 19th in order to be fit and fresh for an attack planned for the next morning. When he was woken he did not even wait to drink the coffee his orderly brought to the plane. 'He'd slept well and was full of energy,' the man said, 'he waved to me and shouted that he'd have the coffee when he came back.' But hardly had the plane taken off before it crashed and burst into flames. His comrades declared later that my husband had made too steep a curve and that his plane had slipped as a result, but this would seem to be in contradiction with the assurance he

240

had given me at Kiev. I received the news of his death as we were celebrating the feast of St. Stephen at the hospital on the morning of August 20th, 1942."

To this I must add that my son had already been recalled; several Members of Parliament and members of the government had insisted on his return. On August 20th, he was to visit the Hungarian troops in his sector of the front, after which he was intending to return to Budapest to resume his functions as Deputy Regent.

Whether the conversations between Stephen and his wife were overheard or not, my son's views were generally known in German circles, as is evident from the unambiguous entries in Goebbel's diaries and writings. I need not dwell on the distress caused me by the German display that marked his death. The German Reich had not seen fit to congratulate him on his election to the Deputy Regency; he had never received any form of military award during his lifetime. But now Herr von Ribbentrop arrived in person to confer two high posthumous orders. I was too shattered by my bereavement to realize to the full the diabolical hypocrisy of the German condolences.

In connection with these funeral rites, certain foreign publications have spoken about negotiations going forward at that time to crown King-Emperor Victor Emmanuel with St. Stephen's Crown. As a similar story had already been circulated about the Duke of Aosta, the Italian General in the East African campaign, I must give the facts here. If such plans did exist, I was never consulted about them; nor was I likely to have initiated them, since in no circumstances would I have been prepared to countenance them. This statement is not intended to reflect on the personality of either the Italian monarch or of the Duke of Aosta. The latter I had met while I was on holiday at the Villa d'Este on Lake Como, and I had liked him very much. I gather that when Mussolini was told of these plans, he emphatically rejected them.

It might be thought that the people who asserted that I wished to see the establishment of a Savoy monarchy would have realized that this assertion was in conflict with the accusation that I was striving to secure St Stephen's Crown for the 'House of Horthy'. Yet there are publications imputing both schemes to me simultaneously. The truth is that I had no dynastic ambitions and I can therefore only regret that I seem to have been suspected of having them in certain Hungarian circles. The choice of my son to be my deputy, and I repeat: without the right of succession, was due to unusual circumstances. It was the outcome of the particular political views held by my son and of the remarkable coincidence of our opinions. As it proved impossible for me to find such another, his place remained vacant.

In October, a law was passed to honour my son in bestowing upon him the title, 'Hero of the Nation'. To his memory are dedicated the words, spoken on August 26th, 1942, before Parliament by the Hungarian Prime Minister, Nicholas Kállay:

"As Prime Minister, I speak not only on behalf of the Cabinet and of my own party, but also on behalf of all political parties represented in Parliament. I believe that I can say this, for I feel it, I know it: every true Hungarian, throughout the country, is at this moment in full agreement with me. Since this tragedy on the Eastern front overwhelmed our nation, the country has been in mourning. It mourns the Deputy Regent of the realm, his loss to the country, it mourns a soldier who died a hero's death. It weeps for a glorious young life and shares in the sorrow of a father. For glorious indeed was the man who embodied the flower of Hungarian manhood. Outstanding in mind and body, stately, healthy, strong and noble, he was a courageous fighter. Stephen Horthy was a man able to think profoundly and constructively concerning the problems of life and the problems of his country.

Perhaps too few of us knew him well enough to grasp the great qualities of his mind, the range of his intelligence and the strength of his sense of duty. In the whole of my life, I have met but few of our countrymen who were his equal. Now he is no longer with us, I can say this openly. Had he been with us to hear these words, they would have embarrassed him. In his relations with his fellow-men, he always did his best to put others at ease; never did he trade on his birth and position. For months, he worked in the United States of America in the guise of a simple labourer, and, unknown, a man among men, he felt contentment in his independence. Those who knew him well loved and respected him. He was called to high office by the nation, though he himself never wished to have it thrust upon him. He accepted the task entrusted to him only when an appeal was made to his sense of duty.

Modesty, comradeship and a sense of duty were the fundamental traits of his character. As a labourer, as an official, as President of the Railways, he was conscientious and zealous in his work. When he presented himself for military service, he did so as a first lieutenant of reserve, the first reservist in the Air

242

Force and perhaps the oldest among fighter pilots; his qualities, and, above all, his unusual degree of courage, were impressive.

On St. Stephen's Day, he set out on his hundredth flight, his twenty-fifth combat flight. He was our best fighter pilot, yet he fell a victim to his heavy task. As always, he was flying unaccompanied. He went forth alone. Today, the whole nation accompanies his remains."

19. The Search for the Way Out

Information sent me by my son Stephen from the Eastern front shortly before his death gave me a very sombre picture of the situation. The deadlock of Stalingrad and the defeat of El Alamein were clear evidence that the tide had turned. In Germany itself and even more beyond the German borders, belief in a German victory was rapidly dwindling. Everywhere, even in Germany, people were beginning to speculate on the possibility of ending the war. Mussolini tried to convince Hitler that he ought to conclude peace with Stalin; the invariable answer to this frequently reiterated advice was a stereotyped, "The East is a military problem."

The appointment of Kállay to the Premiership brought a change that was in close inner relationship with the change in the whole military and political situation.

On March 10th, 1942, I called upon Nicholas Kállay, a leading figure in our political world, to take over from Bárdossy. Foreigners have been inclined to regard his well-defined features: high forehead, bushy eyebrows, prominent cheekbones, aquiline nose and firm chin, as the fundamental traits of the Magyar. Kállay was certainly an embodiment of the traditions of our race, of a people that, encircled by inimical foreign races, had been forced to fight for self-preservation throughout the centuries.

As Minister of Agriculture Kállay had rendered his country meritorious service, but not until he attained the Premiership did his talents find their full outlet. He combined a penetrating intelligence with a shrewdness that knew when to use cunning in the face of overwhelming odds; when no other method was appropriate.

His aim, as Premier, was to regain Hungary's freedom of action and to return, if possible, to a state of non-belligerence. War fatigue was growing. Apprehension of the might of our eastern neighbour, heightened by historical and geographical considerations, was intermingled with a growing distaste for the totalitarianism of the Third Reich and with esteem for the Western powers and their democratic forms of government. These tensions were becoming increasingly obvious in the domestic politics of Hungary. The extreme right wing of Parliament, which consisted of the former Premiers Bárdossy and Imrédy and their adherents, and of course the Arrow-Cross disciples, demanded an intensification of the war effort. Meanwhile the left wing, consisting of the Smallholders' Party under Bajcsy-Zsilinszky[1] and the Social Democrats, demanded more or less openly that we should withdraw from the war. In addition, the first pamphlets of a Communist underground movement were being circulated.

Kállay took these trends into account while outwardly pursuing the policy of his predecessor. Between him and myself, there was an unspoken agreement that he should have a free hand without referring details to me in taking measures that would, while safeguarding our relations with Hitlerite Germany, draw us closer to the British[2] and Americans without entailing active support of the Soviet Union. This was a delicate problem, and in face of Roosevelt's policy with regard to Stalin an insoluble one. The secret agreement that we entered into with the Western powers that we should allow their planes to fly over Hungary unmolested provided they refrained from bombing Hungarian towns was not entirely to the disadvantage of the Germans, in that it left important railway links and war factories undamaged. In the summer of 1942, our first contact was made with Great Britain[3].

1 Endre Bajcsy-Zsilinszky (1886-1944) was arrested by the Gestapo after a fire fight on March 20, 1944 upon the German occupation of Hungary. Before he was shot and captured, he succeeded in making a phone call to Dr. Endre Fall, anti-Nazi director of the Revisional League, to warn him of the Gestapo attack. Fall escaped to Kisujszállás and went into hiding. He survived the war. Bajcsy-Zsilinszky was executed in Sopron-Kôhida prison on December 24, 1944.

2 Attempts to establish covert contacts with British diplomats in neutral countries were coordinated by the executive director of the Revisional League, Dr. Endre Fall. Starting with Ambassador Aladár Szegedy-Maszák in Sweden in 1942, Hungarian diplomats Dezsô Ujváry and László Veress, newspaperman András Frey, and Nobel Laureate Albert Szent-Györgyi relayed Hungary's interests in an armistice in Istambul in May of 1943. Similar feelers were made in Switzerland, and Portugal. However, the British government opposed any direct contacts. Indirect contacts were made with officers of the Special Operations Executive, (SOE), their interests, however, was in generating partizan activities behind German lines. (Bokor, Peter: *Endplay by the Danube*, Budapest: RTV-Minerva, 1982, transcript of TV interviews with participants. In Hung.)

3 Through friends in the Polish government in exile, Andor Wodianer, Hungarian minister to Lisbon made the first contact with the British government in

246

However, more than a year passed before the talks could be arranged. Kállay and Szombathelyi, the Chief of the General Staff, took charge of these[4].

In July, Kállay had been received by Hitler for military discussions at his headquarters. Our Premier raised the special problems of Hungarian-Rumanian relations. Hitler seems to have regarded this as an evasive measure, judging by a comment that appeared in his 'table talks'.[5] Nor could Hitler approve of our preoccupation with a reform of our Upper House and with other problems of a domestic nature during the emergencies of war. When our Premier, in a speech made in the Upper House on December 17th, 1942, stressed the "emphatic demands of Hungarian national sovereignty and independence", what he meant was clear enough. This statement went far to increase the mistrust Hitler had felt for Kállay from the outset.

Hitler's exalted mood was very obvious to me during a visit I paid him at Klessheim from the 16th to the 18th of April, 1943. Immediately before my arrival, Mussolini, together with Bastianini[6], Ciano's successor, and the Rumanian Marshal Antonescu[7], had called on him and told him bluntly that he should sue for peace. Mussolini, who, as soon as the loss of the whole of North Africa was certain, was becoming apprehensive about the approaching

January, 1943. To avoid German intelligence, the negotiations were transferred to Turkey. Kállay also enlisted the help of Archduke Otto Habsburg in March, 1943, who was well connected with Roosevelt. These contacts were broken with the German occupation. (Vigh, Károly: *Jump into the Dark,* Budapest: Magvetô, 1980, p. 111. In Hung.)

4 At the request of British diplomats in Turkey, Szombathelyi sent Lt. Col. Otto Hatz to Istambul on Dec. 16, 1943. During his return trip, Hatz, former military attache to Bulgaria, contacted Otto Wagner German Counter-Intelligence officer in Sofia and briefed him on his mission. This report was in Berlin before Hatz arrived to Budapest (Gosztonyi, P.: *Ferenc Szombathelyi's Memoirs*, New Brunswick: Occidental Press, 1980. In Hung.)

5 Henry Picker: Hitlers Tishgespräche in Fuehrerhauptquartier 1941-42, Bonn, 1951.

6 Giuseppe Bastianini (1899-1961)

7 Marshal Ion Antonescu (1882-1946). From 1940 the Fascist Rumanian regime's leader ("Conducator"). He was responsible of massacres of Jews in Rumania with some 350 thousand victims. Executed as war criminal in 1946. In the early 1990's he was rehabilitated in Rumania, there are streets named after him.

invasion of Sicily. He had again insisted that the Axis should come to terms with Stalin. Antonescu, on the other hand, thought that all forces should be marshalled to stem the tide from the East and was in favour of coming to terms with the Western powers. Hitler's hysterical excitement had mounted in face of their 'defeatism', to use a favourite Nazi expression of the time. After his efforts to instil some confidence into them, his excitement had by no means ebbed away by the time I arrived. No doubt it had its effect on the way he received me. Even Goebbels, who had always been ill-disposed towards me and Hungary, wrote in his diary: "The Fuehrer minced no words and especially pointed out to Horthy how wrong his policies were.... The Fuhrer was very outspoken." Well, Goebbels was not present at that conversation, which was entirely private, and it is unlikely that he was told that I vigorously countered Hitler's accusations and demands.

Hitler declared that the Hungarian troops had fought badly during the previous winter offensive, to which I replied that the best of troops cannot put up a good show against an enemy superior in number and arms; that the Germans had promised us armoured vehicles and guns but had not supplied them; and that the heavy losses of our troops were the best testimony to the strength of their morale. Then Hitler went on to lecture me on the Jewish question, shouting that "the Jews must either be exterminated or put in concentration camps". I saw no reason why we should capitulate to Hitler and change our views on this subject, especially as in October of the previous year we had introduced a special levy on Jewish capital as a 'war contribution' and had also restricted the Jewish tenure of land. Although these were measures that had been taken by the Kállay Government, Hitler proceeded to vilify Kállay, declaring that he was preparing a Hungarian defection. He demanded that Kállay be dismissed from the Premiership. I refused categorically to yield on that point and asked Hitler to refrain from interfering with my official functions. A Prime Minister, and above all a Chief of State, must be at liberty to gain information of the position and views of his opponents by all the means at his disposal.

In our afternoon discussion, Hitler was in slightly better control of his emotions. We talked, among other things, of the German element in Hungary. I told him plainly that during recent years the friendly relations between Germans and Magyars had been ruined by the interference of German official bodies in Hungarian affairs. Hitler reverted to the subject of Kállay, who, he said, should be dismissed "in the interests of

German-Hungarian friendship". I again rejoined, "I see no reason whatever for his dismissal." Hitler apparently was under the illusion that his *Lebensraum* doctrine entitled him to decide who should be appointed Prime Minister of an allied sovereign state.

We parted with no trace of friendliness. Subsequently no joint communiqué was issued. The versions that were published in Berlin and in Budapest were utterly at variance. As to Hitler's real thoughts, we must again turn to Goebbels as the most reliable witness, for, after a statement concerning my "humanitarian attitude" in the matter of the Jewish question, he wrote in his diary, "From all this, the Fuehrer deduced that all the rubbish of small nations still existing in Europe must be liquidated as fast as possible." And that was to be done by the Germans, who could consider themselves fortunate that "in the future organization of Europe" they would have to fear "no serious competitors" in the Italians. No one was ever so explicit to my face, nor to any other Hungarian. Nor was it necessary, what Hitler meant was clear enough.

We were not at that time to know that even the Western democracies would be unwilling or unable to prevent the 'organizing' of Europe by Stalin on similar and even more radical principles though under different auspices. In his memoirs, Cordell Hull notes a remark made by Roosevelt on February 12th, 1943, to the effect that all nations that had fought on the side of Germany could be dealt with only under the Casablanca formula, unconditional surrender. In June the *London Times* expressly stated this in a leading article on the Hungarian peace attempts. At the Teheran Conference of late November to early December, 1943, and even later, the British had been in favour of establishing a second front in the Balkans, if only to create a diversion during the invasion of France. I am firmly convinced that an invasion of the Balkans in 1943, in view of the German dependence on Rumanian oil, Hungarian bauxite and Yugoslav ore and on the food supplied by the countries of south-east Europe, would have hastened the end of the war. I admit that we could hardly have envisaged Great Britain totally relinquishing her interests in our part of Europe. And so it came about that our government, though without my knowledge, established radio communication with the Allied Headquarters at Cairo. Before my visit to Klessheim, Prime Minister Kállay had called on Mussolini in Rome and had made a proposal to him of joint action by Italy, Hungary and Rumania with, if possible, the support of Greece and Turkey. Mussolini, however, wanted to see first how events would develop before he was prepared to come into the open. Apparently he believed that an attempt to invade Sicily could be beaten off. A few months later[8], the Duce was deposed, by his closest collaborators, the Fascist Grand Council, with the support of Badoglio[9] and the Italian Royal House.

In Budapest, no one doubted that the arrest of Mussolini would bring about the passing over of Italy to the Allied camp. It seemed as if a landing on the Dalmatian coast were imminent. These expectations were not realized. The Germans seized their opportunity to stabilize themselves in Italy. With the Italian capitulation on September 8th, they had expected the immediate seizure of Rome by the Allies, if not an Allied landing in the Pisa - La Spezia area.

A fact that is no longer in dispute is that the demand for 'unconditional surrender' put forward by Roosevelt at Casablanca, and agreed to by Churchill, enabled Hitler to protract the war for nearly two years after defeat was a practical certainty. The prospect of having to surrender, of being at the enemy's absolute mercy, inspired the German people and the German troops to fight with the courage of despair. Even in our country, certain elements, either in a spirit of defiance, feeling that they had gone too far to withdraw, or from fear of Communism, wished for the first time to throw all our resources into the German effort[10]. I had, at Kállay's suggestion, prorogued Parliament on May 4th for an indefinite period, but that did not succeed in suppressing the agitation of either the extreme right or the extreme left wings. The Smallholders' Party drew up a memorandum on July 31st, 1943, demanding that "everything possible should be done to regain Hungary's independence, freedom, and neutrality in the war", if necessary by fighting on the British

8 On July 26, 1943.

9 General Pietro Badoglio (1871-1956), formerly viceroy of Ethiopia, was the chief of the Italian general staff. After the fall of Mussolini he became the premier of Italy, and he negotiated the armistice.

10 The Stalinist massacre of 4,800 Polish officers at Katyn was well known by all army officers fighting on the Russian front, whether they were German, Rumanian, Italian, Slovak, Hungarian, Finnish, Croatian, or something else. They were ill disposed to surrender to the Soviets unconditionally. It may be surmised that Roosevelt and Churchill, with their Casablanca Accords, extended the war by two years, causing the death of millions. The condition was later relaxed for countries other than Germany and Japan. The requirements and procedures set for armistice arrangements were, inexplicably, never communicated to the governments in question.

side. The Hungarian Second Army, under the command of General Jány, had arrived back from the Eastern front to Budapest. Both the government and I thought it essential to have troops of our own at hand for any eventuality. For this reason, I did not comply with Hitler's request that three Hungarian divisions should be sent to the Balkans, where German troops were being increasingly harried by partisans. However, at the Germans' strong request I allowed some forces to remain in Russia guarding the lines of communication.

Premier Kállay was also in charge of Foreign Affairs. At his suggestion, I appointed Jenö Ghyczy[11] Foreign Minister on July 24th, 1943, and Andor Szentmiklóssy[12] as his Parliamentary Secretary. Ghyczy was in Kállay's confidence and was useful in drawing away some of the German fire.

Relations with Berlin deteriorated from month to month as the foreign press reported Hungarian approaches to neutral countries and, incorrectly, Hungarian efforts to obtain a separate peace. A separate peace was not feasible as all our frontiers were at too great a distance from the frontiers of the Western powers[13]. It was undoubtedly on account of these press reports that Ribbentrop sent a special envoy on a secret mission to Budapest at the end of the year. Information sent him by his Minister, von Jagow[14], seemed to him either inadequate or unreliable. The special envoy, Dr. Edmund Veesenmayer[15], hid his political activities behind a feigned interest in the

11 Jenö Ghyczy (1893-1982). He was instrumental of initiating several 'feelers' through Hungarian legations in neutral countries to seek an armistice.

12 Andor Szentmiklóssy (1893-1945). Former Minister to Brazil, Deputy Foreign Minister. He was arrested by the Germans and died at the Dachau concentration camp.

13 In July, 1943, Horthy told Col. Gyula Kádár, chief of the military intelligence: "Many people advise me to bail out of the war, but no one tells me how. I can not step out to the balcony of the palace and shout: I changed sides! The Germans would bring in Szálasy in 24 hours". (Gosztonyi: Air Raid.., op. cit.)

14 SS General Dietrich von Jagow (1892-1945). He was Germany's ambassador to Hungary between 1941 and 1944. Committed suicide at the end of the war.

15 SS Colonel Edmund Veesenmayer (1904-1977). Earlier, he was German Plenipotentiary to Slovakia and Croatia, setting up the Nazi puppet regimes. He was convicted to twenty years in prison in the Nuremberg Trials but was paroled soon after. In a 1962 interview he stated that "Horthy was irreplaceable in Hungary and he knew it" (Gosztonyi: Air Raid... op. cit.)

Hungarian oil industry, and engaged in discussions with the former Premier, Imrédy, and his group. We were not accustomed to these unofficial methods in diplomacy, and I demanded and achieved the recall of Dr. Veesenmayer. This affair and other matters I discussed with von Papen, the German Ambassador in Ankara, who had accepted an invitation to a hunting expedition in December. On that occasion, I showed him a document sent by the German Volksbund to Neubacher[16], the German economic attaché to the south-east, outlining a plan to divide Hungary into its ethnic units and incorporate these on a federal basis in the National-Socialist Reich. Von Papen knows that I made no secret of this in giving the Germans my views on it. Later I was accused, so I heard, of having secretly conspired behind the Germans' backs. Von Papen's son has, since the war, kindly supplied me with a transcript of the letter which his father sent in December, 1943, to Werkmeister, the German charge d'affaires in Budapest. Von Papen wrote that his personal impression was that much could be gained by re-establishing cordial relations with Hungary. The conviction that we were in the same boat and must sink or swim together was general, he said. So was the feeling of despair and fear of what the future might bring, especially since victory by force of arms was no longer considered possible. In this letter, he also stated that, with regard to the feelers which Hungary had put out abroad, I had often discussed these with him and had stressed their usefulness in obtaining information, as it was essential for Hungary to know the British or American views. On December 12th, the American Secretary of State, Cordell Hull, had addressed a 'warning' to the governments of Hungary, Bulgaria and Rumania. In this he said that it must now be clear to them that they would have to share the results of the crushing defeat that the United Nations were preparing to inflict upon Germany.

But how could mutual trust between us and the Hitler Government have been re-established after Hungary found herself on the Nazi list of condemned countries? Between the realization that, in the reorganization of Europe, no matter what form it took, we should be made a vassal state and our determined will to defend Hungary's right to independence, no compromise was possible.

Yet, simple as the situation appears now, at the time it was far from simple. The complexity of our position led to a harsh clash of opinions in our country. I cannot conceal the fact that every man in a responsible position felt within himself the conflict of conscience. The right wing of the governing party had,

16 Hermann Neubacher (1893-1960).

in February, 1944, submitted a memorandum to the Prime Minister, questioning the belief that the British had already won the war. A victory of the joint enemy coalition, the memorandum argued aptly enough, would not eliminate the Communist menace. "If Germany suffers a defeat, Communism will triumph, and then woe betide Europe."

Conditions in southern Italy had led to the deposition of King Victor Emmanuel III. In Yugoslavia, the British had disowned Mihailovic and had recognized Tito. Russia had broken off diplomatic relations with the Polish Government in exile. The signs of the times were not heartening. These omens could not be dismissed as trivial, though the left-wing opposition tried to dismiss them as such, for which they were severely criticized in the memorandum. The promulgators of the memorandum did their cause considerable harm, however, by a threatening insistence that the German armies should at least retain their defensive positions in our country, if not as allies, then as an occupying force. It was precisely this that our government and I wanted by all means to prevent. The German course, to give that name to the policy advocated in the memorandum, was made none the more commendable by its implication to the infamous 'final solution' of the Jewish question. That is, that we should agree to the extermination of some 800,000 Jews. I made a personal effort to make the situation clear to Hitler, both in conversation and in a letter I wrote him, pointing out that a violent solution which, in any case, would be contrary to humanity and morals would not only undermine law and order but would have a deleterious effect on production.

Our small ship of state was tossing between Scylla and Charybdis. Our Premier, Kállay, did all he could to gain time. I devoted my main attention to military matters so that we should not be caught unprepared, from whichever direction danger loomed.

"Hungary," I wrote to Hitler in approximately these words, *"gazes anxiously upon her troops, stationed so far from home, mindful as she is of her heavy losses*[17] *in the 1942 winter campaign through the Hungarian Second Army being badly equipped in its severe contest far from its homeland. The historical and spiritual ties binding Hungarians to their native borders are strong. Those frontiers are the limits of their political ambitions, the limits also of their spiritual strength. For Hungarians to fight their best, those frontiers must be near. The recall of these*

17 In the Battle of Voronezh, commenced on January 22, 1943, the 200,000 strong, ill equipped Second Hungarian Army lost 147,000 men.

troops has become necessary for yet other reasons. The scene of war is shifting nearer Hungary and these troops will soon be needed for the defence of their own land. Our light materiel can be used effectively only in the Carpathians. I need not repeat that we are firmly resolved to defend our country against every attack with all our strength. Moreover, it is important that we should stand alone in defending our borders, taking all responsibility upon ourselves. That we owe to our nation. One of the most painful experiences of 1918 was absence of Hungarian troops for the defence of our own land. Now we are being threatened from the East. The front is drawing ever closer. We need our army and its equipment, for they can render Hungary and our common cause a greater and more valuable service at home than abroad. Their recall is for Hungary's defence."

In the same letter, I went on to say that the Hungarian participation in the occupation of south Transylvania proposed by Germany would be of doubtful value in face of the hatred of the Rumanian people for Hungary, fanned as it had been by propaganda. A possible rising of the Rumanians both there and in north Transylvania would have to be taken into consideration. We had been informed of the communications passing between Benes and Julius Maniu[18], the Transylvanian leader the Rumanian Agrarian Opposition Party, and of Benes's reassurances that Soviet Russia would help the Rumanians regain Transylvania. Finally, in that letter to Hitler, I stressed our anxiety concerning Budapest, which was the absolute "spiritual, political, economic and also war-industrial center" of the land, so that we dare not endanger it by consenting to a concentration of German forces near it, since that would without doubt attract heavy air-raids.

I waited in vain for Hitler's reply. My letter had been the signal for him to set into operation the Plan Margarete I: the military maneuvre that was "to secure Hungary." We heard that German troops were being concentrated in Burgenland, and, far from denying such rumours, the German Minister, von Jagow, confirmed them when he called on Ghyczy, our Foreign Minister, to protest vehemently against the slanderous imputations that they were gathering there in readiness for the occupation of Hungary. In its original form, Plan Margarete I, as I was to learn later, was based on joint German, Slovak and Rumanian military action and aimed at getting rid of me in the political field.

18 Iuliu Maniu (1873-1953), mentioned earlier in connection with Francis Ferdinand.

254

That a decision had to be taken became clear when the German Minister von Jagow, a party member who had replaced Herr von Erdmannsdorff[19], the last of the professional German diplomats, called on me at the Palace late in the evening after I had attended a performance at the Opera on our national holiday, March 15th[20], to transmit to me a message from Hitler. The message was to the effect that Hitler apologized for having been unable to answer my letter earlier owing to indisposition. The questions I had raised would be settled at Klessheim and, as Hitler was in a hurry to return to his headquarters, he requested me to go and see him at Klessheim within forty-eight hours.

19 Otto von Erdmannsdorff (1888-1978). His unpublished memoirs contain many quotations from Horthy. A review was published by P. Gosztonyi in "Air Raid, Budapest, op. cit.. For instance, after the attack of the Soviet Union, Horthy is quoted as saying: "After 22 years of waiting for this day, I am happy. Mankind will be grateful to Hitler for this deed. 189 million Russians will be freed from the yoke forced on them by two million Bolsheviks. This decision of Hitler's will bring about a peace. England and the United States will have to realize that Germany can not be conquered militarily".

20 March 15 is the anniversary of the beginning of the Hungarian Revolution of 1848-49.

20. The Occupation of Hungary

I sent von Jagow away without giving him a definite answer. Whether to accept Hitler's invitation or not was a question needing careful consideration. I therefore summoned the Prime Minister, the Foreign Minister, the Minister of War and the Chief of the General Staff. Kállay and Csatay[1], the Minister of War, advised me not to go. Szombathelyi, the Chief of the General Staff, and the Foreign Minister disagreed with them, the latter pointing out that Hitler had just received Tiso and Antonescu and that a refusal on my part could only acerbate the tension. As I learned later, Ghyczy the Foreign Minister, was cautious enough to draw up the text of a telegram to be sent to his deputy in warning if Hungary were to be occupied. This telegram was actually received in Budapest. If the Foreign Minister was in favour of the visit in spite of his fears, it was because he, realizing that resistance was impossible, was prepared to approve any step that might lead to a compromise.

I could see little use in undertaking the journey to Klessheim but could not deny the cogency of the arguments in favour. The determining factor in my decision to see Hitler was the thought that in a personal interview I could press for the return of the Hungarian troops which were now stationed abroad. I set out for Klessheim, therefore, on March 17th, 1944, accompanied by Ghyczy, Csatay and Szombathelyi.

March 17th was a Friday, and it is an old superstition of the sea that one should never set out on a Friday. And, indeed, in my sea days, I had never done so. I had always waited until eight bells had heralded a new day. On March 17th, I was untrue to my old custom. I set out with an uneasy feeling that was soon to be justified. Details may have slipped my mind, but I still clearly remember twice putting my revolver in my pocket and twice taking it out again before leaving the train. I knew that I would not be searched as Hitler's Generals were; but justice was to be meted out to him by a higher tribunal. I left my revolver in my coach[2].

---

1   General Lajos Csatay (1886-1944), minister of war from June 12 to October 16, 1944. He committed suicide in a German prison.

For the time being, events followed the usual procedure. As my train drew in on Saturday morning, Hitler, Ribbentrop, Keitel and others were at the station. I had the impression that Hitler stooped more and looked much older than when I had last seen him. As we were driven to Schloss Klessheim, an estate belonging to Archduke Louis Victor, the brother of the late Emperor, I asked Hitler if he desired our Foreign Minister and the Generals to be present at our discussion. He replied that he did not.

We went straight to his study, followed by Paul Schmidt[3], Hitler's interpreter. I had nothing against Herr Schmidt, whom I considered an intelligent and kindly man, and to whom we now owe the account of the exceedingly dramatic events of my stay at Klessheim which he has recorded in his book, (Paul Schmidt: Statist auf diplomatischer Bühne 1923 - 1945.). However, as none of my people were present and as no interpreter was needed between myself and Hitler, I queried his presence, and he withdrew. Later I regretted this, for, had I not protested, there would have been a witness to our talk.

Hitler was very ill at ease and seemed to find it difficult to begin. Instead of broaching the subject of the repatriation of our troops, he began with the Italian 'betrayal', which had put Germany in a difficult position. Since, according to his information, Hungary also was contemplating a change of sides, he felt he was obliged to take precautionary measures[4] in order to avoid being caught unawares a second time.

Upon my dry request for 'proofs', he repeated his accusations against Premier Kállay and our Legations in neutral countries. I countered sharply with the reply that Magyars had never been traitors. "Without my consent, there can never be the change of sides that you have described," I declared. "Should

2   Later Horthy mentioned his fleeting intent to kill Hitler to the commander of his gendarme guard detachment at Gödöllô, Colonel István Balló (personal communication, Ed.) While, if successfully carried out, killing Hitler would have shortened the war by a year, but it would have been catastrophic for Hungary.

3   Paul Otto Schmidt (1899-1970) chief interpreter of the German Foreign Ministry.

4   "March 15, 1944: German troops massed along the Hungarian border, preparing to occupy the territory of their shaky ally" - page 309 of Goralski, R. : World War II Almanac, 1931-1945, New York: Putnam, 1981.

events force my hand one day so that, to safeguard our very existence, I have to ask the enemy for an armistice, I assure you that I shall openly and honestly inform the German Government of such negotiations beforehand. We would, in any case, never be the first to take up arms against our German comrades."

The conversation continued for some time and we both grew heated. "I do not know what you mean by 'taking precautionary measures'," I said to Hitler. "If by that phrase you mean military measures, or in other words the occupation of an independent and sovereign state which has made many sacrifices on Germany's behalf, that would be an unspeakable crime. I can only warn you against the execution of so injudicious a step, which would cause unparalleled hatred for your regime to flare up."

From his excited answers, I realized that intelligent discussion was impossible. I interrupted him with the vehement words: "If everything has been decided upon already, there is no point in prolonging this discussion. I am leaving." Saying this, I walked quickly to the door with the intention of going to the rooms allocated to me on a higher floor. Hitler ran after me.

I sent for my fellow countrymen and told them what had happened. We decided to leave Klessheim forthwith. I requested Baron Dörnberg, who was in charge of arrangements, to see to the immediate departure of our special train. Today I know what I did not know then: that Hitler's 'precautionary measures' had already been set on foot and that orders had been given, should I prove 'stubborn', for my arrest in Vienna on my way home.

Hitler's immediate move, however, no doubt on the advice of his entourage, was an attempt to prevent our departure. To this end, an air alarm was sounded. The castle was put under a smoke screen and we were informed that bombs had severed the telephone communications. Together with that message, I received an invitation from Hitler to lunch and a request that we should continue our discussions in the afternoon. In the hope that he would have reconsidered his attitude, I agreed. The atmosphere during lunch could not be described as cordial. Hitler picked nervously at his vegetarian food. I felt little inclined to make conversation, nor apparently did the eight others assembled around the oval table in the handsome dining-hall.

259

After the meal, several separate discussions sprang up. Hitler endeavoured to give Szombathelyi the impression that he regretted his project[5]. That was probably all part of the game. He even went so far as to summon Field Marshal Keitel to ask him whether the occupation of Hungary could not be countermanded. Keitel replied that it could not as the troops were already on the march.

Having heard this from Szombathelyi, I said to Hitler during our second interview, "Then I shall, of course, lay down my office." Hitler thereupon began to plead with me. He had, he declared, always loved Hungary. He would not dream of interfering with Hungary's sovereignty. We know now that it was not only to the Rumanians that he had often said the contrary. He knew that Hungary had always been a sovereign state, "unlike Bohemia," he added, "which used to belong to the Holy Roman Empire, that is to say, Germany." His military measures were intended only to safeguard Hungary. "I give you my word that the German troops shall be withdrawn as soon as a new Hungarian Government that has my confidence has been formed." I replied that I had to reserve judgment on that point, and withdrew once more to my own apartments.

What was I to do? It was plain that my resignation would not prevent the military occupation, would indeed merely give Hitler and opportunity to introduce a hundred per cent Nazi Arrow-Cross regime. The precedent of the Italian debacle with its horrible attendant circumstances constituted a timely warning. So long as I continued head of the state, the Germans would have to show a certain circumspection. They would have to leave the Hungarian Army under my orders, and would therefore be unable to incorporate it into the German Army. While I was in charge, they could not attempt putting the Arrow-Cross Party into office to do their deadly work of murdering Hungarian patriots, of exterminating the 800,000 Hungarian Jews and the tens of thousands of refugees who had sought sanctuary in Hungary. It would have been easier for me to make the great gesture of abdication. I would have been spared many a denunciation. But to leave a sinking ship, especially one that needed her captain more than ever, was a step I could not bring myself to

5   While together in a Nazi prison in 1944, Szombathelyi told General Vilmos Nagybaconi Nagy, former Minister of War, that he has talked Hitler out of arresting Horthy on the spot. (Nagy, V. N.: Years of Destiny, Budapest: Gondolat, 1986. p. 244. In Hung.)

260

take. At the time it was more important to me that Hitler promised to withdraw his troops from Hungary as soon as a government acceptable to him had been appointed.

One thing was clear to me: whatever 'proofs' Hitler may have had of our negotiations with the enemy, his treachery in overrunning our country after having lured me and my Ministers away from Budapest was so wicked that henceforward we should be entirely released from any obligations to Nazi Germany.

The cup of Klessheim, however, had not yet been drained to the last dreg. As nothing more had been said about the time of departure of my train, I asked whether I was to consider myself a prisoner. Baron Dörnberg hastened to tell me that, the air alarm being over, my train would be ready to leave at eight o'clock that night. As I was preparing to go, the Foreign Minister of the Reich, Ribbentrop, came to read me the text of the communiqué covering my 'visit'. This document stated that the entry of German troops into Hungary was by 'mutual consent'. I protested angrily against this new lie. "You might as well have added," I fulminated, "that I begged Hitler to have Hungary occupied by Slovak and Rumanian troops, which was another of the threats he made." Ribbentrop wriggled desperately, putting forward the plea that in life minor untruths were often necessary. Phrased as it was, the communiqué made the occupation appear less hostile. I had been aware that this was the intention from the outset. I therefore insisted on the deletion of that particular lie. Ribbentrop at last agreed. But in the German press, the communiqué was published in its original form.

At eight o'clock that night we left. On the platform at Klessheim I saw Hitler for the last time before he committed suicide in the bunker of the Reich Chancellery, escaping by this act the justice of his earthly judges. A death which was announced to the world as death in action.

Our train was held up for a long time at Salzburg and at Linz. I was not intended to return to Budapest until the occupation had been accomplished. On the morning following our departure, during our journey, the Minister, von Jagow, came with the news that he had been recalled and that his successor, who was also on the train, wished to be introduced to me. This successor was none other than Dr. Edmund Veesenmayer, who had recently been in Budapest for some months. He was not only to be Minister but also bear the title of Plenipotentiary of the Reich. I gave Herr Veesenmayer my views on the occupation of our country. He assured me that it was his aim to carry out his assignment in complete accord with me. In how far he carried out his instructions in the months to come, or in how far the many inexorable measures taken were due to his own initiative, I cannot judge. To me he was the final arbiter representing the Nazi Government, as I declared later at Nuremberg.

Even while we were still travelling to Hungary, Dr. Veesenmayer began to discuss the formation of a new government, at the head of which he wished to see the former Premier, Béla Imrédy. That was out of the question.

The occupation of Hungary by eleven divisions, including several armoured divisions, had gone forward without giving rise to serious incidents. The general public, even our officers and soldiers, had little idea of the hollowness of the much-vaunted "friendship and comradeship of arms". For the rest, the main body of our troops were at the eastern and south-eastern frontiers and there had been no one present to give military orders.

The Prime Minister, Kállay met me at the railway station and as we drove to the Palace he rapidly told me what had been happening in Budapest. The Gestapo had arrested nine members of the Upper House and thirteen of the Lower House. They had seized the police headquarters and had requisitioned the Hotel Astoria for their use. Upon arrival, we found German sentries on guard outside the Palace gates.

At the meeting of the Crown Council, which I convened immediately, I gave the government a resumé of events at Klessheim. This was followed by the reports of the men who had accompanied me. Csatay, who had talked with Keitel, declared that the Germans had insisted that the Regent should not resign. Were he to do so, they would give the Slovaks, Croats and Rumanians a free hand in Hungary. Ghyczy, who had talked with Ribbentrop, and Szombathelyi, who had also talked with Hitler, confirmed this[6].

---

6   According to a Nuremberg trial document (D-679), a memorandum ad-
     dressed to Hitler by Colonel Wilhelm Höttl of the S.S. Secret Service, the
     original plan was to occupy Hungary with the aid of Slovak and Romanian
     troops. Höttl's warned Hitler not to do this. Ultimately Hitler followed the Höttl
     recommendation rather than the original army headquarters plan.

Kállay thanked me in the name of the government and of the nation for having saved the Supreme Command of our National Army. He expressly urged me not to relinquish my office, however much pressure was brought to bear on me. It gave me immense satisfaction to hear him, of all people, confirming the arguments I had put forward at Klessheim. When Kállay went on to ask me to accept his government's resignation, I assured him that I would be prepared to do so only under extreme pressure, as he had always enjoyed my unlimited confidence. We all knew full well that difficult times lay ahead. Kállay and his family escaped arrest only by slipping away through underground passages, dating from the time of Turkish occupation, to our apartments in the Palace, whence he alone was driven away by the Turkish Minister in his car[7]. Count Stephen Bethlen also managed to elude the secret police who had been sent to arrest him. The Minister for Home Affairs, Keresztes-Fischer, and his brother[8], the former Chief of the Military Chancellery, were arrested on March 20th[9].

I had been able to reject Dr. Veesenmayer's proposal that Imrédy should be appointed to the Premiership on the grounds that this leader of a small extreme-right-wing opposition had no backing in the country. A more difficult task was to find a man of whom Hitler would approve and who at the same time would be acceptable to us. We thought of creating a government of civil servants, but the Germans refused to accept this plan and insisted that a

---

7   He stayed at the Turkish Legation until the Fall of 1944 when he gave him-
    self up to the Germans. He survived imprisonment in the Mauthausen con-
    centration camp. His memoirs, written in New York, were published quite
    early after the war.

8   General Lajos Keresztes-Fisher (1884-1948). Both he and his brother
    Ferenc survived their imprisonment in the Buchtenwald concentration
    camp.

9   SS Lt. Gen. Alfred Trenker came to Hungary on March 19 as Gestapo Chief
    of Budapest. He had a list of 150 prominent anti-Nazi Hungarians to be ar-
    rested immediately. Another 310 were to be detained later. (Gosztonyi, Pe-
    ter: Storm over Eastern Europe, Budapest: Népszava, 1990. In Hung.) The
    fact that the Germans has planned Hungary's occupation for a long time is
    further proven by the fact that their list was so outdated that some persons
    listed were dead for years or out of the country for a long time, as recounted
    by Swedish diplomat Per Anger who was in Hungary at the time. (Letters
    and Dispatches 1924-1944, Raoul Wallenberg, U. S. Holocaust Memorial
    Museum, 1995.)

parliamentary government be formed. My choice finally fell on our Berlin Ambassador, General Döme Sztójay[10]. He had been present at the Klessheim discussions, had spent years in Berlin and was *persona grata* with Hitler. On March 23rd, he and the new members of the Cabinet were sworn in by me. Sztójay took the Ministry for Foreign Affairs as well as the Premiership. His deputy was Jenô Rácz[11]. Andor Jaross[12] became the new Minister for Home Affairs; Lajos Reményi-Schneller[13], Minister of Finance; Lajos Szász[14], Minister of Industry; Antal Kunder[15], Minister of Commerce and Transport; Béla Jurcsek[16], Minister of Agriculture; István Antal[17], Minister of Justice and Education; Lajos Csatay, Minister of War. Rácz, Jaross and Kunder belonged to the Imrédy Party. Reményi-Schneller, Szász, Jurcsek and Antal were members of the right wing of the government party.

The next few months constituted a depressing chapter in Hungarian history. I need hardly say that Hitler's promises to withdraw his troops as soon as a government which met with his approval had been formed, and to cease his interference in Hungarian Government matters, were not kept. The Balkan

10 Major General Döme Sztójay (1883-1946), former head of intelligence, dip-
    lomat, was a personal friend of Veesenmayer.

11 General Jenô Rátz (1882-1952) resigned his position on July 20 in protest
    when Horthy refused to sign into law some anti-Semitic measures. Later he
    became Speaker in the Pairlament during the Nazi regime. Convicted to life,
    he died in prison.

12 Andor Jaross (1896-1946).

13 Dr. Lajos Reményi-Schneller (1892-1946) was an economist. He was a
    member of the cabinet, on and off, in varous capacities from 1938. He was
    Minister of Finance in the Szálasi government. His coupled Hungarian Ger-
    man name, one of the many in this book, shows that a large number of Hun-
    gary's bureaucrats were of German origin. An even greater number of these
    were among the professional officer corps. Many of these were in sympathy
    with the Nazis.

14 Dr. Lajos Szász (1888-1946), lawyer, banker, politician. Occupied various
    cabinet positions during the war.

15 Antal Kunder (1900-1968).

16 Béla Jurcsek (1903-1945).

17 István Antal (1896-1975), lawyer, politician. Held several cabinet positions
    such as propaganda, justice, religion minister.

Army, under the command of Field Marshal Baron Weichs[18], which had behaved with exemplary discipline, did indeed leave the country, but only to make room for new formations of the Waffen-SS and the Gestapo.

On April 2nd, Dr. Veesenmayer had been instructed by the German Foreign Office that I should be excluded from all political activity. Sztójay and his government thenceforth carried out as promptly as they could the orders given them by Dr. Veesenmayer and the German occupation authorities.

I found it very gratifying that our Ministers accredited in neutral countries, and their diplomatic staffs, refused to accept instructions from the Sztójay Government, as a protest against the occupation of Hungary. A few of the Ministers resigned, and remained in touch with me. That Hungary's position was rightly summed up became clear when the governments of these neutral countries refused to accredit Ministers appointed by the Sztójay Government. Sztójay had to content himself with sending out charge's d'affaires to replace the Ministers who had resigned.

I have said that, while writing these memoirs, I have not had at hand the relevant official documents. I have in my possession, however, copies of the minutes of some of the Cabinet meetings held during the period of German occupation, though I cannot guarantee that they are complete. On reading them, the sentences "The Germans demand, The Cabinet agrees" occur with monotonous regularity. Sztójay began by proposing that Parliament should not discuss the arrest of the members of the two Houses; the Minister for Home Affairs supported this proposal by letting it be known that anyone broaching the subject would be arrested.

Obviously, all German demands concerning the availability of labour, food supplies and war materials were fulfilled. Demands for more troops were frequent. In 1943, we had created a highly trained elite cavalry corps, equipped with armoured vehicles and motorized heavy artillery. I had considered it vital to keep these reliable troops in Hungary, and I had

18 General Baron Maximilian von Weichs (1881-1954) wrote in his diary that the German Army Headquarters insisted on a 'strong arm policy': disarming the Hungarian armed forces, and plundering the economy. He and Veesenmayer disagreed with the O.K.W., Weich called the plan "sheer madness". Finally, Weichs and Veesenmayer has prevailed. (Gosztonyi, P.: Air Raid, Budapest!, Budapest: Népszava, 1958, in Hung.)

repeatedly refused German requests to send them to the Eastern front. The Germans had then invited our Chief of the General Staff, Szombathelyi, to call at the Fuehrer's headquarters. He returned with the impression that a continued refusal would lead to serious reprisals of a violent nature. Only then, in May 1944, with great reluctance, did I permit this corps to be moved to our frontiers after both Hitler and Keitel had agreed to my proviso that it was to remain on the left wing of our Army. That proviso was, of course, not honoured. Hardly had the corps reached the frontier before it was sent further north. On its way through the Pripet Marshes it lost a considerable part of its armoured vehicles and motorized artillery, besides being attacked by Soviet armoured divisions and suffering heavy losses. The German front was already wavering and the Hungarian regiments had, in accordance with the orders of the German High Command, been given the task of covering a withdrawal under orders to hold out to the last man. Lieutenant Field Marshal Vattay[19] did not obey these orders but followed the retreating German regiments. Our cavalry corps finally found itself in the Warsaw sector.

The Nazis now imposed a sharply anti-Semitic policy. The Sztójay Government was forced to compel all Jews to wear a clearly displayed Star of David and to degrade them to second-class citizenship. It was certainly no fault of this government that their persecution and deportations still did not reach the pitch that Berlin prescribed. A protest made by the Prince-Primate Cardinal Serédi against the anti-Semitic measures was rejected[20] Horthy's demand was disregarded[21]. The Minister of Commerce ordered all Jewish firms to be closed. The technical execution of the deportations was entrusted to the parliamentary secretaries, Baky[22], and Endre[23], two notorious anti-Semites who, at Cabinet meetings, were often heard to declare that "humanitarian considerations were immaterial"[24]. On July 7th, Hitler summoned Sztójay, complimented him on certain of the measures taken against the Jews but, maintaining that much was still to be done, said that the Gestapo would remain in Hungary "until the Jewish problem had been completely settled". Only the courageous and loyal Minister of War, Csatay, tried repeatedly to resist the inhumanity of the measures taken against the

19 General Antal Vattay (1891-1966). On October, 1944, he was imprisoned by the Nazis. Having survived that, he was imprisoned the the Communist secret police on false charges in 1949 and was not released until the 1956 revolution.

Jews[26]. After the events of October 15th, Csatay and his wife took their own lives.

20 Upon learning truth about the deportations, Horthy wrote the following letter to the Prime Minister:

"Dear Sztójay:

I was aware that the Government in the given forced situation has to take many steps that I do not consider correct, and for which I can not take responsibility. Among these matters is the handling of the Jewish question in a manner that does not correspond to the Hungarian mentality, Hungarian conditions, and, for the matter, Hungarian interests. It is clear to everyone that what among these were done by Germans or by the insistence of the Germans was not in my power to prevent, so in these matters I was forced into passivity. As such, I was not informed in advance, or I am not fully infored now, however, I have heard recently that in many cases in inhumaneness and brutality we exceeded the Germans. I demand that the handling of the Jewish affairs in the Ministry of Interior be taken out of the hands of Deputy Minister László Endre. Furthermore, László Baky's assignment to the management of the police forces should be terminated as soon as possible."

21 Bokor, Peter: *Deadend*, Budapest: RTV-Minerva, 1985. In Hung. P. 31.

22 László Baky (1898-1946) a retired officer of the gendarmes. He prepared the list of those to be arrested by the Gestapo. (Bokor, P.: *Endplay*... op. cit., p. 134.) Executed in 1946.

23 László Endre (1895-1946), deputy minister of the interior. Executed after the war.

24 General Antal Náray, in his 1945 memoirs (op. cit.) that were hidden for 38 years, described an audience with Horthy on June 18, on Horthy's 76-th birthday. Horthy related to him his experiences with Hitler at Klessheim that fully agrees with Horthy's description. Another interesting quote: "What they do to the Jews exceeds inhumanity" said Horthy, upon which he turned quiet, looked away at length, and cried, wrote Náray.

26 According to General Faragho, Horthy related to him in a confidential conversation that German officials in Switzerland screened a film, staged by the Gestapo, that depicted the barbarian treatment of Jews by Hungarian gendarmes, followed by humanitarian scenes by German nurses, upon transfer of the Jews into German custody. No copy of this film is known to exist. According to a member of the Jewish Council, Samu Stern, the Council called the film to Horthy's attention, as an example of the anti-Hungarian propaganda by the Nazis (See App. by S. Balogh).

267

For a long time I was helpless before German influence, for, in Budapest and its vicinity, I lacked the means to check or thwart the joint action of the Germans and the Ministry for Home Affairs. As the defeat of Germany drew nearer, I regained, though slowly and imperfectly, a certain freedom of action. In the summer, I succeeded at last in having the possibility of freeing the Jews from the prohibitions and restrictions imposed on them by law. Of the innumerable requests that poured in, I rejected none. The deportations were supposed to be made to labour camps. Not before August did secret information reach me of the horrible truth about the extermination camps. It was Csatay, the Minister of War, who raised the matter at a Cabinet meeting and demanded that our government should insist on the Germans clarifying the situation. This demand was not met by the Cabinet. The Churches, I must here add, did what they could for those in distress by providing them with certificates of baptism. In this, they acted in accordance with the true wishes of our people.

The next step taken by the Germans deliberately flouted the elementary sense of justice of our nation and added much to the odium in which the Germans came to be held. My son Nicholas had established a special chancellery[27] which was in constant communication with the Hungarian Jewish Committee, so that I was kept informed of events and was able to intervene when the opportunity offered[28]. Up until June, more than 400,000 persons had been deported. In August, Budapest was to be 'cleaned up'. 170,000 Jews were registered in the capital and another 110,000 were in hiding at their Magyar friends'. The Deputy Secretaries, Baky and Endre, had planned a surprise action to arrest and deport the Budapest Jews. As soon as news of this reached my ears, I ordered the armoured division which was stationed near Esztergom to be transferred to Budapest[29]. Furthermore, I instructed the Chief of the Budapest gendarmerie to assist in preventing the forceful removal of Jews. The fact that this action saved the Jews of Budapest has been confirmed by the members of the Jewish Committees in Hungary, Samu Stern[30], Dr. Ernô Petô and Dr. Károly Wilhelm, in written statements they made under oath on February 3rd, 1946. I still have photocopies and an

27 Directed by Horthy's son Nicholas Horthy Jr.

28 Adolf Eichmann's statement, "resistance [to the deportations] in Hungary was offered by Horthy and his close associates" confirms this. (Jochen von Lang, Ed.: *Eichmann Interrogated, - Transcripts from the Archives of the Israeli Police,* New York: Farrar, Straus & Giroux, 1983, pp.232.)

English translation of these statements, endorsed by the Swedish Embassy in Rome.[31]

The Red Cross and, at the request of King Gustav[32] of Sweden, the Wallenberg[33] Mission tried to persuade the Germans to agree to grant the Jews unmolested passage to Palestine. Through my Cabinet, I gave full support to this attempt, but in vain. Dr. Veesenmayer entered a protest to the Sztójay Government against my interfering in the Jewish question. Nevertheless, in August I duly informed the Government of the Reich that I would do my utmost to prevent a removal of Jews from Budapest. As the Germans were still striving to keep up the pretence of Hungarian sovereignty, they decided to forgo taking further measures.

Action similar to that taken against the Jews had also been taken against the Polish, Italian and other refugees who had sought in Hungary asylum from

29 This is confirmed by Swedish Diplomat Per Anger who was in Budapest at the time. Anger also states that a colonel of the gendarmes, Ferenczy, to-gether with Endre and Baky planned to depose Horthy at that time. (Letters and Dispatches 1924-1944, Raoul Wallenberg, U.S. Holocaust Memorial Museum, 1995.) Baky's putsch was planned for July 6. He moved armed Ar-row Cross members to Budapest, dressed as gendarmes. On Horthy's com-mand, Colonel Ferenc Koszorus (1899-1974), chief of staff of the battle-hardened First Armored Division, occupied strategic positions with his tanks in and around Budapest in a surprise move. Baky backed down; Eichmann, who directed the deportations, left Hungary. (P. 38, Bokor, P.: Deadend, Budapest: RTV-Minerva, 1985.) The story is described in detail in the Appendix by sons of two participating officers.

30 Samu Stern (1874-1946). See April 26, 1994 letter to the *New York Times* in the Appendix for his memoirs.

31 On July 29, 1944, in a report to his government Raoul Wallenberg wrote: "His (Horthy's) position is illustrated by the very real fact that the deporta-tions were canceled per his order, but also by a number of smaller interven-tions. Among them, two verified instances of trains loaded with prisoners being ordered to turn back just before reaching the border. That Horthy's power is a factor to be reckoned with is shown by the fact that while the above- mentioned trainload of intellectuals was sent across the border, the entire Jewish Council was detained by the Gestapo, so that they would not be able to report the matter to the head of state, who was judged to have enough power to order the train to turn back." (U.S. Holocaust Museum: Raoul Wallenberg: *Letters and Dispatches 1924-1944*; New York: Arcade, 1995, p. 241.)

the Nazis. The Polish schools and the only Polish University outside Poland, other than the one in England, were closed. I gave whatever help I could to these victims also. I was not always as successful in my attempts as I was on one occasion when I was able to prevent a hundred prisoners from being taken from Budapest for deportation. The news had been smuggled out of the prison by a prisoner's wife who carried it to my wife. I had the prison surrounded by troops and the transportation party failed to arrive. I heard later that those prisoners lived to see the end of the war.

As a result of German pressure, Imrédy had been taken into the Government in May, albeit as Minister without portfolio. The uncertainty of Imrédy's ancestry, however, had not been cleared up, and in spite of the issue of a German statement that the documents in question had been forged. The Arrow-Cross Party insisted that he had Jewish blood and refused to collaborate with him. Imrédy and his political friends Kunder and Jaross left the Cabinet on August 7th.

The Allied invasion of France was successful. Hitler's last hope of a military victory had faded. In June, Sztójay had still been able to   return from the Fuehrer's headquarters with the news that the Germans were looking forward

32 On June 30, 1944, King Gustav of Sweden (1858-1950) wrote Horthy the following telegram: *"Having received word of the extraordinarily harsh methods your government has applied against the Jewish population of Hungary, I permit myself to turn to Your Highness personally, to beg in the name of humanity, that you take measures to save those who still remain to be saved of the unfortunate people. This plea has been evoked by my long-standing feelings of friendship for your country and my sincere concern for Hungary's good name and reputation in the community of nations."* On July 12 Horthy replied as follows: *"I have received the telegraphic appeal sent me by Your Majesty. With feelings of the deepest understanding, I ask Your Majesty to be persuaded that I am doing everything that, in the present situation, lies in my power to ensure that the principles of humanity and justice are respected. I esteem to a high degree the feelings of friendship for my country that animate Your Majesty and I ask that Your Majesty preserve these feelings toward the Hungarian people in these times of severe trial."* (U.S. Holocaust Museum, op. cit.; pp. 218-219.)

33 Raoul Wallenberg (1912- ?) Swedish diplomat noted for his extraordinary heroism in saving Hungarian Jews from Nazi deportation. He was arrested by the Soviet army in 1945 for no discernible reason and died in Soviet prison. News stories in 1996 revealed that the Soviets suspected him to be an OSS spy.

to the invasion, which could only end in a fiasco for the British and Americans. Simultaneously, the Russians were pressing forward. Early in August, in an interview with Dr. Veesenmayer, I had advised the occupation of the Transylvanian Carpathians. Veesenmayer had replied that it was impossible to raise the necessary forces.

"You do not need extra forces," I told him. "The German troops within and around Budapest alone would suffice." Our experience in the First World War had shown that the passes could be held by relatively weak forces.

I am not in a position to say whether, had my advice been taken, the advance of the Russian forces into the Hungarian plains could have been prevented after Rumania had changed sides. According to General Guderian's[34] published memoirs (Guderian: *Erinnerungen eines Soldaten*,[35] Heidelberg, 1951) Marshal Antonescu declared himself willing, after a visit to the Fuehrer's headquarters, to evacuate Moldavia and fall back on a front from Galatz via Focsani to the ridge of the Carpathians. The Chief of the Southern Ukraine Army, Major-General Friessner[36], who had been appointed in July, agreed with Antonescu's plan. But Hitler listened to neither the one nor the other. He believed he had time enough to make up his mind and he was no doubt strengthened in this belief by incorrect reports from Bucharest. The military and civilian bodies which had hitherto given an invariably favourable account of the state of affairs in Rumania now hesitated to confess their mistakes and their over-optimism. The surprise of the Germans was therefore all the greater when, after a dramatic interview, young King Michael[37] dismissed Marshal Antonescu on August 23rd. As a result, twenty-one

34 Gen. Heinz Wilhelm von Guderian (1888-1954).

35 In English: *Panzer Leader*, London, 1952; New York, 1967.

36 General Hans Friessner (1892-1971). His experiences as German commander in the Hungarian front are described in his book: *Verratene Schlachten*, Hamburg: Holsten Verlag. He met Horthy on September 9, 1944. Horthy's personality impressed him, but he commented on the "medieval pomp" in the Palace. Horthy's request to spare Hungary and her people puzzled him, "how does one fight a humane war, particularly against the Soviets?"

37 King Michael of Hohenzollern-Sigmaringen (1921-) exiled to Switzerland after the Communist takeover in 1949. In the early 1990's he made repeated attempts to return to Romania.

German divisions were cut off and taken prisoner. The Plan Margarete II, prepared for just such an emergency, could no longer be put into operation, as the troops needed for it were out of action[38].

This gave me the long-sought opportunity to act[39]. Events abroad and at home coincided to make it impossible for Sztójay to continue in office. On August 24th, I sent the Premier's Parliamentary Secretary, István Bárczy[40], and the Chief of my Cabinet Chancellery, Gyula Ambrózy[41], to call on Sztójay, who was at that time in a sanatorium, with my request for his resignation. Sztójay resigned. To my surprise and also to the surprise of others, the German Plenipotentiary raised no objection. If Dr. Veesenmayer is to be believed, this was due to the fact that he wished to work with me and not against me. He was prepared to call on the Arrow-Cross men only in an extreme emergency. I myself think that the general political and military situation was the deciding factor. The Germans influence in Hungary has weakened. But the time for a forceful action had not yet arrived[42].

All that the new government could do was to save what could be saved. I could not agree under any condition to the German proposal that Hungary should be declared an operational area, regardless of the future. We had every reason

38 Hungary's military attaché to Bucharest learned about the putsch before-hand and advised the Germans. They, however, dismissed this information as a typical example of Hungarian mischief against the Rumanians. (Gosztonyi, P.: *Storm over Eastern Europe,* Budapest: Népszava, 1990, p. 170; in Hung.)

39 On August 28 Horthy sent a cable to György Bakách-Bessenyey, former minister to Berne, to initiate negotiations for an armistice. He was advised by representatives of the Western Powers to seek contact with Moscow. As Berne had no diplomatic relations with the Soviets this approach was un-successful. (Vigh, K.: *Jump into the Dark,* op. cit., p.65.)

40 István Bárczy (1882-1952), Chief of Protocol of the Prime Minister's office. On June 28, 1944, murderers hired by Baky attempted to kill him at his home. Instead they killed one of their own before fleeing.

41 Gyula Ambrózy (1884-1954), chief Cabinet Office, Horthy's right hand. He was a major player in feeling out the Western Powers about an armistice.

42 This was a clear miscalculation by Horthy. There were far more Hungarian forces than German in Hungary at the time. This was the last occasion the bailout may have succeeded. (Vigh: *Jump...*; op. cit.; p. 101.)

to fear that if we entered voluntarily a joint Hungarian-German 'fight to the bitter end', the victors would wipe Hungary out permanently. Before the Rumanians changed sides, I had already sent General Béla Dálnoky-Miklós with a special message to Hitler. He was received on July 21st[43]. He informed the Germans, in accordance with what I had said at Klessheim, that if Hungary were not given the aid that had been promised her, she would have to withdraw from the war. Towards the end of August, with the Russians at the gates of Bucharest[44], Hitler sent General Guderian to me. As Guderian has himself stated, I gave him no assurances. He seemed even to sympathize with our point of view, for he agreed to the recall of the Hungarian cavalry division which was still fighting in the Warsaw sector.

On August 29th, at eleven o'clock at night, the new government was sworn in at the Palace. I had appointed Major-General Géza Lakatos[45] Prime Minister and General Gustáv Hennyey[46] Foreign Minister. At the request of the Germans, I agreed to the inclusion of Reményi-Schneller and Jurcsek in the Cabinet. They were henceforth Veesenmayer's informers, keeping him apprised with all that happened at the meetings of the Cabinet and of the Crown Council.

On that August 29th, immediately after the Cabinet had been sworn in, it was convened and the decision was taken to carry on the war against Russia. We were swayed by our wish to prevent Hungary from becoming a battlefield and to this end it was necessary that the southern area round Belgrade and the

---

43 One day after the assassination attempt by Col. Stauffenberg and other officers.

44 The Red Army entered Bucharest on August 8.

45 General Géza Lakatos (1890-1967). Seeing the recent losses of the Germans, Horthy felt that with Lakatos the foreign policy of Kállay could again be pursued: seeking an armistice. His memoirs are published in English: "As I Saw It (The Tragedy of Hungary)", Englewood, NJ: Universe Publishing, 1996. Lakatos stated that Horthy attempted to appoint him prime minister twice before, on July 8, and on July 18, but the Germans thwarted both of these attempts.

46 General Gusztáv Hennyey (1888-1977). He lived in Switzerland after the war, and conducted an extensive and systematic correspondence on the matters of the war. This valuable collection is now held by the Institute Military History in Budapest.

Dukla Pass in the north should be held. The weak Hungarian Army, for the bulk of the Hungarian troops were abroad, was to be strengthened by the German troops in Hungary, about 500,000 men, who had been taken out of the line to be re-established there. The German High Command agreed, but nothing was done before mid-October, by which time it was too late. On the occasion of an earlier visit I had paid to Hitler's headquarters, the 'Wolfschanze', near Rastenberg in East Prussia, Hitler told me that the war would be lost should the Russians overrun the Hungarian plains. This eventuality was now at hand. After the way that Hitler had behaved to me personally and after all he had done to Hungary, I need not have felt myself bound to adhere to the promise I had made at Klessheim, that I would inform him when I sued for an armistice. Yet I did, because of my friendship with the German people, who had finally fallen victims to Hitler, and were also, like ourselves, in danger of being overwhelmed by the Communist flood.

The Rumanians had turned their arms against us. In his first proclamation King Michael had called for the 'liberation of Transylvania'. On August 26th, the day after Paris had been retaken by the Allies, Sofia announced that Bulgaria was withdrawing from the war. However, the Bulgarian attempt to secure an armistice with Britain and the United States of America, failed. The Soviet Union, with which Bulgaria had not hitherto been at war, frustrated the attempt by declaring war on Bulgaria[47]. It was to us a bitter demonstration of the power relations between the Allies.

On September 7th, we received the news that five Soviet armoured divisions were approaching. I called the members of the government together, and summoned János Vörös[48], who had succeeded Szombathelyi as Chief of the General Staff in April. Together we decided that Hungary was no longer able to resist without immediate and considerable assistance. Rumania had declared war on us. A Finnish delegation had travelled to Moscow to negotiate for an armistice. At my request, Premier Lakatos called on the German Plenipotentiary and on the German military attaché, General von Greifenberg[49], that same evening after the Cabinet meeting, and informed them of our Cabinet's decision. The situation demanded that five motorized

---

47 September 5, 1944.

48 General János Vörös (1891-1968). Most of his contemporaries describe him as a vacillating careerist, who bore most of the responsibility for the failed armistice attempts.

divisions should at once be thrown in. Otherwise Hungary would be unable to continue fighting.

Even in this solemn hour, as always, I sought the advice of those men who, throughout the years of my Regency, had shown themselves true servants of the Fatherland and had thereby won my confidence. I made arrangements for Count Stephen Bethlen to be brought safely from his place of hiding outside Budapest to the Palace. There he presided at the meeting held on September 10th, to which, as well as the members of the government, Lakatos and Hennyey, I had invited the Speakers of the two Houses of Parliament, Kánya, the former Foreign Minister, Major-General Rôder, the Counts Maurice Esterházy and Gyula Károlyi, Bánffy, the former Minister of Agriculture, and Count Béla Teleki[50], the leader of the Magyars in Transylvania. After listening to a military report read by General Vörös, Count Bethlen declared that any further bloodshed would be senseless, and that an attempt should therefore be made to end the war forthwith. All who were present were in full agreement[51].

These grave moments were relieved by one tragicomic incident. It had been relatively easy to smuggle Count Bethlen into the Palace. But it was not so simple to secure his safe return to his hiding-place. His characteristic moustache was too recognizable. Bethlen was talked into shaving it off; and did so on the spot; his white upper lip stood out like a beacon in his sunburnt face. My daughter-in-law had the brilliant idea of using a sunray lamp and with its help the colour of his upper lip was darkened to match the rest of his face. In uniform, his cap pulled down over his eyes, Count Bethlen left the town as he had arrived, unobserved.

49 General Hans von Greiffenberg (1893-1951)

50 Count Béla Teleki (1888-1979) was the leader of the Hungarian Party of Transylvania. He was closely associated with the anti-Nazi underground that included friends of the imprisoned Bajcsy-Zsilinszky, such as Endre Fall, leader of the Revisionist League, Baron Ede Atzél, Transylvanian activist who first crossed over to the Soviets to discuss an armistice, and others.

51 On this meeting the Transylvanian leaders insisted that if Horthy does not ask for an armistice than they will act on their own. (Bokor: *Endplay,* op. cit.; p. 235.)

An extraordinary Cabinet meeting held on September 21th caused a certain delay. According to the minutes, of which I have only an unauthenticated copy, Premier Lakatos made the following statement:

"The Regent conferred on September 7th with the Government, on September 10th with his twelve secret counsellors, and has assured himself of the gravity of the war situation and political events abroad. He has reached the conclusion that further expenditure of blood would be useless, and that the great superiority of the Red Army makes the continuation of the war impossible. The Regent has asked me to call on him tomorrow and has instructed me to inform the Government that he will wait no longer. He is firmly determined to ask the enemy today for the terms of an armistice. The Regent desires to learn only one thing from the Government, which members of the Government are prepared to bear their share in the political responsibility for this step, and which are not. The decision of the Regent will in no way be influenced by the answer I shall give him."

The Premier than called upon those present to speak; in order not to influence their decisions, he offered to speak last. A variety of arguments was put forward at the meeting to decline the assumption of political responsibility; only Lakatos, Csatay and Hennyey pronounced in favour of an armistice. Therefore the Cabinet decided to offer me their resignation[52].

Even taking into account the fact that Lakatos and his Ministers had to bear in mind that their colleagues Reményi-Schneller and Jurcsek would immediately make their report to Veesenmayer, their decision came as a surprise to me. I did not hide my feelings from Lakatos and repeated that my determination remained fixed. I noted their resignation but asked the government to remain in office for the time being.

Soon after, the government sent the Chief of the General Staff, Vörös, to Hitler to enquire what help Hitler was prepared to give Hungary. Hitler, it seemed, was fully informed concerning the meetings of September 7th and 10th, but mistrusted the declared intention of the Lakatos Government to carry on the war. Vörös was given no definite assurances of military aid.

---

52 The reason was that Lakatos, in his maiden speech in parliament, promised to continue the war as long as he remained in office.

On September 22nd, I despatched General Náday[53] and the British Colonel Howie[54] by plane to the Allied Headquarters at Caserta, near Naples. Colonel Howie, who had escaped to Hungary from a German prison camp, had been taken by Polish intermediaries to my son, who had had him smuggled into the Palace. He had hidden in the apartments of my aide-de-camp, Tost[55] until the time came for him to fly to Caserta.

At Caserta, General Náday talked with General Maitland Wilson[56] and Sir John Slessor[57], the Commander-in-Chief and Air Forces Chief of the Eighth Army respectively, who told him that Hungary must find a way of communicating with the Russians, as their own hands were tied. Radio communications being much disturbed, this message reached us in a mutilated form, but we were able to guess at the missing part as a similar message already reached us via Berne. The Germans soon learned of the departure of Náday. The pilot[58] had taken his wife with him, which had attracted attention, though they failed to discover in whose company he had gone.

While, on the one hand, the Arrow-Cross Party, seeing the approach of their great chance, were preparing to seize power[59], the political resistance movement, on the other, was becoming more active and was trying to establish contact with me through my son Nicholas[60]. The political activities of the opposition parties, the Smallholders' Party, the Social Democrats and

---

53 General István Náday (1888-1954) was an openly pro-British officer, convinced from the beginning of the final victory of the Allies. He had the habit of writing his personal notes in English. Gen. Vattay's memoirs claim that upon Náday's visit, the Americans arranged for Msgr. Gyula Magyary, a Vatican theologian, to fly the Slovakian partizans by a U.S. plane, from where he traveled to Budapest, bringing communication codes for future radio contacts personally to Horthy. Magyary was sent by Gábor Apor, Hungary's minister to the Vatican, who was in close contact with American authorities in Italy.

54 South African Artillery Colonel Charles Telfer Howie (1905 - ?).

55 Lt. Colonel Gyula Tost (1903-1944).

56 British General Sir Henry Maitland Wilson (1881-1964).

57 Air Marshal Sir John Cotesworth Slessor (1897-1979).

58 János Majoros, an official of the Hungarian Airlines.

the Communists, lacked unity of leadership. The Social Democrats had been weakened, in March, by the arrest of their leader, Károly Peyer[61], and his successor, Árpád Szakasits[62], had relatively little authority among his fellow members. The Smallholders' Party was in much the same position, having lost its real leader, Tibor Eckhardt[63], while his successor, Zoltán Tildy[64], a former clergyman of the Reformed Church, had played a more than questionable role. There were also a few legitimist elements who were in contact with the

59 On September 1, Horthy ordered the arrest of all Arrow Cross leaders but it was disregarded by pro-Nazi officials in the Ministry of Interior.Instead, they were placed into the protection of the Gestapo. (Vigh: *Jump..*; op. cit.; p. 200.)

60 Nicholas Horthy, Jr. (1907-1982), oldest son of the Regent, former Hungarian envoy to Brazil. Gen. Antal Náray (op. cit.), director of the Hungarian Radio and Newsbureau MTI was a personal friend of both of Horthy's sons. In his 1945 memoirs, hidden for 38 years, Náray states that among alternatives of "bailing out" one was the possibility of Horthy and his cabinet flying to exile, while general Szombathelyi was to establish a military dictatorship in covert contact with Horthy. Alternatively, Horthy was to move into the protection of the 300,000 strong army in the Carpathians before his declaration of armistice. Horthy Jr. supposedly told his father: "Father, if we don't do something soon, we will have to leave the palace with a shopping bag in hand." (Vigh: *Jump...;* op. cit.; p. 103.)

61 Károly Peyer (1881-1956), Social Democrat politician.

62 Árpád Szakasits (1888-1965) leader of the Social Democrats who has later fully embraced the post-war Communist government. He offered Horthy to organize a general strike in support of his armistice, and asked for 5,000 weapons to arm the workers of Budapest. The weapons in question ended up in the hand of the Arrow Cross. (Vigh: *Jump...*; op. cit.; p. 255.) According to Mrs Ilona Bowden, Horthy's daughter-in-law, the distribution of arms was planned for between October 17 and 20, the planned day for the proclamation. Political prisoners were prepared to be released at the same time. (Pers. info. Ed.)

63 He spent the war years in Washington lobbying for Hungary under instructions from Horthy and Teleki. His trip was financed by the Hungarian National Bank, and one of his extensive reports sent from Washington is still extant.

64 Zoltán Tildy (1889-1961) left leaning reformed minister who became the first post-war president of Hungary. His Smallholders' party gained absolute majority on the first election, yet he still entered into coalition and gave most powerful cabinet posts to the Communists.

political underground movement, while the Communists, led by László Rajk[65], were waiting for the Russians and retained but a nominal contact with it. The Chief of the State Security Police, General Ujszászy[66], was chosen as contact man, for he was known to be a keen opponent of Communism and was therefore unlikely to rouse the suspicions of the Germans. A number of discussions were held between General Ujszászy and the representatives of the different groups. Among the subjects discussed was the arming of the workers to enable them to guard factories, bridges, roads and railways. Major-General Bakay[67], the Commander of the Budapest Army Corps, was to supervise the distribution of arms. On October 11th, I received Tildy and Szakasits, who had come to see me at my request. Our discussion had no practical results.

65 László Rajk (1909-1949) participated in the Spanish civil war in the Communist International Brigade. He was one of the leaders on the underground Communist Party in Hungary, and became a minister during the Communist Reign of Terror (1949-56). The Communist secret police charged him with pro-American spying, and after a show trial he was hanged. Supposedly, Frank Wiesner of the CIA, under Allan Dulles, had framed him. (Mosley, Leonard: Dulles, New York: Dial Press, 1978.) His rehabilitation and ceremonial re-burial in October, 1956, signaled the end of the reign of terror.

66 Lt. General István Újszászy (1894-1945). Head of Military Intelligence, founder of State Security Center (Államvédelmi Központ), 1942. His incompetence in covert tradecraft earned him worldwide notoriety among intelligence services. At the end of 1943 Kállay established contact with Allen Dulles, OSS representative in Switzerland. On Dulles' suggestion a three men military delegation, led by Col. Florimond Duke successfully parachuted into S.W. Hungary on March 18 and were taken to Budapest. Ujszászy, after arrested and interrogated by the Gestapo, caused the capture of the Americans. In 1944 he was captured by the Soviets, handed over to the Hungarian Communist Security, committed suicide (or killed) in 1945. According to newspaper reports (Népszabadság. June 21, 1997, p. 27) in 1943 Ujszászy was instrumental in arranging the revered Jewish caddik, Rabbi Aharon Rokéah of Belz, Poland, escape to Palestine through Hungary.

67 Major General Szilárd Bakay (1892-1946). In the days before the Nazi occupation, as the commander of the western military district, he is credited with sending the following cable to headquarters: "Russians are in front, Germans behind, British above, send instructions." He was kidnapped by Germans on October 8, 1944, and was taken to Mauthausen. After the war he returned to Hungary on his own will. In 1946 he was arrested, and executed as a war criminal by the Soviets.

21. Appealing for Armistice. My Imprisonment

I was still hesitating before the last irrevocable step. It is always bitter to have to beg for an armistice. The fact that England and America had referred us to the Russians, and to the Russians alone, transformed our misfortune into a tragedy. The first reports were coming in of incredible brutalities committed by the Russian fighting forces against the defenceless population. I had to take the humiliating step of appealing to Moscow.

The laws of self-preservation demanded that we come to terms with the enemy. Should anyone be inclined to criticize us on this score, he should remember that we were not, as we had been in the First World War, Germany's ally by treaty. We had been forced against our will into a war that was waged to forward Hitler's expansionist aims. The basis of our participation in the war against Russia was comparable to that of Germany only in that we were both fighting Communism. But Hungary made no territorial claims on Russia. We knew full well that we could not count on Germany's gratitude for our entry into the war nor for our having supplied her with war materials, for which a debt of three billion pengôs was never settled. We wished to fight the battle against Communism, but only so long as it was in our own interests, not merely to further Hitler's war aims and not to the point of suicide. When a war has plainly been lost, it is time to arrange peace.

Towards the end of September, I sent to Moscow the Chief of the Hungarian gendarmerie, Lieutenant General László Faragho[1], who spoke fluent Russian, having formerly been our military attaché in Moscow. He was accompanied by Professor Count Géza Teleki[2], the son of the Prime Minister, Count Paul Teleki, who had so tragically sacrificed his life, and by Councillor Domonkos Szent-Iványi[3], representing the Ministry for Foreign Affairs[4] During the

---

1 Gen. Gábor Faragho (1890-1953) was supervisor of Horthy's famed gendarmerie, in charge of training. While in Moscow, he was personally acquainted with Stalin. Later Faragho served in the Provisional Government as the minister of food supply. He spent the years of Communism without any harassment on a farm, protected by his extensive number of friends in Moscow.

2 Count Géza Teleki (1911-1983) became Minister of Education in the Provisional Government set up by the occupying Soviet army. Later he emigrated

---

negotiations further delay was caused by the fact that the Soviets did not accept this letter as a formal authorization to negotiate. Hence Lt. Col. József Nemes was sent through the front carrying the requested document[5]. A Magyar landowner in Slovakia[6], who had contacts with the partisans, was the intermediary in the preparations for their journey.

to the United States where he was a professor of geology at George Washington University.

3   Domokos Szentiványi (1898-1980), diplomat, foreign policy advisor of Horthy's son. Served in the Provisional Government set up by the Soviet occupational forces.

4   The delegation carried a three page letter addressed to Stalin written in English by Horthy, in which he asked for armistice. A copy of this handwritten letter turned up decades later:

"Marshal:

I turn to you in the name, and in the interest of my people which is in mortal danger. In the name of the Hungarian people that can not be blamed for the outbreak of this war. For a thousand years, but particularly during the last decade, the fate of our people was influenced by the neighboring German colossus. We were swept into this unfortunate war against the Soviet Union under this influence.

I have to emphasize the fact that my poor country was flooded by the 'fifth column' of the Germans. This major infiltration began at the time when the German armies entered Rumania and Bulgaria. As a result, German agents closely supervised every movement in Hungary, and the most important news and reports were kept from me. I have just been informed that after the air attack of Kassa and Munkács Foreign Minister Molotov, -through the Hungarian envoy-, expressed the peaceful intentions of the Soviet Union toward Hungary. If it is true, it is tragic, since it did not reach me in time.

For the sake of truth, I wish to inform you that we had no intention to take away any piece of land from anyone that we did not have a right to. In contrast, Romania captured Bessarabia from her ally after the first world war, and during the second world war she attempted to capture a large share of southern Russia with the aid of the Germans. Moreover, when we wished to put an end to the cruel treatment of Hungarians in Transylvania in 1940, again, it were the Rumanians who asked for German help, asking Hitler to assist them in keeping at least a part by the Vienna Accord.

When sending my plenipotentiary delegates to the armistice negotiations, I ask you to spare this unfortunate country, -which has it's historical merits-, and whose people shows so many similar traits with the Russian people.

Our representatives were instructed to negotiate for an armistice if possible on the following terms: immediate cessation of hostilities, British and American participation in the occupation of Hungary, and the unhindered withdrawal of German troops from Hungary.

On October 11th, an agreement was initialled in Moscow. No date was as yet fixed, but it was to be a basis for further negotiations. But meanwhile our plans had been upset.

Major-General Bakay, the Commander of the troops in Budapest, who had worked out a detailed plan to defend the Palace in the event of a German attack, was seized and taken away by Gestapo men on his return from an inspection at dawn on October 8th, 1944, as he was stepping out of his car to enter his apartment in the Hotel Ritz. I thereupon sent a message to Moscow by means of the secret transmitter[7] that had been installed in the Palace and was worked by my son Nicholas and my aide-de-camp Tost. I asked that the armistice should be made effective from October 20th. The Russians wished to precipitate matters, as the Americans, during a visit of Churchill and Eden

Be so kind to use your great influence among your allies to set armistice conditions that are congruent with the interests and honor of our people, as this people deserves a peaceful life and a secure future. I take the opportunity to express to you, Marshal Stalin, my highest respect.

Sincerely,

Horthy

P.S. Since our troops are still at the borders, and we are occupied by strong German forces, I ask you to hold my letter in confidence until we can overcome the present situation." (Vigh: *Jump...* op. cit.; p. 145.)

5   Gosztonyi, P. *There is War*, Budapest: Népszava, 1989, p. 70, in Hung.

6   Count Ladomér Zichy (1904-1981). He had land holdings both in Hungary and in Slovakia. In the latter, he had contact with anti-Nazi partisans. This allowed him to arrange Horthy's armistice delegation to fly to Moscow.

7   This was no little feat as a 50 men German radio-broadcast-seeking detachment was encamped only a block away from the Palace. As it turned out later, one of the radio operators was a Nazi spy. However, the decoding of the messages was done by Colonel Tost and the widow of Stephen Horthy, assuring confidentiality.

to Moscow, were protesting against their exclusion from the negotiations with Hungary. Moscow was hoping to put before them a *fait accompli*. The Russians insisted that the effective date should be October 16th, and on the 14th demanded by radio that an answer should be given before 8 a.m. on the 16th.

Meanwhile, several confused incidents had occurred in Budapest. Their sequence is difficult to determine and will probably never be accurately known, for so many people were occupied with so many different activities and the majority are no longer able to speak for themselves. These turbulent events made it impossible for us to keep to the time limit imposed by the Russians. Moscow later made use of this inability to declare our agreement null and void.

Hitler had learned of the Moscow negotiations and was soon informed about the departure of Faragho and his colleagues. He wanted to prevent a Hungarian armistice at all costs. We know now that he was planning coercive measures. Politically, it had been arranged that, with German aid, a meeting of the 'National Opposition' should be held at Esztergom to depose me and proclaim Szálasi head of the state. The military part of this undertaking, the capture of the Palace and the complete occupation of Budapest, was to be entrusted to the SS General von dem Bach-Zelewski[8] and the Lieutenant-Colonel of the Waffen-SS, Otto Skorzeny[9], famed for his liberation of Mussolini. To support Dr. Veesenmayer, Dr. Rudolf Rahn[10], the German Ambassador at Fasano, was sent to Budapest. The telegram containing Veesenmayer's final instructions was received by the German Legation in Budapest during the night of October 13th to 14th, as I learned later.

8   SS General Erich von dem Bach-Zelewski (1899-1972).Commandant of the German forces that suppressed the Warsaw uprising of the Polish Home Army earlier that year.

9   SS Lt. Col. Otto Skorzeny (1908-1975). Legendary German commando leader. He freed Mussolini earlier from Gran Sasso where he was interned by Badoglio. It was his soldiers who captured Horthy's son. He commanded the German forces against the Palace. As a part of "Operation Bazooka", the German plan for takeover initiated soon after the appointment of the Lakatos government, he already reconnoitred the site on September 20 under the disguise of Dr Wolff from Cologne.

10   Rudolf Rahn (1900-1975) was German ambassador to Italy at the time.

On October 14th, I decided that on the following day, a Sunday, I would address the nation over the radio on the proposed armistice. I invited Dr. Veesenmayer to call on me at noon on October 15th at the Palace, with the purpose of informing him of my intention. Immediately after my talk with him, I was to give my broadcast. The script of my address lay ready at the Palace.

I was fully aware that a dramatic race was in progress. I knew that the Germans would do all they could to prevent Hungary from concluding an armistice which I saw as the only way out. Like our Finnish cousins, we had fought the Communist menace as long as there seemed to remain a chance of success. If I wished to spare Hungary the horror of warfare on her own soil and to assure Hungary's existence as a state being recognized by the victors, now was my very last chance. Hitler, on the other hand, had every incentive to keep the war away from Germany's frontiers as long as possible. I could not know the details of his plan, so that I do not know whether the events of that Sunday morning were part of his general plan or not.

The German Security Service had informed my son Nicholas[11] through intermediaries that envoys of Tito wished to talk with him. Nicholas had not kept a first appointment on observing suspicious-looking persons lurking in the vicinity of the proposed meeting-place. Another meeting was fixed for October 15th early in the morning at the offices of Felix Bornemisza[12], the Director of the Hungarian Danube harbours, on Eskü Square on the Pest side. Thinking it possible that there were envoys from Tito who might have important information to give, I had, on the assumption that the meeting would take place in the Palace, empowered Nicholas to negotiate. My son did not realize that I had made that assumption and went into town accompanied by three Guardsmen. He told them to come to his assistance should they observe anything untoward, or should he be away longer than ten minutes.

11 Nicholas Horthy Jr. directed the of the secret "Bailout Bureau" which was set up by Horthy in 1943 ostensibly to deal with the affairs of Hungarians living abroad. Under this cover, the Bureau collected information and facilitated contact with Jews and anti-Nazi opposition groups. After the German invasion in March, 1945, it issued "letters of safe conduct by the Regent" to Jews usually for "activities in the service of the nation", with no requirement to investigate details. Thousands of such letters were issued. (Pers. info. from Mrs. Ilona Bowden.)

12 The same Felix Schmidt-Bornemisza who was comrade-at-arms of Horthy in the navy during WWI.

His suspicions proved only too well founded. He had hardly set foot in the building before he was attacked by fifteen armed Gestapo men who beat him mercilessly until he fell to the ground and feigned unconsciousness. He was then rolled in a carpet and carried to a van that was waiting outside, but before he was thrust into the van he succeeded in giving a cry for help. In the fight shots were fired and one Hungarian and one German were killed. This abduction had obviously been planned well beforehand. Nicholas was to be a hostage to force my hand.

The news of his abduction reached me just before a meeting of the Crown Council that was scheduled for 10 a.m. The meeting did not begin until ten-forty-five. Facing me across the rectangular table sat Vörös, the Chief of the General Staff; on either side of me sat the members of the government and the Chiefs of the Cabinet and Military Chancelleries. I can here refer to the minutes which give my address as follows:

"I have called together the members of the Cabinet in this darkest hour of Hungary's history. Our situation is gravely critical. That Germany is on the verge of collapse is no longer in doubt; should that collapse occur now, the Allies would find that Hungary is Germany's only remaining ally. In that case, Hungary might cease to exist as a State. Hence I must sue for an armistice. I have made sure that we shall receive acceptable conditions from the enemy, but it is certain that we shall be subjected to German atrocities when that armistice is concluded. We shall have much to suffer; our troops may be dispersed. But against that suffering must be set the fact that if we continue this hopeless fight, our race and our fatherland will be in jeopardy and will surely be destroyed. We have no alternative. We must decide to sue for an armistice."

The Chief of the General Staff gave a survey of the military situation. The troops of Marshal Tolbuchin[13] were on the southern outskirts of Belgrade. There was fighting between Szeged and Csongrád to force a passage across the Tisza. South of Debrecen armoured units were engaged in a violent battle. Vörös went on to say that the Russians might be battering at the gates of Budapest itself in two days' time. He told us that at 10.10 a.m. he had received an imperative order from Guderian:

" The entire area of Hungary has been declared a German operational area. Only the German Supreme Command may issue orders. The orders for withdrawal

13 Soviet Marshal Fjodor Ivanovich Tolbuchin (1894-1949).

286

issued to the First and Second Hungarian Armies are hereby countermanded and this counter-order must be implemented within twelve hours."

Practically all those present took part in the discussion which followed. Premier Lakatos declared that the government accepted in full the arguments put forward by the Regent of the Realm but was unable to pronounce in favour of negotiating for an armistice, and therefore had to resign. The reason given for this resignation was that the government had not consulted Parliament before assenting to negotiations or an armistice. I replied that I was about to inform Dr. Veesenmayer of my decision and that the right to ask for an armistice was not vested in Parliament but in me as Supreme Head of the Armed Forces. A conclusion of peace needed the sanction of Parliament, but as a result of the occupation and numerous arrests, this Parliament could no longer be regarded as a fully constitutional body. I therefore asked the government to continue in office. All present, including Reményi-Schneller and Jurcsek, agreed to do so. ·

Dr. Veesenmayer arrived before there had been time for the new government to be sworn in. The meeting of the Crown Council was interrupted while I received the German Plenipotentiary in the presence of the Prime Minister, Lakatos, and the Foreign Minister, Hennyey. With great indignation I protested against the abduction of my son, and when Dr. Veesenmayer denied that he knew anything about it, I confronted him with the German cartridge-cases found on the scene of the abduction. Veesenmayer tried to evade the issue by making the counter-attack that my son had been justly arrested for conspiring with the enemy. Later I learned that the Germans had taken him to an airfield, where a plane was waiting. He had been flown to Vienna and from there was transported to the concentration camp of Mauthausen.

I told Veesenmayer that our decision concerning the armistice had been taken. The colour drained from his face, and he appealed to me, stressing the mystique of the name Horthy. He begged me to postpone my decision, if only for a short time, until I had seen the ambassador, Rahn, who had arrived in Budapest with a special message from Hitler. I replied that I was ready to meet Herr Rahn, but that the decision I had taken was irrevocable. I then returned to the meeting of the Crown Council and the members of the new Cabinet were sworn in.

At 1 p.m., Rahn called. He too tried every means to. make me change my mind. I could only reply that Hungary's willingness to conclude an armistice had already been broadcast. The message containing the text of the proclamation[14] had been taken to the radio station immediately after Dr. Veesenmayer had departed and this text had been broadcasted at 1 p.m.

Veesenmayer, it seemed, had not informed Rahn of the gist of our conversation. Rahn expressed surprise and spoke of the military dangers that would confront the German armies on the cessation of active participation by the Hungarian troops. As I had modelled Hungary's move for an armistice on the Finnish rather than on the Rumanian example, I was prepared to discuss methods by which the Russian troops could be prevented from attacking the Germans in the rear. I was unable, however, to give Rahn the necessary assurances.

Once more I returned to the Crown Council and the minutes recorded on the spot include a short statement made by me:

"I have informed Herr Rahn that he came too late, as I have already asked the enemy for an armistice. We are entering on difficult times, but this step had to be taken. I have burned my boats. I regret that I must place so many difficulties before the members of the Government."

I then shook hands with all present and left the council chamber.

The Arrow-Cross group took my radio proclamation as a signal to go forward with their plans for seizing power. One of the first buildings they occupied

14 The text of the proclamation is included in the Appendix. Horthy by this time mistrusted Vörös. He did not show the proclamation's text to them beforehand. One fateful mistake by Horthy was that he did not specifically state that the preliminary armistice agreement, in fact, was already signed on October 11, 8:57 PM, Moscow time. This allowed the Nazis to obfuscate the matter by their announcements later. It also confused the Hungarian troops. Some writers feel that Horthy should have informed the Soviets about his impending proclamation. Furthermore, Horthy's continued insistence on a gentlemanly 'fair play' toward the Germans suggests a high degree of naiveté. In September, 1946, Horthy explained to a Swiss reporter: "I don't attack from behind, not even a Hitler. I am not a traitor. I promised Hitler that I advise him promptly if I want to make a separate peace. I kept my word." (Gosztonyi, P: Regent Nicholas Horthy and the Emigration, Budapest: Szaz. Publ., 1992, in Hung. p. 134.)

with German aid was the radio station. An Arrow-Cross Party member drew up a counter-proclamation, allegedly in the name of Vörös, the Chief of the General Staff, which was broadcast. It served its purpose. My military orders had not yet reached the troops[15] and everything was thrown into the utmost confusion. The two units of the Army that were still in Budapest went over to the Arrow-Cross after their commander, Bakay, had been arrested and his second in command, Aggteleky[16], had disappeared. It is not known to this day how Vörös's signature came to be appended to the false proclamation. Vörös assured me personally that he had had no knowledge whatsoever of the communiqué sent out in his name[17].

Indescribable excitement reigned in Budapest. To many, my radio proclamation had come as a relief after almost unbearable suspense. A number of political prisoners were released. The underground movement began to carry out its plans. At the same time, there was fear of German reprisals and countervailing measures; the Germans had quickly sent some Tiger tanks to patrol the streets. Those who had hoped for an armistice were now thrown into despair by the spurious Vörös' orders. These conflicting emotions made it easier for the Arrow-Cross supporters to achieve their ends. In the afternoon, the radio sent out the first speech of Szálasi, accompanied by blaring Hungarian and German marches.

15 It was sabotaged by Nazi sympathizer Staff-Colonel Albin Kapitánfy (born Kratzner), who was placed in charge of radioing the Order of the Day to all army units. Later he bragged about this.

16 Major General Béla Aggteleky (1890-1977). He was arrested on the morning of the 15th by his adjutant Iván Hindy, who turned him over to the Gestapo. Later Hindy was the commander of the surrounded Hungarian forces in Budapest and was captured by the Soviets at the end of the siege as he and his entourage emerged from a storm sewer.

17 Vörös escaped from Budapest and hid as a monk in Kecskemét until the Soviet front passed through. He reported to the Red Army and was taken to Moscow. He tried to give the impression to be Horthy's personal representative. He was asked by the Soviets to write a declaration addressed to Hungarian soldiers. It was published in the Pravda on November 15, 1944 under the following title: "Forward for a free and democratic Hungary under the leadership of Regent Horthy." This was not likely to have pleased Moscow's Hungarian Communists. Later Vörös became the minister of war in the Provisional Government. In 1949, after the Communist takeover, he was falsely charged to be an American spy and convicted to life in prison. The 1956 revolution freed him.

The Palace was in a state of siege. The approaches had been mined, incidentally isolating the German Embassy on the Palace Hill. As we learned during the night, the German attack on the Palace had been timed for the early hours of the morning of October 16th[18].

We had just lain down, fully dressed, when Lieutenant Field Marshal Vattay, Chief of the Military Chancellery, and Ambrózy, head of the Cabinet Chancellery, were announced. They had come to deliver the message that the Fuehrer 'offered' me asylum, provided I abdicated, relinquished all powers, and surrendered the Palace. I refused this 'offer' and emphatically told the messengers that I was not to be approached again concerning this matter.

Shortly afterwards, the two men returned with my *aide-de-camp*, Lieutenant-Colonel Tost, to urge my daughter-in-law to persuade me to accept the 'offer'. My daughter-in-law, who, like my son Nicholas, gave me unceasing help and had, in these last days especially, proved to be an indefatigable collaborator, knew me too well to lend herself to such a project. All their entreaties were of no avail, not even the threat that an attack on the Palace was imminent.

Lieutenant-Colonel Tost pleaded with her to change her mind, saying: "Think of the safety of your family, and especially of your son. It is to your advantage." She terminated the conversation by telling them that she would be the last person to attempt to influence me.

In expectation of the attack, I sent my wife, daughter-in-law and grandson at four o'clock in the morning under guard to the residence of the Nuncio, who had in the past offered us sanctuary.

Yet, what was the sense of allowing the situation to develop into a fight? In view of the enemy's superior strength in men and artillery, we had nothing to oppose to their armoured vehicles, a fight could lead only to the decimation of our faithful Guards. Though I had been unable to achieve my aim of bringing peace to Hungary, my radio proclamation had nevertheless proved to the world that Hungary was not willingly submitting to occupation. But I intended to ask no one to lay down his life for me. I therefore ordered that no

18 According to Skorzeny's memoirs, Hitler expected Horthy's attempt to 'bail out' as early as the middle of September. (Dombrády, L. - Toth, S.: The Royal Hungarian Army: 1919-1945; Budapest: Zrinyi, 1987. In Hung.)

resistance should be made. This order failed to reach only one unit in the Palace park, a unit that was commanded by the son of the former Premier, Kállay. Shots were fired, and four German soldiers were killed[19]. Andreas Kállay[20] was taken prisoner and sent to Dachau.

Shortly before 6 a.m., Dr. Veesenmayer appeared and asked me to go to the Hatvany Palace, "to spare me the pain of seeing the occupation of the Royal Palace". That, I thought, was a definite, if courteous, form of arrest. On our arrival at the Hatvany Palace, the headquarters of the SS, Dr. Veesenmayer said, "Here Your Highness is under the Fuehrer's protection."

My reply to that was that I had sought no one's protection and did not consider that I needed it in my own country. Dr. Veesenmayer stared at me in amazement. My words were as incomprehensible to him as his behaviour was to me.

Not until considerably later, the autumn of 1947, in fact, did I obtain the explanation of this mutual misunderstanding. I received my information from a man whose name I cannot give but to whose reliability and veracity I can testify. According to his account, which tallies with the testimonies of witnesses made during the Budapest trial of Szálasi in February, 1946, these were the events of that October night from the 15th to the 16th:

"On October 15th, at 11 p.m., Ambrózy, the head of the Cabinet Chancellery, and Vattay, the Chief of the Military Chancellery, went to the Prime Minister's office, where they found Premier Lakatos in conference with the Ministers, Ivan Rakovszky, Gustav Hennyey, Louis Csatay, Baron Peter Schell[21] and Parliamentary Secretary Stephen Fáy[22]. Vattay declared that he feared that the life of the Regent of the Realm was in danger. The only way by which he and his family

19 The commanders of the opposing German and Hungarian forces agreed the night before not to start hostilities, and to meet at 10 AM. the next day. The Hungarian Guards laid out a mine-field in the approach routes to the Palace. By accident, a lamplighter of the gas street lamps, named Mihály Rekenye, while doing his rounds caused a mine to explode.He survived, with his clothing torn off. Both opponents believed that the other started an attack, and a firefight ensued. (Bokor: *Deadend...*, op. cit.; p.264.)

20 Captain of the Guards András Kállay (1919-).

21 Baron Peter Schell (1898-1974) Interior Minister .

22 István Fáy (1881-1959) Member of Parliament, Deputy Minister.

291

could be saved was to place them under the protection of the German Reich. The Premier rejoined that if that was indeed his opinion, it was Vattay's duty to propose that course to the Regent. Vattay declared himself willing to do so, left with Ambrózy, and returned alone at midnight while the Ministers were still in session. He claimed to have brought the Regent's answer: 'His Serene Highness has agreed to the proposed solution. He makes only one condition, that he may take with him his close collaborators, so that these shall not fall victims to Arrow-Cross revenge.' Vattay then gave the names of Ambrózy, Lehár, and himself. Premier Lakatos, who had no reason for doubting that this was indeed the Regent's answer, undertook to inform the German Embassy. This then was the basis for later developments. The Germans, going by what the Premier had told them, thought that the Regent had completely capitulated before midnight, both politically and militarily. Premier Lakatos undertook the part of intermediary in arranging for the abdication to take place on the afternoon of the 16th. As he saw it, and was bound to see it, capitulation demanded a formal abdication."

This statement clarified what had been to me an inexplicable change of attitude. It showed that Premier Lakatos had based his actions on the false statements made by Vattay in his second interview with the Premier at midnight. What could have been Vattay's motive in bringing an 'answer' which in reality had never been given, an answer, moreover, that was in utter conflict with my clearly expressed views? I can explain his behaviour only if I postulate that Vattay, who had never failed in loyalty to me, took this otherwise inexplicable course of action in order to save my life and the lives·of my family.

This account agrees also with the German statements. According to them, at one o'clock in the morning Lakatos telephoned the German Embassy, which was being evacuated before fighting took place. He spoke to Counsellor Feine[23], who informed Dr. Veesenmayer at once. During the night, a number of express telephone calls were made to the Fuhrer to obtain Hitler's acceptance of the conditions of my supposed capitulation. According to the Germans, Hitler did agree, and Lakatos was informed of this by Counsellor Feine personally at half-past two in the morning. He was asked to come to the German Embassy as quickly as possible and to go to the Palace with Dr. Veesenmayer; I was to leave the Palace before 6 a.m., as it was not certain that the attack on the Palace timed for that hour could be countermanded. A

23 Gerhart Feine (1894-1959).

peaceful solution had been regarded as no longer possible at the Fuehrer's headquarters.

Two rooms were assigned to me at the SS headquarters. Guards swarmed in the corridors and an SS man was stationed on guard in my room. As I was about to take an aspirin, he snatched it with the glass of water from my hand in the belief that I was attempting suicide.

Lakatos, Vattay and Tost were with me. After a while, a German officer came in and announced that "the Premier wished to speak with me". Very surprised, I went into the next room and found Ferenc Szálasi. Giving me a Nazi salute, he made the request that I should appoint him Premier. In the whole of my long career, I had never before had a man asking me to appoint him to office. I advised Szálasi to have himself appointed by the Germans if they had not already done so. "As I am a prisoner here," I added, "I cannot perform my official duties, and in any case you are the last person I should choose to appoint to that function." That snub did not discourage this Arrow-Cross man from making another attempt that same afternoon, receiving, of course, the same reply.

The melancholy hours dragged by. Each one of us had his own sad thoughts. Not one of us could eat the food that was put before us. I soon withdrew to my own room, while the others went to another. Suddenly I heard a shot: Lieutenant-Colonel Tost had risen to his feet and, before anyone had realized what he was about to do, he had shot himself and collapsed by the window, streaming with blood. By his death, I lost one of my most faithful officers; no doubt he preferred to escape by suicide from prolonged imprisonment and Gestapo interrogations which he knew might force him to betray others[24].

As I had brought no personal belongings with me, I asked to be taken to the Palace to pack necessary articles. At 6 p.m., Counsellor Feine came to accompany me. I had been prepared to find that a search had been made, but the disorder of the scene mocked my wildest imaginings. Skorzeny's men had made themselves comfortable on the damask-upholstered furniture. Cupboards and drawers had been broken open. My apartments had already been pillaged and these barbarians had helped themselves to everything that seemed to them of value, from my wife's jewellery to the servants' savings. A

24 Toward the end of December Tost's 70 year old father was also shot to death by Arrow Cross thugs in Kassa.

touch of comedy lightened even this macabre experience. As I approached the bathroom to fetch my toilet articles, the door opened and a man came out wearing my dressing-gown. He had just finished taking his bath. The apartments of my dead son Stephen and of my abducted son Nicholas had also been looted.

I gave my old servant instructions to pack what clothes, linen and other necessities remained. As I was still standing in the bathroom, three guards with sub-machine-guns in attendance, Lakatos suddenly appeared, together with Veesenmayer. Lakatos handed me a sheet of paper on which was set out in German the announcement of my abdication and the appointment of Szálasi as Premier.

I quickly ran my eye over the typewritten page; at the bottom of the German text I read the typewritten words, 'Signed, Horthy'. I returned the sheet to Lakatos saying: "What's this? Am I supposed to sign this?" Lakatos said that I was. I replied that he must know that Szálasi had twice asked me that day to appoint him, and that I had twice refused. That, I thought, closed the conversation, and I went on packing. Lakatos continued to hover about in an obvious state of uncertainty, and it occurred to me that he did not understand my behaviour; I asked him why he wished me to sign the document. Surely, in answer to a direct question, he could only advise me not to sign it. He then indicated that it was a question of my son's life.

I called Veesenmayer, who was standing outside the bathroom, and he confirmed Lakatos's statement that my son's life and eventual return did indeed depend on that signature. I realized that, with or without my signature, the sheet would be published as 'signed Horthy' and it would be proclaimed that I had abdicated after appointing Szálasi. This meant, I said to myself, that while I could change nothing by refusing my signature, I might save my only remaining sons life if I did sign.

I said to Veesenmayer: "I see that you seek to give your *coup d'etat* an air of legality. Will you give me your word of honour that my son will be liberated and will join us if I sign?" "Yes, Your Highness," Veesenmayer replied. "I give you my word of honour." I then told him that I neither resigned nor appointed Szálasi Premier, I merely exchanged my signature for my son's life. A signature wrung from a man at machine-gun point can have little legality.

Dr. Veesenmayer and Rahn were overjoyed at having blocked Hungary's attempt to conclude an armistice and at keeping Hungary in the war 'by peaceful means', as they had been instructed to achieve both these tasks 'if they valued their necks'. (Later I learned that Veesenmeyer had made repeated attempts to keep his word by obtaining my son's return, approaching Ribbentrop, Baron Dörnberg and others in the Foreign Ministry, and Himmler himself with Winkelmann, a high SS official in Budapest.)

The document that I had signed, a prisoner's forced signature, was obviously invalid, though this did not prevent a proclamation in Hungarian being issued. It was a translation of the German document that I had signed, and appended to it was a signed statement from Lakatos, attesting to the accuracy of the translation. I, of course, had never issued any such proclamation, and the signature to Lakatos's attestation had been obtained while he himself was a prisoner. Proof of this is the chit, 'Certificate of Release from Imprisonment', which Lakatos[25] was given on regaining his freedom.

On October 21st, Szálasi thanked Hitler by telegram for the 'true comradeship' that had been so 'inspiringly manifested' on October 15th and 16th in the 'mutuality of the German-Hungarian fate'. In his reply, Hitler referred to Szálasi as the 'responsible Premier' and assured him "that the German Reich will never fail Hungary". Not until after this interchange did Parliament meet again, on November 2nd. Since so many of the members had been arrested, considerably more than under the Sztójay Government, it could only be called a Rump Parliament. At the opening of the session, the Speaker, Tasnádi-Nagy[26], read out two declarations of mine which must have been the 'documents' referred to earlier. There is no evidence that they were ever submitted to the House. The election of a Regent of the Realm was deferred. Parliament 'took notice' of the fact that 'Premier' Szálasi would "provisionally perform the functions of Regent", and would henceforth assume the tide 'Leader of the Nation'. This Parliament could, of course, no longer claim to be a representative body. All attempts of the '*Nemzetvezetô*', the Leader of the Nation, to have his 'Government' officially recognized in neutral countries failed dismally.

25 Subsequently Lakatos was imprisoned by the Nazis but later he escaped. After the war he was imprisoned, then interned, and later deported by the Communists. In 1965 he was allowed to visit his daughter in Australia where he completed his memoirs. He died in 1967.

26 András Tasnády-Nagy (1882-1956)

When my packing was finished as far as my circumstances permitted, I returned from the Palace to the SS headquarters, where I was visited that night by my wife and daughter-in-law. They had been brought from the Nuncio's[27] residence in a German Legation car, after armed SS men had intruded on this extraterritorial soil.

On October 17th, I left the capital and my country a prisoner. At half-past four in the afternoon, Counsellor Feine of the German Legation came to accompany me to the railway station. Under heavy military escort, our car drove to Kelenföld station. The special train, in which my wife and daughter-in-law with her small son were already seated, was waiting to leave the station. Dr. Veesenmayer had asked me, the day before, which members of my entourage I wished to take with me. I had named Ambrózy, Lázár[28], Vattay, and also my aide-de-camp Tost, who was then still alive. Veesenmayer had raised no objections to any of these names, but in the train I found only Vattay and Lieutenant Field Marshal Brunswick[29], whom I had not mentioned at all.

This was the saddest journey of my life. For almost a quarter of a century, I had stood at the head of my country, watching it grow steadily in strength until Hitler had plunged Europe into war and precipitated an unwilling Hungary into the maelstrom. Now I was perforce leaving Hungary; a usurper had thrust me aside with the aid of foreign arms and had set up a regime unworthy of Hungary.

Air alarms had been sounded at every Hungarian station we passed through, and we arrived in Vienna at midnight in the deepest depression. Here, Veesenmayer had told me, my son would join us. I strained my eyes in the hope of seeing my son Nicholas, but probably succeeded only in making myself ridiculous to the man in charge of the train. Neither in Vienna nor at Linz nor in Bavaria did we find him. We did not even know where he was or whether he was still alive. Our request to be allowed to receive a word from him for Christmas was not granted. Ribbentrop merely advised my

27 Msgr.Angelo Rotta. Earlier, he handed out thousands of Vatican letters of protection to Hungarian Jews.

28 Major General Károly Lázár (1890-1968) commander of the Guards.

29 General György Brunswik (1888- ?), logistics commander. According to some, he was a Nazi stool pigeon. (Vigh: *Jump..*; op. cit.)

daughter-in-law in a letter that he was 'suitably housed', a cynical description of his residence in the Mauthausen concentration camp.

At Munich, Baron Dörnberg joined our train. From him we at last learned our destination: Schloss Hirschberg in the neighbourhood of Weilheim, which, for camouflage, had had its name changed to 'Waldbichl'. We later heard that it was there that Mussolini had been taken after his liberation by the Germans. We arrived at Weilheim at eleven o'clock and were taken by car to the pleasantly situated castle. Baron Dörnberg showed us the apartment that had been prepared for us. A room had even been set aside for my son. But what could the Ministry for Foreign Affairs do after Hitler himself had dubbed me a 'shameful traitor'? I was allowed to have in my possession neither money nor valuables. A unit of one hundred men of the Waffen-SS were detailed to patrol the gardens within the barbed-wire fence. Inside the castle were twelve Gestapo men with three police dogs. On our walks, we were invariably accompanied by armed men[30]. From a letter of April 8th, 1947, written by Eric Mayer of the International Red Cross, we learned that his wife, who was active in the Prisoners of War Delegation, had personally brought a Red Cross letter addressed to my daughter-in-law to the castle in February, 1945. The Gestapo Chief, affecting ignorance of the name of Horthy, had I refused to accept it and had told her that there was only an office in the castle, though at that very moment my daughter-in-law and her son were in the garden. "The members of the Horthy family," the delegate informed the International Red Cross, "are prisoners of the Gestapo, to whom not even Red Cross messages can be delivered."

We had no complaint to make about the comfort of our prison; the furnishings of the castle came partly from a Munich palace and partly from Italy. The service also was good at first. After December 1st, however, we received insufficient food. This was due to a personal whim of the Gestapo Chief, who asserted that we could no longer claim special diplomatic rations. The arrival of my brother Eugen[31], therefore, was all the more welcome. Accompanied by a Gestapo agent, he drove up in his car on January 3rd. His car was taken from him, but he was allowed to keep the food he had brought. A small radio set he also had with him was overlooked and at first caused us considerable anxiety, for there was a death penalty attached to the possession

30 The only official contact allowed to Horthy was Chief Consul Horst Hellenthal, assigned there by the German Foreign Ministry.

31 Jenô Horthy (1877-1954) hunter, Africa explorer, writer.

of undeclared radio sets and to listening to foreign stations. We took the risk of using it, however, relieved that we were no longer forced to rely solely on the meagre information contained in the newspapers; behind closed doors and with every possible precaution, we contrived to learn something of the fate of our unhappy Fatherland and the advance of the Allied armies.

From what my brother was able to tell me and from the radio news, the following picture emerged: the Szálasi regime had surpassed our worst fears. The Arrow-Cross Party, drawing much of their support from the hooligan elements in the population, had upon seizing power perpetrated acts of unmitigated vandalism. They had filled, as rapidly as possible, a number of official posts with party members, men who had no inkling of the problems of government or of economics, so that affairs swiftly fell into the utmost confusion. The 'Leader of the Nation' withdrew to an estate near Sopron, where he continued to work on his 'Diary'. It was something along the lines of Mein Kampf, a copy of which was to be handed to every newly married couple and was to become a standard book for every examination.

As early as October 22nd, 1944, a government decree had drawn all male Jews between the ages of ten and sixty into a Defence Labour Force. On November 4th, all Jewish property was confiscated by the state. Hitler found time to receive Szálasi, and on December 4th the two Fuehrers vied with each other in self-delusion when they published a joint official communiqué on the "firm determination of the German people and the Hungarian people united under the revolutionary movement of Hungarists" to "carry on the defensive struggle with all the means in their possession and in the spirit of the traditional and well-tried comradeship-in-arms and friendship of the two nations.

By the time this communiqé was published, the encirclement of Budapest by the armies of Marshal Malinovski[32] and Marshal Tolbuchin was almost complete. The circle was closed on Christmas Eve[33].

32 Soviet Marshal Rogion Jakovlevich Malinovsky (1898-1967).

33 The Siege of Budapest did not end until February 13, 1945. There was a total of 70 thousand German and Hungarian forces encircled under the command of SS General Karl Pfeffer-Wildenbruch. The fight went on from house to house. All seven bridges on the Danube were dynamited. Against Hitler's command, Pfeffer-Wildenbruch decided at the end to stage a breakout. The Soviets were secretly informed of this, and the German forces were massacred on what was later named Malinovsky Boulevard. Only 785 Germans

Then followed what I had hoped to spare my country when I tried to conclude an armistice: the hordes from the East avenged themselves with plunder and destruction on Szálasi's Hungary for its purposeless protraction of the war. Bridges and railways had been blown up by the defeated and retreating German Army. During those last weeks of the collapse of the Third Reich, Hungary became the scene of bloody fighting. Our fine capital was used as a hedgehog position and laid in ruins, as were so many other towns and villages. The remnants of the Hungarian troops, despite the hopelessness of the situation, fought on bravely, to be beaten by the overwhelming superiority of the Red Army. The spoliation of this aftermath of war caused indescribable moral and material loss. The Asiatic barbarians remained true to their past.

The devastation in Budapest itself can be gauged from a report to the Berne Ministry for Foreign Affairs by the Swiss Legation, which left Budapest towards the end of March, 1945:

"Half the city at a rough estimate is in ruins. Certain quarters have, according to the Russians, suffered more than Stalingrad. The quays along the Danube, and in particular the Elisabeth Bridge and the Chain Bridge, are utterly destroyed. On Palace Hill, there is practically nothing left standing. The Royal Palace has been burnt to the ground. The Coronation Church has collapsed. The Parliament Buildings are badly damaged, though their facade is still intact. The Ritz, Hungaria, Carlton, Vadászkürt and Gellért Hotels are in ruins. Part of the Bank Buildings and the National Casino have been destroyed by fire."

Must I describe the state of our feelings during those last weeks of our imprisonment at Schloss Hirschberg? Apart from our fears concerning our home, our friends and relatives, we were anxious about our son and about our own safety. It was as well we did not know till later that Hitler had ordered our extermination before the Americans came, so that no one should ever know who had been imprisoned at Waldbichl. It seems that the Commander of the SS was ready to carry out this order. It was due to the efforts of Consul-General Hellenthal, who had been seconded to us by the German Ministry for Foreign Affairs and to whom we shall always owe gratitude for his

reached their own lines. Pfeffer-Wildenbruch was freed from Soviet prison in 1955, upon Adenauer's Moscow visit. After the siege, Russians commented that Budapest looked worse than Stalingrad. Western media carried little of this matter as it was engaged with reporting on the Battle of the Bulge.

intervention in many instances when intervention was not easy, that the execution was delayed and postponed. Two days before the Americans arrived, the SS men and the Gestapo, including their Commander, put on civilian clothes and fled.

On May 1st, 1945, the vanguard of the American Army arrived at Schloss Hirschberg. We believed that the hour of our liberation had come.

22. The Arrival of the Americans

We were mistaken. The world was so thoroughly out of joint that it took time for the balance to be re-established, even to a slight extent. The clash of arms had died away, but the effects of propaganda were still potent. Too much injustice had been done, too many horrors perpetrated and endured, for people to be able to suppress their urge to seek revenge and to exact punishment. The victors turned a blind eye to the fact that the Soviets had also committed countless crimes against humanity. By reason of their pact with Hitler, their partition of Poland, their attack on Finland, their rape of the Baltic Republics, their war of aggression, their war crimes: Katyn, to cite only one.

In Hungary's case, her 'crime' consisted in having recognized the Soviet Union for what she was: Hungary's implacable enemy. With the collapse of Poland and later through the unsuccessful German attack on Russia, the Communist menace drew nearer our borders, enhancing the danger of the whole south-east of Europe. Today there are few people left throughout the world who see either wisdom or justice in the measures of the Morgenthau plan, in the insistence on unconditional surrender, in the decisions of Teheran, Yalta and Potsdam, in the Paris Peace Treaties of 1947, in the methods of denazification and demilitarization or finally in the trials of the vanquished by the victors. These measures were dominated by Soviet influence and safeguarded Soviet interests above all others. That Germans and Japanese should, seven years after the war ended, be welcomed as allies of the free nations would in 1945 have been regarded as the ravings of a fevered imagination. I feel no urge to say "I told you so", nor to express bitterness at the experiences that have been forced upon me. Rather, I feel wonder and amazement at the vagaries of humanity.

The three American Generals who entered Schloss Hirschberg on May 1st, 1945, the Commander of the 36th Division of the Seventh Army, his Chief of the General Staff and his Artillery Chief, impressed me very favourably. They asked to be allowed to meet my wife and they invited us to tea. The next day they moved on.

In the afternoon, an American Colonel appeared who, his manner courteous and correct, informed me that General Patch, the Commander of the Seventh Army, wished to meet me and invited me to call at his headquarters. Without suspicion, I packed my bag for an absence of several days. We travelled via Augsburg to Göppingen, arriving there at nine o'clock in the evening. I was concerned at keeping General Patch waiting so long.

The villa outside which our car drew up had small resemblance to an Army Headquarters. Nor could I understand why I should be kept waiting in the car for a quarter of an hour before being asked to enter the house. I was taken to a drawing-room where some young American officers were making themselves at home. When I was asked for my personal papers and whether I had any money, arms or medicine on me, I decided that the joke had gone too far, and I demanded that the officer should take me forthwith to General Patch. I was then told that General Patch was in Paris, that I had to consider myself a prisoner of war and that I must spend the night where I was. A lieutenant who spoke Hungarian conducted me to a small room on the first floor, in which the furniture consisted only of a bedstead.

I refused to tolerate this, and after long deliberations I was finally taken to another villa. There I was taken into a room which contained two beds, one of which was already occupied. Again I protested and, as apparently there was no other accommodation available, I declared I should spend the night in the car. As I said this, the occupant of the bed sat up and said: "Your Serene Highness might perhaps wish to stay. I am Field Marshal List."

The next day we were both moved to another villa, where we found Field Marshals Leeb, Baron Weichs and Rundstedt. I was, therefore, in good company, and at our common meals and during our walks we talked animatedly. I heard many details about Hitler's methods of warfare and about the war in Hungary, enough to make one, according to one's temperament, weep with grief or roar with fury. What was not pleasant was that we were, in a sense, on show. The first invasion was made by two dozen journalists from Paris; this incident passed with no outstanding display of tactlessness. After four days, we were all moved to Augsburg, together with the Headquarters.

We went from the frying-pan into the fire. Instead of being housed in a villa, we were now immured in a labour camp which was guarded by noisy Puerto Ricans. My quarters, however, two rooms and a kitchen, were clean and tidy.

The food was chiefly tinned, and we were given the freedom to continue our talks while walking in a large meadow.

There is nothing quite like military secrecy. If General Patch had really wanted to make my acquaintance, he went about fulfilling it in a very unusual way. One morning, a stranger asked me how I was; I countered by asking with whom I had the honour of speaking. My interlocutor replied that he was General Patch. He was accompanied by his whole staff. His tall, slender, military figure impressed me favourably and I should have preferred to have talked with him privately; I could have dispensed with the ubiquitous photographers. I was still given no inkling of what the future held for me.

Meanwhile, the camp was gradually filling. Cars and coaches were constantly depositing new prisoners, including Hermann Göring. He, however, was segregated from the rest. One day, Ferenc Szálasi arrived; he was later handed over to the Budapest Government, tried and convicted. He was executed on March 13th, 1946. The Hungarian-speaking American officer who had been detailed to assist me put me in touch with Colonel Pajtás, the Commander of the Crown Guard, who, together with five NCO's, had succeeded in smuggling the iron chest containing the coronation regalia out of Hungary. Colonel Pajtás told me that the Americans had placed the locked chest in a place of safety. The Holy Crown, however, was not in the chest. As before in Hungarian history, it had been buried in Austrian ground. Later I heard that it also was safely in American hands.

The tidings I received concerning Hungary were horrifying. The looting, rape and violence that had followed upon the entry of the Red Army into Budapest surpassed the horrors with which we had grown familiar in reports from Vienna and Berlin. Neither small girls nor old women were spared. Cases were known of women in Russian uniforms knocking down men who would not do their bidding. Commando troops with special equipment searched for gold and other precious metals. In the banks, safes were broken open, and the contents, whether they belonged to Hungarians, foreigners or even allies, were looted. The pillage went on for weeks, and banks, business firms and private houses were searched time and time again. The Jews were treated no better than the rest of the population, who were picked off the streets and set to work. This was the fate even of the Minister of Education and of one of the Mayors of Budapest, and they were freed only after days had passed. In the neighbourhood of Gödöllö the first of the concentration camps was built, and deportations to the East began in earnest.

I remember May 8th, V.E. Day, which fell during my Augsburg period, as a happy day. First an NCO brought me a radio message to say that my son Nicholas, together with Kállay, Leon Blum, Schuschnigg, Badoglio's son and a few other former inmates of Dachau and Mauthausen concentration camps had been liberated by American troops at the Pragser Wildsee in South Tirol. It was the first news that I had had of my son for seven months. On the same day, I was allowed a visit to my family, who were still at Hirschberg; parting with them after a few hours, due to the uncertainty of my further fate, was very sad.

Before long, I was being moved from place to place. I had the pleasure of meeting the brothers Keresztes-Fischer, whom I had believed to be dead; one of them had for several years been our best Minister for Home Affairs, the younger had for a long time been the Chief of my Military Chancellery. The invitation of the Camp Commandant to dinner, at which my friends were to tell me the rest of the story of their escape, I was unable to attend, as I was suddenly being flown to the Headquarters of General Eisenhower. I was prepared for unpleasant surprises, but this time my luck was in. On May 11th, 1945, I was taken to the delightful little castle of Lesbioles, near Spa, which was provided with every comfort. The Commandant was a Major of the British Intelligence Service. Not only were we excellently cared for, but we received many attentions: we could play the piano, have a game of billiards or chess; there were opportunities for interesting conversations, especially with Ambassador Franz von Papen. The former German Minister of Food, Darré, was also at Lesbioles while I was there; he had fallen out of favour with Hitler as early as 1942.

Of General Eisenhower we saw nothing. We had no idea why we had been brought to this place. Three years later, the answer was given us. One of my friends, who now lives in Belgium, wrote me that he had been invited to Lesbioles. During his visit, the owner of the castle had told him that Lesbioles had been occupied by the Americans as they advanced. After they had moved on eastward, he was allowed to return and found everything in perfect order, except that, to his surprise, he found that in every room, on the ceilings above the lamps, plaster rosettes had been placed. He had them removed and in each was found a microphone. It is obvious, therefore, that it was known to the

Americans that I was friendly with von Papen, and that it was hoped that, in discussing various matters openly, they might be able to find out something interesting. To make the presence of von Papen less obvious, a third person had been included, quite a clever scheme.

I was assured that I was not a prisoner of war but merely in 'protective custody'. On Whit Monday, May 21st, our Odyssey continued. As the Headquarters was moved to France, we had to leave Spa and were taken to the Luxembourg resort Mondorf, some ten miles from the capital of Luxembourg, where several high-ranking 'war criminals' and prisoners of war were concentrated. Here comfort was lacking. In spite of my protests, I was taken to a markedly dirty little hotel. If my old valet had not brought bed-linen and a fur rug, I should have had to sleep under a medley of garments as the others did. The food was mainly cold and unpalatable; it made me feel sick. One day, as I was rising to go to my room, I fainted. The perturbation of the camp doctor and the camp Commandant, who came rushing up, was so great that I decided to exploit my indisposition. I stayed in bed for two days, and after that conditions improved materially.

As the guard-towers of the camp were not yet ready, we were not allowed to go for walks. I was depressed by hearing nothing from my family, especially as I was very worried about my son's health, after the many months he had spent in a concentration camp. Apart from that, the news we were receiving was not of a nature to hearten us. The American papers contained very little about Hungary. Of course, would it have been pleasant to read detailed accounts of the inhuman behaviour of the Communist soldiery, whose excesses were on the level of those of the concentration camp guards. The newspapers gave space only to the latter. The political news soon made it clear that Benes, as in 1918 and 1919, was trying to act as an omniscient adviser on south European questions, naturally at the expense of Hungary. He was plainly unaware that the treaty he had concluded with Russia during the war would be of no use in preventing the transformation of Czechoslovakia into a 'people's democracy' a few years later.

At this stage, they began to take an interest in me. Of my resistance to Hitlerism, for which I had had to pay with imprisonment and danger of life, the Allies knew nothing or pretended to know nothing. From the American newspapers, I gathered that Tito had placed my name on the list of war criminals, holding me responsible for the atrocities committed at Ujvidék in

1942. Later I was told that Tito's request for my extradition had been refused by Britain and the United States of America.

Opposite our 'hotel' at Mondorf, a prison camp was under construction. A three-storied hotel, surrounded by barbed wire, was reserved for political prisoners and prisoners of war; among them were Göring, Ribbentrop, Keitel and Dönitz. I was asked if we wished to enlarge our circle by including one or two of the 'gentlemen across the way'. After a word with von Papen and Darré, I named Baron Steengracht, the Parliamentary Secretary of the Ministry for Foreign Affairs, and Artillery-General Boetticher; these two men did indeed join us on June 25th. The youthful Baron Steengracht had displayed intelligence and courage, and had apparently been able to circumvent several of the plans of his Chief, Ribbentrop. He told us many things that confirmed the 'organized disorganization' of the Third Reich, as he termed it. "The fundamental trait in Hitler's character was mistrust," he told us, "which led to many sound people being thrust aside while a ready ear was lent to those who advocated violence or who voiced irresponsible suspicions."

All prisoners at Mondorf, except for our small group, were under the command of the American Colonel Andrus. Later he became the head of Internal Security in Nuremberg, where he was not particularly liked by his underlings. He did all he could to get the five of us in his power, and finally he succeeded. His first act was to order my luggage to be searched and everything with which I could have hanged or injured myself to be removed. All my valuables were taken from me, in exchange for receipts. He ordered my valet, who had been with me for twenty-four years and had never been a soldier, to be moved into the prison camp. I sent in a written protest, but in vain.

On August 9th, we were moved again, this time to Wiesbaden, after spending the last night in the Mondorf Palace Hotel. Why? Twenty-five of us were billeted in two villas in the friendly, peaceful little city. I was assigned to the house of a famous eye specialist, where I once more had the use of a bathroom. Our meals we ate in common. During our walks in the garden, I came to know the brother-in-law of the former Crown Prince and later King Umberto of Italy, Prince Philip of Hesse; Schwerin-Krosigk, the Reich Minister of Finance, Field Marshal Kesselring, Major-General Blaskowitz, Grand-Admiral Dönitz and other high-ranking naval officers. From Prince Philip, who had tragically lost his wife in a concentration camp, I heard the details of the sufferings of the Mauthausen inmates. He also told me that my son, after his liberation, had been taken to Capri. Nicholas, he said, had believed throughout that he was to be executed, but had endured all physical and psychological torture remarkably well.

Grand-Admiral Dönitz, whom I came to know well, I found an exceedingly interesting man. He told me details of his short period as head of the state at Flensburg, during which he had made a last vain attempt to conclude an armistice in the West to enable him to hold out a little longer in the East. Dönitz also told me of the submarine warfare. I was amazed to hear that, in the autumn of 1939 to 1940, there had been only thirty to forty seaworthy U-boats available. The first phase of the U-boat war had been terminated by the British radar system, and after that the snorkel device had been developed. He told me that the losses of U-boat personnel had been 25,000 dead out of a total of 40,000. Dönitz was removed from Wiesbaden after a fairly short time. I was to meet him twice more. At the request of the other naval officers, I occupied the room his departure had left vacant.

My first interrogation took place shortly before this, on August 28th, nearly four months after I had been taken prisoner. The pleasant American major who conducted the interrogation was especially interested in the importance of Hungary during the war and the part she played, and also in the details of my arrest by Hitler. I owe it to his kindness that I soon after received my first letter from my wife since I had left Schloss Hirschberg.

I was taken next to Oberursel, near Frankfurt, a camp which most of the inmates will remember as detestable. We were a group of fifty, well housed, well cared for, allowed to play bridge every evening. But, irrespective of person, rank or age, we had to perform menial tasks, to clean our rooms, for instance. A naval officer and, after he left, a vice-admiral, in spite of my protests, very kindly insisted on doing my share. On September 24th, we were moved, again by lorry, to another unknown destination. It proved to be Nuremberg.

I thought of Dante's famous words, "Lasciate ogni speranza voi ch'entrate", as we entered the courtyard of the high walled-in five-story penitentiary. The four wings formed a cross. We were placed, in solitary confinement, in one of the wings.

Although Colonel Andrus had assured us that we were only to be witnesses, three weeks passed before we were moved to another wing. The cells were no different there, but the doors were kept open, and in the mornings and afternoons we were allowed to go for two-hour walks, a pleasant concession in that beautiful autumn of 1945. It was less pleasant to have to join a huge queue for food, though the Germans arranged that I should not have to wait. We had to clean our own utensils in enormous tubs, another annoyance to which one had to grow accustomed. We were at any rate spared one hardship meted out to the 'war criminals', who had to go about shackled to a guard. Nor were our cells lit by searchlights from dusk till dawn as were theirs. We were given soap, clean linen, razors. Our washroom, mending room and bathroom also alleviated our situation considerably. We were at last given postal facilities so that I was able at least to keep in touch with my family.

Among the witnesses were generals and field marshals, diplomats, cabinet ministers and deputy secretaries. Small language groups were formed, and chess enthusiasts organized a tournament. Books were exchanged and lively discussions arose over the news we read in the American soldiers' paper Stars and Stripes, the dropping of the first atom bomb, for instance, and the end of the war in the Far East. At that time, elections were being organized in Hungary which, to the astonishment of the Communists and the all-powerful Marshal Voroshilov, gave an absolute majority to the Smallholders' Party, for whom all with patriotic leanings voted. That was their response to the Communist methods of 'liberation', and it clearly revealed the Magyar spirit of independence. Those circles who had believed in the possibility of a Hungarian democracy were soon disappointed. By his behaviour, Zoltán Tildy, the President of the Smallholders' Party, facilitated the Communist domination of the country. When we spoke of Hungary at Nuremberg, and innumerable questions were asked me about it, I found my German fellow prisoners full of understanding for the millstone predicament in which we had found ourselves. Questions concerning Hungarian matters played no part at all in the frequent interrogations. They only wanted information against Hitler and against the two Nuremberg prisoners, Ribbentrop and Keitel. When, in November, the American judge handed me a questionnaire in which to write my answers, he put an unexpected question to me. He asked whether I did not need the assistance of my son, who was in Rome. My reply was an eager "Yes". The judge smiled and said, "Well, I will send for him." On December 1st I had the over whelming joy of embracing my only remaining child. The American judge left us alone for an hour and a half; after our separation of fourteen months, and what events those months had seen, we had much to say. Not before this moment had I known that he had been in solitary confinement in that ill-famed concentration camp of Mauthausen, over the crematorium and next to the torture chamber, so that night and day he smelt burning flesh and heard the screams of the tortured. He had expected every day to be his last, for he had been told that he had been condemned to die by strangulation. One hundred and fifty people, of whom he was one, had been taken from Mauthausen to the Dachau concentration camp, then to Villa Bassa, where they had been liberated by American soldiers of the Fifth Army on May 4th. The leader of the prisoners' convoy, an SS Hauptsturmfuehrer, was found to have on him an order from Himmler to the effect that all political prisoners were to be killed lest they should fall into Allied hands. My son described the fervour with which the newly liberated prisoners had attended a religious service in a small mountain chapel at which Pastor Niemöller had preached the sermon and Mgr. Neuhäusler had said Mass. The spirit of community at that moment had appeared to him a guarantee of a happy future and a lasting peace, but his hopes were soon shattered. Allied nationals were segregated from other nationals, and even when they were transferred to Capri and Naples, full freedom was denied them.

My son was housed in a requisitioned villa and we were able to meet daily. He was present when the American Chief Justice Jackson came to inform me that no prosecution against me was pending from the American side, and that Tito had been informed of this. I surmised that my arrest had indeed been for protective custody, so that, had the Russians insisted on extradition, the United States of America could prevent it by laying claim to my person.

Jackson enquired most courteously after my wishes. "My home," I told him, "is occupied by the Russians. I cannot return there. You will understand that a man of seventy-eight has only one wish: to spend his remaining days in the midst of his own family. Whether in Bavaria or elsewhere, it is immaterial to me." Jackson replied that, though he sympathized with me, the decision did not rest with him. He would have to consult Washington.

I was expecting that months would pass before any decision was made. Three days later, on December 17th, I was released from Nuremberg penitentiary. In the night, at 1:45 a.m., the light was suddenly switched on in my cell. An American officer who was a stranger to me came in and asked me to pack my effects as speedily as possible. The car was waiting. "Where are we going?" I queried. "I can't tell you," was his answer, which filled me with renewed apprehension. This was not lessened when Wiedemann, the former German Consul General in San Francisco and before that Hitler's aide-de-camp, joined me. We put all our luggage, my valuables had been returned to me in the office, in a closed car and soon Nuremberg was left behind. It was easy to guess the direction in which we were heading; the waning moon was on our starboard beam. We were therefore driving south towards Munich.

I began to think I had rejoiced too soon as we turned off the main road and drew up outside a prison. But only Wiedemann was asked to alight, and the rest of us merely made a halt for breakfast. When we set out again, the American officer whispered in my ear, "Weilheim."

Weilheim was the town in which my family was staying. For the whole eight months of my imprisonment, I had been longing for this moment of happiness. So great was my emotion that I could only clasp the officer's hand in silence. Just on nine o'clock, we arrived at Weilheim and then had to search for the house to which my family had moved. I stayed in the car while the officer rang the bell. As my wife opened the door, I heard him say, "I have brought you a Christmas present." "From my husband?" "No. Your husband himself."

Since that day, I have been a private person. Only once more have I had to play my part as Regent of Hungary: at the Nuremberg trial of Dr. Veesenmayer in March 1, 1948. I limited myself to answering the questions put to me which dealt chiefly with the nature of Dr. Veesenmayer's function in Hungary and with the persecution of the Jews.

As I learned much later, a Hungarian lawyer on U.S. Government mission in Nuremberg, Dr. Alexander Páthy, was instrumental in having me and my son brought to Nuremberg. I never met him personally but I had known his brothers well. One of them had been closely associated with my son for a number of years and the two others have been respectively the Hungarian Consul General and Consul in Egypt. Instead of conducting the routine interrogation and cross-examination, he wrote a questionnaire for me to answer in my own way and words. He created an objective and unbiased atmosphere around me, which permitted me and my son to be evaluated without prejudice. I am grateful to him for all that he did. I appreciate the fact

310

that he did not reveal his identity to me throughout his and my stay in Nuremberg, or, for that matter, even after he left.

I cannot, unfortunately, make a similar acknowledgment to another Hungarian lawyer, whose name I prefer not to mention. He also was present during one of my interrogations and he did his utmost to discredit me. The kind of questions he tried to put to me indicated that they were inspired by the prevailing Hungarian regime. He was, however, refused permission to ask these silly questions and vanished from a scene he should never have entered.

We spent four years at Weilheim with no means of subsistence of our own, depending entirely on the help of kind friends. First UNRRA supported us; when that Organization closed down, we received care parcels from American friends, in particular from the last two American Ministers in Budapest, Montgomery and Pell. After the many disappointments and disillusionments of the recent years, the ready help given us by our American friends was profoundly moving, and will never be forgotten by us. Our gratitude to His Holiness Pope Pius XII is also very deep. He, as Cardinal Secretary of State and Papal Legate had been our guest during the Eucharistic Congress of 1938. Our plight was made known to him and he arranged for money to be sent to us. We were thus preserved from the sad necessity of having to sell items from the care parcels, a practice that was perforce common in Germany. Our grateful thanks are also due to the many German and American families who threw open their homes to us and gave us so much hospitality and so many happy hours.

Our home naturally tended to become a focal meeting-point for my countrymen. Many of them who had come to Germany before the end of the war, either voluntarily or under compulsion, tried to carve themselves a new life. Western Germany, however, was filled to overflowing with refugees from the East. Only the unemployable, the old and the sick tended to remain and were usually in sorry circumstances. Thousands of the able-bodied emigrated; others returned home when, after the great electoral victory of the Smallholders' Party, Ferenc Nagy became Prime Minister and a free and democratic development of Hungary, in accordance with the tenets of the Atlantic Charter, was generally expected. But before long, these expectations were dashed. Our hearts sank as we heard eye-witness accounts of the horrors being perpetrated by the Soviets and their Communist disciples. Though, in spite of the Russian occupation, eighty-three percent of the electorate, demonstrating to the West their true feelings, had rejected Communism in the election held on November 4th, 1945. The Communists soon found a way to exert pressure on the Minister for Home Affairs, who controlled the key positions of State Police, Economic Police and Security Police, so that they dominated the economic life of the country and were able gradually to oust the Smallholders' Party. Until the Paris Peace Treaty of February, 1947, which redrew the Hungarian frontiers as they had been fixed by the Treaty of Trianon, except for certain alterations favouring the restored state of Czechoslovakia, the Russians maintained the outward forms of democracy. In the elections held on August 31st, 1947, such scruples were no longer necessary. The Smallholders' Party lapsed into insignificance. The Communist 'Agrarian Reform', which aimed at creating holdings too small to be economically self-supporting in order to drive the peasants into communal farming, turned the Hungary that in 1946 had been a wheat exporting country into a wheat-importing country. Meanwhile, the peasantry had to content itself with the assurance that "the Hungarian Communist Party aims at a prosperous peasantry".

The whole of the free world now knows what the Soviet concepts of 'democracy' and 'free elections' mean. Behind the Iron Curtain, the rule of brutal terror prevails, depriving the individual of all rights, which was made manifest in the spectacular trial of Prince Primate Cardinal Joseph Mindszenty. The Cardinal now lies in gaol, a Hungarian martyr of the Catholic faith, and there is not a Hungarian in the world, whatever his faith may be, who does not utter his name with the most profound reverence. His lot is shared by many a bishop and by many a cleric; no denomination is exempt. And there are also the hundreds of thousands of the innocent nameless who have been condemned with no semblance of justice and deported. They cry out against a regime which can only be maintained by hermetic isolation, by barbed-wire fences and minefields. But even though the Communist rulers can impose silence on the Hungarian nation, yet beneath this cloak of oppression the Hungarian heart still beats and the Hungarian spirit of liberty survives. They are the guarantee that one day Hungarian servitude shall come to an end.

From the shores of the Atlantic Ocean, my thoughts turn constantly eastward, to the banks of the Danube, to my beloved Fatherland. No country on earth, however beautiful, can take the place of my own land in my affections. Though conditions in Germany improved considerably after the currency reform, we had to leave Bavaria's raw climate on account of my wife's health and seek a new asylum. That our choice fell on Portugal can be ascribed to a fortunate chance. My son knew the Portuguese Minister in Berne; he kindly offered to provide us with a visa. Owing to his efforts and those of the American Consul General in Munich, Mr. Sam Woods, the military authorities granted us a 'Temporary Travel Document in lieu of Passport', and on December 18th, 1948, we left Weilheim. After a short stay in Switzerland, we travelled through Italy to Genoa, where we boarded a steamer for Lisbon. Before our departure, we had the joy of meeting Premier Kállay at Rapallo.

Friends placed at our disposal a villa in the beautiful flower-starred Estoril. Here we found old friends and rapidly made new ones. From all over the world, we receive letters from our Hungarian countrymen expressing their attachment, which gives us great satisfaction. We are deeply grateful for the hospitality that has been given us. It is with the utmost interest that I follow the rise of Portugal under the leadership of her wise Prime Minister, Dr. Oliveira Salazar. May his country have the happy future to which the diligence of its lovable people entitles it.

23. A Last Glance in Retrospect and Outlook on the Future

At the beginning of these memoirs, I recorded that the Austro-Hungarian Navy, when I joined it, still consisted partly of sailing ships. I may live to see ships driven by atomic power. In the year 1931, the flight, undertaken with Lord Rothermere's kind assistance, of the Hungarian pilots, Endresz[1] and Magyar, from America to Hungary in the plane "Justice for Hungary", was hailed as a bold pioneering achievement. Today, four-engined planes roar over my house daily on the Lisbon route across the Atlantic. In my time, the pride of the Hungarian Army was its cavalry; today the heroic charge has the quality of tales of bows and arrows. And not only have weapons changed; so also has the spirit of man. Of the honourable warfare of an earlier age, little was left in the Second World War; total war does not distinguish between combatants and non-combatants. It can also be regarded as a retrogression of mankind to a condition which the Hague and Geneva Conventions were believed to have outlawed.

The diplomats were no better than the warlords. Neither at Versailles nor at Trianon was the conquered who had fought bravely recognized as *hostis justus*, (rightful enemy) to whom, after the dust of battle had settled, the victor held out his hand, and since Versailles and Trianon there has been no peace in the world. The First World War, which was allegedly fought to make the world 'safe for democracy', terminated, at the dictates of hatred-fed electorates, in treaties which were a breeding-ground for Communism, Fascism and National Socialism. The Second World War, in which again millions upon millions of people lost their lives, has not ended in the proclamation of the four freedoms and the Atlantic Charter which were its declared aim. Where today is the freedom of religion, freedom of speech, freedom from need and freedom from fear? Admittedly, no one in the Western world is persecuted for belonging to a particular sect or for not belonging to some other, and everyone is allowed to criticize the government. But are not *want* and *fear* greater than ever in many of the countries of this free world? Meanwhile, a quarter of the

---

1   György Endresz (1893-1933), Sándor Magyar (1898-1981).

315

human race is forced to live under a new tyranny that has but one aim: to bring the other three-quarters under its sway.

The secret diplomacy and the 'autocracy' of the old monarchies have been much condemned. But the secret diplomacy of the Congress of Vienna preserved Europe from the suffering and misery of a major war for over a century. Nationalism, radiating from France and infecting one European country after another, finally overthrew the balance on which peace was based. A well-meaning idealist, ignorant of European affairs, American President Woodrow Wilson, inscribed the self-determination of the peoples on his banner. But he could not prevent the first application of that principle from being falsified to suit the interests of the victors of 1918 and their henchmen. The mistakes of his successor, Franklin D. Roosevelt, led finally to the utter destruction of self-determination in Central Europe by Stalin.

Hungary, for her participation in Hitler's war, has been called an unwilling satellite. It would have been truer to say that Hungary tried, with the relatively small means at her disposal, to defend herself against two encroaching forces: against the Soviets with all her available arms; against the Nazi ideology with all her diplomatic powers. Nor am I willing to admit that present-day[2] Hungary is a vassal state, for even between lord and vassal there are relations of reciprocal rights and duties. Hungary is an occupied country, governed by foreign masters, and I speak literally, for the Communist Ministers in power are mostly Soviet citizens[3].

How the liberation of Hungary, for which we work and pray, will finally come about, no one can say. Many people behind the Iron Curtain look forward in their despair to a third world war. But would there be a Hungarian nation left at the end of it? Would not Europe, of which Hungary is an integral part, be so completely ruined and devastated that the destruction brought by the Thirty Years' War and the Wars of the Turks would pale into insignificance?

By whatever means Soviet Imperialism may one day be thrust back behind its boundaries, a process in which the United Nations are bound to play the major part, this much is certain: that we must prepare ourselves for the day to come. I belong to the few still alive who have actively served the brilliant Habsburg monarchy, who have known the kind and wise Emperor Francis Joseph ruling over his contented people. I have lived through the collapse of that empire and the vain attempts to create a workable order in its place. Had the dismemberment of the realm of St. Stephen's Crown brought happiness to the people 'liberated', we might have discerned reason in the general injustice. But that was not the case. Bowed down beneath the costly burden of armaments, forced by the injustices committed into a political war on several fronts, robbed of the advantages of a well-balanced concert of industry and agriculture within a unified customs area, our neighbours failed to experience the happiness they had anticipated. That the Czechs were never so contented as they had been under the old monarchy was admitted by Jan Masaryk[4] to Duff Cooper, the British Ambassador in Paris, in a confidential conversation. He could not have pronounced a harsher indictment of his father's policy. Even the Transylvanian Rumanians were dissatisfied with the Bucharest rule, however much they tried to exploit their new-won position as masters of the Transylvanian Magyars and Saxons. Like Czechoslovakia, Yugoslavia soon fell asunder when the external pressure which had respectively held Czechs and Slovaks, Croats and Serbs together ceased to exist. The Slovaks, who had been deceived by Masaryk's promises incorporated in the Pittsburgh Treaty of 1917, will never, after the Second World War, forgive Benes and his regime for the death sentence passed on Father Tiso. If today we can speak of a leader of the Croats, that leader is Archbishop Stepinac, who was admittedly released from prison under the 1951 Communist regime of Belgrade but who was not allowed to resume his function. When, after the war, representatives of the Hungarian Smallholders' Party presented their claim on the Magyar areas outside of Hungary's borders, they were designated 'Enemies of Peace' by the Communists and were politically silenced.

To divide the Danube basin with its many racial mixtures into national states is as impossible[5] as squaring the circle. The more I have thought about the problem, the clearer it has become to me that the peace and prosperity of all the peoples between the Tirol and Bukovina, between the Banat and the Sudetenland, can only be re-established within a reconstruction of their old

These Soviet imports were Prime Minister Mátyás Rákosi (Rosenfeld), Secret Police leaders Mihály Farkas and his son Vladimir, Economics Minister Ernô Gerô (Singer), Minister of Industry Zoltán Vas (Weinberger), chief ideologue József Révai, and propagandist Ferenc Münnich. They were all Soviet citizens. Horthy delicately omits mentioning that they were all Jewish.

4   Jan Masaryk (1886-1948), son of Thomas G. Masaryk, was Czechoslovakia's Foreign Minister. He was murdered by the Communists.

5   U.S. Senator Daniel Patrick Moynihan is in complete agreement. He devoted a whole book to this subject: *Pandaemonium: Ethnicity in International Politics*, New York: Oxford University Press, 1993.

historic unit. It may be said that the same experiment should not be tried twice. I realize that it is impracticable simply to return to the old regime. But oppression and tutelage, favouritism and exploitation can easily be circumvented by giving complete autonomy on the Swiss model or on that of any other federated state, or in accordance with the plans of Emperor Charles, which were never implemented owing to the outbreak of the 1918 revolution.

In government, in industry, in any kind of society, the best method of sharing is that of the nursery, "You divide, I choose." Since legislation aims at giving each party a fair deal, not one of the partners in a federal state need be at a disadvantage, for if in a given area the ethnic majority were to place a minority at a disadvantage, in another area the position might well be reversed, which would be to no one's advantage.

The period between the wars, and the war itself, showed how tragic was the position of the small Danubian and Balkan countries, the Great Powers using them as pawns on a gigantic chessboard. The mutual enmity of the small states facilitated the machiavellian policy of the great. If a large state were again to be created, consisting of all these parts, covering roughly the area of the old Austro-Hungarian Empire, it would be a stabilizing factor in European affairs[6]. The stabilizing factor which Austria-Hungary was, and was recognized to be, throughout the nineteenth century.

Bismarck was certainly not the last to recognize this. In a talk with the Hungarian poet, Maurus Jókay[7], on February 27th, 1887, he gave a detailed formulation: "It is necessary that there should be a well-consolidated state in Central Europe such as the Austro-Hungarian monarchy. I was aware of that when, in 1866, I hastened to conclude a peace which displeased many of our friends. To found small national states in Eastern Europe is an impossibility; only historical states can survive." Bismarck, at that time, conceded only Germans and Hungarians to have "administrative talent and a knowledge of statesmanship" and the other nationalities to have merely good military qualities. That judgment must now be revised, yet the fundamental truth of his contention remains. It has also been stated by the eminent Czech historian, F. Palacky[8], "If Austria did not exist, it would be necessary to create

6   *The Economist* (Nov. 18, 1995) whole heartedly endorses Horthy's assessment in a survey article, entitled "The Return of the Habsburgs".

7   Mór Jókay (1825-1904) famous Hungarian novelist, one of the leaders of the reformist revolutionary youth in 1848.

her." To Bismarck, it was obvious that the historic house of Habsburg should stand at the head of the historic state. It may be looking too far ahead to concern ourselves with this at the present moment, but it would seem evident, were the unity of this new-old state to be re-created, that at its head should be placed a person who stood indisputably above the strife of nationalities. I would rejoice if, at the helm of a mighty and happy Federation of Danubian States, I were to see the rightful heir of the Habsburg dynasty[9].

Whatever the future may bring, I beg and pray all Magyars worthy of that name, whether living in silence under foreign overlords or in exile far from their homes, to hold together, to forget party strife, and to keep before their eyes a single purpose: the restoration of Hungary's freedom. Let us remember, lest their sacrifice was in vain, all those who gave their lives for their fatherland and those prisoners of war who have not yet returned home. The Hungarian people, and especially the Magyar peasants, are noble-minded. If the peasantry, the backbone of our nation, can succeed in retaining its well-tried, centuries-old national sense, its moral integrity, its martial courage and its joy in labour, even in times of terror and subjugation, if it refuses to heed those political agitators who preach class hatred and kindle the passions of the multitude, then, one day, Hungary will regain her freedom. To her defence and protection I dedicated my life.

8 Frantisek Palacky (1898-1976).

9 Horthy refers to Otto von Habsburg.

APPENDICES

1.. Horthy's Proclamation Broadcasted by the Hungarian Radio on October 15, 1944

"Ever since the will of the nation put me at the country's helm, the most important aim of Hungarian foreign policy has been, through peaceful revision, to repair, at least partly, the injustices of the Peace Treaty of Trianon. Our hopes in the League of Nations in this regard remained unfulfilled."

"At the time of the beginning of a new world crisis, Hungary was not led by any desire to acquire new territories. We had no aggressive intention against the Republic of Czechoslovakia, and Hungary did not wish to regain by war territories taken from her. We entered the Bácska only after the collapse of Yugoslavia and, at the time, in order to defend our blood brethren. We accepted a peaceful arbitration of the Axis powers regarding the Eastern territories taken from us in 1918 by Rumania."

"Hungary was forced into war against the Allies by German pressure, which weighed upon us owing to our geographical situation. But even so we were not guided by any ambition to increase our own power and had no intention to snatch as much as a square metre of territory from anybody."

"Today it is obvious to any sober-minded person that the German Reich has lost the war. All governments responsible for the destiny of their countries must draw the appropriate conclusions from this fact, for as a great German statesman, Bismarck, once said, "No nation ought to sacrifice itself on the altar of an alliance.""

"Conscious of my historic responsibility, I have the obligation to undertake every step directed to avoiding further unnecessary bloodshed. A nation that allowed the soil inherited from its forefathers to be turned into a theatre of rearguard actions in an already lost war, defending alien interests out of a serflike spirit, would lose the esteem of public opinion throughout the world."

"With grief I am forced to state that the German Reich on its part broke the loyalty of an ally towards our country a long time ago. For a considerable time it has thrown formation after formation of the Hungarian armed forces into battle outside the frontiers of the country against my express wish and will."

"In March of this year, however, the Fuehrer of the German Reich invited me to negotiation in consequence of my urgent demand for the repatriation of Hungary's armed forces. There he informed me that Hungary would be occupied by German forces and he ordered this to be carried out in spite of my protests, even while I was retained abroad. Simultaneously German political police invaded the country and arrested numerous Hungarian citizens, among them several Members of Parliament as well as the Minister of the Interior of my government then in office."

"The Premier himself evaded detention only by taking refuge in a neutral legation. After having received a firm promise by the Fuehrer of the German Reich that he would cancel acts that violated and restricted Hungary's sovereignty, should I appoint a government enjoying the confidence of the Germans, I appointed the Sztójay Government."

"Yet the Germans did not keep their promise. Under cover of the German occupation the Gestapo tackled the Jewish question in a manner incompatible with the dictates of humanity, applying methods it had already employed elsewhere. When war drew near our frontiers, and even passed them, the Germans repeatedly promised assistance, yet again they failed to honour their promise."

"During their retreat they turned the country's sovereign territory over to looting and destruction. These actions, contrary to an ally's loyalty, were crowned by an act of open provocation. Lieutenant-General Szilárd Bakay, military commander of Budapest, was treacherously attacked and abducted by Gestapo agents in the very center of the city, exploiting the bad visibility of a foggy October morning when he was getting out of his car in front his home."

"Subsequently German aircraft dropped leaflets against the government in office. I received reliable information that troops of pro-German tendency intended to raise their own men to power by using force to effect a political upheaval and the overthrow of the legal Hungarian Government which I had in the meantime appointed, and that they intended to turn their country's territory into a theatre of rearguard actions for the German Reich."

"I decided to safeguard Hungary's honour even against her former ally, although this ally, instead of supplying the promised military help, meant finally to rob the Hungarian nation of its greatest treasure, its freedom and independence."

"I informed a representative of the German Reich that we were about to conclude a military armistice[1] with our former enemies and to cease all hostilities against them."

"Trusting in your love of truth, I hope to secure, of one accord with you, the continuity of our nation's life in the future and the realization of our peaceful aims."

"Commanders of the Hungarian Army have received appropriate orders from me. Accordingly, the troops, loyal to their oath and following an Order of the Day now issued simultaneously, must obey the commanders appointed by me. I appeal to every honest Hungarian to follow me on this path, beset by sacrifices, that will lead to Hungary's salvation."

2. Recollections by Mrs. Ilona Bowden, Widow of Stephen Horthy, Deputy-Regent of Hungary, Cascais, Portugal, 1993

I have been asked many times to give interviews by the Hungarian Radio, Television and newspapers about my father-in-law, Admiral Horthy, but never once by the American media. I am also aware of the misinformation about Admiral Horthy in the United States. This is due to the lies and distortions that have been spread by Nazi and Communist propaganda. Even by American films, like the one that was made about the Swedish diplomat Raoul Wallenberg, which was a defamatory fiction as it referred to the Regent.

I sometimes read comments on the Regent by people who have not known him personally, and who seem to be able to know what he thought about things and why he made decisions in his life. I myself have lived with my parents-in-law since the day I married their eldest son Stephen Horthy in 1940. We lived in my husband's small flat in the Royal Palace in Budapest. It was connected by a small staircase from his parents apartment. I stayed there with them after my husband was killed in 1942. We were all arrested together

1

323

by the Gestapo and taken to Germany in 1944, with my son who then was only three years old.

After our liberation by the American troops, we went on living together in Germany for four years. Then, with the generous help of John Flournoy Montgomery, who in the United States collected funds for us, we moved to Portugal and settled there. John Montgomery was American Minister to Hungary between 1933 and 1941. In 1947 he wrote a book entitled: *Hungary, the Unwilling Satellite*, (New York, The Devin-Adair Company[2], 1947). He knew Admiral Horthy personally and had become a personal friend. Later he brought together a small group of people in the United States, who committed themselves to provide us with enough means to be able to live in exile. This group consisted of four people: Montgomery himself, Francis Chorin, who had been one of the most important Jewish personalities in banking and trade in Hungary, Dr. László Páthy, lawyer and counsellor at law, also Jewish, and the American born Countess Madeleine Apponyi.

Our gratitude to these friends has no bounds. Without them we could never have left Germany, where my mother-in-law's health suffered much from the cold climate and we were seriously worried about her.

I have intentionally mentioned the Jewish origin of our friends because there were many false rumors about the Jewish question in connection with the Regent. I suppose that not many remember that when due to German pressure the anti-Semitic laws started to be introduced in Hungary, the Regent always resisted and tried to prevent them. Usually he was silenced by being told that as a constitutional head of state he must accept parliamentary majority.

Very few people have knows, that after the war, when we still were in Bavaria, we were visited by Dr. Ruben Hecht, a passionate Zionist politician, who had been the personal adviser to Israeli Prime Minister Begin. Hecht came to see us, to thank Regent Horthy for what he had done for the Jews in Hungary and for his support of the plan to re-settle all the Jews from Hungary to Israel. He knew that the failure of this plan was not the fault of the Regent. When Ruben Hecht saw how we lived in Bavaria, he went to Switzerland to facilitate our passage to Portugal. We always remained in touch with him. Only recently

2   Republished in 1993 by Vista Books, P.O. Box 1766, Morristown, NJ 07962.

324

did I receive the sad news that this many sided, incredibly capable friend had a heart attack and passed away. I keep many letters of his as souvenirs.

Having lived for sixteen years with Admiral and Mrs. Horthy, I am certain that I know them both better than anyone else. It is only during our captivity by the Gestapo and in our life in exile, when we had to depend on each other, that I really and truly learned to know the Regent.

After having been head of state for a quarter of a century, here, with very little means to live, he never complained, always tried to help, even by helping to do the beds while we lived in Germany. He never said bad things about other people and did not change in any way with the changed circumstances. He had the strong hope that he will live to see his country free again. After the war he received letters from Hungarians from all over the world and answered them all. I helped him with his correspondence and with the publishing of his memoirs. Jokingly he called me his minister of interior, exterior, and finance...

For all the members of the Horthy family whom I have known, working, serving your country and doing your duty was the outstanding feature of their character. The Admiral loved his country perhaps above everything else. During his regency he never tried to enrich himself. When all ministers salaries were raised, he did not allow his salary to be improved. His private property in the County of Szolnok was, in 1919, 723 hectares (about 1,700 acres) and remained unchanged till the end of the Second World War. His marriage was a very happy one, we celebrated their golden wedding here in Portugal which was a very joyous occasion.

There was this persisting rumor of him wanting to create a dynasty. I can testify that it is untrue. It is certainly misleading to hear that his son was elected Deputy Regent, but knowing the precise circumstances, one gets a different picture. The Deputy Regent had no right of succession. If the Regent had died he would only be Deputy Regent until a new Regent was chosen. Stephen had been elected by Parliament because of his personal merits, his outspoken anti-Nazi feelings, and his personal achievements. He was a mechanical engineer. On his own initiative, he had gone to the Ford Motor Works in Detroit for a year and a half. There he worked his way up from simple workman to engineer. After he returned home he became the manager in charge of the largest steel factory in Hungary and later the head of the Hungarian Railways. He also was an outstanding pilot. After his death there were some people, although not many, who brought up the idea of proclaiming his two year old son as king of Hungary. It was an absurd idea. My father-in-law flatly rejected it. As the mother of this child, I was worried and went to see him myself, to ask his sincere opinion. He then told me quite clearly that he would never ever reach for the crown of Hungary, whether for himself or anyone of his family. He told me with his own words: "if I would ever do that, I think that my own brother would regard me as unworthy and refuse to shake my hand".

Here in exile, in Portugal, my father-in-law asked me that if I am still alive when his country becomes free, that is, when the last Russian soldier has left Hungary, then I take his remains home to the family crypt in his home town in Kenderes. It seems to me like a miracle that I have lived to see my country free again and so I tried to fulfill my promise to my father-in-law and take both their remains home to the family crypt. In Hungary all private property was taken over by the Communist state, and our home is no longer ours, but by some strange coincidence the family crypt has never been nationalized, it was just forgotten. It is the only place that we, the Horthy family still own. This is also where their beloved children are buried.

The re-burial of the Regent and Madame Horthy took place on the 4th of September, 1993. We considered it a family affair. We have not asked for any help, but the response has been enormous. The Hungarian Seamen, the Maltese and St. John's Orders, the local authorities in Kenderes, and many others have given me a helping hand. I have received hundreds of letters from all over Hungary, and from Hungarians abroad, even as far as Australia, who wanted to come to the re-burial, to pay their respect and show their affection. The Hungarian Radio and Television have come to Portugal to interview me and my son, and to take pictures of the British Cemetery where they have been buried in exile. It is very touching and a lovely homage for a head of state, who died in exile after having served his country all his life. He had not even received a pension in consideration of past services. Only defamatory rumors were spread about him in the past 40 odd years. I trust that in spite of all, the truth is known and will be revealed.

Mrs Bowden's answers to the Editors question about the deportation of Jews:

To the question of "when and in what matter did the Regent found out the truth about the Nazi concentration camps?" Mrs. Stephen Horthy answered as follows:

"After the German occupation, that is, after March 19th, when the deportations commenced, a small 'conspiratory, news gathering' group has formed, of which I was a member too. Often we met in my apartment in the Palace. This group brought to me the writer Sándor Török, who was the vice-president of the Association of Christian Jews of Hungary. Later, he used to visit me on his own through a side entrance, taking off his yellow star. His alias was 'Bardócz the bookbinder', he used this name on the phone also. He brought all kinds of news with the purpose of informing the Regent.

Fortunately, I wrote a diary, in which the memorable day is marked: on July 3rd, 1944, he delivered the "Auschwitz Notebook" to me. I read this tremendously shocking description of the gas chamber-equipped extermination camp in his presence. One could feel that every word of it is true, as something like this could not be fabricated. I immediately brought this to my father-in-law's chambers. - Three days later, on July 6th, the Hungarian Government halted the deportation of the Jews. Prime-Minister Sztójay advised the German plenipotentiary that under the instructions of the Regent, the Government forbids the deportation of more Jews.German acceptance of this move was only possible as they by that time were in trouble on all fronts. They wanted to keep up the seemingly good relations towards the outside world and not rish a conflict in Hungary. Unfortunately, by this time the deportations from the outlying areas have been completed. The details of these we learned only long after the war.

Some people assert that the Regent knew about the extermination camp, but in my opinion this is impossible because after reading the the "Notebook" he would have said that he knows about this already. He would have had no reason to keep this a secret and put on a show in front of his wife and me."
(Personal letter, dated July 31, 1966, to the Editor.)

327

3.. 'Letters to the Editor' on Horthy's Re-Burial in Hungary

János Blumgrund of Vienna, Austria, a Hungarian Jew, appeared on a Hungarian TV interview on the occasion of Regent Horthy's re-burial in Hungary, with a caption "Jewish wreaths on Horthy's grave". A news photo was published widely at the time showing hand held placard at the scene, with the legend: "The Grateful Jewry" on it. It was Mr. Blumgrund who held the sign. Letters to editors criticizing Mr. Blumgrund's action were written by other Hungarian Jews. One of them was written by György Gadó. Gadó's letter follows:

"To Mr. János Blumgrund, Vienna, Austria

Dear Mr. Blumgrund:

I saw with some astonishment in the September 16th issue of the *Pesti Hirlap* the information under the title "Jewish wreaths of Horthy's grave" along with your photograph.

I wouldn't have believed from the champion of human rights as I have known you , and for what I respected you until now, that you would stand up for someone like Horthy who have gravely limited human as well as civil rights (and not only in regard of Jews) from the beginning of his reign until the very end.

And you did it right at the time when the extreme right, and their allies in all practicality, the Hungarian right wing of Antall[3], with the name of "Christian Nationalist Alliance", essentially continue the rebuilding of the counter-revolutionary regime (counter-revolution in terms of countering the 1919 revolution too). The re-burial of Horthy in the prevailing circumstances, that is, not as a family ceremony but in an pseudo-official one, is one of the campaign actions of an ever more obvious counter-revolutionary politics.

As to Horthy's relationship with the Jews, only those can consider it good who are not familiar with the facts; and others who, in their assimilative and "Christian-National" enthusiasm consider it important to have credence

---

3   Refers to József Antall, then prime minister of Hungary.

among the supporters and beneficiaries of the anti-Semitic Hungarian right-wing.

By the way, on what right do you call yourself a "Hungarian Jew"? Perhaps by the right of your baptism and under the blessing of the Pope? Only those should call themselves who are faithful to the Jewry. You are not.

September 21, 1993

Sincerely: György Gadó"

Mr Blumgrund's reply as it appeared in the Budapest daily "*Pesti Hirlap*", on October 11, 1993:

"Dear Mr. Gadó:

I stood up in defense of Regent Nicholas Horthy explicitly as a advocate of human rights. One of the fundamental human rights is to be buried according to one's last wishes. It is a fact of history that Nicholas Horthy has never been convicted of any crime, not even been charged with one.

Even the 'great Stalin', who can not be labeled as soft hearted, advised our prime minister, Ferenc Nagy "to leave the old gentleman alone".

It is true that Regent Nicholas Horthy restricted the operation of the Communist Party (as well as that of the Arrow Cross), but interestingly so did the United States, until the 1940's, for example. And I have not heard that President Roosevelt was called a Fascist for that.

In 1919 there was, of course, a Counter-Revolution in Hungary. It followed the Károlyi Government's Fall revolution that turned into the bloody terrorist dictatorship of Béla Kun.

During the 133 days of the Soviet Republic of Hungary, the Lenin Boys of Tibor Szamuely executed 590 people, 44 of whom were Jews. That reign of horror could only be swept away by a Counter-Revolution. This, as is known, began in Arad, Vienna, and Szeged. It was so 'anti-Semitic' that the first counter-revolutionary government's Minister of Justice in Arad was Lajos Pálmai Jewish notary. (See Hungarian Jewish Lexicon, Budapest, 1929, page 220.) It's administrative and propaganda expenses were procured by János Wolf and Samu Krausz, both Jews. Samu Biedl, the president of the local Jewish community, had a large share in the establishment of the Anti-Bolshevik Committee of Szeged. The earliest formation of the Nationalist Battalions that occupied the barracks had 72 officers; 15 of these were Jewish. (op. cit.)

From the many other references available, I quote a segment of the diary of General Harry Hill Bandholtz, who was the commander of the American Military Mission in Hungary. He refers to the report by Colonel Horowitz upon visiting Admiral Horthy in Transdanubia (September 29, 1919), in which Horowitz claims that Horthy does everything possible to prevent the persecution of Jews. "Indeed", he goes on, " there were many Jews among the Bolsheviks, hence there is a strong anti-Jewish sentiment.

Let me take a leap in time. In September, 1940, I had my *bar mitzvah* in Pozsony (Bratislava); that is when a Jewish boy becomes adult in a religious sense. After the ceremony at the synagogue the whole family and friends celebrated at our home. As this went on, three Hlinka guards rushed into our home and took away our radio. Because from that day on in the independent Slovak state Jews were not allowed to own radios. This was only one of the many other restrictions. And when a few months later we managed to get over to what is now referred to as "Fascist Hungary" we felt like new persons. And while around Hungary the deportation, and killing of Jews went on, the Government of Hungary has done everything possible to save not only the 800,000 Jews in Hungary, but Hungarian citizens of Jewish religion living on areas occupied by the Nazis. In 1945 Mr. Ruben Hecht, who later assisted Israeli Prime Minister Begin, expressed his personal thanks to Nicholas Horthy for this.

I consider ungratefulness a particularly ugly personal treat. I considered it natural to show my gratefulness and respect by giving my last regards to Mr. Nicholas Horthy. I believe that those surviving Jews who think in a honorable manner could have done likewise.

By the way, if you would have watched my TV interview with greater attention, you would know on what ground I can call myself a Hungarian Jew.

With the regard that you deserve:

János Blumgrund"

From the Israeli Hungarian weekly: "A Hét Tükre" ('mirror of the week') [Republished in the September 30, 1993, issue of the "*Magyar Élet*" Hungarian-American weekly.]

"Hungary and the Jews:

The collapse of Communism has a great deal of consequences. Most are positive. That Syria, with assorted contingencies, is willing to make peace with us is one of them. Another is, that the former Soviet state's Jewish citizens are free to travel to Israel, or practice their religion wherever they are. So is the fact that Hungary turned into a democratic country, first time in her history, such that the Jews there can be Jews, without the benefit of secret police agent "rabbis".

So is the fact that day after tomorrow, Saturday the earthly remains of Nicholas Horthy will be buried in Kenderes. It's so because the former Regent asked in his last testament from his daughter-in-law and his grandson, that as soon as the last Soviet soldier gets out of Hungary, make sure that he be buried in the ground of his country. The former regent had absolute right to this.

Based on the foregoings, I do not agree with the cripto-Communists, and with those sophisticates, with some Jews among them, who raise objections, show disgust, display rancor, and, in connection with the burial, call Horthy every bad name using the defunct Rákosi-Kádár regime's whole collection of negative expressions.

It would take a long essay to analyze what the Horthy regime meant, that is, Horthy's 25 years of reign in Hungary. I am not authorized to do this, wouldn't do it here and now. Perhaps I only comment that to determine such

331

things concerns the Hungarian people, and not to György Gadó and his former Communist colleagues. They brought enough trouble on us already, and the time would be right for them to take on discrete silence. I include here the Communist newspapermen of Israel, who are educating the Hungarians about democracy.

What rightfully interests me is Horthy and the Jews. How can one summarize the Horthy regime from a Jewish point of view? What was the condition of the Jews between 1920 and 1945 in Horthy-Hungary?

The Horthy regime inherited in 1920 not only Trianon but the 133 day reign of terror that was defined by the names of Béla Kun and Tibor Szamuely, in which the Magyars, with some justification, have seen a Jewish dictatorship. In spite of this, the regime soon consolidated: there were no significant anti-Jewish atrocities. With the exception of the *numerus clausus* there were no anti-Jewish manifestations until 1939, that is, until the first Jewish laws. Although Horthy boasted here and there saying that "he was the first anti-Semite head of state in Europe", but this had no concrete manifestations. The Jews were behaving as Magyars as before, on the freed lands of Transylvania. Northern areas, etc. the Jews were welcoming the re-entering Horthy on his white horse with enthusiasm. The Jewish Laws, were made in order to conform to the "spirit of the age", or to German pressure, or with the secret intention to take the wind out of the sails of the German Nazis. Until the German occupation, that is, until March 19, 1944, this was more or less successful. A fact: Dr. József Antall, Sr., for whom his son planted a tree at Yad Vasem, could only be a Rightous Gentile, could only save (Polish) Jews in 1942, as it was the Horthy regime and it's Minister of Interior, Ferenc Keresztes-Fisher made it possible for him. I know: there were atrocities with the labor servicemen, there was Kamenec-Podolsk, etc., but I know as well that until the German occupation Hungary appeared almost the oasis of peace and quiet in the eyes of the Jews in the neighboring countries. I was not the Hungarian Jews to escapes to Tiso's Slovakia, but in reverse; it was not the Hungarian Jews that were escaping to Antonescu's Romania, but in reverse.

The dice turned on March 19, 1944. The Germans occupied Hungary. Horthy was pushed aside and from that moment the matter of his responsibility is rather doubtful. Not so that of the Hungarian people, which enthusiastically assisted the commandos of Eichmann in deporting the Jews in record time.

332

Obvious, and it was revealed during the Eichmann trial in Jerusalem that without the cooperation of Hungary's power-organizations (police, gendarmes, soldiers) and the railways it would have been impossible to carry out the deportation of nearly a million Jews.

Horthy, when he could, stopped the deportations, blocked the Baky-Eichmann Plan to move the Jews of Budapest to Auschwitz. He was not a lover of the Jews, he was not a "cadik", could not claim the title of Righteous Gentile, but he was not the devil either as the Communist propaganda painted him. Fact: the Americans did not hand him over to Tito's hoods, and Stalin himself suggested to Rákosi not to ask for his extradition to Hungary as a war criminal. He knew why.

The Horthy regime, as is, was not worse from a Jewish point of view than Kun-Kohn's Commune, or the Rákosi Terror. Such remembrance was drilled into the public opinion by the Communist brainwash. Horthy was anti-Communist. That is true. And so what? So am I. The majority of the world's population is that. This is why this cruelly inhumane system collapsed.

We Jews are not vengeful, neither do we vilify the dead. If Horthy wants to rest in Hungarian soil, may he rest in peace. Peace on his ashes."

Naftali Kraus, Israel

A letter published in the Op/Ed page of *The New York Times* on September 20, 1993. The writer is a military historian in Canada:

"To the Editor:

"Reburial is Both a Ceremony and a Test for Today's Hungary" (Sept. 5) incorrectly states that Adm. Miklós Horthy became an admiral in a country without a navy."

Capt. Miklós Horthy of Nagybánya was promoted rear admiral and fleet commander on March 1, 1918, near the close of World War I in an empire that was about to disappear. But the Imperial and Royal Austro-Hungarian

333

Navy was, in that age of the dreadnought battleship, the fifth largest in Europe after the British, French, Imperial German and Imperial Russian fleets.

During the years he was regent of Hungary, from 1920 to 1944, Horthy maintained his admiral's rank, even though in 1919, postwar Hungary lost both its seacoast and naval bases. The bases were lost when the pre-1914 Hungarian Adriatic province of Croatia became part of the new post-war Kingdom of Yugoslavia.

In our era, when South Slavs are again locked in savage racial conflict, and despite Admiral Horthy's pro-Magyar and, some say, anti-Semitic policies as the long-term Regent of Hungary, the fleet in which he served was the only truly multi-ethnic European navy of the 1914 era.

In 1917, as wartime commander of the Austro-Hungarian light cruiser squadron, his three ship captains were a Croat, Romanian and Hungarian Magyar, respectively.

Since most officers of the navy of the Habsburg monarchy were Austrian, Czech, or Hungarian, and most of the crews were Croats, its officers usually had to know three languages: German, the navy's official language, in addition to their own, if not German, and a working knowledge of Serbo-Croatian. The Austro-Hungarian navy was not defeated by racial conflict, but surrendered as a part of the complete military collapse of the Habsburg Monarchy in early November 1918.

The most famous Austro-Hungarian naval officer was Lieut. Georg Ritter von Trapp, not because he was that navy's top U-boat ace, but as the founder of the Trapp family Singers, whose songs still make sense in any language."

John D. Harbron, Senior Research Fellow, Canadian Institute of Strategic Studies, Toronto, Sept. 11, 1993"

4. New data on Julius Gömbös, former prime-minister of Hungary

by Dr. Károly Dékán, Budapest, Hungary

The "immortal" circles of aristocrats and the big money people, as well as the pro-Habsburg legitimists were not enthusiastic when Nicholas Horthy put the reins of power into the hands of a mere "mortal" on October 1, 1932. Hic Rodus, hic salta!

Son of a village teacher, the prime minister acted in the depths of the Great Depression with the same decisiveness that he exhibited during the second return of King Charles IV. Then the students of the Technical University raised by him halted the king's train at Budaörs as it was approaching Budapest.

The first step was to immediately cancel the martial law introduced by the previous prime minister, Julius Károlyi. He placed into center stage social policies to assist those with large families. He connected such policies with a foreign and trade politics that made it possible to sell the hereto unsaleable wheat stocks of the country.

His first trip was to see Pope Pius XI, who gave a private audience to Gömbös the Lutheran. (Horthy was of the Reformed faith.) On this occasion, in conjunction with the 1927 Friendship Treaty between Italy and Hungary, he paid a visit to Italian king Victor Emmanuel III. The same time he visited with Mussolini, seeking a market for Hungarian wheat.

Upon completing these negotiations, he went home and initiated social reforms. Part of these was the reduction of the price of textbooks, bread, milk, and coal. He broke up the cartel of the coal companies. Stiffened the regulation of banks. On his urging, the Parliament voted in the regular state support of WW1 disabled veterans, war widows and orphans. He reduced the taxes on multi-child families. Along with this, he drastically raised the taxes on the rich. He suspended the auctions of farmers' land, rescheduled farm loans, and reduced unemployment by public investments.

He was aware of the fact that successful social political measures are possible only with a positive foreign trade balance. With this as his aim, he visited leaders of countries friendly toward Hungary: Hitler, Dollfuss, Pilsudszki, the prime ministers of Bulgaria and Turkey, during the first two years of his rule.

Through these visits he established trade agreements with Germany, Italy, and Austria that allowed the exportation of agricultural products of Hungary. As a result, the negative foreign trade balance or 6.1 million (Hungarian Pengô) in 1932 has changed to a positive 55.5 million trade balance by October 31, 1933. Parallel with these, showing a considerable acumen in real-politics, he established diplomatic relations with the Soviet Union in February, 1934.

The active foreign trade politics of Gömbös has shown its effect by 1933-34. The sale of the excess wheat stocks made a positive effect on agriculture, and indirectly on industry. Industrial production, particularly in the field of agricultural machinery, has grown, bringing about a reduction of unemployment. By 1935-36 Hungary ceased to be the oft mentioned "country of three million beggars."

To his credit, he resisted the Nazi racial policies promulgated by the extreme right that started after Hitler came to power in Germany. The existence of the Friendship Treaty with Italy, mentioned earlier, that was negotiated earlier by Prime Minister István Bethlen with Benito Mussolini who professed a Bible-based, Judeo-Christian oriented philosophy, that rested on Fascist-corporational jurisprudence.

Although he was raised in military school, his excessive work habits brought about an incurable illness. He died at an early age, 50, on October 6, 1936. He left an economically and politically stable country to his successors.

The thick shadow of the "immortals" obstructed his life. They did not let him rest even after death. Criminal hands dynamited his statue[4] that was raised during the Premiership of Miklós Kállay.

I trust that with the post-Communist changes Julius Gömbös will take his rightful place in Hungary's history.

---

4 About December 6, 1944, during the Nazi Arrow-Cross terror. More than likely that the perpetrators were from the anti-Nazi underground, who blamed Gömbös for bringing Hungary into the Nazi orbit.

5. On Horthy and the Hungarian Jews

A letter on the same topic: originally published in the Op/Ed pages of *The New York Times* and was reprinted in the January 22, 1994 issue of the *Kanadai Magyarság*.

"Hungary Was the First European Fascist State?

There were two letters published in the January 1st (1994) issue of *The New York Times*, "Horthy and Hitler" and "Hungary and the Serbs", which are potentially misleading.

The first letter states that "Hungary was the first European Fascist State whatever that word means". I suggest that if the writer does not know what Fascism means then he should not use the term in such an accusatory sense!

His statement that Horthy in 1938 took part in "dismembering" Czechoslovakia is highly misleading without pointing out that Czechoslovakia (which recently dismembered itself) was an artificial creation which did not exist until the end of the First World War. Slovakia was a part of Hungary for a thousand years and Horthy re-occupied only that part which had an overwhelming (86.5 %) Hungarian majority population.

The second letter refers to the Hungarian occupation of the Vojvodina section of Yugoslavia as "one of the most shameful episodes of Hungarian history". Indeed, there were atrocities committed by some Hungarian troops in January 1942 but it was not Horthy's doing. The outraged Minister of Defense, Vilmos Nagybaczoni-Nagy initiated an investigation and court-martial proceedings commenced against the ringleaders of the pogrom. The officers responsible for the killings, however, with German help, managed to escape to Germany where they joined the SS and thus were beyond the reach of Hungarian justice.

Horthy was no Nazi and Hungary was not a Fascist State except during the last months of the war after Horthy's futile attempt at an armistice on October 15th, 1944. By that time the Germans occupied the country and their fanatic henchmen, Szálasi and members of his Arrow-Cross Party let all hell loose. Horthy was placed under house arrest guarded by the SS in Hirschberg Castle in Bavaria and his son was kidnapped and deported to Mauthausen.

The tragedy of Horthy and that of Hungary itself was that it was clearly impossible to regain any of the territories lost in the disastrous 1920 treaty of Trianon, without German help. Border revision was the top agenda supported by the whole nation and no leader could survive without advocating it. Horthy's reluctant alliance with Germany did result in recovering the bulk of the Hungarian inhabited lands from surrounding countries, which were of course, lost again at the end of the war.

The Allies recognized this reality and while the Hungarian nation paid a heavy price for its role during the war, Horthy himself was not tried nor was he ever treated as a war criminal.

Dr. Thomas Nonn, Professor and Chairman of the Art Department,

Kingsborough College, New York"

5. On Horthy and the Hungarian Jews: To The Editor, *The New York Times* April 26, 1994

Dear Sir:

I have read with great dismay and disappointment your Budapest correspondent's special report, dated April 17, in your April 18th issue, "Hungary and the Jews: Looking at 1944 Is Difficult." I fully agree with the title, it is difficult for everyone who lived through 1944 in Hungary to look back. For the Jews, of course, it was the year of the Holocaust—unquestionably a most tragic year.

But from the perspective of 1994, it should be easier to look back at least intellectually and evaluate the events of 1944 as they had actually occurred and revise some of the old, inaccurate beliefs. The last few years had brought forth a number of original documents that should help everyone, Jews or non-Jews, to find out the truth. The *New York Times* should be especially careful in sorting out and reporting the truth.

338

One landmark publication on the events of 1944 is a volume examining the role of the Jewish Council ("Judenrat" in German and "Zsid\ Tan<cs" in Hungarian) of Budapest. The volume contains unedited versions of diaries, recollections written shortly after the events by Jewish leaders, and the report of a "mock trial" by a cionist organization examining the role of the Jewish Council. The report of the trial was originally published in the CIONIST WEEKLY REPORT, a Hungarian language newsletter.

The book, "Kollaboracio vagy kooperacio" (Collaboration or cooperation) was edited by Maria Schmidt, a noted scholar of Jewish history in Hungary, and was published in 1990 with the support of the Memorial Foundation for Jewish Culture and the Hungarian Academy of Science-Soros Foundation Committee. Randolph L. Braham of the City College of New York wrote a recommendation to the book. Important documents that are reproduced in this book, including the essay by Samuel Stern, have also been published in English by Braham in Hungarian Jewish Studies III, 1973, New York.

Today there is no excuse for one who writes about 1944 in Hungary for not taking these writings into consideration. It is especially important for a writer for the TIMES, who should not rely on hazy memories of an eighty year old man alone, who had limited access to information in the first place, and had served only as a messenger or a delivery man in 1944—no matter how important the message might have been—when contemporary eye witness accounts are readily available.

The article alleges that a Mr. Elias received a clandestine report, "a description of Auschwitz" to be delivered to the family of Admiral Horthy, without detailing what the document had contained. It is unlikely that it had a full accounting of the atrocities as the article seems to intimate, since it is generally agreed that nobody in Hungary, or even in Europe or the US, was aware of the full details of the crimes. It would be interesting to go back and examine the TIMES 1944 issues to see, when it first reported the existence of gas chambers?

If Hungarians did not know about the existence of the gas chambers or mass killings, how can they be assigned the guilt your reporter and the entire article seems to assign the Hungarian people? Especially the quotes attributed to (and perhaps poorly translated) Mr. Goncz, President of the Republic of Hungary, and castigating Prime Minister Boross for failing to recognize "national responsibility for what happened in World War II, when Hungary fought beside the Nazis" are capable of fueling anti-Hungarian sentiment among your readers. How can an occupied nation that did not even know what was happening be responsible for an act of the occupiers?

If the Hungarian people are guilty for standing by, so are the leaders of the Allied side in Washington for rejecting Hungary's repeated pleas for separate peace and for protection by the allied side against the German aggression before Germany occupied Hungary in March 1944. By the way, there were no commemorations held to remember that date, almost as if it would have spoiled the Jewish anniversary to remember that Hungary was under German occupation at the time. Even if the Allied invasion took place in the Balkan instead of Normandy, as Churchill wanted, most of the Hungarian Jews could have been saved. Yet, the Hungarians, led by Admiral Horthy, resisted as best as they could, even under German military occupation, as the above mentioned book documents.

Still the article slanders Admiral Horthy, Governor of Hungary, by writing that "Admiral Horthy...agreed to German demands for the deportation of the Jews." Admiral Horthy did no such thing! If he had, the 200,000 Jews of Budapest would not have survived. In fact, Horthy did act as a true hero, if one reads Samuel Stern's account of Horthy's role in saving the Hungarian Jews.

Stern had been President of the Budapest Jewish Synagogue since 1929. In 1944 the seventy year old Stern became a member of the Jewish Council. As such, he had been as close to the events as anyone in Hungary could. He was in ill health by the time he dictated his recollections to his secretary in 1945, just one year before his death. The complete document is reproduced in the volume.

Let me present a few concrete examples of Horthy's attitude as presented by Stern: in July Horthy had used army divisions to confront Eishmann's forces and to prevent the deportation of the near 200,000 Jews of Budapest. This so enraged Eichmann, that on July 10 he loaded 1500 Jews on a freight train in Kistarcsa and directed the train to Germany. When Horthy was informed of this, he ordered the gendarmes to stop the train and return it to Kistarcsa.

According to Stein, Eichmann was shocked and jumping in anger, that Horthy, in spite of the military occupation and signed agreement, had repeatedly dared to counter him. So, while the Jewish Council's attention was distracted, he had his SS troops cut the telephone lines at the Kistarcsa internment camp, surrounded and disarmed the gendarmes and had the same Jews re-loaded and spirited them out of Hungary (pp. 84-86).

It seems that Eichmann was determined to deport the Jews of Budapest at any cost. In August, weeks before the appointed date, German forces surrounded the Capital, making sure that the collection and deportation of the Jews cannot be prevented again by the gendarmes or the Hungarian army, so the necessary Hungarian forces had to be sneaked in under false pretenses.

When the deportation appeared inevitable Stern devised a super secret plan to save them: Horthy should go along with Eichman's plans to deport the Jews from Budapest, offer the gendarmes to help in the process, bring all the available armed Hungarian peace-keeping personnel from the countryside to the surrounded Capital, and, once there is sufficient force in Budapest refuse the deportation. To create an excuse for Horthy's apparent change of mind they mobilized the Vatican and other neutral embassies to issue a stern warning to Horthy. Only seven people: three members of the Jewish Council, Horthy, his son, and the commander and deputy commander of the gendarmes knew of the plan. All the outsiders, and even the other members of the Jewish Council, were unaware of the plot, and some frantically tried to escape the certain deportation. Ultimately, though, the plan had worked, and the Germans refused to push for a military confrontation (pp. 87-92). Yet, in the public's mind, including Mr. Elias, it seems, the picture that Horthy was willing to go along with the deportation has persisted to this day, and this view seems to be reflected in Jane Perlez's article.

But this is not the end of Stern's story of Horthy's heroism. The new Lakatos Government was forced to make a new agreement in August; instead of deportation to Germany, it was limited to deportation to work camps in Hungary. Yet, the Hungarians insisted on conditions that enabled the government to sabotage it. Horthy had assured Stern that in spite of the agreement, there will be no deportations from Budapest. The agreement contained a provision, that the places where the Jews were to be collected outside the Capital "had to conform to European standards." With the help of the Hungarian Red Cross, which did the inspection and determination,

341

during the available month and a half (from the end of August to the resignation of Horthy in October) it "did not find one suitable place in Western Hungary", so the deportations did not take place until the Russian attack of Budapest began, and by then the Germans had concerns other than the Jews (pp.93-94).

Thus, Horthy certainly did as much as any Western leader to protect and save the Hungarian Jews, and under the circumstances did a great deal more than our own leaders, or the western media. The fact that the 200,000 Jews in Budapest survived until the arrival of the Soviets, could not have been possible without Horthy's active resistance to the German orders. The article quotes Mr. Elias that "whatever is said about Horthy saving Jews is not true." This is based on total ignorance of the maneuvering behind the scenes, and is contradicted by the testimony of all members of the Jewish Council. How would Mr. Elias know what happened, in the greatest secrecy, behind the scenes, unless he had read the Stern account and the account of the other leaders involved with Horthy?

Hungary was engaged at the time in a death struggle for its independent existence against one of its arch enemies, yet, Hungary and Horthy did not surrender the Hungarian Jews without a struggle, and fifty years later, instead of giving him credit, his memory is attacked and Hungary's reputation is soiled by emotional and short sighted or ignorant individuals with the willing or (hopefully) unwitting assistance of The New York Times.

At the time the Times itself admitted the fair treatment Jews received in Hungary. After saving the Jews of Budapest the first time and after returning the trainload of Jews to Kistarcsa, on July 15, 1944 the TIMES had an article praising Hungary as the last refuge of Jews in Europe, and that "Hungarians tried to protect the Jews." This should not be forgotten fifty years later!

Therefore we hope a correction will be forth coming, at least out of respect for the members of the Budapest Jewish Council, who did everything possible, along with the government of Hungary at the time, supported by thousands of Hungarians, to resist one of the great tragedies of human history. The cooperation of the Jewish Council and Admiral Horthy is one of the most important and positive untold stories of the century.

If *The Times* wants to do its share to make sure that the Holocaust never happens again, it must tell the truth, the whole truth, and nothing but the truth. Only if future generations are told the truth, and if the righteous men are recognized instead of vilified, can we prevent or defeat anti-Semitism. And the lesson of 1944 is that if men of good will work together, they can do miracles. Horthy was a good man and Hungarians a good nation. It took a great deal more than Wallenberg and Tibor Baransky, a good friend of mine, to save the two hundred thousand Jews of Budapest.

There were many who stood up and risked their lives for the Jews of Hungary and who should be recognized on the fiftieth anniversary of the events, from the well known to the almost forgotten to the nameless.

The list certainly should include at its top the son of Horthy, Miklos Horthy Jr., who was readily available to the Jewish Council and often acted as a channel to his father and whose arrest on October 15 by the Germans sparked Horthy's declaration to get out of the war (p.97). Then there were people like Cardinal Mindszenty, who as Bishop of Veszprem was arrested and imprisoned by the Germans and is mentioned by Stern at least twice, along with the Bishop of Gyor, as "two righteous men" (pp. 80, 98), and heroes like Col. Ferenc Koszorus, the commander of an army division who was willing to confront the Germans and Eichmann. The list could continue with Minister of Defense General Janos Csatay (who was arrested by the Germans and committed suicide, together with his wife, in the prison), or another Colonel of the Hungarian Army, Imre Reviczky, whose memory is honored in a synagogue in Sydney with a tablet quoting the Talmud: "The righteous Gentiles have a share in the world to come."

Please, do not deprive these righteous men from their good name and reputation and from their well earned share in the world to come!

I know this might be too long to be published as a letter to the editor, so you may print this as an Op-Ed piece, or publish an edited version in the interest of fairness and of the principle: "et altera pars auditur." Or, if you wish, I would submit the above in an essay format that could be published by your paper.

Sincerely,

Sandor Balogh, Ph.D.

Chair, Exec. Committee, National Federation of American Hungarians

6. The Forgotten Rescue: The Royal Hungarian Army and the Rescue of the Budapest Jews

From material contributed by Frank Koszorus, Esq. and Chris Szabo. Fathers of both have participated in the actions described.

On July 7, 1944 Veesenmayer reported from Budapest to the Wilhelmstrasse[5]: "I just had a one-and half hour discussion with Sztójay. He informed me about the Governor's concerns, who is afraid of the joint putsch of Baky and the Gendarmerie. ... The Governor was very agitated.... Simultaneously, the Gendarmerie units concentrated here were returned to their garrisons."

What was behind this short report commenced with Horthy's order to dismiss the main collaborators in the deportation of Hungary's Jews, Assistant Interior Secretaries László Baky and László Endre, issued on the June 26, 1944, at the Crown Council. Baky disregarded this order saying that there are "higher powers behind him than to follow Horthy's commands." [6]

Preparing a putsch on Adolf Eichmann's advice, Baky attempted to have István Bárczy murdered, and have his keys to the Regent's residence stolen, as mentioned elsewhere in this book. Even though this attempt failed, Baky went on with his plans to concentrate gendarmerie units to Budapest, arrest Horthy, and deport the Jews of Budapest. The ruse to bring in the gendarmerie troops was a ceremony to have Mrs Horthy to consecrate the flags of these units. Horthy's orders to remove these troops were disregarded. Horthy desperately needed reliable army units to enforce his order. He had to circumvent the normal Chain of Command, especially the Chief of Staff, Colonel-General János Vörös, who was not to be trusted. The Commander of

5   *The Wilhelmstrasse and Hungary: German diplomatic documents about Hungary,* Budapest: Kossuth, 1968; in Hungarian.

6   Levai, Jenö: *Jewish fate in Hungary,* in Hungarian.

Horthy's own Guards, Major-General Károly Lázár and other members of Horthy's close circle, arranged for the countermeasures to be taken.

A chance encounter between Guard Commander General Lázár and Colonel of the General Staff Ferenc Koszorus on July 2 changed history[7]. Koszorus commanded the Hungarian First Armored Division which was garrisoned in small towns around Budapest. This command was earlier destroyed on the Soviet front, but subsequently was completely reequipped and ready for action. The existence of the Division war kept from the Germans, ostensibly from keeping it from being sent away to the front, and be at hand for any eventuality.

Koszorus advised General Lázár that his command is ready to follow the Governor's orders, and asked for an audience with the Regent.

Colonel Koszorus was called to an audience with the Regent at the Royal Palace on July 5th, at which time Horthy explained to Colonel Koszorus that armed Gendarmerie battalions were moving into place around Budapest in order to carry out armed action, based on an order from Secretary of State for the Interior, László Baky.

At the July 5 audience, Koszorus had asked what to do in the event of negotiations failing, and was ordered to use force if necessary. However, his request to arrest Baky and publicly humiliate him as a traitor was refused by the ever-chivalrous Regent.

The military force Koszorus had at his disposal was quite considerable. By July 1944, the Hungarian Army had fully recovered from its severe losses in the Soviet Union, incurred in 1942 and 1943. The Hungarian Army had, during 1943, put in place the Szabolcs Plan, aimed at reorganizing and modernizing its under-gunned units as much as possible, based on experience in Russia.

The units immediately available to Col. Koszorus were in Budapest, and near the capital, and comprised mainly tank units, all from the 1st Armored Division. These units were fully equipped, with trained and experienced men, and were also equipped with Hungarian tanks, armored cars and other

---

7   Koszorus, F.: *Mamoirs and Collection of Studies*, Englewood, NJ: Universe Publ., in Hung.

Hungarian-built equipment. It is probable that the number of well-armed men under Koszorus for this operation would have been around 10,000.

The key unit was the 1st Tank Regiment, which was commanded by Colonel vitéz Zoltán Ball, a man with very strong humanitarian credentials, who had done a great deal of work helping Polish POW's in 1939. He and Koszorus had the following units immediately available in the first week of July:

The 1/I Tank Battalion at Párkány-Nána (today, Sturovo, Slovakia), the 1/II Tank Battalion at Jászberény and the I/III Tank Battalion at Rétság, all within a radius of 70 kilometers (cca. 50 miles) of Budapest. The Tank Battalions were powerful units indeed. Their main power was in their 58 40M Turán tanks, 22 of which were equipped with the powerful 75-mm gun. (41M version) Thus, if necessary, the Regent, for once, had at his disposal the power to do something he wanted to do.

Furthermore, the 51st. Motorized Anti-Aircraft Battalion was immediately available. They also had available other elements of the 1st Armored Division; and 1st. Motorized Infantry Regiment, two of whose battalions (the 1st and 2nd Motorized Infantry Battalions) were based in Budapest. These motorized infantry units had the excellent Hungarian-designed and built Raba M38/M42 Botond all-terrain personnel carrier, which held 14 men.

Finally, the 1st Armored Reconnaissance Battalion, equipped with Hungarian-designed and built 39M Csaba Armored Cars; the full Regimental Command Company and Command Structure of the 1st Tank Regiment at Esztergom, near Budapest; with 8 Hungarian-built Turán medium tanks, and three light Hungarian 38M Toldi tanks, as well as a powerful self-propelled artillery unit with Hungarian-built 40M Nimród fighting vehicles, equipped with the famous Swedish Bofors 40mm automatic cannon[8].

Colonel Koszorus, on receiving orders, went to work right away, and by 6 A.M. on the 6th of July, had ordered armored units to close all routes leading into Budapest from the West. His units went as far north as the suburb of Óbuda. He then organized a high-ranking "Officer's Patrol"[9]. This meant

---

8   Lt. Colonel Attila Bonhardt. Archivist at the Military History Archives in Budapest, leading expert on Hungarian tanks and armor. Interviews, private correspondence.

that all the members of the Squad or Platoon in question would be officers, a highly unusual event, aimed at impressing Baky.

This patrol gave Interior Secretary Baky an ultimatum, which said essentially the following: That the Regent had ordered the removal of Baky's troops from the environs of Budapest; that the officers of the armored division would oversee the withdrawal; and that in the event of non-compliance on the part of Baky and his men, there are sufficient forces to hand to enforce the Regent's order.

According to the report, given later by the officer's patrol, this caused no small stir among Baky's supporters. Baky himself tried to get support from various quarters, presumably including the Germans themselves. However, it would appear that the Germans were not in a position to help him, and he seemed to be unable to call on further extreme right-wing elements within Hungary.

Colonel Koszorus wrote[10]: "At nine o'clock," Baky told the patrol-commander, "he can report to me that he (Baky) will follow the terms of the ultimatum."[11] With that, the moment of crisis passed. The Gendarme battalions withdrew from Budapest, Baky left, and the Budapest Jews were not deported. Their deportation, in July 1944, would surely have meant the total annihilation of all the 200,000 Jewish people in Budapest. As late as October the 28th, 1944, the Reich Representative for Hungary reported that 200,000 Jews remained in the Budapest area.[12] Of these, an estimated 50,000 would eventually be deported by the Germans, and a further 15,000 people would be killed by Arrow Cross extremists during the desperate siege of Budapest, despite help given by the Catholic Church and the International Committee of the Red Cross, Raoul Wallenberg, and others.

9   Interviews-discussions with Dr Aladár vitéz Szabó, formerly an officer of the Royal Hungarian Army's Ist. Armored Division. (Retired Hungarian Army 1st. Lieutenant).

10 Ibid.

11 Gosztonyi, Péter: *A Magyar Honvédség a Második Világháborúban* (The Hungarian Defence Forces in the Second World War), Budapest, Europa Publishers, 1995

12 Stark T.: Hungarian Jewry at the time of the Holocaust and after the war. (1941-1955). *Hungarian Quarterly* Volume XXXIV No 132. Winter 1993. p 135

In the immediate aftermath of these actions the surprised Adolf Eichmann said: "In my long experience never happened to me such a thing. .. unacceptable,.... this is not what we agreed on, ... this is entirely impossible." The Israeli Tsvi Erez pointed out that "this is the only occasion when an Axis country applied military force towards the prevention of Jewish deportation."

The Germans reacted soon to the decisive action of the 1st Armored Division. Within weeks it was disbanded as one unit after the other was transferred to the Soviet Front. What would have been Horthy's active reserve force to be used at the time of the "bailout", was thrown away in defense of the Jews of Budapest. The whole country has paid the price for this courageous action later.

Colonel Koszorus could barely escape the Gestapo in the following November, during the Arrow Cross rule. He escaped from Budapest, survived the war, and lived to write his memoirs in the United States.

The decisive action of Colonel Koszorus, Admiral Horthy and those under their command certainly led to the eventual survival of at least 130,000 Jewish people at war's end. Some fifty years after these events, it should be natural for such an act to be, if not honored, at least remembered by the present generation.

9 780966 573435

Printed in the United States
2062